Mike Holt's Illustrated Guide to

Understanding NEC® Requirements for

SOLAR PHOTOVOLTAIC SYSTEMS

Based on the 2011 NEC®

Since 1974
www.MikeHolt.com

Mike Holt Enterprises, Inc.

888.NEC.CODE (632.2633) • www.MikeHolt.com • Info@MikeHolt.com

D0813667

NOTICE TO THE READER

Mike Holt's Illustrated Guide to Understanding NEC® Requirements for Solar Photovoltaic Systems

First Printing: January 2011

Technical Illustrator: Mike Culbreath
Cover Design: Madalina Iordache-Levay
Layout Design and Typesetting: Cathleen Kwas

COPYRIGHT © 2011 Charles Michael Holt
ISBN 978-1-932685-54-1

For more information, call 888.NEC.CODE (632.2633), or E-mail Info@MikeHolt.com.

NEC, NFPA, and *National Electrical Code* are registered trademarks of the National Fire Protection Association.

This logo is a registered trademark of Mike Holt Enterprises, Inc.

If you are an instructor and would like to request an examination copy of this or other Mike Holt Publications:

Call: 888.NEC.CODE (632.2633) • Fax: 352.360.0983
E-mail: Info@MikeHolt.com • Visit: www.MikeHolt.com

You can download a sample PDF of all our publications by visiting www.MikeHolt.com

I dedicate this book to the
Lord Jesus Christ,
my mentor and teacher.
Proverbs 16:3

One Team

To Our Instructors and Students:

We're committed to providing you the finest product with the fewest errors, but we're realistic and know that there'll be errors found and reported after the printing of this book. The last thing we want is for you to have problems finding, communicating, or accessing this information. It's unacceptable to us for there to be even one error in our textbooks or answer keys. For this reason, we're asking you to work together with us as One Team.

Students: Please report any errors you may find to your instructor.

Instructors: Please communicate these errors to us by sending an email to corrections@mikeholt.com.

Our Commitment:

We'll continue to list all of the corrections that come through for all of our textbooks and answer keys on our Website. The most up-to-date answer keys will always be available to instructors to download from our instructor Website. We don't want you to have problems finding this updated information, so we're outlining where to go for all of this below:

To view textbook and answer key corrections: Students and instructors go to our Website, www.MikeHolt.com, click on "Books" in the sidebar of links, and then click on "Corrections."

To download the most up-to-date answer keys: Instructors go to our Website, www.MikeHolt.com, click on "Instructors" in the sidebar of links and then click on "Answer Keys." On this page you'll find instructions for accessing and downloading these answer keys.

If you're not registered as an instructor you'll need to register. Your registration will be sent to our educational director who in turn will review and approve your registration. In your approval E-mail will be the login and password so you can have access to all of the answer keys. If you have a situation that needs immediate attention, please contact the office directly at 888.NEC.CODE (632.2633).

Call 888.NEC.CODE (632.2633) or visit us online at www.MikeHolt.com

Table of Contents

Introduction

Mike Holt's Illustrated Guide to Understanding NEC Requirements for Solar Photovoltaic Systems

This textbook covers the *NEC* requirements for Solar Photovoltaic Systems (solar power). Solar power is new to most in the electrical industry and this expanding and exciting industry has created many *NEC* challenges for the designer, contractor, installer, inspector, and instructor. The writing style of this textbook, and in all of Mike Holt's products, is meant to be informative, practical, useful, informal, easy to read, and applicable for today's electrical professional. Also, just like all of Mike Holt's textbooks, it contains hundreds of full-color illustrations to help you see the safety requirements of the *National Electrical Code* in practical use, as they apply to today's electrical installations.

This illustrated textbook contains cautions regarding possible conflicts or confusing *NEC* requirements, tips on proper electrical installations, and warnings of dangers related to improper electrical installations. In spite of this effort, some rules may seem to be unclear or need additional editorial improvement.

We can't eliminate confusing, conflicting, or controversial *Code* requirements, but we do try to put them into sharper focus to help you understand their intended purpose. Sometimes a requirement is so confusing nobody really understands its actual application. When this occurs, this textbook will point the situation out in an upfront and straightforward manner. We apologize in advance if that ever seems disrespectful, but our intention is to help the industry understand the current *NEC* as best as possible, point out areas that need refinement, and encourage *Code* users to be a part of the change process that creates a better *NEC* for the future.

The *Code* is updated every three years to accommodate new electrical products and materials, changing technologies, and improved installation techniques, and to make editorial refinements to improve readability and application. While the uniform adoption of each new edition of the *NEC* is the best approach for all involved in the electrical industry, many inspection jurisdictions modify the *Code* when it's adopted. In addition, the *NEC* allows the authority having jurisdiction, typically the "Electrical Inspector," the flexibility to waive specific *Code* requirements, and to permit alternative wiring methods contrary to the *NEC* requirements. This is only allowed when he or she is assured the completed electrical installation is equivalent in establishing and maintaining effective safety [90.4].

Keeping up with the *Code* should be the goal of everyone involved in the safety of electrical installations. This includes electrical installers, contractors, owners, inspectors, engineers, instructors, and others concerned with electrical installations.

About the 2011 *NEC*

The actual process of changing the *Code* takes about two years, and it involves thousands of individuals making an effort to have the *NEC* as current and accurate as possible. Let's review how this process works:

Step 1. Proposals—November, 2008. Anybody can submit a proposal to change the *Code* before the proposal closing date. Over 5,000 proposals were submitted to modify the 2011 *NEC*. Of these proposals, over 300 rules were revised that significantly effect the electrical industry. Some changes were editorial revisions, while others were more significant, such as new articles, sections, exceptions, and Informational Notes.

Step 2. *Code*-Making Panel(s) Review Proposals—January, 2009. All *Code* proposals were reviewed by *Code*-Making Panels. There were 19 panels in the 2011 *Code* process who voted to accept, reject, or modify them.

Step 3. Report on Proposals (ROP)—July, 2009. The voting of the *Code*-Making Panels on the proposals was published for public review in a document called the "Report on Proposals," frequently referred to as the "ROP."

Step 4. Public Comments—October, 2009. Once the ROP was available, public comments were submitted asking the *Code*-Making Panel members to revise their earlier actions on change proposals, based on new information. The closing date for "Comments" was October, 2009.

Step 5. Comments Reviewed by *Code* Panels—December, 2009. The *Code*-Making Panels met again to review, discuss, and vote on public comments.

Step 6. Report on Comments (ROC)—April, 2010. The voting on the "Comments" was published for public review in a document called the "Report on Comments," frequently referred to as the "ROC."

Step 7. Electrical Section—June, 2010. The NFPA Electrical Section discussed and reviewed the work of the *Code*-Making Panels. The Electrical Section developed recommendations on last-minute motions to revise the proposed *NEC* draft that would be presented at the NFPA annual meeting.

Step 8. NFPA Annual Meeting—June, 2010. The 2011 *NEC* was voted by the NFPA members to approve the action of the *Code*-Making Panels at the annual meeting, after a number of motions (often called "floor actions") were voted on.

Step 9. Standards Council Review Appeals and Approves the 2011 *NEC*—July, 2010. The NFPA Standards Council reviewed the record of the *Code*-making process and approved publication of the 2011 *NEC*.

Step 10. 2011 *NEC* Published—September, 2010. The 2011 *National Electrical Code* was published, following the NFPA Board of Directors review of appeals.

> **Author's Comment:** Proposals and comments can be submitted online at the NFPA Website (www.nfpa.org). From the homepage, click on "Codes and Standards" at the top of the page, then from the Codes and Standards page click on "Proposals and Comments" in the box on the right-hand side of the page. The deadline for proposals to create the 2014 *National Electrical Code* is November 5, 2011. If you would like to see something changed in the *Code*, you're encouraged to participate in the process.

The Scope of This Textbook

This textbook, *Mike Holt's Illustrated Guide to Understanding NEC Requirements for Solar Photovoltaic Systems*, covers the general installation requirements contained in the *NEC* from Article 90 through 705 that Mike and his team consider to be of critical importance, and is based on the following conditions:

1. Alternating-Current Power Systems and Voltage. When a voltage is referenced in this textbook, it's relating to the alternating current of one of the following, unless identified otherwise:

   2-wire, single-phase, 120V
   3-wire, single-phase, 120/240V
   4-wire, three-phase, 120/240V Delta
   4-wire, three-phase, 120/208V or 277/480V Wye

2. Electrical Calculations. Unless the question or example specifies three-phase, they're based on a single-phase power supply. In addition, all amperage calculations are rounded to the nearest ampere in accordance with Section 220.5(B).

3. Conductor Material. Conductors are considered copper, unless aluminum is identified or specified.

4. Conductor Sizing. Conductors are sized based on a THHN/THWN copper conductor terminating on a 90°C terminal in accordance with 110.14(C)(1), unless the question or example identifies otherwise.

5. Overcurrent Device. The term "overcurrent device" refers to a molded-case circuit breaker, unless specified otherwise. Where a fuse is specified, it's a single-element type fuse, also known as a "one-time fuse," unless the text specifies otherwise.

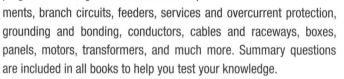

Mike Holt's Detailed *NEC* Library

If you want to really understand the 2011 *National Electrical Code,* then Mike Holt's Detailed *Code* Library is ideal for you. This program covers general installation requirements, branch circuits, feeders, services and overcurrent protection, grounding and bonding, conductors, cables and raceways, boxes, panels, motors, transformers, and much more. Summary questions are included in all books to help you test your knowledge.

This program includes 3 textbooks and 10 DVDs:

- *Understanding the National Electrical Code Volume 1* textbook
- *Understanding the National Electrical Code Volume 2* textbook
- *NEC Exam Practice Questions* book
- General Requirements Part 1 DVD and Part 2 DVD
- Grounding vs. Bonding Part 1 DVD and Part 2 DVD
- Wiring Methods Part 1 DVD and Part 2 DVD
- Equipment for General Use DVD
- Special Occupancies DVD
- Special Equipment DVD
- Limited Energy and Communication Systems DVD

Order the Mike Holt's Detailed *Code* Library by calling 888.NEC.CODE (632.2633).

About This Textbook

This textbook is to be used along with the *NEC*, not as a replacement for it, so be sure to have a copy of the 2011 *National Electrical Code* handy. Compare what Mike is explaining in this book to what the *Code* book says, and discuss any topics that you find difficult to understand with others.

You'll notice that in this book, a great deal of the *NEC* wording has been paraphrased, and some of the article and section titles appear different from the wording in the actual *Code*. Mike believes doing so makes it easier to understand the content of the rule, so keep this in mind when comparing this textbook against the actual *NEC*.

We hope that as you read through this textbook, you'll allow sufficient time to review the text along with the outstanding graphics and examples, which are invaluable to your understanding.

Textbook Format

This textbook follows the *NEC* format, but it doesn't cover every *Code* requirement. For example, it doesn't include every article, section, subsection, exception, or Informational Note. So don't be concerned if you see the textbook contains Exception 1 and Exception 3, but not Exception 2.

Important Features of This Textbook

In order to better meet the needs of our customers, we have improved the layout of our books with some new features. These features include:

- Special Sections which contain additional information to better help you understand a concept are identified with colored frame.

- Examples or practical application questions with their answer and solution have a light yellow background.

- Graphics that contain a 2011 *Code* change will have a green border with a green 2011 CC icon next to the heading.

- Any *NEC* changes will be in green underlined text in all graphics. If you see a green bordered graphic with no green underlined text, it most likely indicates that the *Code* change is the removal of some text. Graphics without a color border support the concept being discussed, but nothing in the graphic was affected by a change for 2011.

- Any 2011 *Code* is denoted by <u>underlined text and in the corresponding chapter color</u>. For example, in Chapter 1 the change text will be red and underlined; Chapter 2 the change text will be cyan and underlined, and so on.

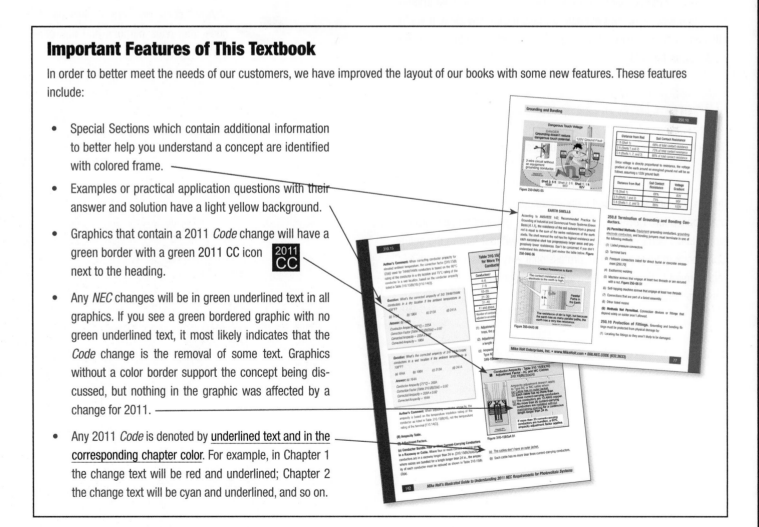

Cross-References and Author's Comments

Cross References. This textbook contains several *NEC* cross-references to other related *Code* requirements to help you develop a better understanding of how the *NEC* rules relate to one another. These cross-references are indicated by *Code* section numbers in brackets, an example of which is "[90.4]."

Author's Comments. "Author's Comments," written by Mike, are intended to help you understand the *NEC* material, and to bring to your attention things of which you should be aware.

Difficult Concepts

As you progress through this textbook, you might find that you don't understand every explanation, example, calculation, or comment. Don't become frustrated, and don't get down on yourself. Remember, this is the *National Electrical Code* and sometimes the best attempt to explain a concept isn't enough to make it perfectly clear. If you're still confused, visit www.MikeHolt.com, and post your question on the *Code* Forum for help.

Different Interpretations

Some electricians, contractors, instructors, inspectors, engineers, and others enjoy the challenge of discussing the *NEC* requirements, hopefully in a positive and productive manner. This give-and-take is important to the process of better understanding the *Code* requirements and application. However, if you're going to get into an *NEC* discussion, please don't spout out what you think without having the actual *Code* book in your hand. The professional way of discussing an *NEC* requirement is by referring to a specific section, rather than talking in vague generalities.

Textbook Errors and Corrections

Humans develop the text, graphics, and layout of this textbook, and since currently none of us are perfect, there may be a few errors. This can occur because the *NEC* is dramatically changed each *Code* cycle; new articles are added, some are deleted, some are relocated, and many are renumbered. We take great care in researching the *NEC* requirements to ensure this textbook is correct. If you believe there's an error of any kind in this textbook (typographical, grammatical, technical, or anything else), no matter how insignificant, please let us know.

Any errors found after printing are listed on our Website, so if you find an error, first check to see if it's already been corrected. Go to www.MikeHolt.com, click on the "Books" link, and then the "Corrections" link (www.MikeHolt.com/bookcorrections.htm).

If you don't find the error listed on the Website, contact us by sending an E-mail to Corrections@MikeHolt.com. Be sure to include the book title, page number, and any other pertinent information.

How to Use the
National Electrical Code

The *National Electrical Code* is written for persons who understand electrical terms, theory, safety procedures, and electrical trade practices. These individuals include electricians, electrical contractors, electrical inspectors, electrical engineers, designers, and other qualified persons. The *Code* isn't written to serve as an instructive or teaching manual for untrained individuals [90.1(C)].

Learning to use the *NEC* is like learning to play the game of chess; it's a great game if you enjoy mental warfare. When learning to play chess, you must first learn the names of the game pieces, how the pieces are placed on the board, and how each piece moves.

Once you understand the fundamentals, you're ready to start playing the game. Unfortunately, at this point all you can do is make crude moves, because you really don't understand how all the information works together. To play chess well, you'll need to learn how to use your knowledge by working on sub-tle strategies before you can work your way up to the more intriguing and complicated moves.

Not a Game

Electrical work isn't a game, and it must be taken very seriously. Learning the basics of electricity, important terms and concepts, as well as the basic layout of the *NEC* gives you just enough knowledge to be dangerous. There are thousands of specific and unique applications of electrical installations, and the *Code* doesn't cover every one of them. To safely apply the *NEC*, you must understand the purpose of a rule and how it affects the safety aspects of the installation.

NEC Terms and Concepts

The *NEC* contains many technical terms, so it's crucial for *Code* users to understand their meanings and their applications. If you don't understand a term used in a *Code* rule, it will be impossible to properly apply the *NEC* requirement. Be sure you understand that Article 100 defines the terms that apply to two or more *Code* articles. For example, the term "Dwelling Unit" is found in many articles; if you don't know what a dwelling unit is, how can you apply the requirements for it?

In addition, many articles have terms unique for that specific article and definitions of those terms are only applicable for that given article. For example, Section 250.2 contains the definitions of terms that only apply to Article 250—Grounding and Bonding.

Small Words, Grammar, and Punctuation

It's not only the technical words that require close attention, because even the simplest of words can make a big difference to the application of a rule. The word "or" can imply alternate choices for equipment wiring methods, while "and" can mean an additional requirement. Let's not forget about grammar and punctuation. The location of a comma can dramatically change the requirement of a rule.

Slang Terms or Technical Jargon

Electricians, engineers, and other trade-related professionals use slang terms or technical jargon that isn't shared by all. This makes it very difficult to communicate because not everybody understands the intent or application of those slang terms. So where possible, be sure you use the proper word, and don't use a word if you don't understand its definition and application. For example, lots of electricians use the term "pigtail" when describing the short conductor for the connection of a receptacle, switch, luminaire, or equipment. Although they may understand it, not everyone does.

NEC Style and Layout

Before we get into the details of the *NEC*, we need to take a few moments to understand its style and layout. Understanding the structure and writing style of the *Code* is very important before it can be used and applied effectively. The *National Electrical Code* is organized into ten major components.

1. Table of Contents
2. Article 90 (Introduction to the *Code*)
3. Chapters 1 through 9 (major categories)
4. Articles 90 through 840 (individual subjects)
5. Parts (divisions of an article)
6. Sections and Tables (*Code* requirements)

7. Exceptions (*Code* permissions)

8. Informational Notes (explanatory material)

9. Annexes (information)

10. Index

1. Table of Contents. The Table of Contents displays the layout of the chapters, articles, and parts as well as the page numbers. It's an excellent resource and should be referred to periodically to observe the interrelationship of the various *NEC* components. When attempting to locate the rules for a particular situation, knowledgeable *Code* users often go first to the Table of Contents to quickly find the specific *NEC* Part that applies.

2. Introduction. The *NEC* begins with Article 90, the introduction to the *Code*. It contains the purpose of the *NEC*, what's covered and what isn't covered along with how the *Code* is arranged. It also gives information on enforcement and how mandatory and permissive rules are written as well as how explanatory material is included. Article 90 also includes information on formal interpretations, examination of equipment for safety, wiring planning, and information about formatting units of measurement.

3. Chapters. There are nine chapters, each of which is divided into articles. The articles fall into one of four groupings: General Requirements (Chapters 1 through 4), Specific Requirements (Chapters 5 through 7), Communications Systems (Chapter 8), and Tables (Chapter 9).

Chapter 1 General

Chapter 2 Wiring and Protection

Chapter 3 Wiring Methods and Materials

Chapter 4 Equipment for General Use

Chapter 5 Special Occupancies

Chapter 6 Special Equipment

Chapter 7 Special Conditions

Chapter 8 Communications Systems (Telephone, Data, Satellite, Cable TV and Broadband)

Chapter 9 Tables—Conductor and Raceway Specifications

4. Articles. The *NEC* contains approximately 140 articles, each of which covers a specific subject. For example:

Article 110 General Requirements

Article 250 Grounding and Bonding

Article 300 Wiring Methods

Article 430 Motors and Motor Controllers

Article 500 Hazardous (Classified) Locations

Article 680 Swimming Pools, Fountains, and Similar Installations

Article 725 Remote-Control, Signaling, and Power-Limited Circuits

Article 800 Communications Circuits

5. Parts. Larger articles are subdivided into parts.

Because the parts of a *Code* article aren't included in the section numbers, we have a tendency to forget what "part" the *NEC* rule is relating to. For example, Table 110.34(A) contains working space clearances for electrical equipment. If we aren't careful, we might think this table applies to all electrical installations, but Table 110.34(A) is located in Part III, which only contains requirements for "Over 600 Volts, Nominal installations." The rules for working clearances for electrical equipment for systems 600V, nominal, or less are contained in Table 110.26(A)(1), which is located in Part II—600 Volts, Nominal, or Less.

6. Sections and Tables.

Sections. Each *NEC* rule is called a "*Code* Section." A *Code* section may be broken down into subsections by letters in parentheses (A), (B), and so on. Numbers in parentheses (1), (2), and so forth, may further break down a subsection, and lowercase letters (a), (b), and so on, further break the rule down to the third level. For example, the rule requiring all receptacles in a dwelling unit bathroom to be GFCI protected is contained in Section 210.8(A)(1). Section 210.8(A)(1) is located in Chapter 2, Article 210, Section 8, Subsection (A), Sub-subsection (1).

Many in the industry incorrectly use the term "Article" when referring to a *Code* section. For example, they say "Article 210.8," when they should say "Section 210.8." Section numbers in this book are shown without the word "Section," unless they begin a sentence. For example, Section 210.8(A) is shown as simply 210.8(A).

Tables. Many *Code* requirements are contained within tables, which are lists of *NEC* requirements placed in a systematic arrangement. The titles of the tables are extremely important; you must read them carefully in order to understand the contents, applications, limitations, and so forth, of each table in the *Code*. Many times notes are provided in or below a table; be sure to read them as well since they're also part of the requirement. For example, Note 1 for Table 300.5 explains how to measure the cover when burying cables and raceways, and Note 5 explains what to do if solid rock is encountered.

7. Exceptions. Exceptions are *Code* requirements or permissions that provide an alternative method to a specific requirement. There are two types of exceptions—mandatory and permissive. When a rule has several exceptions, those exceptions with mandatory requirements are listed before the permissive exceptions.

Mandatory Exceptions. A mandatory exception uses the words "shall" or "shall not." The word "shall" in an exception means that if you're using the exception, you're required to do it in a particular way. The phrase "shall not" means it isn't permitted.

Permissive Exceptions. A permissive exception uses words such as "shall be permitted," which means it's acceptable (but not mandatory) to do it in this way.

8. Informational Notes. An Informational Note contains explanatory material intended to clarify a rule or give assistance, but it isn't a *Code* requirement.

9. Annexes. Annexes aren't a part of the *NEC* requirements, and are included in the *Code* for informational purposes only.

Annex A. Product Safety Standards

Annex B. Application Information for Ampacity Calculation

Annex C. Raceway Fill Tables for Conductors and Fixture Wires of the Same Size

Annex D. Examples

Annex E. Types of Construction

Annex F. Critical Operations Power Systems (COPS)

Annex G. Supervisory Control and Data Acquisition (SCADA)

Annex H. Administration and Enforcement

Annex I. Recommended Tightening Torques

10. Index. The Index at the back of the *NEC* is helpful in locating a specific rule.

Changes to the *NEC* since the previous edition(s), are identified by shading, but rules that have been relocated aren't identified as a change. A bullet symbol "•" is located on the margin to indicate the location of a rule that was deleted from a previous edition. New articles contain a vertical line in the margin of the page.

How to Locate a Specific Requirement

How to go about finding what you're looking for in the *Code* depends, to some degree, on your experience with the *NEC*. *Code* experts typically know the requirements so well they just go to the correct rule without any outside assistance. The Table of Contents might be the only thing very experienced *NEC* users need to locate the requirement they're looking for. On the other hand, average *Code* users should use all of the tools at their disposal, including the Table of Contents and the Index.

Table of Contents. Let's work out a simple example: What *NEC* rule specifies the maximum number of disconnects permitted for a service? If you're an experienced *Code* user, you'll know Article 230 applies to "Services," and because this article is so large, it's divided up into multiple parts (actually eight parts). With this knowledge, you can quickly go to the Table of Contents and see it lists the Service Equipment Disconnecting Means requirements in Part VI.

> **Author's Comment:** The number 70 precedes all page numbers because the *NEC* is NFPA Standard Number 70.

Index. If you use the Index, which lists subjects in alphabetical order, to look up the term "service disconnect," you'll see there's no listing. If you try "disconnecting means," then "services," you'll find that the Index specifies that the rule is located in Article 230, Part VI. Because the *NEC* doesn't give a page number in the Index, you'll need to use the Table of Contents to find the page number, or flip through the *Code* to Article 230, then continue to flip through pages until you find Part VI.

Many people complain that the *NEC* only confuses them by taking them in circles. As you gain experience in using the *Code* and deepen your understanding of words, terms, principles, and practices, you'll find the *NEC* much easier to understand and use than you originally thought.

Customizing Your *Code* Book

One way to increase your comfort level with the *Code* is to customize it to meet your needs. You can do this by highlighting and underlining important *NEC* requirements, and by attaching tabs to important pages. Be aware that if you're using your *Code* book to take an exam, some exam centers don't allow markings of any type.

Highlighting. As you read through this textbook, be sure you highlight those requirements in the *Code* that are the most important or relevant to you. Use yellow for general interest and orange for important requirements you want to find quickly. Be sure to highlight terms in the Index and the Table of Contents as you use them.

Underlining. Underline or circle key words and phrases in the *NEC* with a red pen (not a lead pencil) and use a 6-inch ruler to keep lines straight and neat. This is a very handy way to make important requirements stand out. A small 6-inch ruler also comes in handy for locating specific information in the many *Code* tables.

Tabbing the *NEC*. By placing tabs on *Code* articles, sections, and tables, it will make it easier for you to use the *NEC*. However, too many tabs will defeat the purpose. You can order a set of *Code* tabs designed by Mike Holt online at www.MikeHolt.com, or by calling 1.888.NEC. CODE (632.2633).

About the Author

Mike Holt

Mike Holt worked his way up through the electrical trade from an apprentice electrician to become one of the most recognized experts in the world as it relates to electrical power installations. He has worked as a journeyman electrician, master electrician, and electrical contractor. Mike's experience in the real world gives him a unique understanding of how the *NEC* relates to electrical installations from a practical standpoint. You'll find his writing style to be direct, nontechnical, and practical.

Did you know that he didn't finish high school? So if you struggled in high school or if you didn't finish it at all, don't let this get you down, you're in good company. As a matter of fact, Mike Culbreath, Master Electrician, who produces the finest electrical graphics in the history of the electrical industry, didn't finish high school either. So two high school dropouts produced the text and graphics in this textbook! However, realizing success depends on one's continuing pursuit of education. Mike immediately attained his GED (as did Mike Culbreath) and ultimately attended the University of Miami's Graduate School for a Master's degree in Business Administration (MBA).

Mike Holt resides in Central Florida, is the father of seven children, and has many outside interests and activities. He's a six-time National Barefoot Water-Ski Champion (1988, 1999, 2005, 2006, 2007, and 2008), has set many national records, has competed in three World Championships (2006, 2008, and 2010) and continues to train and work out year-round so that he can qualify to ski in the 2012 World Barefoot Championships at the age of 61!

What sets him apart from some, is his commitment to living a balanced lifestyle; placing God first, family, career, then self.

Mike Holt—Special Acknowledgments

First, I want to thank God for my godly wife who's always by my side and my children, Belynda, Melissa, Autumn, Steven, Michael, Meghan, and Brittney.

A special thank you must be sent to the staff at the National Fire Protection Association (NFPA), publishers of the *NEC*—in particular Jeff Sargent for his assistance in answering my many *Code* questions over the years. Jeff, you're a "first class" guy, and I admire your dedication and commitment to helping others understand the *NEC*. Other former NFPA staff members I would like to thank include John Caloggero, Joe Ross, and Dick Murray for their help in the past.

A personal thank you goes to Sarina, my long-time friend and office manager. It's been wonderful working side-by-side with you for over 25 years nurturing this company's growth from its small beginnings.

About the Graphic Illustrator

Mike Culbreath

Mike Culbreath devoted his career to the electrical industry and worked his way up from an apprentice electrician to master electrician. While working as a journeyman electrician, he suffered a serious on-the-job knee injury. With a keen interest in continuing education for electricians, he completed courses at Mike Holt Enterprises, Inc. and then passed the exam to receive his Master Electrician's license. In 1986, after attending classes at Mike Holt Enterprises, Inc., he joined the staff to update material and later studied computer graphics and began illustrating Mike Holt's textbooks and magazine articles. He's worked with the company for almost 25 years and, as Mike Holt has proudly acknowledged, has helped to transform his words and visions into lifelike graphics.

Special Acknowledgments

I want to thank my wonderful children, Dawn and Mac, who have had to put up with me during the *Code* revision seasons.

I would like to thank Steve Arne, our amazing technical editorial director, Eric Stromberg, an electrical engineer and super geek (and I mean that in the most complimentary manner, this guy is brilliant), and Ryan Jackson, an outstanding and very knowledgeable code guy, for helping me keep our graphics as technically correct as possible.

I also want to give a special thank you to Cathleen Kwas for making me look good with her outstanding layout design and typesetting skills. I would also like to acknowledge Belynda Holt Pinto, our Chief Operations Officer and the rest of the outstanding staff at Mike Holt Enterprises, for all the hard work they do to help produce and distribute these outstanding products.

And last but not least, I need to give a special thank you to Mike Holt for not firing me about 25 years ago when I "borrowed" one of his computers and took it home to begin the process of learning how to do computer illustrations. He gave me the opportunity and time needed to develop my computer graphic skills. He's been an amazing friend and mentor since I met him as a student many years ago. Thanks for believing in me and allowing me to be part of the Mike Holt Enterprises family.

Mike Holt
Enterprises Team

Editorial Team

I want to thank **Toni Culbreath** and **Barbara Parks** who worked tirelessly to proofread and edit the final stages of this publication. Their attention to detail and dedication to this project is greatly appreciated.

Production Team

I want to thank **Cathleen Kwas** who did the layout and production of this book. Her desire to create the best possible product for our customers is greatly appreciated.

Video Team Members

The following special persons provided assistance in the development of this textbook; particularly in ensuring that the technical content is accurate. In addition, they all provided outstanding technical advice as they served on the video team along with author Mike Holt and a guest appearance by graphic illustrator Mike Culbreath.

Steve Arne
Technical Training Consultant
Arne Electro Tech
Rapid City, S.Dak.
ElectricalMaster.com

Steve Arne has worked in various positions in the electrical industry since 1974 including electrician, electrical contractor, full-time instructor, and department chair in technical postsecondary education. Steve has developed and taught curriculum for many electrical training courses as well as university business and leadership courses. He's completed a Bachelor's degree in Technical Education and a Master's degree in Administrative Studies. Currently, he provides electrician exam prep and continuing education *Code* classes in South Dakota, Wyoming, and surrounding states using Mike Holt's textbooks and material. He enjoys seeing a student's

"lights come on" as they come to a point of understanding and have the "ah-ha" experience of learning something new.

Steve has worked for Mike Holt as a technical editor and video team participant since 2002, and used Mike Holt's books in his classes for a number of years before that. Steve is very thankful to have been associated with an industry leader like Mike who provides excellent training products to help students progress in the electrical industry. Steve has been active in the South Dakota Electrical Council, serving on the Board of the Black Hills Chapter in various capacities and is the current Chapter President.

Steve and his wife Deb live in Rapid City, S.Dak. where they're both active in their church and community, and love to spend time with their children and grandchildren. Most of all, Steve and Deb both endeavor to put God first in their lives and in their home.

Bill Brooks, PE
Principal, Brooks Engineering
Vacaville, California
www.brooksolar.com

Bill Brooks, of Brooks Engineering LLC, has 22 years of experience designing, installing, and evaluating grid-connected PV systems. More than 5,000 installers and 5,000 inspectors have attended his courses throughout the U.S. and abroad. His field troubleshooting skills have been valuable in determining where problems occur to focus training on those issues of greatest need.

Bill has written several important technical manuals for the industry that are now widely used in California and beyond. His recent publications include the *Expedited Permit Process for PV Systems,* and *Field Inspection Guidelines for PV Systems,* as well as feature articles in *Photon* and *SolarPro* magazines. Bill is actively involved in the development of PV codes and standards including IEEE–929 (*PV Utility Interconnection*) and for the *National Electrical Code* (*NEC*) Article 690 (*Solar Photovoltaic PV Systems*). He's also a member of *Code*-Making Panel 4 for the *NEC*.

Bill holds Bachelor of Science and Master of Science degrees in Mechanical Engineering from North Carolina State University and is a registered Professional Engineer in North Carolina and California.

David Click
Program Director, PV Project Engineering
Florida Solar Energy Center
Cocoa, Florida
www.floridaenergycenter.org

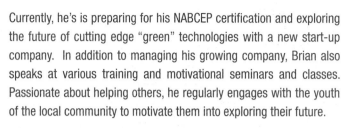

David Click became involved in solar energy through the Department of Energy's first Solar Decathlon. When searching for an undergraduate research project, he found a DOE flyer announcing the 2002 competition and was hooked from the start.

He served as project manager for the engineering team behind the University of Virginia's entry. After receiving his BS and MS degrees in electrical engineering from UVA, he joined Solar Design Associates in Massachusetts from 2004 to 2007, managing and designing PV projects from 3-600 kW dc.

Since 2007, Dave's been working at the Florida Solar Energy Center in Cocoa, FL with projects including training prospective PV installers, leading local efforts in DOE market transformation programs, and educating code officials on proper PV design and installation. He also serves on the North American Board of Certified Energy Practitioners (NABCEP) PV Installers' Exam Committee.

Dave and his wife Barrie live beneath their 5.40 kW hybrid PV/Thermal system in Orlando (in a house). During the system's first 12 months of operation, their electric bills resulted in a year-end utility credit of $33.39!

Daniel Brian House
Dan House Electric, Inc
Ocala, FL
www.DanHouseElectric.com

Brian House is a high-energy entrepreneur with a passion for doing business the right way. Brian is currently the CEO of Dan House Electric, Inc., an unlimited electrical contracting company based in Florida and working throughout the SE United States.

He's been involved in varying aspects of alternative energy and energy conservation since the 1990s and has a passion for constantly improving the combinations of technology offered to his customers, whether designing energy-efficient lighting retrofits, exploring "green" biomass generators, or partnering with solar energy companies as their preferred installer. Brian has experienced the laughs and tears of "the growing up of" alternative energy and looks to the future for more exciting developments.

Currently, he's is preparing for his NABCEP certification and exploring the future of cutting edge "green" technologies with a new start-up company. In addition to managing his growing company, Brian also speaks at various training and motivational seminars and classes. Passionate about helping others, he regularly engages with the youth of the local community to motivate them into exploring their future.

Brian and his wife Carissa have shared the joy of their four children and over 30 foster children during a happy 13 years of marriage. When not at work or church, he's an avid fly fisherman preferring the action-packed intercostals for his angling venue.

Ryan Mayfield
State Licensed PV Installer/NABCEP Certified PV Installer/PV Instructor
Renewable Energy Associates
Corvallis, OR
www.renewableassociates.com

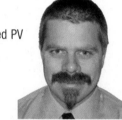

Ryan Mayfield served as Engineering Manager for a national solar distributor and was responsible for the company's design and manufacturing groups. Ryan worked directly with installers and electricians in the field, helping to solve complex design and installation issues.

Now he's the President of Renewable Energy Associates, a consulting firm providing design, support, and educational services for electrical contractors, architectural and engineering firms, and manufacturers and government agencies. Ryan serves as Solar Photovoltaic Systems Technical Editor for *SolarPro* magazine, and authors feature articles in *SolarPro* and *Home Power* magazines. He's a Certified Master Trainer for the PV courses he teaches at Lane Community College. Ryan also teaches various PV courses for electricians, solar professionals, code officials, inspectors, and individuals looking to join the solar industry. Class topics include introduction to PV, *National Electrical Code* and PV systems, commercial PV systems, and preparation for the North American Board of Certified Energy Practitioners (NABCEP) Certified PV Installer test.

Ryan lives in Corvallis, OR with his wife, Amy, and two children, A.J. and Lauren. They enjoy getting outdoors as much as possible, especially when they have the opportunity to get in the canoe for a few days.

Notes

Mike Holt's Illustrated Guide to Understanding 2011 NEC Requirements for Solar Photovoltaic Systems

Introduction to the *National Electrical Code*

INTRODUCTION TO ARTICLE 90—INTRODUCTION TO THE *NATIONAL ELECTRICAL CODE*

Many *NEC* violations and misunderstandings wouldn't occur if people doing the work simply understood Article 90. For example, many people see *Code* requirements as performance standards. In fact, the *NEC* requirements are bare minimums for safety. This is exactly the stance electrical inspectors, insurance companies, and courts take when making a decision regarding electrical design or installation.

Article 90 opens by saying the *NEC* isn't intended as a design specification or instruction manual. The National Electrical *Code* has one purpose only, and that's the "practical safeguarding of persons and property from hazards arising from the use of electricity." It goes on to indicate that the *Code* isn't intended as a design specification or instruction manual. The necessity to carefully study the *NEC* rules can't be overemphasized, and the role of textbooks such as this one is to help in that undertaking. Understanding where to find the rules in the *Code* that apply to an installation is invaluable. Rules in several different articles often apply to even a simple installation.

Article 90 then describes the scope and arrangement of the *NEC*. A person who says, "I can't find anything in the *Code*," is really saying, "I never took the time to review Article 90." The balance of Article 90 provides the reader with information essential to understanding those items you do find in the *NEC*.

Typically, electrical work requires you to understand the first four chapters of the *Code* which apply generally, plus have a working knowledge of the Chapter 9 tables. That knowledge begins with Article 90. Chapters 5, 6, and 7 make up a large portion of the *NEC*, but they apply to special occupancies, special equipment, or other special conditions. They build on, modify, or amend the rules in the first four chapters. Chapter 8 contains the requirements for communications systems, such as telephone systems, antenna wiring, CATV, and network-powered broadband systems. Communications systems aren't subject to the general requirements of Chapters 1 through 4, or the special requirements of Chapters 5 through 7, unless there's a specific reference in Chapter 8 to a rule in Chapters 1 through 7.

90.1 Purpose of the *NEC*.

(A) Practical Safeguarding. The purpose of the *NEC* is to ensure that electrical systems are installed in a manner that protects people and property by minimizing the risks associated with the use of electricity.

(B) Adequacy. The *Code* contains requirements considered necessary for a safe electrical installation. If an electrical installation is installed in compliance with the *NEC*, it will be essentially free from electrical hazards. The *Code* is a safety standard, not a design guide.

NEC requirements aren't intended to ensure the electrical installation will be efficient, convenient, adequate for good service, or suitable for future expansion. Specific items of concern, such as electrical energy management, maintenance, and power quality issues aren't within the scope of the *Code*. Figure 90–1

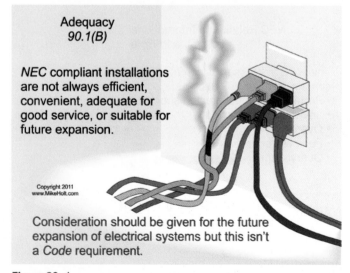

Adequacy
90.1(B)

NEC compliant installations are not always efficient, convenient, adequate for good service, or suitable for future expansion.

Copyright 2011
www.MikeHolt.com

Consideration should be given for the future expansion of electrical systems but this isn't a *Code* requirement.

Figure 90–1

Note: Hazards in electrical systems often occur because circuits are overloaded or not properly installed in accordance with the *NEC*. These often occur if the initial wiring didn't provide reasonable provisions for system changes or for the increase in the use of electricity.

Author's Comments:

• See the definition of "Overload" in Article 100.

• The *NEC* doesn't require electrical systems to be designed or installed to accommodate future loads. However, the electrical designer, typically an electrical engineer, is concerned with not only ensuring electrical safety (*Code* compliance), but also with ensuring the system meets the customers' needs, both of today and in the near future. To satisfy customers' needs, electrical systems are often designed and installed above the minimum requirements contained in the *NEC*. But just remember, if you're taking an exam, licensing exams are based on your understanding of the minimum *Code* requirements.

(C) Intention. The *Code* is intended to be used by those skilled and knowledgeable in electrical theory, electrical systems, construction, and the installation and operation of electrical equipment. It isn't a design specification standard or instruction manual for the untrained and unqualified.

(D) Relation to International Standards. The requirements of the *NEC* address the fundamental safety principles contained in the International Electrotechnical Commission (IEC) standards, including protection against electric shock, adverse thermal effects, overcurrent, fault currents, and overvoltage. **Figure 90–2**

NEC Relation to International Standards
90.1(D) and Note

The *NEC* addresses the safety principles contained in the IEC such as:
• Protection against electric shock
• Adverse thermal effects
• Overcurrent
• Fault currents
• Overvoltage

Figure 90–2

Author's Comments:

• See the definition of "Overcurrent" in Article 100.

• The *NEC* is used in Chile, Ecuador, Peru, and the Philippines. It's also the electrical code for Colombia, Costa Rica, Mexico, Panama, Puerto Rico, and Venezuela. Because of these adoptions, the *NEC* is available in Spanish from the National Fire Protection Association, 1.617.770.3000, or www.NFPA.Org.

90.2 Scope of the *NEC*.

(A) What is Covered. The *NEC* contains requirements necessary for the proper installation of electrical conductors, equipment, and raceways; signaling and communications conductors, equipment, and raceways; as well as optical fiber cables and raceways for the following locations: **Figure 90–3**

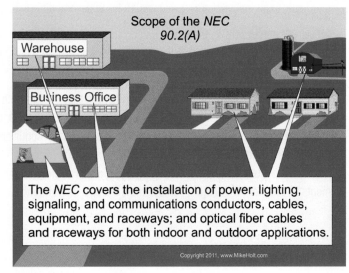

Scope of the NEC
90.2(A)

Warehouse

Business Office

The *NEC* covers the installation of power, lighting, signaling, and communications conductors, cables, equipment, and raceways; and optical fiber cables and raceways for both indoor and outdoor applications.

Copyright 2011, www.MikeHolt.com

Figure 90–3

(1) Public and private premises, including buildings or structures, mobile homes, recreational vehicles, and floating buildings.

(2) Yards, lots, parking lots, carnivals, and industrial substations.

(3) Conductors and equipment connected to the utility supply.

(4) Installations used by an electric utility, such as office buildings, warehouses, garages, machine shops, recreational buildings, and other electric utility buildings that aren't an integral part of a utility's generating plant, substation, or control center. **Figure 90–4**

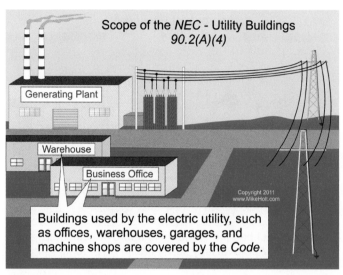

Figure 90–4

90.3 *Code* Arrangement.

The *Code* is divided into an introduction and nine chapters. **Figure 90–5**

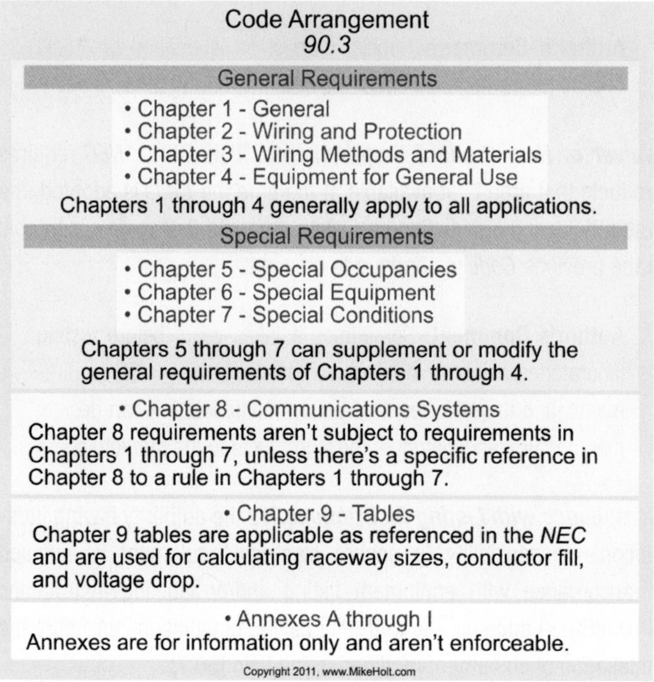

Code Arrangement
90.3

General Requirements
• Chapter 1 - General
• Chapter 2 - Wiring and Protection
• Chapter 3 - Wiring Methods and Materials
• Chapter 4 - Equipment for General Use
Chapters 1 through 4 generally apply to all applications.

Special Requirements
• Chapter 5 - Special Occupancies
• Chapter 6 - Special Equipment
• Chapter 7 - Special Conditions
Chapters 5 through 7 can supplement or modify the general requirements of Chapters 1 through 4.

• Chapter 8 - Communications Systems
Chapter 8 requirements aren't subject to requirements in Chapters 1 through 7, unless there's a specific reference in Chapter 8 to a rule in Chapters 1 through 7.

• Chapter 9 - Tables
Chapter 9 tables are applicable as referenced in the *NEC* and are used for calculating raceway sizes, conductor fill, and voltage drop.

• Annexes A through I
Annexes are for information only and aren't enforceable.

Copyright 2011, www.MikeHolt.com

Figure 90–5

General Requirements. The requirements contained in Chapters 1, 2, 3, and 4 apply to all installations.

Author's Comment: These first four chapters may be thought of as the foundation for the rest of the *Code*, and are the main focus of this textbook.

Special Requirements. The requirements contained in Chapters 5, 6, and 7 apply to special occupancies, special equipment, or other special conditions. These chapters can supplement or modify the requirements in Chapters 1 through 4.

Communications Systems. Chapter 8 contains the requirements for communications systems, such as telephone systems, antenna wiring, CATV, and network-powered broadband systems. Communications systems aren't subject to the general requirements of Chapters 1 through 4, or the special requirements of Chapters 5 through 7, unless there's a specific reference in Chapter 8 to a rule in Chapters 1 through 7.

Author's Comment: An example of how Chapter 8 works is in the rules for working space about equipment. The typical 3 ft working space isn't required in front of communications equipment, because Table 110.26(A)(1) isn't referenced in Chapter 8.

Tables. Chapter 9 consists of tables applicable as referenced in the *NEC*. The tables are used to calculate raceway sizing, conductor fill, the radius of raceway bends, and conductor voltage drop.

Annexes. Annexes aren't part of the *Code*, but are included for informational purposes. There are eight Annexes:

• Annex A. Product Safety Standards
• Annex B. Application Information for Ampacity Calculation
• Annex C. Raceway Fill Tables for Conductors and Fixture Wires of the Same Size
• Annex D. Examples
• Annex E. Types of Construction
• Annex F. Critical Operations Power Systems (COPS)
• Annex G. Supervisory Control and Data Acquisition (SCADA)
• Annex H. Administration and Enforcement

90.4 Enforcement.

The *Code* is intended to be suitable for enforcement by governmental bodies that exercise legal jurisdiction over electrical installations for power, lighting, signaling circuits, and communications systems, such as: **Figure 90–6**

The enforcement of the *NEC* is the responsibility of the authority having jurisdiction (AHJ), who is responsible for interpreting requirements, approving equipment and materials, waiving *Code* requirements, and ensuring equipment is installed in accordance with listing instructions.

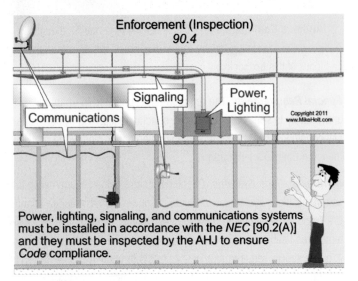

Power, lighting, signaling, and communications systems must be installed in accordance with the *NEC* [90.2(A)] and they must be inspected by the AHJ to ensure *Code* compliance.

Figure 90–6

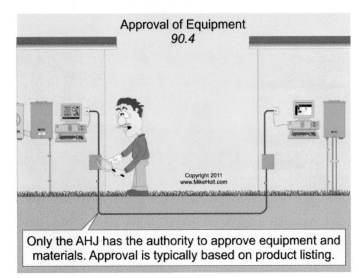

Only the AHJ has the authority to approve equipment and materials. Approval is typically based on product listing.

Figure 90–7

Author's Comment: See the definition of "Authority Having Jurisdiction" in Article 100.

Interpretation of the Requirements. The authority having jurisdiction is responsible for interpreting the *NEC*, but his or her decisions must be based on a specific *Code* requirement. If an installation is rejected, the authority having jurisdiction is legally responsible for informing the installer of which specific *NEC* rule was violated.

Author's Comment: The art of getting along with the authority having jurisdiction consists of doing good work and knowing what the *Code* actually says (as opposed to what you only think it says). It's also useful to know how to choose your battles when the inevitable disagreement does occur.

Approval of Equipment and Materials. Only the authority having jurisdiction has authority to approve the installation of equipment and materials. Typically, the authority having jurisdiction will approve equipment listed by a product testing organization, such as Underwriters Laboratories, Inc. (UL). The *NEC* doesn't require all equipment to be listed, but many state and local AHJs do. See 90.7, 110.2, 110.3, and the definitions for "Approved," "Identified," "Labeled," and "Listed" in Article 100. **Figure 90–7**

Author's Comment: According to the *NEC*, the authority having jurisdiction determines the approval of equipment. This means he or she can reject an installation of listed equipment and can approve the use of unlisted equipment. Given our highly litigious society, approval of unlisted equipment is becoming increasingly difficult to obtain.

Waiver of Requirements. By special permission, the authority having jurisdiction can waive specific requirements in the *Code* or permit alternative methods where it's assured equivalent safety can be achieved and maintained.

Author's Comment: Special permission is defined in Article 100 as the written consent of the authority having jurisdiction.

Waiver of New Product Requirements. If the 2011 *NEC* requires products that aren't yet available at the time the *Code* is adopted, the authority having jurisdiction can allow products that were acceptable in the previous *Code* to continue to be used.

Author's Comment: Sometimes it takes years before testing laboratories establish product standards for new *NEC* requirements, and then it takes time before manufacturers can design, manufacture, and distribute these products to the marketplace.

Compliance with Listing Instructions. It's the authority having jurisdiction's responsibility to ensure electrical equipment is installed in accordance with equipment listing and/or labeling instructions [110.3(B)]. In addition, the authority having jurisdiction can reject the installation of equipment modified in the field [90.7].

Author's Comment: The *NEC* doesn't address the maintenance of electrical equipment because the *Code* is an installation standard, not a maintenance standard. See NFPA 70B—*Recommended Practice for Electrical Equipment Maintenance.*

90.5 Mandatory Requirements and Explanatory Material.

(A) Mandatory Requirements. In the *NEC* the words "shall" or "shall not," indicate a mandatory requirement.

> **Author's Comment:** For the ease of reading this textbook, the word "shall" has been replaced with the word "must," and the words "shall not" have been replaced with "must not." Remember that in many places, we'll paraphrase the *Code* instead of providing exact quotes, to make it easier to read and understand.

(B) Permissive Requirements. When the *Code* uses "shall be permitted" it means the identified actions are permitted but not required, and the authority having jurisdiction isn't permitted to restrict an installation from being done in that manner. A permissive rule is often an exception to the general requirement.

> **Author's Comment:** For ease of reading, the phrase "shall be permitted," as used in the *Code*, has been replaced in this textbook with the phrase "is permitted" or "are permitted."

(C) Explanatory Material. References to other standards or sections of the *NEC*, or information related to a *Code* rule, are included in the form of <u>Informational Notes</u>. Such notes are for information only and aren't enforceable as a requirement of the *NEC*.

For example, Informational Note 4 in 210.19(A)(1) recommends that the voltage drop of a circuit not exceed 3 percent. This isn't a requirement; it's just a recommendation.

> **Author's Comment:** For convenience and ease of reading in this textbook, I'll identify Informational Notes simply as "Note."

(D) <u>Informative</u> Annexes. Nonmandatory information annexes contained in the back of the *Code* book are for information only and aren't enforceable as a requirement of the *NEC*.

90.6 Formal Interpretations.
To promote uniformity of interpretation and application of the provisions of the *NEC*, formal interpretation procedures have been established and are found in the NFPA's *Regulations Governing Committee Projects*.

> **Author's Comment:** This is rarely done because it's a very time-consuming process, and formal interpretations from the NFPA aren't binding on the authority having jurisdiction.

90.7 Examination of Equipment for Product Safety.
Product evaluation for safety is typically performed by a testing laboratory, which publishes a list of equipment that meets a nationally recognized test standard. Products and materials that are listed, labeled, or identified by a testing laboratory are generally approved by the authority having jurisdiction.

> **Author's Comment:** See Article 100 for the definition of "Approved."

Listed, factory-installed, internal wiring and construction of equipment need not be inspected at the time of installation, except to detect alterations or damage [300.1(B)]. **Figure 90–8**

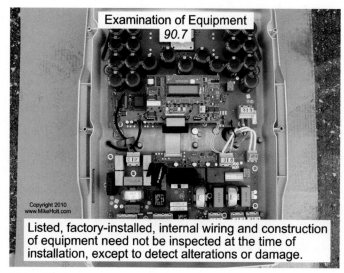

Examination of Equipment
90.7

Listed, factory-installed, internal wiring and construction of equipment need not be inspected at the time of installation, except to detect alterations or damage.

Figure 90–8

ARTICLE 90. INTRODUCTION—PRACTICE QUESTIONS

1. The *NEC* is _____.

    (a) intended to be a design manual
    (b) meant to be used as an instruction guide for untrained persons
    (c) for the practical safeguarding of persons and property
    (d) published by the Bureau of Standards

2. Compliance with the provisions of the *NEC* will result in _____.

    (a) good electrical service
    (b) an efficient electrical system
    (c) an electrical system essentially free from hazard
    (d) all of these

3. The *Code* contains provisions considered necessary for safety, which will not necessarily result in _____.

    (a) efficient use
    (b) convenience
    (c) good service or future expansion of electrical use
    (d) all of these

4. Hazards often occur because of _____.

    (a) overloading of wiring systems by methods or usage not in conformity with the *NEC*
    (b) initial wiring not providing for increases in the use of electricity
    (c) a and b
    (d) none of these

5. The *Code* isn't a design specification standard or instruction manual for the untrained and unqualified.

    (a) True
    (b) False

6. The *NEC* applies to the installation of _____.

    (a) electrical conductors and equipment within or on public and private buildings
    (b) outside conductors and equipment on the premises
    (c) optical fiber cables
    (d) all of these

7. This *Code* covers the installation of _____ for public and private premises, including buildings, structures, mobile homes, recreational vehicles, and floating buildings.

    (a) optical fiber cables
    (b) electrical equipment
    (c) raceways
    (d) all of these

8. Chapters 1 through 4 of the *NEC* apply _____.

    (a) generally to all electrical installations
    (b) only to special occupancies and conditions
    (c) only to special equipment and material
    (d) all of these

9. The material located in the *NEC* Annexes are part of the requirements of the *Code* and shall be complied with.

    (a) True
    (b) False

10. The _____ has the responsibility for deciding on the approval of equipment and materials.

    (a) manufacturer
    (b) authority having jurisdiction
    (c) testing agency
    (d) none of these

11. By special permission, the authority having jurisdiction may waive specific requirements in this *Code* where it is assured that equivalent objectives can be achieved by establishing and maintaining effective safety.

    (a) True
    (b) False

12. The authority having jurisdiction has the responsibility _____.

    (a) for making interpretations of rules
    (b) for deciding upon the approval of equipment and materials
    (c) for waiving specific requirements in the *Code* and permitting alternate methods and material if safety is maintained
    (d) all of these

13. If the *NEC* requires new products that are not yet available at the time a new edition is adopted, the _____ may permit the use of the products that comply with the previous edition of the *Code* adopted by that jurisdiction.

    (a) electrical engineer
    (b) master electrician
    (c) authority having jurisdiction
    (d) permit holder

14. In the *NEC*, the words _____ indicate a mandatory requirement.

    (a) shall
    (b) shall not
    (c) shall be permitted
    (d) a or b

15. When the *Code* uses _____, it means the identified actions are allowed but not required, and they may be options or alternative methods.

    (a) shall
    (b) shall not
    (c) shall be permitted
    (d) a or b

16. Explanatory material, such as references to other standards, references to related sections of the *NEC*, or information related to a *Code* rule, are included in the form of Informational Notes.

    (a) True
    (b) False

17. Nonmandatory information annexes contained in the back of the *Code* book _____.

    (a) are for information only
    (b) aren't enforceable as a requirement of the *Code*.
    (c) are enforceable as a requirement of the *Code*
    (d) a and b

18. Factory-installed _____ wiring of listed equipment need not be inspected at the time of installation of the equipment, except to detect alterations or damage.

    (a) external
    (b) associated
    (c) internal
    (d) all of these

Notes

CHAPTER 1

GENERAL

INTRODUCTION TO CHAPTER 1—GENERAL

A young child doesn't begin reading and writing until they have an understanding of some of the basic words of the language. Similarly, you must be familiar with a few basic rules, concepts, definitions, and requirements that apply to the rest of the *NEC* and you must maintain that familiarity as you continue to apply the *Code*.

Chapter 1 consists of two topics. Article 100 provides definitions so people can understand one another when trying to communicate about *Code*-related matters and Article 110 provides the general requirements needed to correctly apply the rest of the *NEC*.

Time spent learning this general material is a great investment. After understanding Chapter 1, some of the *Code* requirements that seem confusing to other people—those who don't understand Chapter 1—will become increasingly clear to you. The requirements will strike you as being "common sense," because you'll have the foundation from which to understand and apply them. When you read the *NEC* requirements in later chapters, you'll understand the principles upon which many of them are based, and not be surprised at all. You'll read them and feel like you already know them.

- **Article 100—Definitions.** Part I of Article 100 contains the definitions of terms used throughout the *Code* for systems that operate at 600V, nominal, or less. The definitions of terms in Part II apply to systems that operate at over 600V, nominal.

   Author's Comment: This textbook covers the requirements for systems that operate at 600V, nominal, or less.

Definitions of standard terms, such as volt, voltage drop, ampere, impedance, and resistance, aren't listed in Article 100. If the *NEC* doesn't define a term, then a dictionary suitable to the authority having jurisdiction should be consulted. A building code glossary might provide better definitions than a dictionary found at your home or school.

Definitions located at the beginning of an article apply only to that specific article. For example, the definition of a "Swimming Pool" is contained in 680.2, because this term applies only to the requirements contained in Article 680—Swimming Pools, Fountains, and Similar Installations. As soon as a defined term is used in two or more articles, its definition is included in Article 100.

- **Article 110—Requirements for Electrical Installations.** This article contains general requirements for electrical installations for the following:
  - Part I. General
  - Part II. 600V, Nominal, or Less

Notes

Definitions

INTRODUCTION TO ARTICLE 100—DEFINITIONS

Have you ever had a conversation with someone, only to discover that what you said and what he or she heard were completely different? This often happens when people in a conversation don't understand the definitions of the words being used, and that's why the definitions of key terms are located right at the beginning of the *NEC* (Article 100), or at the beginning of each article.

If we can all agree on important definitions, then we speak the same language and avoid misunderstandings. Because the *Code* exists to protect people and property, it's very important to know the definitions presented in Article 100.

Now, here are a couple of things you may not know about Article 100:

Article 100 contains many, but not all, of the terms defined by the *NEC*. In general, only those terms used in two or more articles are defined in Article 100. Those terms used only within one article are located within that article, often near the beginning of the article.

- Part I of Article 100 contains the definitions of terms used throughout the *Code* for systems that operate at 600V, nominal, or less.
- Part II of Article 100 contains only terms that apply to systems that operate at over 600V nominal.

How can you possibly learn all of these definitions? There seem to be so many. Here are a few tips:

- Break the task down. Study a few words at a time, rather than trying to learn them all at one sitting.
- Review the graphics in the textbook. These will help you see how a term is applied.
- Relate them to your work. As you read a word, think about how it applies to the work you're doing. This will provide a natural reinforcement to the learning process.

DEFINITIONS

Accessible (as it applies to equipment). Admitting close approach and not guarded by locked doors, elevation, or other effective means.

Accessible (as it applies to wiring methods). Not permanently closed in by the building structure or finish and capable of being removed or exposed without damaging the building structure or finish. **Figure 100–1**

Author's Comments:

- Conductors in a concealed raceway are considered concealed, even though they may become accessible by withdrawing them from the raceway. See the definition of "Concealed" in this article.

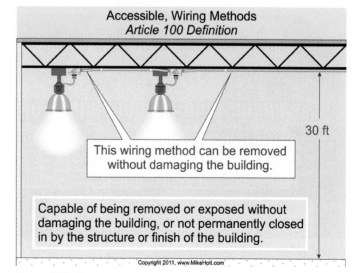

Figure 100–1

- Raceways, cables, and enclosures installed above a suspended ceiling or within a raised floor are considered accessible, because the wiring methods can be accessed without damaging the building structure. See the definitions of "Concealed" and "Exposed" in this article.

Accessible, Readily (Readily Accessible). Capable of being reached quickly without having to climb over or remove obstacles, or resort to portable ladders. **Figures 100–2 and 100–3**

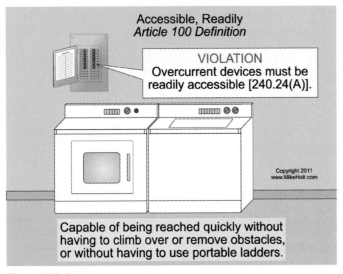

Figure 100–2

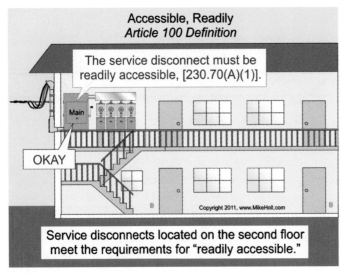

Figure 100–3

Ampacity. The <u>maximum</u> current, in amperes, a conductor can carry continuously, where the temperature of the conductor won't be raised in excess of its insulation temperature rating. **Figure 100–4**

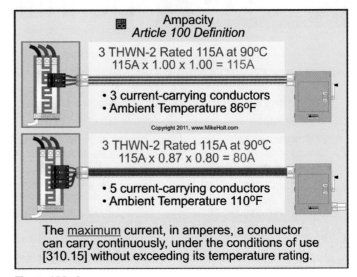

Figure 100–4

Author's Comment: See 310.10 and 310.15 for details and examples.

Approved. Acceptable to the authority having jurisdiction, usually the electrical inspector.

Author's Comment: Product listing doesn't mean the product is approved, but it's a basis for approval. See 90.4, 90.7, 110.2, and the definitions in this article for "Authority Having Jurisdiction," "Identified," "Labeled," and "Listed."

Authority Having Jurisdiction (AHJ). The organization, office, or individual responsible for approving equipment, materials, an installation, or a procedure. See 90.4 and 90.7 for more information.

Note: The authority having jurisdiction may be a federal, state, or local governmental department or an individual, such as a fire chief, fire marshal, chief of a fire prevention bureau or labor department or health department, a building official or electrical inspector, or others having statutory authority. In some circumstances, the property owner or his/her agent assumes the role, and at governmental installations, the commanding officer, or departmental official may be the authority having jurisdiction.

Author's Comments:

- Typically, the authority having jurisdiction is the electrical inspector who has legal statutory authority. In the absence of federal, state, or local regulations, the operator of the facility or his or her agent, such as an architect or engineer of the facility, can assume the role.

- Some believe the authority having jurisdiction should have a strong background in the electrical field, such as having studied electrical engineering or having obtained an electrical contractor's license, and in a few states this is a legal requirement. Memberships, certifications, and active participation in electrical organizations, such as the International Association of Electrical Inspectors (IAEI), speak to an individual's qualifications. Visit www.IAEI.org for more information about that organization.

Bonded (Bonding). Connected to establish electrical continuity and conductivity. **Figure 100–5)**

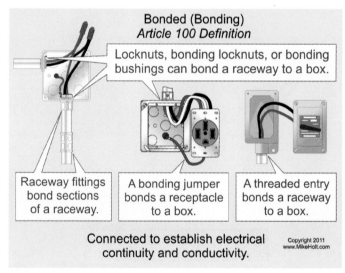

Figure 100–5

Author's Comment: The purpose of bonding is to connect two or more conductive objects together to ensure the electrical continuity of the fault current path, provide the capacity and ability to conduct safely any fault current likely to be imposed, and to minimize potential differences (voltage) between conductive components.

Bonding Conductor or Jumper. A conductor that ensures electrical conductivity between metal parts of the electrical installation. **Figure 100–6**

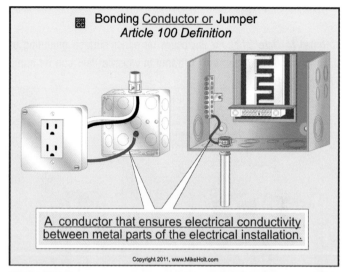

Figure 100–6

Building. A structure that stands alone or is cut off from other structures by fire walls with all openings protected by fire doors approved by the authority having jurisdiction. **Figure 100–7**

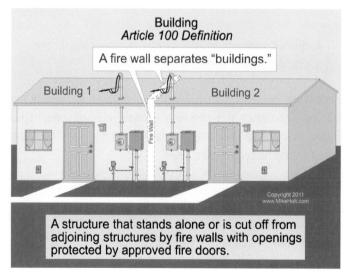

Figure 100–7

Author's Comment: Not all fire-rated walls are fire walls. Building codes describe fire barriers, fire partitions and other fire-rated walls, in addition to fire walls. Check with your local building inspector to determine if a rated wall creates a separate building (fire wall).

Cabinet [Article 312]. An enclosure for either surface mounting or flush mounting provided with a frame in which a door can be hung. **Figure 100–8**

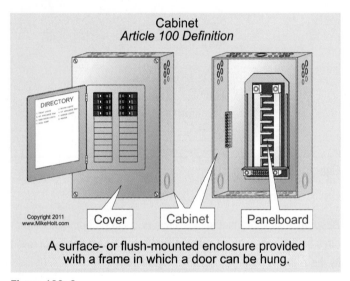

Cabinet
Article 100 Definition

Cover   Cabinet   Panelboard

A surface- or flush-mounted enclosure provided with a frame in which a door can be hung.

Figure 100–8

Author's Comment: Cabinets are used to enclose panelboards. See the definition of "Panelboard" in this article.

Concealed. Rendered inaccessible by the structure or finish of the building. Conductors in a concealed raceway are considered concealed, even though they may be made accessible by withdrawing them from the raceway. **Figure 100–9**

Author's Comment: Wiring behind panels designed to allow access, such as removable ceiling tile, is considered exposed.

Conduit Body. A fitting that's installed in a conduit or tubing system and provides access to conductors through a removable cover. **Figure 100–10**

Connector, Pressure (Solderless). A device that establishes a conductive connection between conductors or between a conductor and a terminal by the means of mechanical pressure.

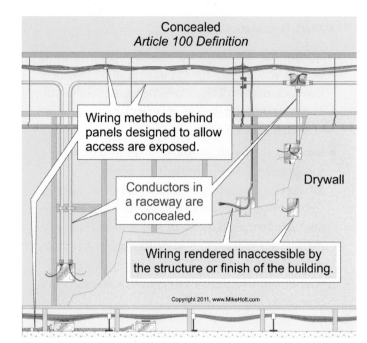

Concealed
Article 100 Definition

Wiring methods behind panels designed to allow access are exposed.

Conductors in a raceway are concealed.

Drywall

Wiring rendered inaccessible by the structure or finish of the building.

Copyright 2011, www.MikeHolt.com

Figure 100–9

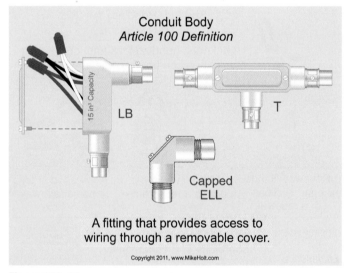

Conduit Body
Article 100 Definition

15 in³ Capacity

LB

T

Capped ELL

A fitting that provides access to wiring through a removable cover.

Copyright 2011, www.MikeHolt.com

Figure 100–10

Cutout Box [Article 312]. Cutout boxes are designed for surface mounting with a swinging door or covers secured directly to the box.

Device. A component of an electrical installation intended to carry or control electric energy as its principal function.

Author's Comment: Devices include wires and busbars, receptacles, switches, illuminated switches, circuit breakers, fuses,
time clocks, controllers, and so forth, but not locknuts or other
mechanical fittings. A device may consume very small amounts
of energy, such as an illuminated switch, but still be classified as
a device based on its principal function.

Disconnecting Means. A device that opens all of the ungrounded circuit conductors from their power source. This includes devices such
as switches, attachment plugs and receptacles, and circuit breakers.
Figure 100–11

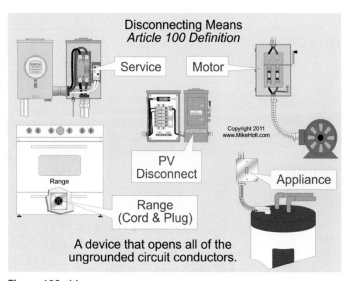

Figure 100–11

Dwelling Unit. A space that provides independent living facilities,
with space for eating, living, and sleeping; as well as permanent facilities for cooking and sanitation. **Figure 100–12**

Enclosed. Surrounded by a case, housing, fence, or wall(s) that prevents accidental contact with energized parts.

Energized. Electrically connected to a source of voltage.

Equipment. A general term including fittings, devices, appliances,
luminaires, machinery, and the like. **Figure 100–13**

Exposed (as applied to live parts). Capable of being touched if not
suitably guarded, isolated, or insulated.

Exposed (as applied to wiring methods). On or attached to the surface of a building, or behind panels designed to allow access.

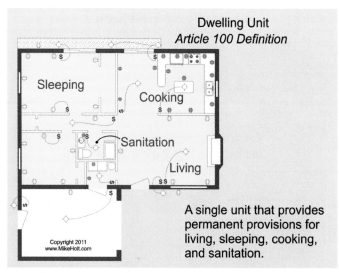

Figure 100–12

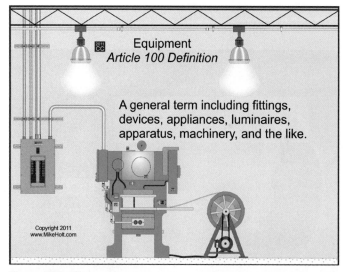

Figure 100–13

Author's Comment: An example is wiring located in the space
above a suspended ceiling or below a raised floor. **Figure
100–14**

Fitting. An accessory, such as a locknut, intended to perform a
mechanical function.

Ground. The earth. **Figure 100–15**

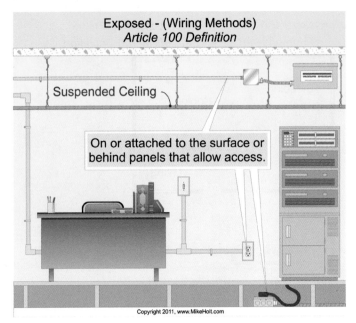

Figure 100–14

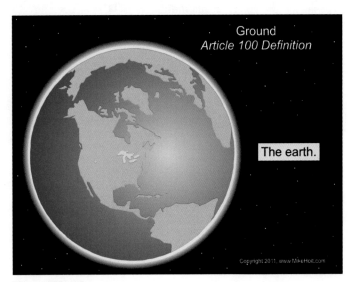

Figure 100–15

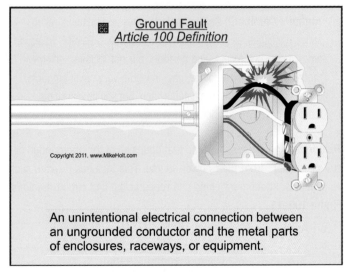

Figure 100–16

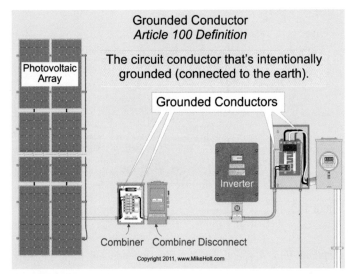

Figure 100–17

Ground Fault. An unintentional electrical connection between an ungrounded conductor and the metal parts of enclosures, raceways, or equipment. **Figure 100–16**

Grounded (Grounding). Connected to ground or to a conductive body that extends the ground connection.

Grounded Conductor [Article 200]. The circuit conductor that's intentionally grounded (connected to the earth). **Figure 100–17**

Grounding Conductor, Equipment (EGC). The conductive path(s) that connect metal parts of equipment to the system neutral conductor, to the grounding electrode conductor, or both [250.110 through 250.126]. **Figure 100–18**

Note 1: The circuit equipment grounding conductor also performs bonding.

Note 2: An equipment grounding conductor can be any one or a combination of the types listed in 250.118. **Figure 100–19**

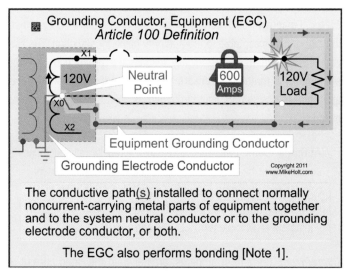

Figure 100–18

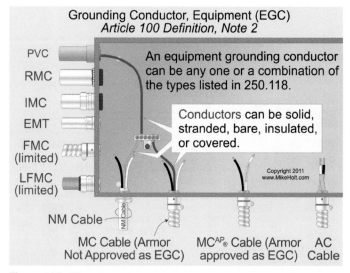

Figure 100–19

Author's Comment: Equipment grounding conductors include:

- A bare or insulated conductor
- Rigid Metal Conduit
- Intermediate Metal Conduit
- Electrical Metallic Tubing
- Listed Flexible Metal Conduit as limited by 250.118(5)
- Listed Liquidtight Flexible Metal Conduit as limited by 250.118(6)
- Armored Cable
- Metal-Clad Cable as limited by 250.118(10)
- Metallic cable trays as limited by 250.118(11) and 392.60
- Electrically continuous metal raceways listed for grounding
- Surface Metal Raceways listed for grounding

Grounding Electrode. A conducting object used to make a direct electrical connection to the earth [250.50 through 250.70]. **Figure 100–20**

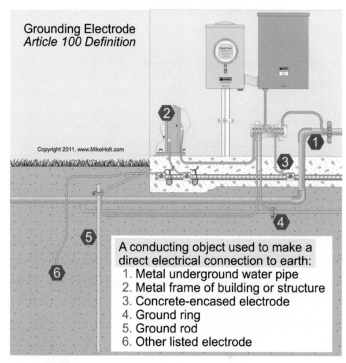

Figure 100–20

Grounding Electrode Conductor (GEC). The conductor used to connect the system grounded conductor (neutral) to a grounding electrode or to a point on the grounding electrode system. **Figure 100–21**

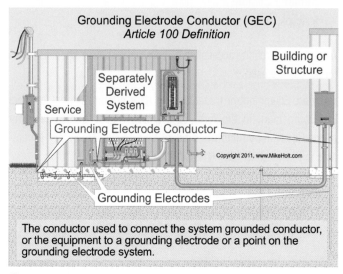

Figure 100–21

Identified Equipment. Recognized as suitable for a specific purpose, function, or environment by listing, labeling, or other means approved by the authority having jurisdiction.

> **Author's Comment:** See 90.4, 90.7, 110.3(A)(1), and the definitions for "Approved," "Labeled," and "Listed" in this article.

In Sight From (Within Sight). Visible and not more than 50 ft away from the equipment. **Figure 100–22**

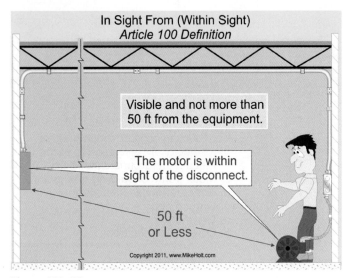

In Sight From (Within Sight)
Article 100 Definition

Visible and not more than 50 ft from the equipment.

The motor is within sight of the disconnect.

50 ft or Less

Copyright 2011, www.MikeHolt.com

Figure 100–22

Interrupting Rating. The highest short-circuit current at rated voltage the device is identified to interrupt under standard test conditions.

> **Author's Comment:** For more information, see 110.9 in this textbook.

Isolated. Not readily accessible to persons serunless special means for access are used.

Labeled. Equipment or materials that have a label, symbol, or other identifying mark in the form of a sticker, decal, printed label, or molded or stamped into the product by a testing laboratory acceptable to the authority having jurisdiction.

> **Author's Comment:** Labeling and listing of equipment typically provides the basis for equipment approval by the authority having jurisdiction [90.4, 90.7, 110.2, and 110.3].

Listed. Equipment or materials included in a list published by a testing laboratory acceptable to the authority having jurisdiction. The listing organization must periodically inspect the production of listed equipment or material to ensure the equipment or material meets appropriate designated standards and is suitable for a specified purpose.

> **Author's Comment:** The *NEC* doesn't require all electrical equipment to be listed, but some *Code* requirements do specifically require product listing. Organizations such as OSHA increasingly require that listed equipment be used when such equipment is available [90.7, 110.2, and 110.3].

Overcurrent. Current, in amperes, greater than the rated current of the equipment or conductors resulting from an overload, short circuit, or ground fault. **Figure 100–23**

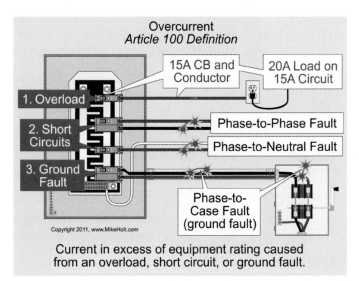

Overcurrent
Article 100 Definition

15A CB and Conductor
20A Load on 15A Circuit

1. Overload
2. Short Circuits
3. Ground Fault

Phase-to-Phase Fault
Phase-to-Neutral Fault
Phase-to-Case Fault (ground fault)

Copyright 2011, www.MikeHolt.com

Current in excess of equipment rating caused from an overload, short circuit, or ground fault.

Figure 100–23

> **Author's Comment:** See the definitions of "Ground Fault" in 250.2 and "Overload" in this article.

Overload. The operation of equipment above its current rating, or current in excess of conductor ampacity. When an overload condition persists for a sufficient length of time, it can result in equipment failure or in a fire from damaging or dangerous overheating. A fault, such as a short circuit or ground fault, isn't an overload.

Panelboard [Article 408]. A distribution point containing overcurrent devices and designed to be installed in a cabinet. **Figure 100–24**

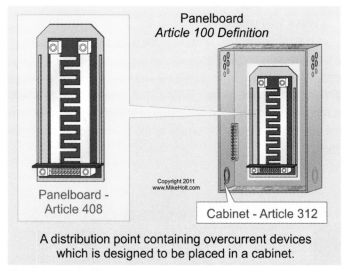

Panelboard
Article 100 Definition

Panelboard - Article 408

Cabinet - Article 312

Copyright 2011
www.MikeHolt.com

A distribution point containing overcurrent devices which is designed to be placed in a cabinet.

Figure 100–24

Author's Comments:

• See the definition of "Cabinet" in this article.

• The slang term in the electrical field for a panelboard is "the guts." This is the interior of the panelboard assembly and is covered by Article 408, while the cabinet is covered by Article 314.

Premises Wiring. The interior and exterior wiring, including power, lighting, control, and signal circuits, and all associated hardware, fittings, and wiring devices. This includes both permanently and temporarily installed wiring from the service point to the outlets, or where there's no service point, wiring from and including the power source to the outlets. **Figure 100–25**

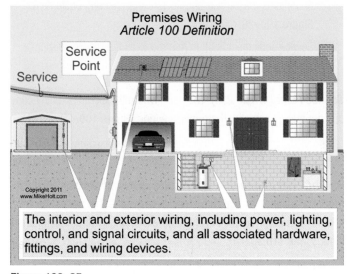

Premises Wiring
Article 100 Definition

Service

Service Point

Copyright 2011
www.MikeHolt.com

The interior and exterior wiring, including power, lighting, control, and signal circuits, and all associated hardware, fittings, and wiring devices.

Figure 100–25

Qualified Person. A person who has the skill and knowledge related to the construction and operation of electrical equipment and its installation. This person must have received safety training to recognize and avoid the hazards involved with electrical systems. **Figure 100–26**

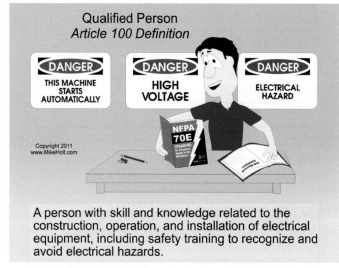

Qualified Person
Article 100 Definition

DANGER
THIS MACHINE STARTS AUTOMATICALLY

DANGER
HIGH VOLTAGE

DANGER
ELECTRICAL HAZARD

NFPA 70E

Copyright 2011
www.MikeHolt.com

A person with skill and knowledge related to the construction, operation, and installation of electrical equipment, including safety training to recognize and avoid electrical hazards.

Figure 100–26

Note: NFPA 70E, *Standard for Electrical Safety in the Workplace*, provides information on safety training requirements expected of a "qualified person."

Author's Comments:

• Examples of this safety training include, but aren't limited to, training in the use of special precautionary techniques, of personal protective equipment (PPE), of insulating and shielding materials, and of using insulated tools and test equipment when working on or near exposed conductors or circuit parts that can become energized.

• In many parts of the United States, electricians, electrical contractors, electrical inspectors, and electrical engineers must complete from 6 to 24 hours of *NEC* review each year as a requirement to maintain licensing. This in itself doesn't make one qualified to deal with the specific hazards involved with electrical systems.

Raceway. An enclosure designed for the installation of conductors, cables, or busbars. Raceways in the *NEC* include:

Raceway Type	Article
Electrical Metallic Tubing	358
Electrical Nonmetallic Tubing	362
Flexible Metal Conduit	348
Intermediate Metal Conduit	342
Liquidtight Flexible Metal Conduit	350
Liquidtight Flexible Nonmetallic Conduit	356
Metal Wireways	376
Rigid Metal Conduit	344
PVC Conduit	352

Author's Comments: A cable tray system isn't a raceway; it's a support system for cables and raceways [392.2].

Service [Article 230]. The conductors from the electric utility that deliver electric energy to the wiring system of the premises.

Author's Comment: Conductors from a UPS system, solar photovoltaic system, generator, or transformer aren't service conductors. See the definitions of "Feeder" and "Service Conductors" in this article.

Service Conductors. The conductors from the service point to the service disconnecting means. Figure 100–27

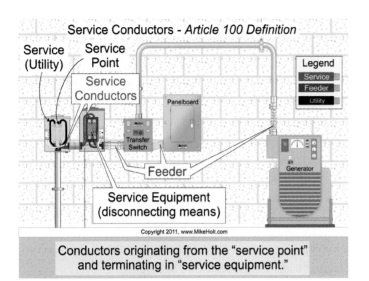

Conductors originating from the "service point" and terminating in "service equipment."

Figure 100–27

Author's Comment: These conductors fall within the requirements of Article 230, since they are not under the exclusive control of the electric utility.

Service Equipment [Article 230]. Circuit breaker(s) or switch(es) connected to the load end of service conductors, intended to control and cut off the service supply to the building/structure. Figure 100–28

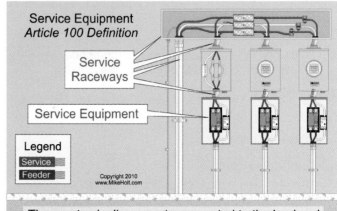

The one to six disconnects connected to the load end of service conductors intended to control and cut off the supply to the building or structure.

Figure 100–28

Author's Comments:

- It's important to know where a service begins and where it ends in order to properly apply the *NEC* requirements. Sometimes the service ends before the metering equipment. Figure 100–29
- Service equipment is often referred to as the "service disconnect" or "service disconnecting means."

Service Point [Article 230]. The point where the electrical utility conductors make contact with premises wiring. Figure 100–30

Note: The service point is the point where the serving utility ends and the premises wiring begins.

Short-Circuit Current Rating. The prospective symmetrical fault current at a nominal voltage that electrical equipment is able to be connected to without sustaining damage exceeding defined acceptance criteria. See 110.10.

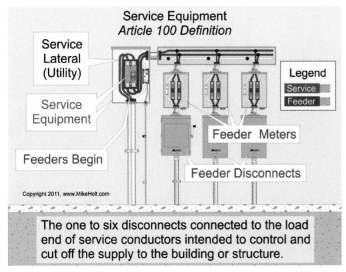

Figure 100–29

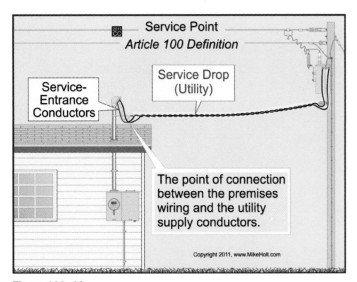

Figure 100–30

Special Permission. Written consent from the authority having jurisdiction.

Author's Comment: See the definition of "Authority Having Jurisdiction" in this article.

Structure. That which is built or constructed.

Ungrounded. Not connected to the ground (earth) or a conductive body that extends the ground (earth) connection. Figure 100–31

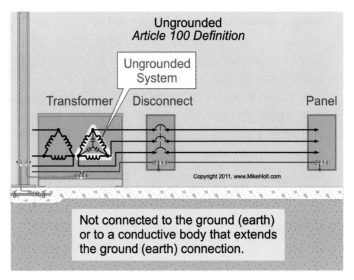

Figure 100–31

Author's Comment: The use of this term relates to an ungrounded system, where one of the system's current-carrying conductors isn't grounded (connected to the earth) [250.4(B) and 250.30(B)].

Utilization Equipment. Equipment that utilizes electricity for electronic, electromechanical, chemical, heating, lighting, or similar purposes.

Voltage, Nominal. A value assigned for the purpose of conveniently designating voltage class, such as 120/240V, 120/208V, or 277/480V [220.5(A)]. Figure 100–32

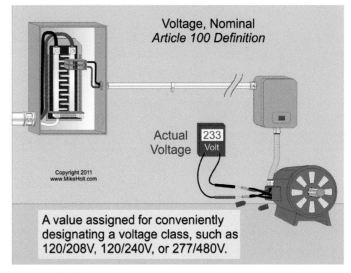

Figure 100–32

Author's Comment: The actual voltage at which a circuit operates can vary from the nominal within a range that permits satisfactory operation of equipment. In addition, the common voltage ratings of electrical equipment are 115V, 200V, 208V, 230V, and 460V. The electrical power supplied might be at the 240V, nominal voltage, but the voltage at the equipment will be less. Therefore, electrical equipment is rated at a value less than the nominal system voltage.

ARTICLE 110

Requirements for Electrical Installations

INTRODUCTION TO ARTICLE 110—REQUIREMENTS FOR ELECTRICAL INSTALLATIONS

Article 110 sets the stage for how you'll implement the rest of the *NEC*. This article contains a few of the most important and yet neglected parts of the *Code*. For example:

- How should you terminate conductors?
- What kinds of warnings, markings, and identification does a given installation require?
- What's the right working clearance for a given installation?
- What do the temperature limitations at terminals mean?
- What are the *NEC* requirements for dealing with flash protection?

It's critical that you master Article 110, and that's exactly what this Illustrated Guide to Understanding the National Electrical *Code* is designed for. As you read this article, you're building your foundation for correctly applying the *NEC*. In fact, this article itself is a foundation for much of the *Code*. The purpose for the National Electrical *Code* is to provide a safe installation, but Article 110 is perhaps focused a little more on providing an installation that's safe for the installer and maintenance electrician, so time spent in this article is time well spent.

PART I. GENERAL REQUIREMENTS

110.1 Scope. Article 110 covers the general requirements for the examination and approval, installation and use, access to and spaces about electrical equipment; as well as general requirements for enclosures intended for personnel entry (manholes, vaults, and tunnels).

110.2 Approval of Conductors and Equipment. The authority having jurisdiction must approve all electrical conductors and equipment. Figure 110–1

> **Author's Comment:** For a better understanding of product approval, review 90.4, 90.7, 110.3 and the definitions for "Approved," "Identified," "Labeled," and "Listed" in Article 100.

110.3 Examination, Identification, Installation, and Use of Equipment.

(A) Guidelines for Approval. The authority having jurisdiction must approve equipment. In doing so, consideration must be given to the following:

Approval of Equipment
110.2

Conductors and equipment can be installed only if they're approved.

The authority having jurisdiction must approve all electrical conductors and equipment.

Figure 110–1

(1) Suitability for installation and use in accordance with the *NEC*

Note: Suitability of equipment use may be identified by a description marked on or provided with a product to identify the suitability of the product for a specific purpose, environment, or application. Special conditions of use or other limitations may be marked on the equipment, in the product instructions, or appropriate listing and labeling information. Suitability of equipment may be evidenced by listing or labeling.

(2) Mechanical strength and durability

(3) Wire-bending and connection space

(4) Electrical insulation

(5) Heating effects under all conditions of use

(6) Arcing effects

(7) Classification by type, size, voltage, current capacity, and specific use

(8) Other factors contributing to the practical safeguarding of persons using or in contact with the equipment

(B) Installation and Use. Equipment must be installed and used in accordance with any instructions included in the listing or labeling requirements. Figure 110–2

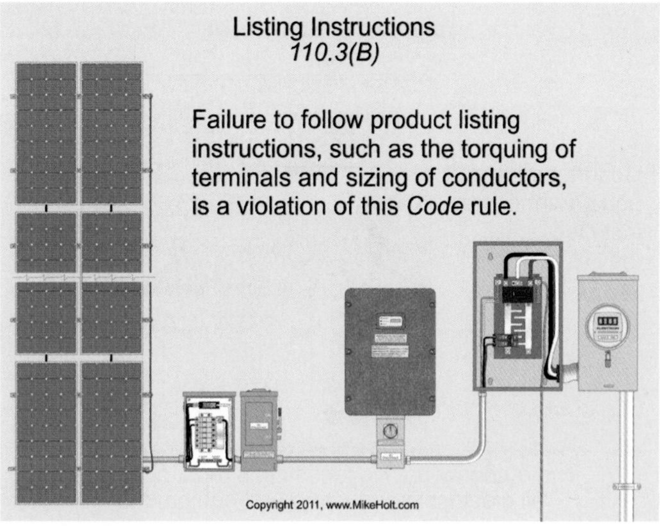

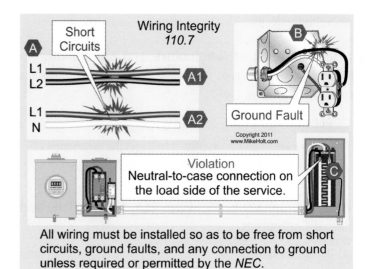

Figure 110–2

110.5 Copper Conductors.

110.5 Copper Conductors. If the conductor material isn't specified in a rule, the material and the sizes given in the *Code* (and this textbook) are based on copper.

110.6 Conductor Sizes.

110.6 Conductor Sizes. Conductor sizes are expressed in American Wire Gage (AWG), typically from 18 AWG up to 4/0 AWG. Conductor sizes larger than 4/0 AWG are expressed in kcmil (thousand circular mils). Figure 110–3

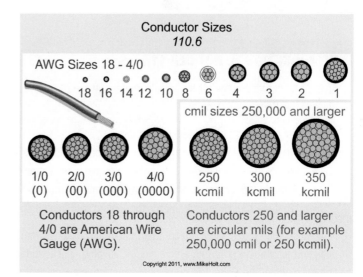

Figure 110–3

110.7 Wiring Integrity.

110.7 Wiring Integrity. All wiring must be installed so as to be free from short circuits, ground faults, and any connection to ground (such as a neutral conductor connection to the circuit equipment grounding conductor), unless required or permitted by this *Code*. Figure 110–4

Figure 110–4

Author's Comments:

- Short circuits and ground faults often arise from insulation failure due to mishandling or improper installation. This happens when, for example, wire is dragged over a sharp edge, when insulation is scraped on boxes and enclosures, when wire is pulled too hard, when insulation is nicked while being stripped, or when cable clamps and/or staples are installed too tightly.

- To protect against accidental contact with energized conductors, the ends of unused conductors must be covered with an insulating device identified for the purpose, such as a twist-on or push-on wire connector [110.14(B)].

110.8 Suitable Wiring Methods. Only wiring methods recognized as suitable are included in the *NEC*, and they must be installed in accordance with the *Code*. **Figure 110–5**

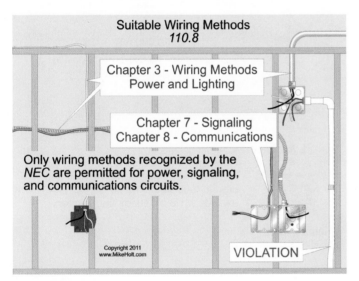

Figure 110–5

Author's Comment: See Chapter 3 for power and lighting wiring methods, Chapter 7 for signaling, remote-control, and power-limited circuits, and Chapter 8 for communications circuits.

110.9 Interrupting Protection Rating. Overcurrent devices such as circuit breakers and fuses are intended to interrupt the circuit, and they must have an interrupting rating <u>not less than</u> the nominal circuit voltage and the current that's available at the line terminals of the equipment. **Figure 110–6**

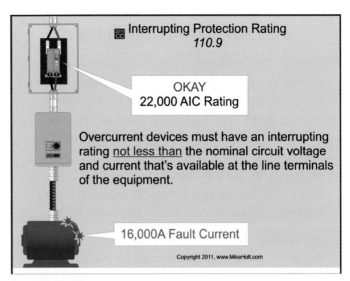

Figure 110–6

Author's Comments:

- See the definition of "Interrupting Rating" in Article 100.

- Unless marked otherwise, the ampere interrupting rating for circuit breakers is 5,000A [240.83(C)], and for fuses it's 10,000A [240.60(C)(3)]. **Figure 110–7**

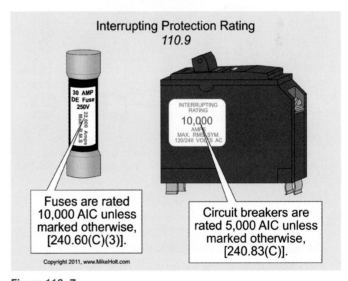

Figure 110–7

AVAILABLE SHORT-CIRCUIT CURRENT

Available short-circuit current is the current, in amperes, available at a given point in the electrical system. This available short-circuit current is first determined at the secondary terminals of the utility transformer. Thereafter, the available short-circuit current is calculated at the terminals of service equipment, then at branch-circuit panelboards and other equipment. The available short-circuit current is different at each point of the electrical system. It's highest at the utility transformer and lowest at the branch-circuit load.

The available short-circuit current depends on the impedance of the circuit, which increases moving downstream from the utility transformer. The greater the circuit impedance (utility transformer and the additive impedances of the circuit conductors), the lower the available short-circuit current. **Figure 110–8**

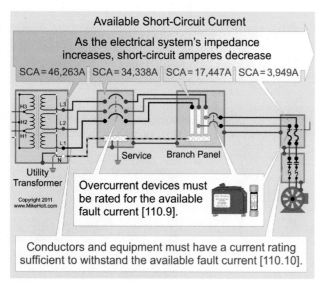

Figure 110–8

The factors that affect the available short-circuit current at the utility transformer include the system voltage, the transformer kVA rating, and the circuit impedance (expressed in a percentage on the equipment nameplate). Properties that have an impact on the impedance of the circuit include the conductor material (copper versus aluminum), conductor size, conductor length, and motor-operated equipment supplied by the circuit.

Author's Comment: Many people in the industry describe Amperes Interrupting Rating (AIR) as "Amperes Interrupting Capacity" (AIC).

DANGER: *Extremely high values of current flow (caused by short circuits or ground faults) produce tremendously destructive thermal and magnetic forces. If the circuit overcurrent device isn't rated to interrupt the current at the available fault values at its listed voltage rating, it can explode while attempting to open the circuit overcurrent device resulting from a short circuit or ground fault, which can cause serious injury or death, as well as property damage.* **Figure 110–9**

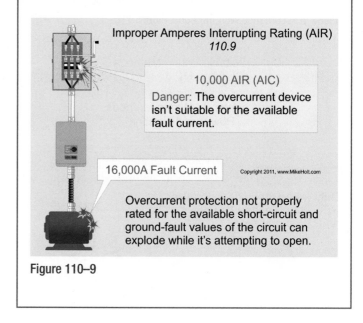

Figure 110–9

110.10 Circuit Impedance, Short-Circuit Current Rating, and Other Characteristics. Electrical equipment
must have a short-circuit current rating that permits the circuit protective device to open from a short circuit or ground fault without extensive damage to the electrical equipment of the circuit. This fault is assumed to be either between two or more of the circuit conductors or between any circuit conductor and the equipment grounding conductor(s) permitted in 250.118. Listed equipment applied in accordance with their listing is considered to have met the requirements of this section.

Author's Comment: For example, a motor controller must have a sufficient short-circuit rating for the available fault current. If the fault exceeds the controller's 5,000A short-circuit current rating, the controller can explode, endangering persons and property. **Figure 110–10**

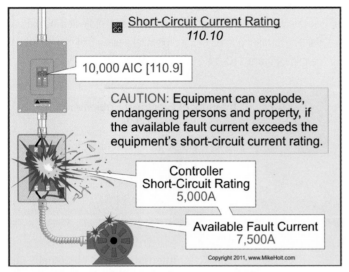

Figure 110–10

110.11 Deteriorating Agents.
Electrical equipment and conductors must be suitable for the environment and conditions of use. Consideration must also be given to the presence of corrosive gases, fumes, vapors, liquids, or other substances that can have a deteriorating effect on the conductors or equipment. **Figure 110–11**

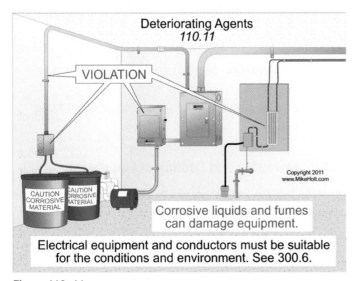

Figure 110–11

Author's Comment: Conductors must not be exposed to ultraviolet rays from the sun unless identified for the purpose [310.10(D)].

Note 1: Raceways, cable trays, cablebus, cable armor, boxes, cable sheathing, cabinets, elbows, couplings, fittings, supports, and support hardware must be of materials that are suitable for the environment in which they're to be installed, in accordance with 300.6.

Note 2: Some cleaning and lubricating compounds contain chemicals that can cause deterioration of the plastic used for insulating and structural applications in equipment.

Equipment not identified for outdoor use and equipment identified only for indoor use must be protected <u>against damage</u> from the weather <u>during construction.</u>

Note 3: See *NEC* Table 110.<u>28</u> for appropriate enclosure-type designations.

110.12 Mechanical Execution of Work.
Electrical equipment must be installed in a neat and workmanlike manner.

Note: Accepted industry practices are described in ANSI/*NECA* 1, *Standard Practices for Good Workmanship in Electrical Contracting.*

Author's Comment: The National Electrical Contractors Association (*NECA*) created a series of National Electrical Installation Standards (NEIS)® that established the industry's first quality guidelines for electrical installations. These standards define a benchmark or baseline of quality and workmanship for installing electrical products and systems. They explain what installing electrical products and systems in a "neat and workmanlike manner" means. For more information about these standards, visit www.neca-neis.org/.

(A) Unused Openings. Unused openings, other than those intended for the operation of equipment or for mounting purposes, or those that are part of the design for listed products, must be closed by fittings that provide protection substantially equivalent to the wall of the equipment. **Figure 110–12**

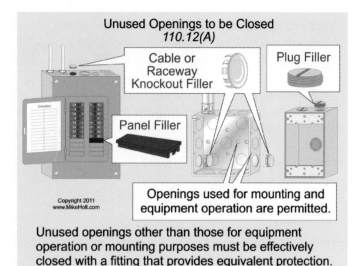

Figure 110–12

Author's Comments:

- See the definition of "Fitting" in Article 100.

- Unused openings for circuit breakers must be closed using identified closures, or other means approved by the authority having jurisdiction, that provide protection substantially equivalent to the wall of the enclosure [408.7]. **Figure 110–13**

- Openings intended to provide entry for raceways or cables in cabinets, cutout boxes, and meter socket enclosures must be adequately closed [312.5(A)].

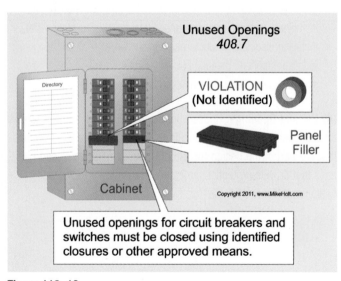

Figure 110–13

(B) Integrity of Electrical Equipment. Internal parts of electrical equipment must not be damaged or contaminated by foreign material, such as paint, plaster, cleaners, and so forth.

Author's Comment: Precautions must be taken to provide protection from contamination of the internal parts of panelboards and receptacles during building construction. Make sure that electrical equipment is properly masked and protected before painting or other phases of the project take place that can cause damage. **Figure 110–14**

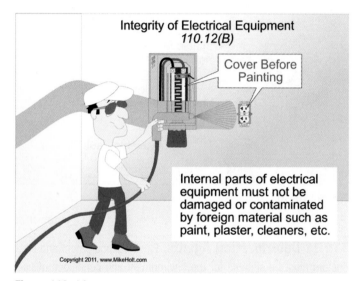

Figure 110–14

Electrical equipment that contains damaged parts may adversely affect safe operation or mechanical strength of the equipment and must not be installed. This includes parts that are broken, bent, cut, or deteriorated by corrosion, chemical action, or overheating.

Author's Comment: Damaged parts include cracked insulators, arc shields not in place, overheated fuse clips, and damaged or missing switch handles or circuit-breaker handles. **Figure 110–15**

110.13 Mounting and Cooling of Equipment.

(A) Mounting. Electrical equipment must be firmly secured to the surface on which it's mounted.

Author's Comment: See 314.23 for similar requirements for boxes.

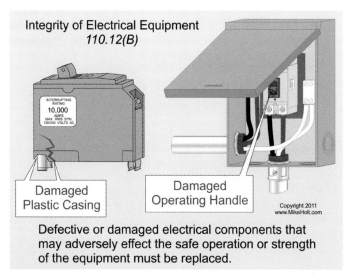

Integrity of Electrical Equipment
110.12(B)

Damaged Plastic Casing

Damaged Operating Handle

Copyright 2011
www.MikeHolt.com

Defective or damaged electrical components that may adversely effect the safe operation or strength of the equipment must be replaced.

Figure 110–15

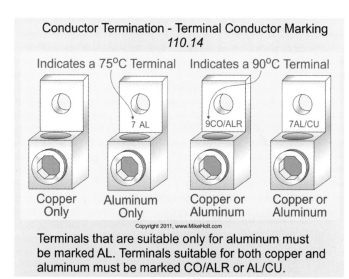

Conductor Termination - Terminal Conductor Marking
110.14

Indicates a 75°C Terminal   Indicates a 90°C Terminal

7 AL   9CO/ALR   7AL/CU

Copper Only   Aluminum Only   Copper or Aluminum   Copper or Aluminum

Copyright 2011, www.MikeHolt.com

Terminals that are suitable only for aluminum must be marked AL. Terminals suitable for both copper and aluminum must be marked CO/ALR or AL/CU.

Figure 110–16

(B) Cooling. Electrical equipment that depends on natural air circulation must be installed so walls or adjacent equipment don't prevent airflow over the surfaces. The clearances between top surfaces and adjacent surfaces must be maintained to dissipate rising warm air for equipment designed for floor mounting.

Electrical equipment constructed with ventilating openings must be installed so free air circulation isn't inhibited.

> **Author's Comment:** Transformers with ventilating openings must be installed so that the ventilating openings aren't blocked. The required wall clearances must be clearly marked on the transformer case [450.9].

110.14 Conductor Termination and Splicing. Conductor terminal and splicing devices must be identified for the conductor material and they must be properly installed and used. **Figure 110–16**

Connectors and terminals for conductors more finely stranded than Class B and Class C, as shown in Table 10 of Chapter 9, must be identified for the conductor class. **Figure 110–17**

Copper and Aluminum Mixed. Copper and aluminum conductors must not make contact with each other in a device unless the device is listed and identified for this purpose.

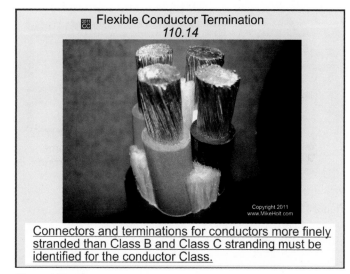

Flexible Conductor Termination
110.14

Copyright 2011
www.MikeHolt.com

Connectors and terminations for conductors more finely stranded than Class B and Class C stranding must be identified for the conductor Class.

Figure 110–17

> **Author's Comment:** Few terminations are listed for the mixing of aluminum and copper conductors, but if they are, that will be marked on the product package or terminal device. The reason copper and aluminum shouldn't be in contact with each other is because corrosion develops between the two different metals due to galvanic action, resulting in increased contact resistance at the splicing device. This increased resistance can cause the splice to overheat and cause a fire.

> **Note:** Many terminations and equipment are marked with a tightening torque.

Author's Comment: Conductors must terminate in devices that have been properly tightened in accordance with the manufacturer's torque specifications included with equipment instructions. Failure to torque terminals can result in excessive heating of terminals or splicing devices due to a loose connection. A loose connection can also lead to arcing which increases the heating effect and also may lead to a short circuit or ground fault. Any of these can result in a fire or other failure, including an arc-flash event. In addition, this is a violation of 110.3(B), which requires all equipment to be installed in accordance with listing or labeling instructions. **Figure 110–18**

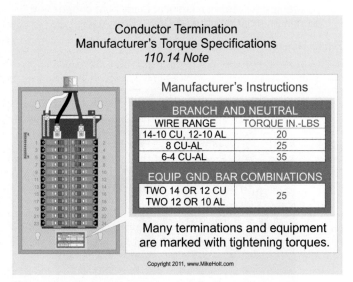

Figure 110–18

Question: What do you do if the torque value isn't provided with the device?

Answer: Call the manufacturer, visit the manufacturer's website, or have the supplier make a copy of the installation instructions.

(A) Terminations. Conductor terminals must ensure a good connection without damaging the conductors and must be made by pressure connectors (including set screw type) or splices to flexible leads.

Author's Comment: See the definition of "Connector, Pressure" in Article 100.

Question: What if the conductor is larger than the terminal device?

Answer: This condition needs to be anticipated in advance, and the equipment should be ordered with terminals that will accommodate the larger conductor. However, if you're in the field, you should:

- *Contact the manufacturer and have them express deliver you the proper terminals, bolts, washers, and nuts, or*

- *Order a terminal device that crimps on the end of the larger conductor and reduces the termination size.*

Terminals for more than one conductor and terminals used for aluminum conductors must be identified for this purpose, either within the equipment instructions or on the terminal itself. **Figure 110–19**

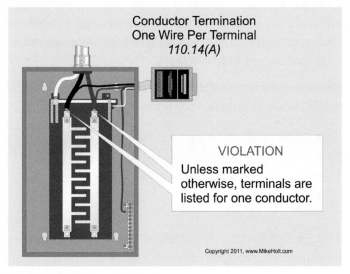

Figure 110–19

Author's Comments:

- Split-bolt connectors are commonly listed for only two conductors, although some are listed for three conductors. However, it's a common industry practice to terminate as many conductors as possible within a split-bolt connector, even though this violates the *NEC*. **Figure 110–20**

- Many devices are listed for more than one conductor per terminal. For example, some circuit breakers rated 30A or less can have two conductors under each lug. Grounding and bonding terminals are also often listed for more than one conductor under the terminal.

- Each neutral conductor within a panelboard must terminate to an individual terminal [408.41].

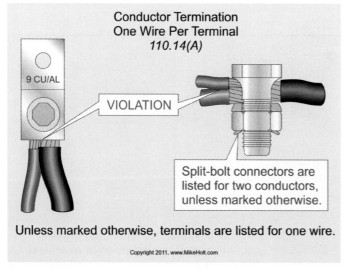

Figure 110–20

(B) Conductor Splices. Conductors must be spliced by a splicing device identified for the purpose or by exothermic welding.

Author's Comment: Conductors aren't required to be twisted together prior to the installation of a twist-on wire connector, unless specifically required in the installation instructions. **Figure 110–21**

Unused circuit conductors aren't required to be removed. However, to prevent an electrical hazard, the free ends of the conductors must be insulated to prevent the exposed end of the conductor from touching energized parts. This requirement can be met by the use of an insulated twist-on or push-on wire connector. **Figure 110–22**

Author's Comment: See the definition of "Energized" in Article 100.

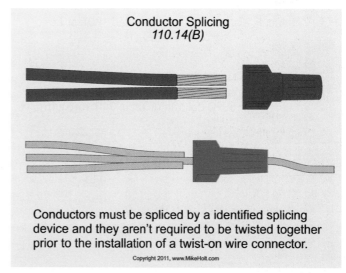

Figure 110–21

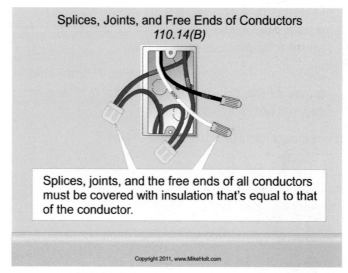

Figure 110–22

(C) Temperature Limitations (Conductor Size). Conductors are to be sized using their ampacity from the insulation temperature rating column of Table 310.15(B)(16) that corresponds to the lowest temperature rating of any terminal, device, or conductor of the circuit.

(1) Equipment Temperature Rating Provisions. Unless the equipment is listed and marked otherwise, conductor sizing for equipment terminations must be based on Table 310.15(B)(16) in accordance with (a) or (b):

(a) Equipment Rated 100A or Less. Figure 110–23

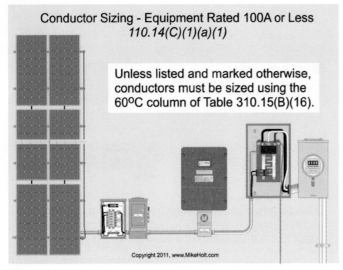

Figure 110–23

(1) Conductors must be sized using the 60°C temperature column of Table 310.15(B)(16) if the terminal temperature rating isn't marked or not given in an exam question.

(3) Conductors terminating on terminals rated 75°C are sized in accordance with the ampacities listed in the 75°C temperature column of Table 310.15(B)(16)

(b) Equipment Rated Over 100A. Figure 110–24

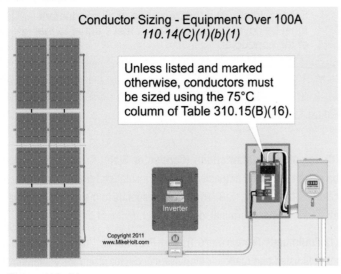

Figure 110–24

(2) Conductors are sized in accordance with the ampacities listed in the 75°C temperature column of Table 310.15(B)(16), provided the conductors have an insulation rating of at least 75°C.

110.16 Arc-Flash Hazard Warning. Electrical equipment such as switchboards, panelboards, industrial control panels, meter socket enclosures, and motor control centers in other than dwelling units that are likely to require examination, adjustment, servicing, or maintenance while energized must be field-marked to warn qualified persons of the danger associated with an arc flash from short circuits or ground faults. The field-marking must be clearly visible to qualified persons before they examine, adjust, service, or perform maintenance on the equipment. Figure 110–25

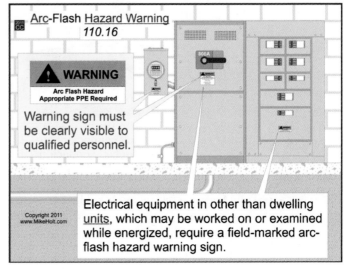

Figure 110–25

Author's Comments:

- See the definition of "Qualified Person" in Article 100.

- This rule is meant to warn qualified persons who work on energized electrical systems that an arc flash hazard exists so they'll select proper personal protective equipment (PPE) in accordance with industry accepted safe work practice standards.

Note 1: NFPA 70E, *Standard for Electrical Safety in the Workplace*, provides assistance in determining the severity of potential exposure, planning safe work practices, and selecting personal protective equipment.

110.22 Identification of Disconnecting Means.

(A) General. Each disconnecting means must be legibly marked to indicate its purpose unless located and arranged so the purpose is evident. The marking must be of sufficient durability to withstand the environment involved. Figure 110–26

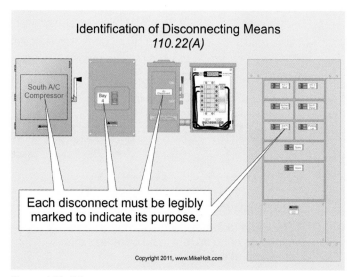

Figure 110–26

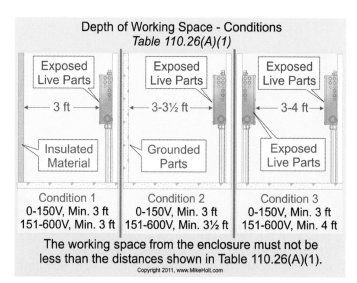

Figure 110–27

PART II. 600V, NOMINAL, OR LESS

110.26 Spaces About Electrical Equipment. For the purpose of safe operation and maintenance of equipment, access and working space must be provided about all electrical equipment.

(A) Working Space. Equipment that may need examination, adjustment, servicing, or maintenance while energized must have working space provided in accordance with (1), (2), and (3):

> **Author's Comment:** The phrase "while energized" is the root of many debates. As always, check with the AHJ to see what equipment he or she believes needs a clear working space.

(1) Depth of Working Space. The working space, which is measured from the enclosure front, must not be less than the distances contained in Table 110.26(A)(1). Figure 110–27

Table 110.26(A)(1) Working Space

Voltage-to-Ground	Condition 1	Condition 2	Condition 3
0–150V	3 ft	3 ft	3 ft
151–600V	3 ft	3½ft	4 ft

- Condition 1—Exposed live parts on one side of the working space and no live or grounded parts, including concrete, brick, or tile walls are on the other side of the working space.
- Condition 2—Exposed live parts on one side of the working space and grounded parts, including concrete, brick, or tile walls are on the other side of the working space.
- Condition 3—Exposed live parts on both sides of the working space.

(a) Rear and Sides. Working space isn't required for the back or sides of assemblies where all connections and all renewable or adjustable parts are accessible from the front. Figure 110–28

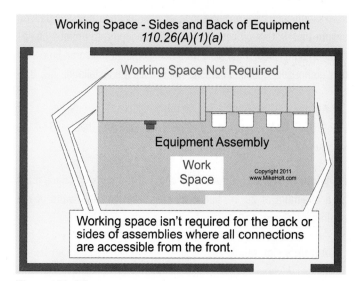

Figure 110–28

(b) Low Voltage. If special permission is granted in accordance with 90.4, working space for equipment that operates at not more than 30V ac or 60V dc can be less than the distance in Table 110.26(A)(1). Figure 110–29

> **Author's Comment:** See the definition of "Special Permission" in Article 100.

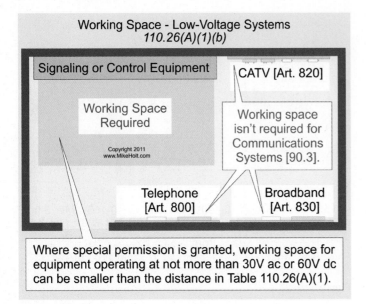

Figure 110–29

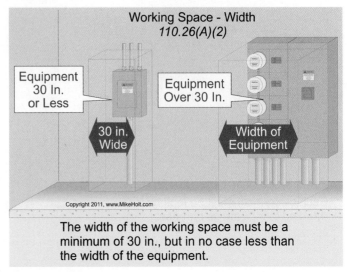

The width of the working space must be a minimum of 30 in., but in no case less than the width of the equipment.

Figure 110–30

(c) Existing Buildings. If electrical equipment is being replaced, Condition 2 working space is permitted between dead-front switchboards, panelboards, or motor control centers located across the aisle from each other where conditions of maintenance and supervision ensure that written procedures have been adopted to prohibit equipment on both sides of the aisle from being open at the same time, and only authorized, qualified persons will service the installation.

> **Author's Comment:** The working space requirements of 110.26 don't apply to equipment included in Chapter 8—Communications Circuits [90.3].

(2) Width of Working Space. The width of the working space must be a minimum of 30 in., but in no case less than the width of the equipment. **Figure 110–30**

> **Author's Comment:** The width of the working space can be measured from left-to-right, from right-to-left, or simply centered on the equipment, and the working space can overlap the working space for other electrical equipment. **Figure 110–31**

In all cases, the working space must be of sufficient width, depth, and height to permit all equipment doors to open 90 degrees. **Figure 110–32**

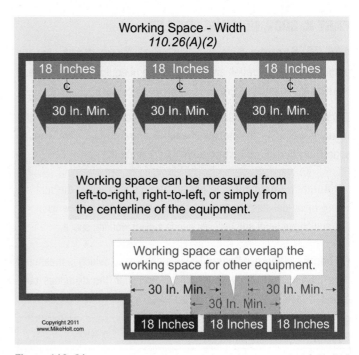

Figure 110–31

(3) Height of Working Space (Headroom). The height of the working space in front of equipment must not be less than 6½ ft, measured from the grade, floor, platform, or the equipment height, whichever is greater. **Figure 110–33**

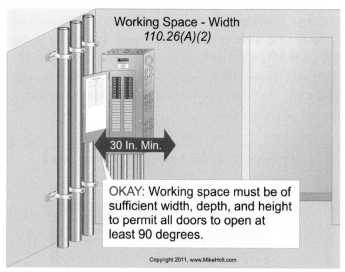

Figure 110–32

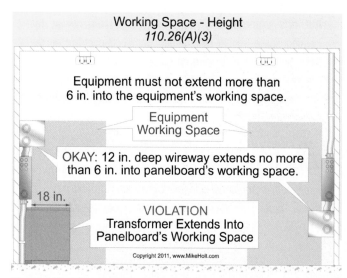

Figure 110–34

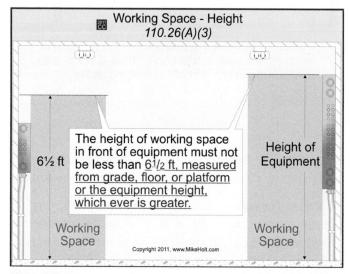

Figure 110–33

Equipment such as raceways, cables, wireways, cabinets, panels, and so on, can be located above or below electrical equipment, but must not extend more than 6 in. into the equipment's working space. **Figure 110–34**

Ex 1: The minimum headroom requirement doesn't apply to service equipment or panelboards rated 200A or less located in an existing dwelling unit.

Author's Comment: See the definition of "Dwelling Unit" in Article 100.

Ex 2: Meters are permitted to extend beyond the other equipment.

(B) Clear Working Space. The working space required by this section must be clear at all times. Therefore, this space isn't permitted for storage. When normally enclosed live parts are exposed for inspection or servicing, the working space, if in a passageway or general open space, must be suitably guarded. **Figure 110–35**

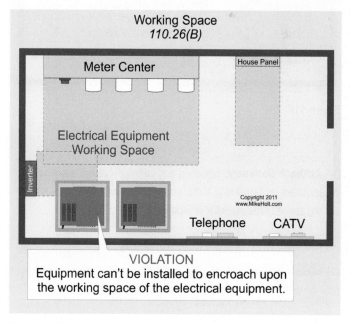

Figure 110–35

Author's Comment: When working in a passageway, the working space should be guarded from occupants using the passageway. When working on electrical equipment in a passageway one must be mindful of a fire alarm evacuation with numerous occupants congregated and moving through the passageway.

⚠️ **CAUTION:** *It's very dangerous to service energized parts in the first place, and it's unacceptable to be subjected to additional dangers by working around bicycles, boxes, crates, appliances, and other impediments.* **Figure 110–36**

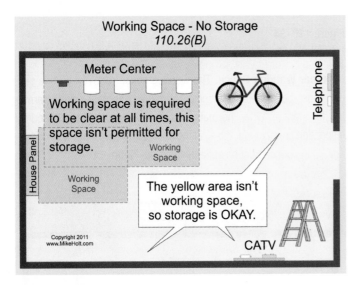

Figure 110–36

Author's Comment: Signaling and communications equipment must not be installed in a manner that encroaches on the working space of the electrical equipment.

(C) Entrance to and Egress from Working Space.

(1) Minimum Required. At least one entrance of sufficient area must provide access to and egress from the working space.

Author's Comment: Check to see what the authority having jurisdiction considers "Sufficient Area." Building codes contain minimum dimensions for doors and openings for personnel travel.

(2) Large Equipment. An entrance to and egress from each end of the working space of electrical equipment rated 1,200A or more that's over 6 ft wide is required. The opening must be a minimum of 24 in. wide and 6½ ft high. **Figure 110–37.** A single entrance to and egress from the required working space is permitted where either of the following conditions is met.

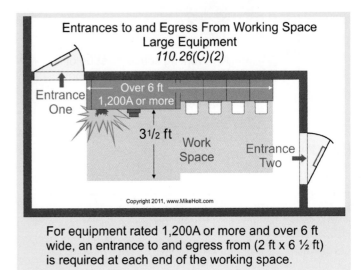

For equipment rated 1,200A or more and over 6 ft wide, an entrance to and egress from (2 ft x 6 ½ ft) is required at each end of the working space.

Figure 110–37

(a) Unobstructed Egress. Only one entrance is required where the location permits a continuous and unobstructed way of egress travel.

(b) Double Workspace. Only one entrance is required where the required working space depth is doubled, and the equipment is located so the edge of the entrance is no closer than the required working space distance. **Figure 110–38**

(3) Personnel Doors. If equipment with overcurrent or switching devices rated 1,200A or more is installed, personnel door(s) for entrance to and egress from the working space located less than 25 ft from the nearest edge of the working space must have the door(s) open in the direction of egress and be equipped with panic hardware or other devices that open under simple pressure. **Figure 110–39**

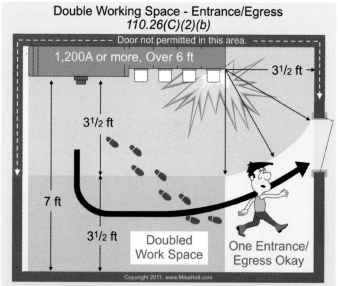

One entrance/egress is permitted where the required working space is doubled, and equipment is located so the edge of the entrance is no closer than the required working space distance.

Figure 110–38

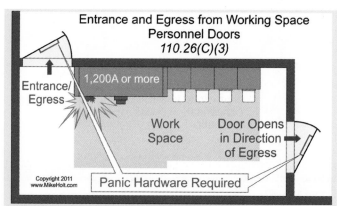

For equipment rated 1,200A or more, personnel door(s) located less than 25 ft from the nearest edge of working space must open in the direction of egress and have panic hardware or devices that open under simple pressure.

Figure 110–39

Author's Comments:

- History has shown that electricians who suffer burns on their hands in electrical arc flash or arc blast events often can't open doors equipped with knobs that must be turned.

- Since this requirement is in the *NEC*, the electrical contractor is responsible for ensuring that panic hardware is installed where required. Some electrical contractors are offended at being held liable for nonelectrical responsibilities, but this rule is designed to save the lives of electricians. For this and other reasons, many construction professionals routinely hold "pre-construction" or "pre-con" meetings to review potential opportunities for miscommunication—before the work begins.

(D) Illumination. Service equipment, switchboards, panelboards, as well as motor control centers located indoors must have illumination located indoors and must not be controlled by automatic means only. Figure 110–40

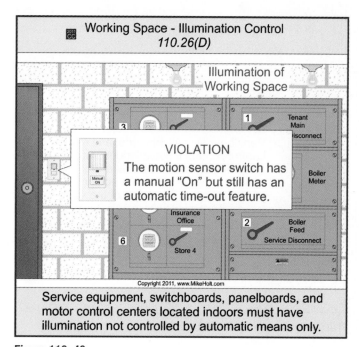

Service equipment, switchboards, panelboards, and motor control centers located indoors must have illumination not controlled by automatic means only.

Figure 110–40

Author's Comment: The *Code* doesn't provide the minimum foot-candles required to provide proper illumination. Proper illumination of electrical equipment rooms is essential for the safety of those qualified to work on such equipment.

(E) Dedicated Equipment Space. Switchboards, panelboards, and motor control centers must have dedicated equipment space as follows:

(1) Indoors.

(a) Dedicated Electrical Space. The footprint space (width and depth of the equipment) extending from the floor to a height of 6 ft above the equipment or to the structural ceiling, whichever is lower, must be dedicated for the electrical installation. No piping, ducts, or other equipment foreign to the electrical installation can be installed in this dedicated footprint space. **Figure 110–41**

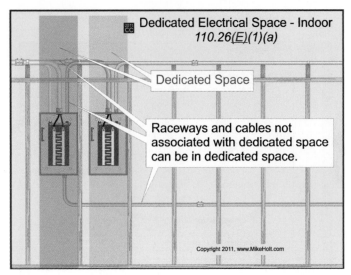

Figure Figure 110–42

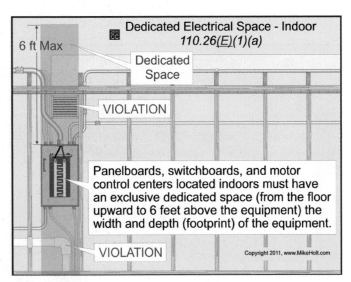

Figure 110–41

Ex: Suspended ceilings with removable panels can be within the dedicated footprint space [110.26(E)(1)(d)].

Author's Comment: Electrical raceways and cables not associated with the dedicated space can be within the dedicated space. These aren't considered "equipment foreign to the electrical installation." **Figure 110–42**

(b) Foreign Systems. Foreign systems can be located above the dedicated space if protection is installed to prevent damage to the electrical equipment from condensation, leaks, or breaks in the foreign systems, which can be as simple as a drip-pan. **Figure 110–43**

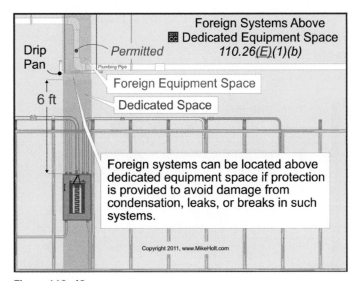

Figure 110–43

(c) Sprinkler Protection. Sprinkler protection piping isn't permitted in the dedicated space, but the *NEC* doesn't prohibit sprinklers from spraying water on electrical equipment.

(d) Suspended Ceilings. A dropped, suspended, or similar ceiling isn't considered a structural ceiling.

(F) Locked Electrical Equipment Rooms or Enclosures. Electrical equipment rooms and enclosures housing electrical equipment can be controlled by locks because they are still considered to be accessible to qualified persons who require access. **Figure 110–44**

Author's Comment: See the definition of "Accessible as it applies to equipment" in Article 100.

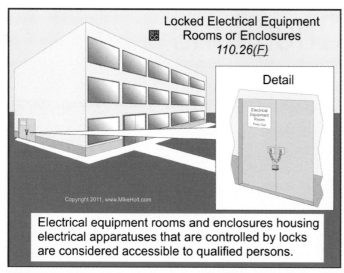

Figure 110–44

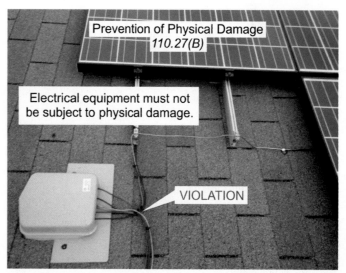

Figure 110–45

110.27 Guarding.

(A) Guarding Live Parts. Live parts of electrical equipment operating at 50V or more must be guarded against accidental contact. This can be done by:

(1) Locating them in a separate room, vault, or enclosure.

(2) Guarding with a partition or screen.

(3) Locating them on a balcony or platform.

(4) Elevating them 8 ft or more above the floor or working surface.

(B) Prevent Physical Damage. Electrical equipment must not be installed where subject to physical damage, unless enclosures or guards are arranged and they are of sufficient strength to prevent damage. **Figure 110–45**

(C) Warning Signs. Entrances to rooms and other guarded locations containing exposed live parts must be marked with conspicuous signs forbidding unqualified persons from entering.

110.28 Enclosure Types. Enclosures must be marked with an enclosure-type number and be suitable for the location in accordance with Table 110.28.

The enclosures aren't intended to protect against condensation, icing, corrosion, or contamination that might occur within the enclosure or that enters via the raceway or unsealed openings.

Note: Raintight enclosures include Types 3, 3S, 3SX, 3X, 4, 4X, 6, and 6P; rainproof enclosures are Types 3R, and 3RX; watertight enclosures are Types 4, 4X, 6, and 6P; driptight enclosures are Types 2, 5, 12, 12K, and 13; and dusttight enclosures are Types 3, 3S, 3SX, 3X, 5, 12, 12K, and 13.

CHAPTER 1. GENERAL

Article 100. Definitions

1. Admitting close approach, not guarded by locked doors, elevation, or other effective means, is referred to as _____.

   (a) accessible (as applied to equipment)
   (b) accessible (as applied to wiring methods)
   (c) accessible, readily
   (d) all of these

2. Capable of being removed or exposed without damaging the building structure or finish, or not permanently closed in by the structure or finish of the building is known as _____.

   (a) accessible (as applied to equipment)
   (b) accessible (as applied to wiring methods)
   (c) accessible, readily
   (d) all of these

3. Capable of being reached quickly for operation, renewal, or inspections without resorting to portable ladders and such is known as _____.

   (a) accessible (as applied to equipment)
   (b) accessible (as applied to wiring methods)
   (c) accessible, readily
   (d) all of these

4. The maximum current in amperes a conductor can carry continuously, where the temperature will not be raised in excess of the conductor's insulation temperature rating is called its _____.

   (a) short-circuit rating
   (b) ground-fault rating
   (c) ampacity
   (d) all of these

5. "_____" means acceptable to the authority having jurisdiction.

   (a) Identified
   (b) Listed
   (c) Approved
   (d) Labeled

6. Where no statutory requirement exists, the authority having jurisdiction can be a property owner or his/her agent, such as an architect or engineer.

   (a) True
   (b) False

7. Bonded can be described as _____ to establish electrical continuity and conductivity.

   (a) isolated
   (b) guarded
   (c) connected
   (d) separated

8. A reliable conductor that ensures electrical conductivity between metal parts of the electrical installation that are required to be electrically connected is called a _____.

   (a) grounding electrode
   (b) auxiliary ground
   (c) bonding conductor or jumper
   (d) tap conductor

9. The *NEC* defines a(n) _____ as a permanent structure having a roof and walls that stands alone or that is cut off from adjoining structures by fire walls or fire barriers, with all openings therein protected by approved fire doors and used to enclose an occupancy.

   (a) unit
   (b) apartment
   (c) building
   (d) utility

10. An enclosure for either surface mounting or flush mounting provided with a frame in which a door can be hung is called a(n) _____.

    (a) enclosure
    (b) outlet box
    (c) cutout box
    (d) cabinet

11. Cables are considered _____ if rendered inaccessible by the structure or finish of the building.

    (a) inaccessible
    (b) concealed
    (c) hidden
    (d) enclosed

12. A separate portion of a raceway system that provides access through a removable cover to the interior of the system, defines the term _____.

    (a) junction box
    (b) accessible raceway
    (c) conduit body
    (d) cutout box

13. A solderless pressure connector is a device that _____ between conductors or between conductors and a terminal by means of mechanical pressure.

    (a) provides access
    (b) protects the wiring
    (c) is never needed
    (d) establishes a connection

14. _____ are designed for surface mounting with a swinging door.

    (a) Outlet boxes
    (b) Cabinets
    (c) Cutout boxes
    (d) none of these

15. A unit of an electrical system that carries or controls electric energy as its principal function is a(n) _____.

    (a) raceway
    (b) fitting
    (c) device
    (d) enclosure

16. A(n) _____ is a device by which the conductors of a circuit can be disconnected from their source of supply.

    (a) feeder
    (b) enclosure
    (c) disconnecting means
    (d) conductor interrupter

17. A _____ is a single unit that provides independent living facilities for persons, including permanent provisions for living, sleeping, cooking, and sanitation.

    (a) one-family dwelling
    (b) two-family dwelling
    (c) dwelling unit
    (d) multifamily dwelling

18. Surrounded by a case, housing, fence, or wall(s) that prevents persons from accidentally contacting energized parts is called _____.

    (a) guarded
    (b) covered
    (c) protection
    (d) enclosed

19. As used in the *NEC*, equipment includes _____.

    (a) fittings
    (b) appliances
    (c) machinery
    (d) all of these

20. When the term exposed, as it applies to live parts, is used in the *Code*, it refers to _____.

    (a) capable of being inadvertently touched or approached nearer than a safe distance by a person
    (b) parts that are not suitably guarded, isolated, or insulated
    (c) wiring on, or attached to, the surface or behind panels designed to allow access
    (d) a and b

21. For wiring methods, on or attached to the surface, or behind access panels designed to allow access is known as _____.

    (a) open
    (b) uncovered
    (c) exposed
    (d) bare

22. An accessory, such as a locknut, intended to perform a mechanical function best describes a _____.

    (a) part
    (b) equipment
    (c) device
    (d) fitting

23. The word "Earth" best describes what *NEC* term?

    (a) Bonded
    (b) Ground
    (c) Effective ground-fault current path
    (d) Guarded

24. A(n) _____ is an unintentional, electrically conducting connection between an ungrounded conductor of an electrical circuit, and the normally noncurrent-carrying conductors, metallic enclosures, metallic raceways, metallic equipment, or earth.

    (a) grounded conductor
    (b) ground fault
    (c) equipment ground
    (d) bonding jumper

25. Connected to ground or to a conductive body that extends the ground connection is called _____.

    (a) equipment grounding
    (b) bonded
    (c) grounded
    (d) all of these

26. A circuit conductor that is intentionally grounded is called a(n) "_____."

    (a) grounding conductor
    (b) unidentified conductor
    (c) grounded conductor
    (d) grounding electrode conductor

27. The installed conductive path that connects normally noncurrent-carrying metal parts of equipment together and to the system grounded conductor or to the grounding electrode conductor, or both, is known as a(n) "_____."

    (a) grounding electrode conductor
    (b) grounding conductor
    (c) equipment grounding conductor
    (d) none of these

28. A conducting object through which a direct connection to earth is established is a _____.

    (a) bonding conductor
    (b) grounding conductor
    (c) grounding electrode
    (d) grounded conductor

29. A conductor used to connect the system grounded conductor or equipment to a grounding electrode or to a point on the grounding electrode system is called the "_____" conductor.

    (a) main grounding
    (b) common main
    (c) equipment grounding
    (d) grounding electrode

30. Recognized as suitable for the specific purpose, function, use, environment, and application is the definition of "_____."

    (a) labeled
    (b) identified (as applied to equipment)
    (c) listed
    (d) approved

31. Within sight means visible and not more than _____ ft distant from the equipment.

    (a) 10
    (b) 20
    (c) 25
    (d) 50

32. The highest current at rated voltage that a device is identified to interrupt under standard test conditions is the _____.

    (a) interrupting rating
    (b) manufacturer's rating
    (c) interrupting capacity
    (d) withstand rating

33. _____ means that an object is not readily accessible to persons unless special means for access are used.

    (a) Isolated
    (b) Secluded
    (c) Protected
    (d) Locked

34. Equipment or materials to which a symbol or other identifying mark of a product evaluation organization that is acceptable to the authority having jurisdiction has been attached is known as _____.

    (a) listed
    (b) labeled
    (c) approved
    (d) identified

35. Equipment or materials included in a list published by a testing laboratory acceptable to the authority having jurisdiction is said to be _____.

    (a) book
    (b) digest
    (c) manifest
    (d) listed

36. Any current in excess of the rated current of equipment or the ampacity of a conductor is called _____.

    (a) trip current
    (b) fault current
    (c) overcurrent
    (d) short circuit

37. An overload is the same as a short circuit or ground fault.

    (a) True
    (b) False

38. A panel, including buses and automatic overcurrent devices, designed to be placed in a cabinet or cutout box and accessible only from the front is known as a "_____."

    (a) switchboard
    (b) disconnect
    (c) panelboard
    (d) switch

39. Premises wiring includes _____ wiring from the service point or power source to the outlets.

    (a) interior
    (b) exterior
    (c) underground
    (d) all of these

40. The *NEC* defines a(n) _____ as one who has skills and knowledge related to the construction and operation of the electrical equipment and installations and has received safety training to recognize and avoid the hazards involved.

    (a) inspector
    (b) master electrician
    (c) journeyman electrician
    (d) qualified person

41. NFPA 70E — *Standard for Electrical Safety in the Workplace*, provides information to help determine the electrical safety training requirements expected of a qualified person.

    (a) True
    (b) False

42. A raceway is an enclosure designed for the installation of wires, cables, or busbars.

    (a) True
    (b) False

43. The conductors and equipment from the electric utility that deliver electric energy to the wiring system of the premises is called a "_____."

    (a) branch circuit
    (b) feeder
    (c) service
    (d) none of these

44. Service conductors originate at the service point and terminate at service disconnecting means.

    (a) True
    (b) False

45. The _____ is the necessary equipment, usually consisting of a circuit breaker(s) or switch(es) and fuse(s) and their accessories, connected to the load end of service conductors, and intended to constitute the main control and cutoff of the supply.

    (a) service equipment
    (b) service
    (c) service disconnect
    (d) service overcurrent device

46. The _____ is the point of connection between the facilities of the serving utility and the premises wiring.

    (a) service entrance
    (b) service point
    (c) overcurrent protection
    (d) beginning of the wiring system

47. The prospective symmetrical fault current at a nominal voltage to which an apparatus or system is able to be connected without sustaining damage exceeding defined acceptance criteria is known as the "_____."

    (a) short-circuit current rating
    (b) arc flash
    (c) overcurrent rating
    (d) available fault current

48. Special permission would be the written consent from the _____.

    (a) testing laboratory
    (b) manufacturer
    (c) owner
    (d) authority having jurisdiction

49. A structure is that which is built or constructed.

    (a) True
    (b) False

50. Ungrounded describes not connected to ground or a conductive body that extends the ground connection.

    (a) True
    (b) False

51. Utilization equipment is equipment that utilizes electricity for _____ purposes.

    (a) electromechanical
    (b) heating
    (c) lighting
    (d) any of these

52. A value assigned to a circuit or system for the purpose of conveniently designating its voltage class, such as 120/240V, is called _____ voltage.

    (a) root-mean-square
    (b) circuit
    (c) nominal
    (d) source

Article 110. Requirements for Electrical Installations

1. In judging equipment for approval, considerations such as the following shall be evaluated:

    (a) mechanical strength
    (b) wire-bending space
    (c) arcing effects
    (d) all of these

2. Listed or labeled equipment shall be installed and used in accordance with any instructions included in the listing or labeling.

    (a) True
    (b) False

3. Conductors shall be _____ unless otherwise provided.

    (a) bare
    (b) stranded
    (c) copper
    (d) aluminum

4. Conductor sizes are expressed in American Wire Gage or _____.

    (a) inches
    (b) circular mils
    (c) square inches
    (d) cubic inches

5. Wiring shall be installed so that the completed system will be free from _____, other than as required or permitted elsewhere in the *Code*.

    (a) short circuits
    (b) ground faults
    (c) connections to the earth
    (d) all of these

6. Only wiring methods recognized as _____ are included in this *Code*.

    (a) expensive
    (b) efficient
    (c) suitable
    (d) cost-effective

7. Equipment intended to interrupt current at fault levels shall have an interrupting rating not less than the nominal circuit voltage and the current that is available at the line terminals of the equipment.

    (a) True
    (b) False

8. The _____ of a circuit shall be selected and coordinated to permit the circuit protective devices to clear a fault without extensive damage to the electrical equipment of the circuit.

    (a) overcurrent devices
    (b) total circuit impedance
    (c) equipment short-circuit current ratings
    (d) all of these

9. Unless identified for use in the operating environment, no conductors or equipment shall be _____ having a deteriorating effect on the conductors or equipment.

    (a) located in damp or wet locations
    (b) exposed to fumes, vapors, liquids or gases
    (c) exposed to excessive temperatures
    (d) all of these

10. Some cleaning and lubricating compounds can cause severe deterioration of many plastic materials used for insulating and structural applications in equipment.

    (a) True
    (b) False

11. The *NEC* requires that electrical work be _____.

    (a) installed in a neat and workmanlike manner
    (b) installed under the supervision of a licensed person
    (c) completed before being inspected
    (d) all of these

12. Accepted industry workmanship practices are described in ANSI/*NECA* 1-2006, *Standard Practices for Good Workmanship in Electrical Contracting*, and other ANSI-approved installation standards.

    (a) True
    (b) False

13. Unused openings other than those intended for the operation of equipment, intended for mounting purposes, or permitted as part of the design for listed equipment shall be _____.

    (a) filled with cable clamps or connectors only
    (b) taped over with electrical tape
    (c) repaired only by welding or brazing in a metal slug
    (d) effectively closed to afford protection substantially equivalent to the wall of the equipment

14. Internal parts of electrical equipment, including _____, shall not be damaged or contaminated by foreign materials such as paint, plaster, cleaners, abrasives, or corrosive residues.

    (a) busbars
    (b) wiring terminals
    (c) insulators
    (d) all of these

15. Wooden plugs driven into holes in _____ or similar materials shall not be used for securing electrical equipment.

    (a) masonry
    (b) concrete
    (c) plaster
    (d) all of these

16. Electrical equipment that depends on _____ for cooling of exposed surfaces shall be installed so that airflow over such surfaces is not prevented by walls or by adjacent installed equipment.

    (a) outdoor air
    (b) natural circulation of air and convection principles
    (c) artificial cooling and circulation
    (d) magnetic induction

17. Conductor terminal and splicing devices must be _____ for the conductor material and they must be properly installed and used.

    (a) listed
    (b) approved
    (c) identified
    (d) all of these

18. Connectors and terminals for conductors more finely stranded than Class B and Class C, as shown In Table 10 of Chapter 9, must be _____ for the specific conductor class or classes.

    (a) listed
    (b) approved
    (c) identified
    (d) all of these

19. Many terminations and equipment are marked with _____.

    (a) an etching tool
    (b) a removable label
    (c) a tightening torque
    (d) the manufacturer's initials

20. Connection of conductors to terminal parts shall ensure a thoroughly good connection without damaging the conductors and shall be made by means of _____.

    (a) solder lugs
    (b) pressure connectors
    (c) splices to flexible leads
    (d) any of these

21. Connection by means of wire-binding screws, studs, or nuts having upturned lugs or the equivalent shall be permitted for _____ or smaller conductors.

    (a) 12 AWG
    (b) 10 AWG
    (c) 8 AWG
    (d) 6 AWG

22. Soldered splices shall first be spliced or joined so as to be mechanically and electrically secure without solder and then be soldered.

    (a) True
    (b) False

23. The temperature rating associated with the ampacity of a _____ shall be so selected and coordinated so as not to exceed the lowest temperature rating of any connected termination, conductor, or device.

    (a) terminal
    (b) conductor
    (c) device
    (d) all of these

24. Conductor ampacity shall be determined using the _____ column of Table 310.15(B)(16) for circuits rated 100A or less or marked for 14 AWG through 1 AWG conductors, unless the equipment terminals are listed for use with conductors that have higher temperature ratings.

    (a) 30°C
    (b) 60°C
    (c) 75°C
    (d) 90°C

25. For circuits rated 100A or less, when the equipment terminals are listed for use with 75°C conductors, the _____ column of Table 310.15(B)(16) shall be used to determine the ampacity of THHN conductors.

    (a) 30°C
    (b) 60°C
    (c) 75°C
    (d) 90°C

26. Conductors shall have their ampacity determined using the _____ column of Table 310.15(B)(16) for circuits rated over 100A, or marked for conductors larger than 1 AWG, unless the equipment terminals are listed for use with higher temperature-rated conductors.

    (a) 30°C
    (b) 60°C
    (c) 75°C
    (d) 90°C

27. Separately installed pressure connectors shall be used with conductors at the _____ not exceeding the ampacity at the listed and identified temperature rating of the connector.

    (a) voltages
    (b) temperatures
    (c) listings
    (d) ampacities

28. Electrical equipment such as switchboards, panelboards, industrial control panels, meter socket enclosures, and motor control centers that are in other than dwelling units, and are likely to require _____ while energized shall be field-marked to warn qualified persons of potential electric arc flash hazards.

    (a) examination
    (b) adjustment
    (c) servicing or maintenance
    (d) any of these

29. Each disconnecting means shall be legibly marked to indicate its purpose unless located and arranged so _____.

    (a) that it can be locked out and tagged
    (b) it is not readily accessible
    (c) the purpose is evident
    (d) that it operates at less than 300 volts-to-ground

30. Access and _____ shall be provided and maintained about all electrical equipment to permit ready and safe operation and maintenance of such equipment.

    (a) ventilation
    (b) cleanliness
    (c) circulation
    (d) working space

31. A minimum working space depth of _____ to live parts operating at 277 volts-to-ground is required where there are exposed live parts on one side and no live or grounded parts on the other side.

    (a) 2 ft
    (b) 3 ft
    (c) 4 ft
    (d) 6 ft

32. The minimum working space on a circuit that is 120 volts-to-ground, with exposed live parts on one side and no live or grounded parts on the other side of the working space, is _____.

    (a) 1 ft
    (b) 3 ft
    (c) 4 ft
    (d) 6 ft

33. Concrete, brick, or tile walls are considered _____, as it applies to working space requirements.

    (a) inconsequential
    (b) in the way
    (c) grounded
    (d) none of these

34. The required working space for access to live parts operating at 300 volts-to-ground, where there are exposed live parts on one side and grounded parts on the other side, is _____.

    (a) 3 ft
    (b) 3½ ft
    (c) 4 ft
    (d) 4½ ft

35. The required working space for access to live parts operating at 300 volts-to-ground, where there are exposed live parts on both sides of the workspace is _____.

    (a) 3 ft
    (b) 3½ ft
    (c) 4 ft
    (d) 4½ ft

36. Working space distances for enclosed live parts shall be measured from the _____ of equipment or apparatus, if the live parts are enclosed.

    (a) enclosure
    (b) opening
    (c) a or b
    (d) none of these

37. The working space in front of the electric equipment shall not be less than _____ wide, or the width of the equipment, whichever is greater.

    (a) 15 in.
    (b) 30 in.
    (c) 40 in.
    (d) 60 in.

38. Equipment associated with the electrical installation can be located above or below other electrical equipment within their working space when the associated equipment does not extend more than _____ from the front of the electrical equipment.

    (a) 3 in.
    (b) 6 in.
    (c) 12 in.
    (d) 30 in.

39. The minimum height of working spaces about electrical equipment, switchboards, panelboards, or motor control centers operating at 600V, nominal, or less and likely to require examination, adjustment, servicing, or maintenance while energized shall be 6½ ft or the height of the equipment, whichever is greater, except for service equipment or panelboards in existing dwelling units that do not exceed 200A.

    (a) True
    (b) False

40. Working space shall not be used for _____.

    (a) storage
    (b) raceways
    (c) lighting
    (d) accessibility

41. When normally enclosed live parts are exposed for inspection or servicing, the working space, if in a passageway or general open space, shall be suitably _____.

    (a) accessible
    (b) guarded
    (c) open
    (d) enclosed

42. For equipment rated 1,200A or more and over 6 ft wide that contains overcurrent devices, switching devices, or control devices, there shall be one entrance to and egress from the required working space not less than 24 in. wide and _____ high at each end of the working space.

    (a) 5½ ft
    (b) 6 ft
    (c) 6½ ft
    (d) any of these

43. For equipment rated 1,200A or more that contains overcurrent devices, switching devices, or control devices; and where the entrance to the working space has a personnel door less than 25 ft from the working space, the door _____.

    (a) shall open either in or out with simple pressure and shall not have any lock
    (b) shall open in the direction of egress and be equipped with panic hardware or other devices so the door can open under simple pressure
    (c) shall be equipped with a locking means
    (d) shall be equipped with an electronic opener

44. Illumination shall be provided for all working spaces about service equipment, switchboards, panelboards, and motor control centers _____.

    (a) over 600V
    (b) located indoors
    (c) rated 1,200A or more
    (d) using automatic means of control

45. All switchboards, panelboards, and motor control centers shall be _____.

    (a) located in dedicated spaces
    (b) protected from damage.
    (c) in weatherproof enclosures
    (d) a and b

46. The minimum height of dedicated equipment space for motor control centers installed indoors is _____above the enclosure,or to the structural ceiling, whichever is lower.

    (a) 3 ft
    (b) 5 ft
    (c) 6 ft
    (d) 6½ ft

47. For indoor installations, heating, cooling, or ventilating equipment shall not be installed in the dedicated space above a panelboard or switchboard.

    (a) True
    (b) False

48. The dedicated equipment space for electrical equipment that is required for panelboards installed indoors is measured from the floor to a height of _____ above the equipment, or to the structural ceiling, whichever is lower.

    (a) 3 ft
    (b) 6 ft
    (c) 12 ft
    (d) 30 ft

49. The dedicated space above a panelboard extends to a dropped or suspended ceiling, which is considered a structural ceiling.

    (a) True
    (b) False

50. Electrical equipment rooms or enclosures housing electrical apparatus that are controlled by a lock(s) shall be considered _____ to qualified persons.

    (a) readily accessible
    (b) accessible
    (c) available
    (d) none of these

51. To guard live parts over 50V but less than 600V, equipment is permitted to be _____.

    (a) located in a room accessible only to qualified persons
    (b) located on a balcony accessible only to qualified persons
    (c) elevated 8 ft or more above the floor or other working surface
    (d) any of these

52. Live parts of electrical equipment operating at _____ or more shall be guarded against accidental contact by approved enclosures or by suitable permanent, substantial partitions, or screens arranged so that only qualified persons have access to the space within reach of the live parts.

    (a) 20V
    (b) 30V
    (c) 50V
    (d) 100V

53. In locations where electrical equipment is likely to be exposed to _____, enclosures or guards shall be so arranged and of such strength as to prevent such damage.

    (a) corrosion
    (b) physical damage
    (c) magnetic fields
    (d) weather

54. Entrances to rooms and other guarded locations containing exposed live parts shall be marked with conspicuous _____ forbidding unqualified persons to enter.

    (a) warning signs
    (b) alarms
    (c) a and b
    (d) neither a nor b

55. The term rainproof is typically used in conjunction with Enclosure-Type Number _____.

    (a) 3
    (b) 3R
    (c) 3RX
    (d) b and c

CHAPTER 2

WIRING AND PROTECTION

INTRODUCTION TO CHAPTER 2—WIRING AND PROTECTION

Chapter 2 provides general rules for wiring and the protection of conductors. The rules in this chapter apply to all electrical instal-lations covered by the *NEC*—except as modified in Chapters 5, 6, and 7 [90.3].

As you go through Chapter 2, remember its purpose. Chapter 2 is primarily concerned with correctly sizing and protecting circuits. Every article in Chapter 2 deals with a different aspect of this purpose. This differs from the purpose of Chapter 3, which is to cor-rectly install the conductors that make up those circuits.

Chapter 1 introduced you to the *NEC* and provided a solid foundation for understanding the *Code*. Chapters 2 (Wiring and Protection) and 3 (Wiring Methods and Materials) continue building the foundation for applying the *NEC*. Chapter 4 applies the pre-ceding chapters to general equipment. It's beneficial to learn the first four chapters of the *Code* in a sequential manner because each of the first four chapters builds on the preceding chapter. Once you've mastered the first four chapters, you can learn the next four in any order you wish.

- **Article 200—Use and Identification of Grounded Conductors.** This article contains the requirements for the use and identification of the grounded conductor and its terminals.

- **Article 230—Services.** Article 230 covers the installation requirements for service conductors and equipment. It's very important to know where the service begins and ends when applying Article 230.

- **Article 240—Overcurrent Protection.** This article provides the requirements for overcurrent protection and over-current devices. Overcurrent protection for conductors and equipment is provided to open the circuit if the current reaches a value that will cause an excessive or dangerous temperature on the conductors or conductor insulation.

- **Article 250—Grounding and Bonding.** Article 250 covers the grounding requirements for providing a low-imped-ance path to the earth to reduce overvoltage from lightning, and the requirements for a low-impedance fault current path necessary to facilitate the operation of overcurrent devices in the event of a ground fault.

Notes

Use and Identification of Grounded Conductors

INTRODUCTION TO ARTICLE 200—USE AND IDENTIFICATION OF GROUNDED CONDUCTORS

This article contains the requirements for the identification of the grounded conductor and its terminals.

PART I. GENERAL

200.1 Scope. Article 200 contains requirements for the use and identification of grounded conductors and terminals.

200.6 Grounded Conductor Identification.

(A) 6 AWG or Smaller. Grounded conductors 6 AWG and smaller must be identified by one of the following means: **Figure 200–1 and Figure 200–2**

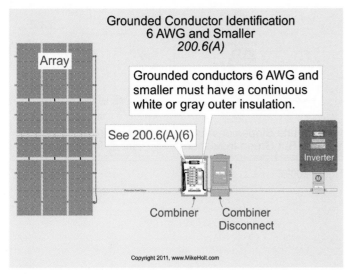

Figure 200–1

(1) By a continuous white outer finish.

(2) By a continuous gray outer finish.

(3) By three continuous white stripes along its entire length on other than green insulation.

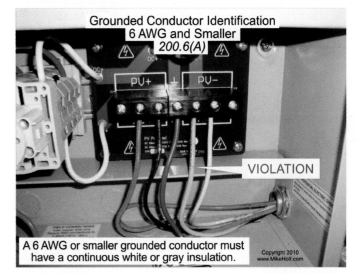

A 6 AWG or smaller grounded conductor must have a continuous white or gray insulation. Copyright 2010 www.MikeHolt.com

Figure 200–2

(4) Wires that have their outer covering finished to show a white or gray color but have colored tracer threads in the braid identifying the source of manufacture are considered to meet the provisions of this section.

Author's Comment: The use of white tape, paint, or other methods of identification isn't permitted for grounded conductors 6 AWG or smaller. **Figure 200–3**

(6) A single-conductor, sunlight-resistant, outdoor-rated cable used for the source circuit grounded conductor in PV systems as permitted by 690.31(B) can be identified by white marking at all terminations. **Figure 200–4 and 200–5**

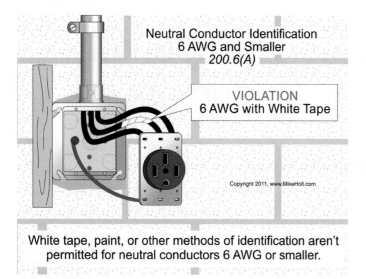

Neutral Conductor Identification
6 AWG and Smaller
200.6(A)

VIOLATION
6 AWG with White Tape

Copyright 2011, www.MikeHolt.com

White tape, paint, or other methods of identification aren't permitted for neutral conductors 6 AWG or smaller.

Figure 200–3

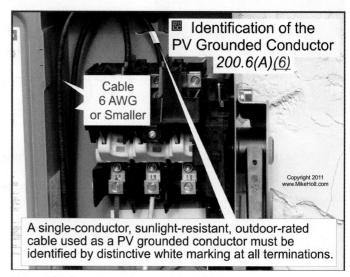

Identification of the
PV Grounded Conductor
200.6(A)(6)

Cable
6 AWG
or Smaller

Copyright 2011
www.MikeHolt.com

A single-conductor, sunlight-resistant, outdoor-rated cable used as a PV grounded conductor must be identified by distinctive white marking at all terminations.

Figure 200–5

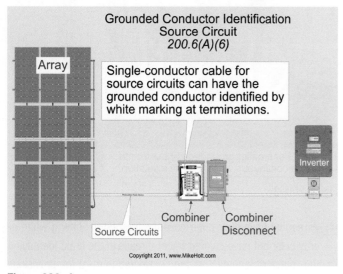

Grounded Conductor Identification
Source Circuit
200.6(A)(6)

Array

Single-conductor cable for source circuits can have the grounded conductor identified by white marking at terminations.

Inverter

Combiner   Combiner Disconnect

Source Circuits

Copyright 2011, www.MikeHolt.com

Figure 200–4

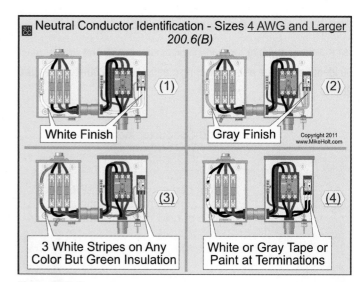

Neutral Conductor Identification - Sizes 4 AWG and Larger
200.6(B)

White Finish   (1)

Gray Finish   (2)

Copyright 2011
www.MikeHolt.com

(3)

(4)

3 White Stripes on Any Color But Green Insulation

White or Gray Tape or Paint at Terminations

Figure 200–6

(B) Size 4 AWG or Larger. Grounded conductors 4 AWG or larger must be identified by one of the following means: **Figure 200–6**

(1) A continuous white outer finish along its entire length.

(2) A continuous gray outer finish along its entire length.

(3) Three continuous white stripes along its length.

(4) White or gray tape or markings at the terminations.

ARTICLE
230

Services

INTRODUCTION TO ARTICLE 230—SERVICES

This article covers the installation requirements for service conductors and service equipment. The requirements for service conductors differ from those for other conductors. For one thing, service conductors for one building/structure can't pass through the interior of another building or structure [230.3], and you apply different rules depending on whether a service conductor is inside or outside a building/structure. When are they "outside" as opposed to "inside?" The answer may seem obvious, but 230.6 should be consulted before making this decision.

Let's review the following definitions in Article 100 to understand when the requirements of Article 230 apply:

- Service Point—The point of connection between the serving utility and the premises wiring.
- Service Conductors—The conductors from the service point to the service disconnecting means. Service-entrance conductors can either be overhead or underground.
- Service Equipment—The necessary equipment, usually consisting of circuit breakers or switches and fuses and their accessories, connected to the load end of service conductors at a building or other structure, and intended to constitute the main control and cutoff of the electrical supply. Service equipment doesn't include individual meter socket enclosures [230.66].

After reviewing these definitions, you should understand that service conductors originate at the serving utility (service point) and terminate on the line side of the service disconnecting means.

PART I. GENERAL

230.1 Scope. Article 230 covers the installation requirements for service conductors and service equipment.

PART IV. SERVICE-ENTRANCE CONDUCTORS

230.43 Wiring Methods. Service-entrance conductors must be installed with one of the following wiring methods:

(1) Open wiring on insulators

(3) Rigid metal conduit

(4) Intermediate metal conduit

(5) Electrical metallic tubing

(6) Electrical nonmetallic tubing

(7) Service-entrance cables

(8) Wireways

(9) Busways

(11) PVC Conduit

(13) Type MC Cable

(15) Flexible metal conduit or liquidtight flexible metal conduit not longer than 6 ft

(16) Liquidtight flexible nonmetallic conduit

(17) High-Density Polyethylene Conduit (HDPE)

(18) Nonmetallic Underground Conduit with Conductors (NUCC)

(19) Reinforced Thermosetting Resin Conduit (RTRC)

PART V. SERVICE EQUIPMENT—GENERAL

230.66 Listed as Suitable for Service Equipment. The service disconnecting means must be listed as suitable for use as service equipment.

> **Author's Comment:** "Suitable for use as service equipment" means, among other things, that the service disconnecting means is supplied with a main bonding jumper so that the grounded conductor can be bonded to the case, as required in 250.24(C). **Figure 230–1**

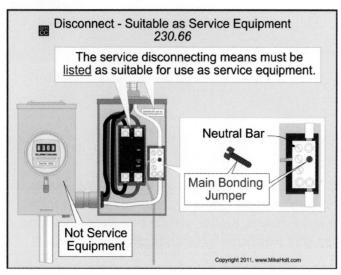

Figure 230-1

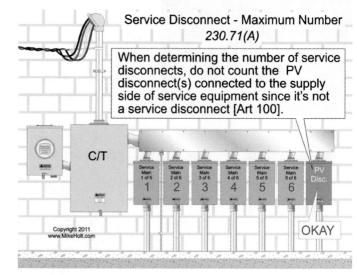

Figure 230-2

230.71 Number of Disconnects.

(A) Maximum. There must be no more than six service disconnects for each service permitted by 230.2, or each set of service-entrance conductors permitted by 230.40 Ex 1, 3, 4, or 5.

The service disconnecting means for each service grouped in one location can consist of up to six switches or six circuit breakers mounted in a single enclosure, in a group of separate enclosures, or in or on a switchboard.

> **Author's Comment:** Disconnecting means for photovoltaic systems connected to the supply-side of service equipment as permitted by 230.82(6) and 705.12(A) are not considered a service disconnecting means. **Figure 230-2**

230.82 Connected on Supply Side of the Service Disconnect. Electrical equipment must not be connected to the supply side of the service disconnect enclosure, except for the following:

(6) Solar photovoltaic systems in accordance with 705.12(A). **Figure 230-3**

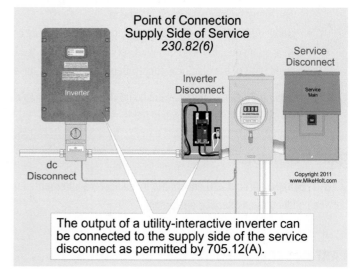

Figure 230-3

ARTICLE 240

Overcurrent Protection

INTRODUCTION TO ARTICLE 240—OVERCURRENT PROTECTION

This article provides the requirements for selecting and installing overcurrent devices. Overcurrent exists when current exceeds the rating of equipment or the ampacity of a conductor. This can be due to an overload, short circuit, or ground fault [Article 100].

Overload. An overload is a condition where equipment or conductors carry current exceeding their current rating [Article 100]. A fault, such as a short circuit or ground fault, isn't an overload. An example of an overload is plugging two 12.50A (1,500W) hair dryers into a 20A branch circuit.

Ground Fault. A ground fault is an unintentional, electrically conducting connection between an ungrounded conductor of an electrical circuit and the normally noncurrent-carrying conductors, metallic enclosures, metallic raceways, metallic equipment, or the earth [Article 100]. During the period of a ground fault, dangerous voltages will be present on metal parts until the circuit overcurrent device opens.

Short Circuit. A short circuit is the unintentional electrical connection between any two normally current-carrying conductors of an electrical circuit, either line-to-line or line-to-case.

Overcurrent devices protect conductors and equipment. Selecting the proper overcurrent protection for a specific circuit can become more complicated than it sounds. The general rule for overcurrent protection is that conductors must be protected in accordance with their ampacities at the point where they receive their supply [240.4and 240.21]. There are many special cases that deviate from this basic rule, such as the overcurrent protection limitations for small conductors [240.4(D)] and the rules for specific conductor applications found in other articles, as listed in Table 240.4(G). There are also a number of rules allowing tap conductors in specific situations [240.21(B)]. Article 240 even has limits on where overcurrent devices are allowed to be located [240.24].

An overcurrent protection device must be capable of opening a circuit when an overcurrent situation occurs, and must also have an interrupting rating sufficient to avoid damage in fault conditions [110.9]. Carefully study the provisions of this article to be sure you provide sufficient overcurrent protection in the correct location.

PART I. GENERAL

240.1 Scope. Article 240 covers the general requirements for overcurrent protection and the installation requirements of overcurrent devices. **Figure 240–1**

> **Author's Comment:** Overcurrent is a condition where the current exceeds the rating of equipment or ampacity of a conductor due to overload, short circuit, or ground fault [Article 100]. **Figure 240–2**

Note: An overcurrent device protects the circuit by opening the device when the current reaches a value that will cause excessive or dangerous temperature rise (overheating) in conductors. Overcurrent devices must have an interrupting rating sufficient for the maximum possible fault current available on the line-side terminals of the equipment [110.9]. Electrical equipment must have a short-circuit current rating that permits the circuit's overcurrent device to clear short circuits or ground faults without extensive damage to the circuit's electrical components [110.10].

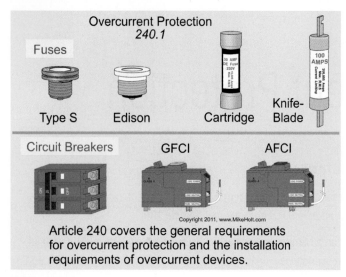

Figure 240–1

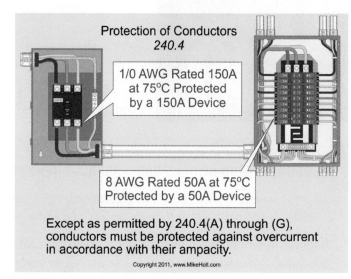

Figure 240–3

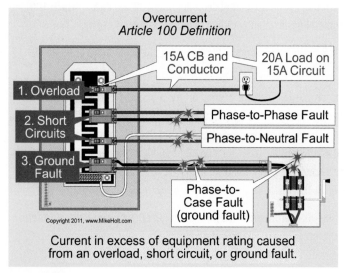

Figure 240–2

240.4 Protection of Conductors. Except as permitted by (A) through (G), conductors must be protected against overcurrent in accordance with their ampacity after ampacity adjustment, as specified in 310.15. **Figure 240–3**

Author's Comment: Conductor overcurrent protection is not required for PV circuit conductors when four or fewer conductors are in a raceway, see 690.9(A) Ex.

(B) Overcurrent Devices Rated 800A or Less. The next higher standard rating of overcurrent device listed in 240.6 (above the ampacity of the ungrounded conductors being protected) is permitted, provided all of the following conditions are met:

(2) The ampacity of a conductor, after the application of ambient temperature correction [310.15(B)(2)(a)], conductor bundling adjustment [310.15(B)(3)(a)], or both, doesn't correspond with the standard rating of a fuse or circuit breaker in 240.6(A).

(3) The overcurrent device rating doesn't exceed 800A. **Figure 240–4**

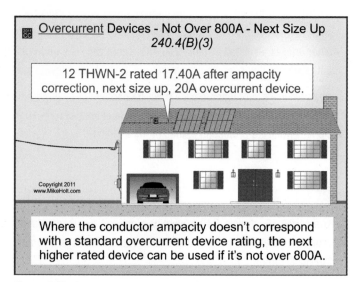

Figure 240–4

(C) Overcurrent Devices Rated Over 800A. If the circuit's overcurrent device exceeds 800A, the conductor ampacity (after the application of ambient temperature correction [310.15(B)(2)(a)], conductor bundling adjustment [310.15(B)(3)(a)], or both, must have a rating of not less than the rating of the overcurrent device defined in 240.6.

(D) Small Conductors. Unless specifically permitted in 240.4 (E) or (G), overcurrent protection must not exceed the following: **Figure 240–5**

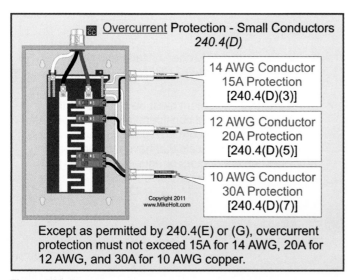

Figure 240–5

(3) 14 AWG Copper—15A

(5) 12 AWG Copper—20A

(7) 10 AWG Copper—30A

240.6 Standard Ampere Ratings.

(A) Fuses and Fixed-Trip Circuit Breakers. The standard ratings in amperes for fuses and inverse time breakers are: 15, 20, 25, 30, 35, 40, 45, 50, 60, 70, 80, 90, 100, 110, 125, 150, 175, 200, 225, 250, 300, 350, 400, 450, 500, 600, 700, 800, 1,000, 1,200, 1,600, 2,000, 2,500, 3,000, 4,000, 5,000 and 6,000. **Figure 240–6**

> **Author's Comment:** Article 100 defines a "Supplementary Overcurrent Device" as a device intended to provide limited overcurrent protection for specific applications and utilization equipment. This limited protection is in addition to the protection provided in the required branch circuit by the branch-circuit overcurrent device.

240.15 Ungrounded Conductors.

(A) Overcurrent Device Required. A fuse or an overcurrent trip unit of a circuit breaker must be connected in series with each ungrounded conductor. A combination of a current transformer and overcurrent relay is considered equivalent to an overcurrent trip unit for the purpose of providing overcurrent protection of conductors. Part II. Location

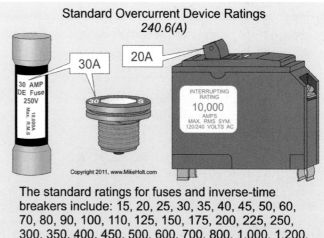

Figure 240–6

240.21 Overcurrent Protection Location in Circuit.

(H) Battery Conductors. Overcurrent protection is installed as close as practicable to the storage battery terminals.

240.24 Location of Overcurrent Devices.

(A) Readily Accessible. Circuit breakers and fuses must be readily accessible, and they must be installed so the center of the grip of the operating handle of the fuse switch or circuit breaker, when in its highest position, isn't more than 6 ft 7 in. above the floor or working platform, except for: **Figure 240–7**

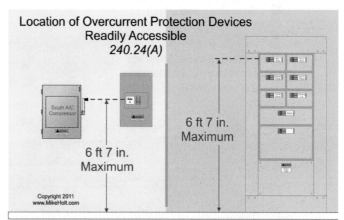

Figure 240–7

(4) Overcurrent devices located next to equipment can be mounted above 6 ft 7 in., if accessible by portable means [404.8(A) Ex 2]. **Figure 240–8**

Note: Electrical equipment must be suitable for the environment, and consideration must be given to the presence of corrosive gases, fumes, vapors, liquids, or chemicals that have a deteriorating effect on conductors or equipment [110.11]. **Figure 240–10**

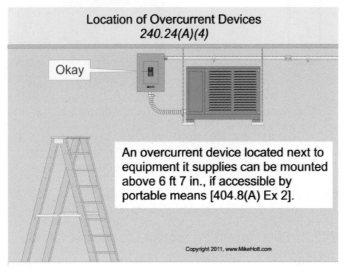

Figure 240–8

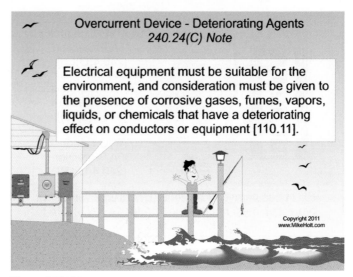

Figure 240–10

(2) Supplementary overcurrent devices in accordance with 240.10.

(C) Not Exposed to Physical Damage. Overcurrent devices must not be exposed to physical damage. **Figure 240–9**

(D) Not in Vicinity of Easily Ignitible Material. Overcurrent devices must not be located near easily ignitible material, such as in clothes closets. **Figure 240–11**

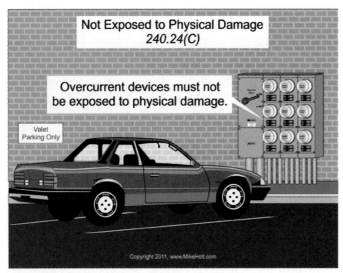

Figure 240–9

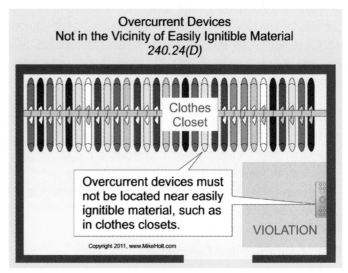

Figure 240–11

(E) Not in Bathrooms. Overcurrent devices aren't permitted to be located in the bathrooms of dwelling units, dormitories, or guest rooms or guest suites of hotels or motels. Figure 240–12

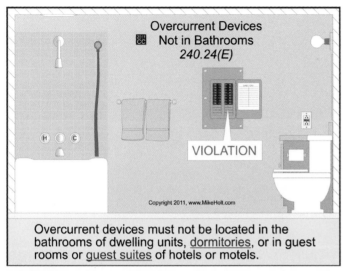

Figure 240–12

(F) Over Steps. Overcurrent devices must not be located over the steps of a stairway. Figure 240–13

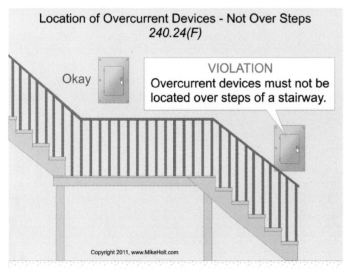

Figure 240–13

Author's Comment: Clearly, it's difficult for electricians to safely work on electrical equipment that's located on uneven surfaces such as over stairways.

PART III. ENCLOSURES

240.32 Damp or Wet Locations. In damp or wet locations, enclosures containing overcurrent devices must prevent moisture or water from entering or accumulating within the enclosure. When the enclosure is surface mounted in a wet location, it must be mounted with not less than ¼ in. of air space between it and the mounting surface. See 312.2.

240.33 Vertical Position. Enclosures containing overcurrent devices must be mounted in a vertical position unless this isn't practical. Circuit-breaker enclosures can be mounted horizontally if the circuit breaker is installed in accordance with 240.81. Figure 240–14

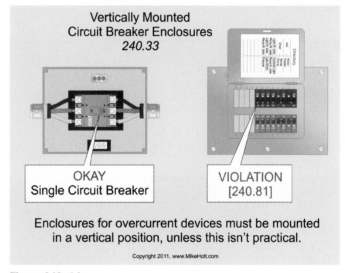

Figure 240–14

Author's Comment: Section 240.81 specifies that where circuit-breaker handles are operated vertically, the "up" position of the handle must be in the "on" position. So, in effect, an enclosure that contains one row of circuit breakers can be mounted horizontally, but an enclosure that contains a panelboard with multiple circuit breakers on opposite sides of each other will have to be mounted vertically.

Notes

Grounding and Bonding

INTRODUCTION TO ARTICLE 250—GROUNDING AND BONDING

No other article can match Article 250 for misapplication, violation, and misinterpretation. Terminology used in this article has been a source for much confusion, but that has improved during the last few *NEC* revisions. It's very important to understand the difference between grounding and bonding in order to correctly apply the provisions of Article 250. Pay careful attention to the definitions that apply to grounding and bonding both here and in Article 100 as you begin the study of this important article. Article 250 covers the grounding requirements for providing a path to the earth to reduce overvoltage from lightning, and the bonding requirements for a low-impedance fault current path back to the source of the electrical supply to facilitate the operation of overcurrent devices in the event of a ground fault.

Over the past five *Code* cycles, this article was extensively revised to organize it better and make it easier to understand and implement. It's arranged in a logical manner, so it's a good idea to just read through Article 250 to get a big picture view—after you review the definitions. Next, study the article closely so you understand the details. The illustrations will help you understand the key points.

PART I. GENERAL

250.1 Scope. Article 250 contains the following grounding and bonding requirements:

(1) What systems and equipment are required to be grounded.

(2) Circuit conductor to be grounded on grounded systems.

(3) Location of grounding connections.

(4) Types of electrodes and sizes of grounding and bonding conductors.

(5) Methods of grounding and bonding.

250.2 Definitions.

Bonding Jumper, Supply-Side. A conductor on the supply side or within a service or separately derived system to ensure the electrical conductivity between metal parts required to be electrically connected. **Figures 250–1 and 250–2**

Effective Ground-Fault Current Path. An intentionally constructed low-impedance conductive path designed to carry fault current from the point of a ground fault on a wiring system to the electrical supply source. **Figure 250–3**

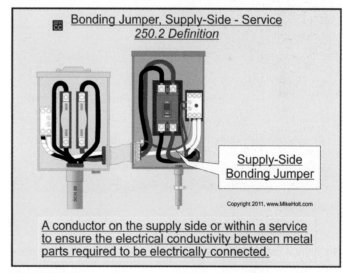

Figure 250–1

Author's Comment: In **Figure 250–3**, "EGC" represents the equipment grounding conductor [259.118], "MBJ" represents the main bonding jumper, "SNC" represents the service neutral conductor (grounded service conductor), and "GEC" represents the grounding electrode conductor.

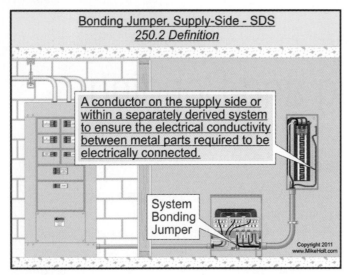

Bonding Jumper, Supply-Side - SDS
250.2 Definition

A conductor on the supply side or within a separately derived system to ensure the electrical conductivity between metal parts required to be electrically connected.

System Bonding Jumper

Figure 250–2

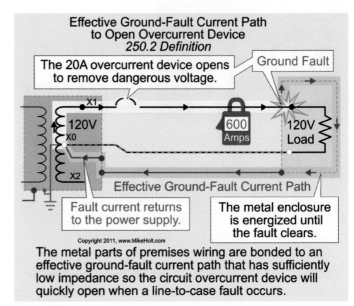

Effective Ground-Fault Current Path to Open Overcurrent Device
250.2 Definition

The 20A overcurrent device opens to remove dangerous voltage.

Ground Fault

120V X1

X0

600 Amps

120V Load

X2

Effective Ground-Fault Current Path

Fault current returns to the power supply.

The metal enclosure is energized until the fault clears.

The metal parts of premises wiring are bonded to an effective ground-fault current path that has sufficiently low impedance so the circuit overcurrent device will quickly open when a line-to-case fault occurs.

Figure 250–4

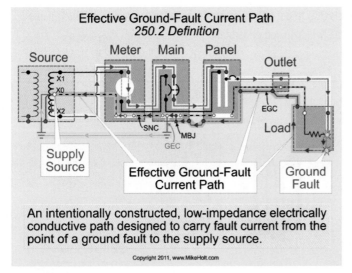

Effective Ground-Fault Current Path
250.2 Definition

Source   Meter   Main   Panel

Outlet

X1
X0
X2

EGC

SNC
MBJ
GEC

Load

Supply Source

Effective Ground-Fault Current Path

Ground Fault

An intentionally constructed, low-impedance electrically conductive path designed to carry fault current from the point of a ground fault to the supply source.

Figure 250–3

Note: The ground-fault current path could be metal raceways, cable sheaths, electrical equipment, or other electrically conductive materials, such as metallic water or gas piping, steel-framing members, metal ducting, reinforcing steel, or the shields of communications cables. **Figure 250–5**

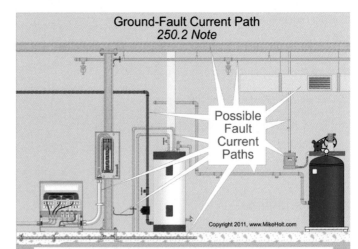

Ground-Fault Current Path
250.2 Note

Possible Fault Current Paths

The ground-fault current path can consist of bonding conductors, metal raceways, metal cable sheaths, metal enclosures, and other electrically conductive materials, such as metallic water or gas piping, steel-framing members, metal ducting, reinforcing steel, or the shields of communications cables.

Figure 250–5

The current path shown between the supply source grounding electrode and the grounding electrode at the service main shows that some current will flow through the earth but the earth is not part of the effective ground-fault current path.

The effective ground-fault current path is intended to help remove dangerous voltage from a ground fault by opening the circuit overcurrent device. **Figure 250–4**

Ground-Fault Current Path. An electrically conductive path from a ground fault to the electrical supply source.

Author's Comment: The difference between an "effective ground-fault current path" and a "ground-fault current path" is the effective ground-fault current path is "intentionally" constructed to provide a low-impedance fault current path to the electrical supply source for the purpose of clearing a ground fault. A ground-fault current path is all of the available conductive paths over which fault current flows on its return to the electrical supply source during a ground fault.

250.4 General Requirements for Grounding and Bonding.

(A) Solidly Grounded Systems.

(1) Electrical System Grounding. Electrical power systems, such as the secondary winding of a transformer are grounded (connected to the earth) to limit the voltage induced by lightning, line surges, or unintentional contact by higher-voltage lines. **Figure 250–6**

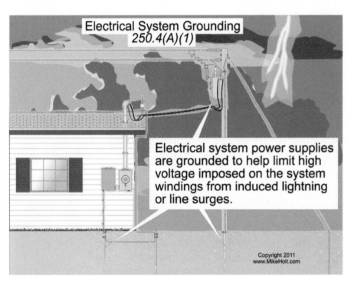

Electrical system power supplies are grounded to help limit high voltage imposed on the system windings from induced lightning or line surges.

Figure 250–6

Author's Comment: System grounding helps reduce fires in buildings as well as voltage stress on electrical insulation, thereby ensuring longer insulation life for motors, transformers, and other system components. **Figure 250–7**

Note: An important consideration for limiting imposed voltage is to remember that grounding electrode conductors shouldn't be any longer than necessary and unnecessary bends and loops should be avoided. **Figure 250–8**

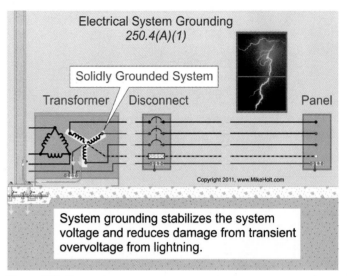

System grounding stabilizes the system voltage and reduces damage from transient overvoltage from lightning.

Figure 250–7

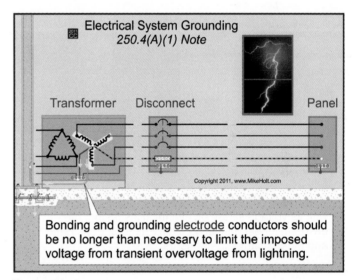

Bonding and grounding electrode conductors should be no longer than necessary to limit the imposed voltage from transient overvoltage from lightning.

Figure 250–8

(2) Equipment Grounding. Metal parts of electrical equipment are grounded (connected to the earth) to reduce induced voltage on metal parts from exterior lightning so as to prevent fires from an arc within the building/structure. **Figure 250–9**

⚠️ **DANGER:** *Failure to ground the metal parts can result in high voltage on metal parts from an indirect lightning strike to seek a path to the earth within the building—possibly resulting in a fire and/or electric shock.* **Figure 250–10**

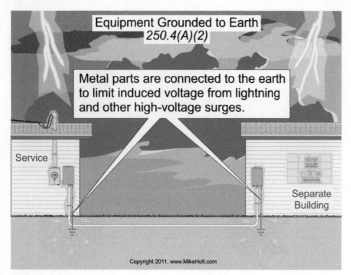

Figure 250–9

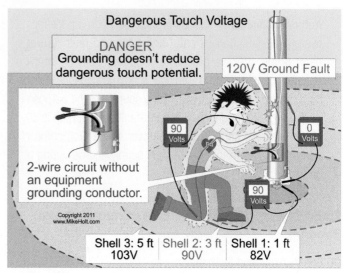

Figure 250–11

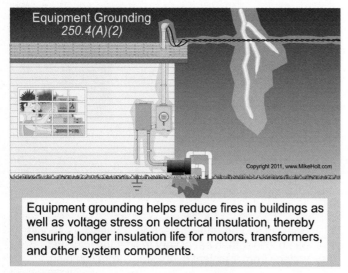

Figure 250–10

Author's Comment: Grounding metal parts helps drain off static electricity charges before flashover potential is reached. Static grounding is often used in areas where the discharge (arcing) of the voltage buildup (static) can cause dangerous or undesirable conditions [500.4 Note 3].

⚠ **DANGER:** *Because the contact resistance of an electrode to the earth is so high, very little fault current returns to the power supply if the earth is the only fault current return path. Result—the circuit overcurrent device won't open and clear the ground fault, and all metal parts associated with the electrical installation, metal piping, and structural building steel will become and remain energized.* **Figure 250–11**

(3) Equipment Bonding. Metal parts of electrical raceways, cables, enclosures, and equipment must be connected to the supply source via the effective ground-fault current path. **Figures 250–12 and 250–13**

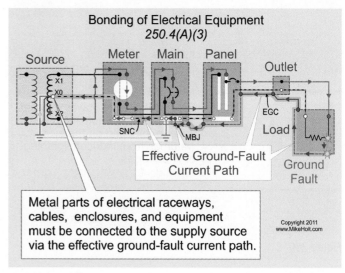

Figure 250–12

Author's Comment: To quickly remove dangerous touch voltage on metal parts from a ground fault, the fault current path must have sufficiently low impedance to the source so that fault current will quickly rise to a level that will open the branch-circuit overcurrent device. **Figure 250–14**

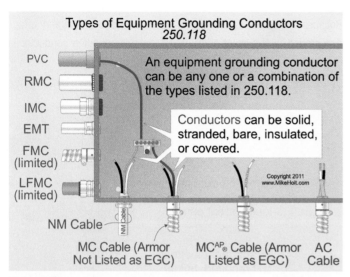

Figure 250–13

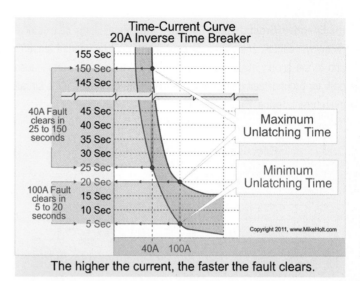

The higher the current, the faster the fault clears.

Figure 250–15

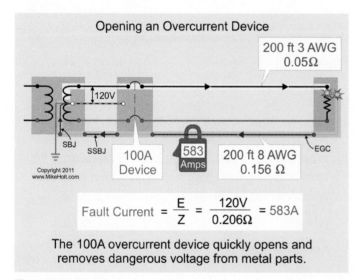

$$\text{Fault Current} = \frac{E}{Z} = \frac{120V}{0.206\Omega} = 583A$$

The 100A overcurrent device quickly opens and removes dangerous voltage from metal parts.

Figure 250–14

Author's Comment: The time it takes for an overcurrent device to open is inversely proportional to the magnitude of the fault current. This means the higher the ground-fault current value, the less time it will take for the overcurrent device to open and clear the fault. For example, a 20A circuit with an overload of 40A (two times the 20A rating) takes 25 to 150 seconds to open the overcurrent device. At 100A (five times the 20A rating) the 20A breaker trips in 5 to 20 seconds. **Figure 250–15**

(4) Bonding Conductive Materials. Electrically conductive materials such as metal water piping systems, metal sprinkler piping, metal gas piping, and other metal-piping systems, as well as exposed structural steel members likely to become energized, must be connected to the supply source via an equipment grounding conductor of a type recognized in 250.118. **Figure 250–16**

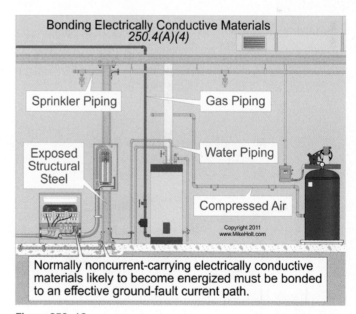

Normally noncurrent-carrying electrically conductive materials likely to become energized must be bonded to an effective ground-fault current path.

Figure 250–16

Author's Comment: The phrase "likely to become energized" is subject to interpretation by the authority having jurisdiction.

(5) Effective Ground-Fault Current Path. Metal parts of electrical raceways, cables, enclosures, or equipment must be bonded together and to the supply system in a manner that creates a low-impedance path for ground-fault current that facilitates the operation of the circuit overcurrent device. **Figure 250–17**

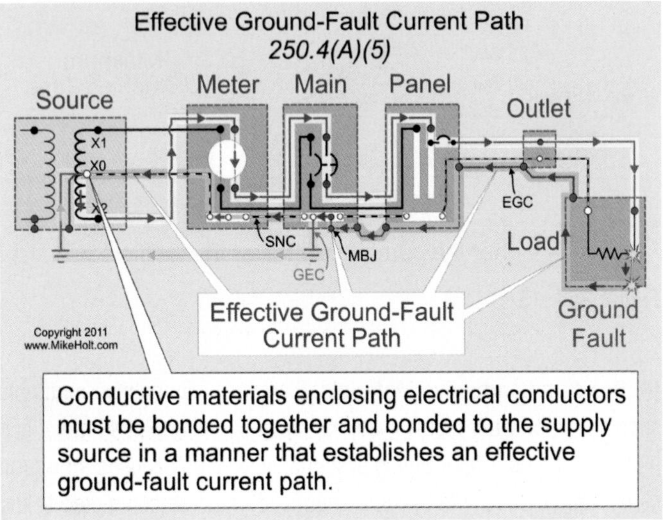

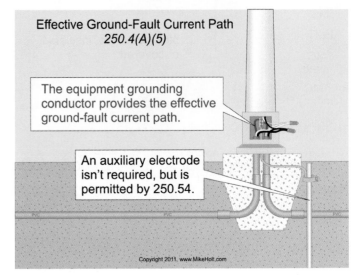

Effective Ground-Fault Current Path
250.4(A)(5)

Conductive materials enclosing electrical conductors must be bonded together and bonded to the supply source in a manner that establishes an effective ground-fault current path.

Figure 250–17

Author's Comment: To ensure a low-impedance ground-fault current path, all circuit conductors must be grouped together in the same raceway, cable, or trench [300.3(B), 300.5(I), and 300.20(A)]. **Figure 250–18**

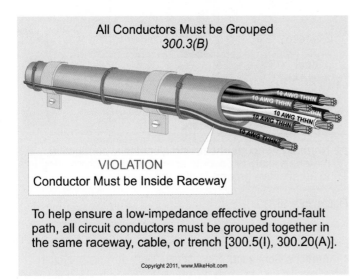

All Conductors Must be Grouped
300.3(B)

VIOLATION
Conductor Must be Inside Raceway

To help ensure a low-impedance effective ground-fault path, all circuit conductors must be grouped together in the same raceway, cable, or trench [300.5(I), 300.20(A)].

Figure 250–18

Because the earth isn't suitable to serve as the required effective ground-fault current path, an equipment grounding conductor is required to be installed with all circuits. **Figure 250–19**

Effective Ground-Fault Current Path
250.4(A)(5)

The equipment grounding conductor provides the effective ground-fault current path.

An auxiliary electrode isn't required, but is permitted by 250.54.

Figure 250–19

Question: What's the maximum fault current that can flow through the earth to the power supply from a 120V ground fault to metal parts of a light pole that's grounded (connected to the earth) via a ground rod having a contact resistance to the earth of 25 ohms? **Figure 250–20**

(a) 4.80A   *(b) 20A*   *(c) 40A*   *(d) 100A*

Answer: *(a) 4.80A*

I = E/R
I = 120V/25 ohms
I = 4.80A

⚠ **DANGER:** *Because the contact resistance of an electrode to the earth is so high, very little fault current returns to the power supply if the earth is the only fault current return path. Result—the circuit overcurrent device won't open and all metal parts associated with the electrical installation, metal piping, and structural building steel will become and remain energized.* **Figure 250–21**

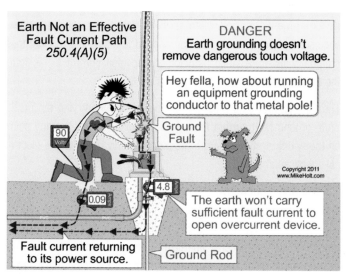

Figure 250–20

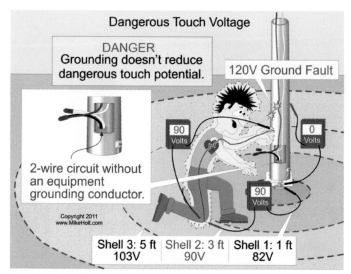

Figure 250–21

EARTH SHELLS

According to ANSI/IEEE 142, *Recommended Practice for Grounding of Industrial and Commercial Power Systems* (Green Book) [4.1.1], the resistance of the soil outward from a ground rod is equal to the sum of the series resistances of the earth shells. The shell nearest the rod has the highest resistance and each successive shell has progressively larger areas and progressively lower resistances. Don't be concerned if you don't understand this statement; just review the table below. **Figure 250–22**

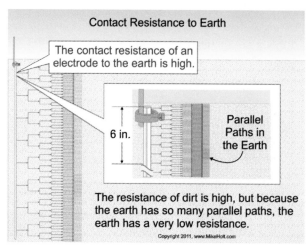

Figure 250–22

Distance from Rod	Soil Contact Resistance
1 ft (Shell 1)	68% of total contact resistance
3 ft (Shells 1 and 2)	75% of total contact resistance
5 ft (Shells 1, 2, and 3)	86% of total contact resistance

Since voltage is directly proportional to resistance, the voltage gradient of the earth around an energized ground rod will be as follows, assuming a 120V ground fault:

Distance from Rod	Soil Contact Resistance	Voltage Gradient
1 ft (Shell 1)	68%	82V
3 ft (Shells 1 and 2)	75%	90V
5 ft (Shells 1, 2, and 3)	86%	103V

(B) Ungrounded Systems.

Author's Comment: Ungrounded systems are those systems with no connection to the ground or to a conductive body that extends the ground connection [Article 100]. **Figure 250–23**

(1) Equipment Grounding. Metal parts of electrical equipment are grounded (connected to the earth) to reduce induced voltage on metal parts from exterior lightning so as to prevent fires from an arc within the building/structure. **Figure 250–24**

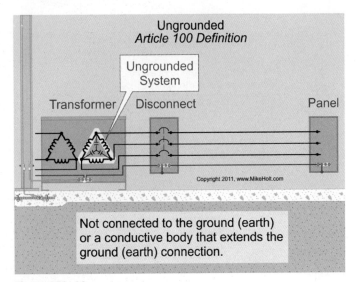

Figure 250–23

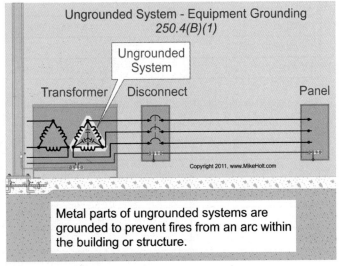

Figure 250–24

Author's Comment: Grounding metal parts helps drain off static electricity charges before an electric arc takes place (flashover potential). Static grounding is often used in areas where the discharge (arcing) of the voltage buildup (static) can cause dangerous or undesirable conditions [500.4 Note 3].

⚠️ **CAUTION:** *Connecting metal parts to the earth (grounding) serves no purpose in electrical shock protection.*

(2) Equipment Bonding. Metal parts of electrical raceways, cables, enclosures, or equipment must be bonded together in a manner that creates a low-impedance path for ground-fault current to facilitate the operation of the circuit overcurrent device.

The fault current path must be capable of safely carrying the maximum ground-fault current likely to be imposed on it from any point on the wiring system where a ground fault may occur to the electrical supply source.

(3) Bonding Conductive Materials. Conductive materials such as metal water piping systems, metal sprinkler piping, metal gas piping, and other metal-piping systems, as well as exposed structural steel members likely to become energized must be bonded together in a manner that creates a low-impedance fault current path that's capable of carrying the maximum fault current likely to be imposed on it. **Figure 250–25**

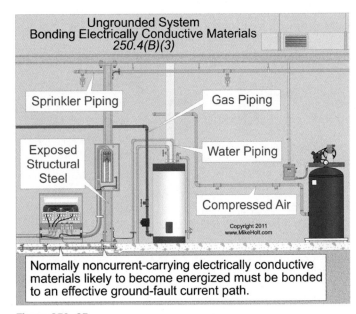

Figure 250–25

Author's Comment: The phrase "likely to become energized" is subject to interpretation by the authority having jurisdiction.

(4) Fault Current Path. Electrical equipment, wiring, and other electrically conductive material likely to become energized must be installed in a manner that creates a low-impedance fault current path to facilitate the operation of overcurrent devices should a second ground fault from a different phase occur. **Figure 250–26**

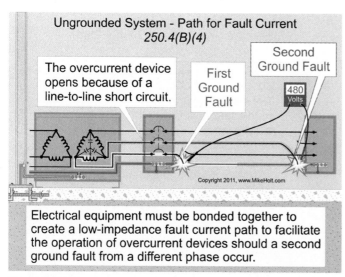

Figure 250–26

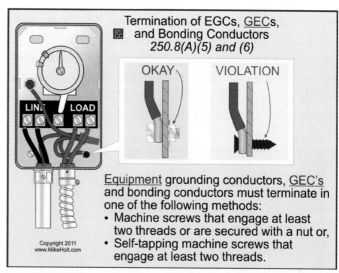

Figure 250–27

Author's Comment: A single ground fault can't be cleared on an ungrounded system because there's no low-impedance fault current path to the power source. The first ground fault simply grounds the previously ungrounded system. However, a second ground fault on a different phase results in a line-to-line short circuit between the two ground faults. The conductive path, between the ground faults, provides the low-impedance fault current path necessary so the overcurrent device will open.

250.8 Termination of Grounding and Bonding Conductors.

(A) Permitted Methods. Equipment grounding conductors, grounding electrode conductors, and bonding jumpers must terminate in one of the following methods:

(1) Listed pressure connectors

(2) Terminal bars

(3) Pressure connectors listed for direct burial or concrete encasement [250.70]

(4) Exothermic welding

(5) Machine screws that engage at least two threads or are secured with a nut, **Figure 250–27**

(6) Self-tapping machine screws that engage at least two threads

(7) Connections that are part of a listed assembly

(8) Other listed means

(B) Methods Not Permitted. Connection devices or fittings that depend solely on solder aren't allowed.

250.10 Protection of Fittings. Grounding and bonding fittings must be protected from physical damage by:

(1) Locating the fittings so they aren't likely to be damaged.

(2) Enclosing the fittings in metal, wood, or an equivalent protective covering.

> **Author's Comment:** Grounding and bonding fittings can be buried or encased in concrete if they're installed in accordance with 250.53(G), 250.68(A) Ex 1, and 250.70.

250.12 Clean Surfaces. Nonconductive coatings, such as paint, must be removed to ensure good electrical continuity, or the termination fittings must be designed so as to make such removal unnecessary [250.53(A) and 250.96(A)].

> **Author's Comment:** Tarnish on copper water pipe need not be removed before making a termination.

PART II. SYSTEM GROUNDING AND BONDING

250.24 Service Equipment—Grounding and Bonding.

(B) Bonding. A main bonding jumper [250.28] must be installed for the purpose of connecting the grounded conductor to the metal parts of the service disconnecting means.

(C) Grounded Conductor Brought to Service Equipment. A service grounded conductor from the electric utility must be <u>routed with the ungrounded conductors</u> and terminate to the service disconnecting means via a main bonding jumper [250.24(B)] that's installed between the service grounded conductor and the service disconnecting means enclosure [250.28]. **Figures 250–28 and 250–29**

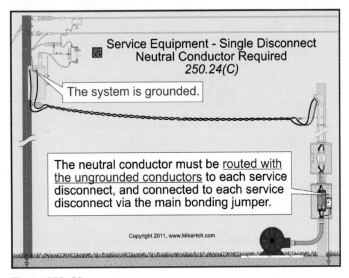

Figure 250–28

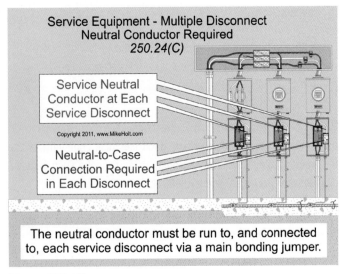

Figures 250–29

Author's Comment: The service grounded conductor provides the effective ground-fault current path to the power supply to ensure that dangerous voltage from a ground fault will be quickly removed by opening the overcurrent device [250.4(A)(3) and 250.4(A)(5)]. **Figure 250–30**

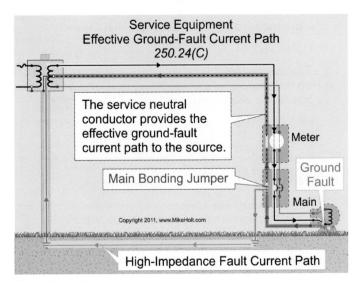

Figure 250–30

⚠ DANGER: *Dangerous voltage from a ground fault won't be removed from metal parts, metal piping, and structural steel if the service disconnecting means enclosure isn't connected to the service grounded conductor. This is because the contact resistance of a grounding electrode to the earth is so great that insufficient fault current returns to the power supply if the earth is the only fault current return path to open the circuit overcurrent device.* **Figure 250–31**

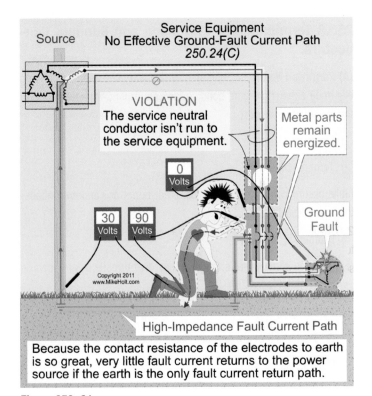

Figure 250–31

Author's Comment: For example, if the grounded conductor is opened, dangerous voltage will be present on metal parts under normal conditions, providing the potential for electric shock. If the earth's ground resistance is 25 ohms and the load's resistance is 25 ohms, the voltage drop across each of these resistors will be half of the voltage source. Since the grounded is connected to the service disconnect, all metal parts will be elevated to 60V above the earth's potential for a 120/240V system. **Figure 250–32**

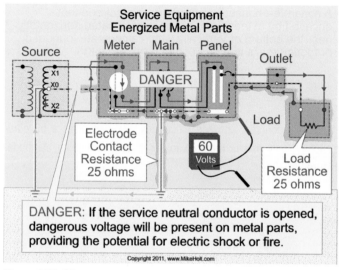

Figure 250–32

Figure 250–33

To determine the actual voltage on the metal parts from an open service grounded conductor, you need to do some complex math calculations. Visit www.MikeHolt.com and go to the "Free Stuff" link to download a spreadsheet for this purpose.

(1) Single Raceway. Because the service grounded conductor serves as the effective ground-fault current path to the source for ground faults, the grounded conductor must be sized so it can safely carry the maximum fault current likely to be imposed on it [110.10 and 250.4(A)(5)]. This is accomplished by sizing the grounded conductor not smaller than specified in Table 250.66, based on the cross-sectional area of the largest ungrounded service conductor. **Figure 250–33**

(2) Parallel Conductors in Two or More Raceways. If service conductors are paralleled in two or more raceways, a grounded conductor must be installed in each of the parallel raceways. The size of the grounded conductor in each raceway must not be smaller than specified in Table 250.66, based on the cross-sectional area of the largest ungrounded service conductor in each raceway. In no case can the grounded conductor in each parallel set be sized smaller than 1/0 AWG [310.10(H)(1)].Part III. Grounding Electrode System and Grounding Electrode Conductor

PART III. GROUNDING ELECTRODE SYSTEM AND GROUNDING ELECTRODE CONDUCTOR

250.52 Grounding Electrode Types.

(A) Electrodes Permitted for Grounding.

(1) Underground Metal Water Pipe Electrode. Underground metal water pipe in direct contact with the earth for 10 ft or more can serve as a grounding electrode. **Figure 250–34**

(2) Metal Frame Electrode. The metal frame of a building/structure can serve as a grounding electrode when it meets at least one of the following conditions:

(1) At least one structural metal member is in direct contact with the earth for 10 ft or more, with or without concrete encasement.

(2) The bolts securing the structural steel column are connected to a concrete-encased electrode [250.52(A)(3)] by welding, exothermic welding, steel tie wires, or other approved means. **Figure 250–35**

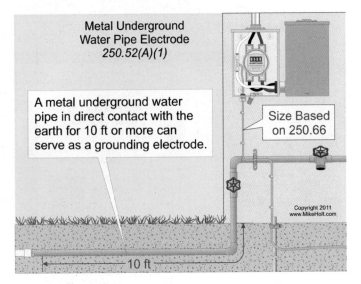

Figure 250–34

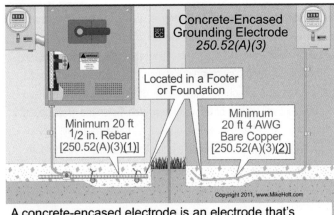

Figure 250–36

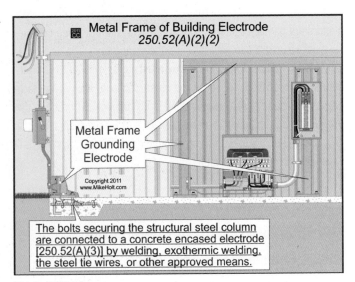

Figure 250–35

(3) Concrete-Encased Electrode. At least 20 ft of either (1) or (2): Figure 250–36

(1) One or more of bare, zinc-galvanized, or otherwise electrically conductive steel reinforcing bars of not less than ½ in. diameter, mechanically connected together by steel tie wires, welding, or other effective means, to create a 20 ft or greater length.

(2) Bare copper conductor not smaller than 4 AWG.

The reinforcing bars or bare copper conductor must be encased by at least 2 in. of concrete located horizontally near the bottom of a concrete footing or vertically within a concrete foundation that's in direct contact with the earth.

If multiple concrete-encased electrodes are present at a building/structure, only one is required to serve as a grounding electrode. Figure 250–37

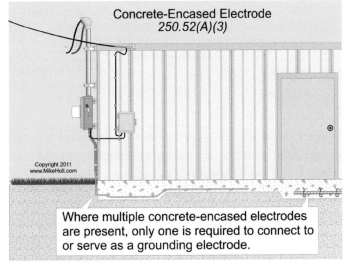

Figure 250–37

Note: Concrete containing insulation, vapor barriers, films or similar items separating it from the earth isn't considered to be in "direct contact" with the earth.

Author's Comments:

- The grounding electrode conductor to a concrete-encased grounding electrode isn't required to be larger than 4 AWG copper [250.66(B)].

- The concrete-encased grounding electrode is also called a "Ufer Ground," named after a consultant working for the U.S. Army during World War II. The technique Mr. Ufer came up with was necessary because the site needing grounding had no underground water table and little rainfall. The desert site was a series of bomb storage vaults in the area of Flagstaff, Arizona. This type of grounding electrode generally offers the lowest ground resistance for the cost.

(4) Ground Ring Electrode. A ground ring consisting of at least 20 ft of bare copper conductor not smaller than 2 AWG buried in the earth encircling a building/structure, can serve as a grounding electrode. Figure 250–38

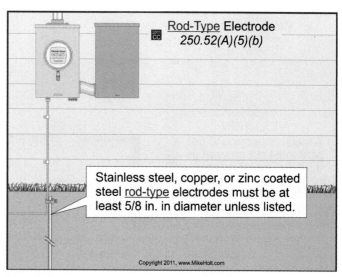

Figure 250–39

Author's Comments:

- The grounding electrode conductor, if it's the sole connection to the ground rod, isn't required to be larger than 6 AWG copper [250.66(A)].

- The diameter of a ground rod has an insignificant effect on the contact resistance of a ground rod to the earth. However, larger diameter ground rods (¾ in. and 1 in.) are sometimes installed where mechanical strength is desired, or to compensate for the loss of the electrode's metal due to corrosion.

(6) Listed Electrode. Other listed grounding electrodes.

(7) Ground Plate Electrode. A bare or conductively coated iron or steel plate with not less than ¼ in. of thickness, or a solid uncoated copper metal plate not less than 0.06 in. of thickness, with an exposed surface area of not less than 2 sq ft.

(8) Metal Underground Systems Electrode. Metal underground piping systems, underground tanks, and underground metal well casings can serve as a grounding electrode.

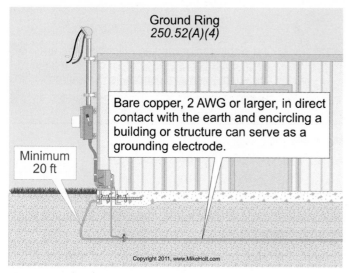

Figure 250–38

Author's Comment: The ground ring must be buried not less than 30 in. [250.53(F)], and the grounding electrode conductor to a ground ring isn't required to be larger than the ground ring conductor size [250.66(C)].

(5) Ground Rod and Pipe Electrode. Ground rod electrodes must not be less than 8 ft in length in contact with the earth [250.53(G)].

(b) Rod-type electrodes must have a diameter of at least ⅝ in., unless listed. Figure 250–39

Author's Comment: The grounding electrode conductor to the metal underground system must be sized in accordance with Table 250.66.

(B) Not Permitted for Use as a Grounding Electrode.

(1) Underground metal gas-piping systems. Figure 250–40

(2) Aluminum

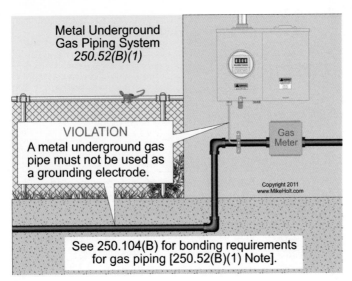

Figure 250–40

250.53 Grounding Electrode Installation Requirements.

(A) Rod, Pipe, or Plate Electrodes.

(1) **Below Permanent Moisture Level.** If practicable, rod, pipe, and plate electrodes must be embedded below the permanent moisture level and be free from nonconductive coatings such as paint or enamel.

(2) **Supplemental Electrode.** A single rod, pipe or plate electrode must be supplemented by an additional electrode of a type specified in 250.52(A)(2) through (A)(8) that's bonded to one of the following: **Figure 250–41**

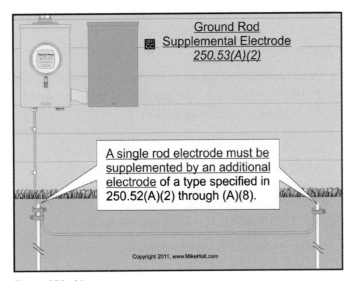

Figure 250–41

(1) The single rod, pipe, or plate electrode

(2) The grounding electrode conductor of the single electrode

(3) The grounded service-entrance conductor

(4) The nonflexible grounded service raceway

(5) The service enclosure

Ex: If a single rod grounding electrode has an earth contact resistance of 25 ohms or less, the supplemental electrode isn't required. **Figure 250–42**

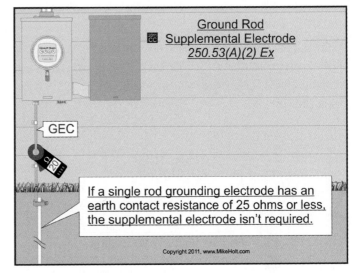

Figure 250–42

(3) **Spacing.** The supplemental electrode for a single rod, pipe, or plate electrode must be installed not less than 6 ft from the single electrode. **Figure 250–43**

> Note: The efficiency of paralleling electrodes is improved by spacing them at least twice the length of the longest rod.

(B) Electrode Spacing. Ground rods used as the required electrode for power systems must be located no closer than 6 ft from lighting protection or photovoltaic system grounding electrodes. Two or more grounding electrodes that are bonded together are considered a single grounding electrode system. **Figure 250–44**

(C) Grounding Electrode Bonding Jumper. Grounding electrode bonding jumpers must be copper when within 18 in. of the earth [250.64(A)], be securely fastened to the surface, and be protected if exposed to physical damage [250.64(B)]. The bonding jumper to each electrode must be sized in accordance with 250.66. **Figure 250–45**

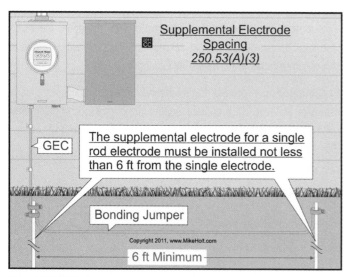

Supplemental Electrode
Spacing
250.53(A)(3)

GEC

The supplemental electrode for a single rod electrode must be installed not less than 6 ft from the single electrode.

Bonding Jumper

Copyright 2011, www.MikeHolt.com

6 ft Minimum

Figure 250–43

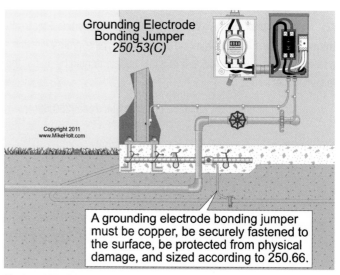

Grounding Electrode
Bonding Jumper
250.53(C)

Copyright 2011
www.MikeHolt.com

A grounding electrode bonding jumper must be copper, be securely fastened to the surface, be protected from physical damage, and sized according to 250.66.

Figure 250–45

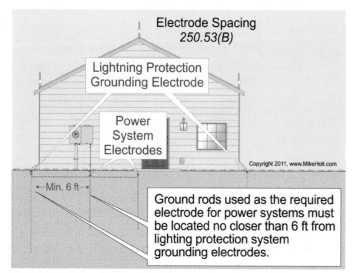

Electrode Spacing
250.53(B)

Lightning Protection
Grounding Electrode

Power
System
Electrodes

Copyright 2011, www.MikeHolt.com

Min. 6 ft

Ground rods used as the required electrode for power systems must be located no closer than 6 ft from lighting protection system grounding electrodes.

Figure 250–44

The grounding electrode bonding jumpers must terminate by the use of listed pressure connectors, terminal bars, exothermic welding, or other listed means [250.8(A)]. When the termination is encased in concrete or buried, the termination fittings must be listed for this purpose [250.70].

(D) Underground Metal Water Pipe Electrode.

(1) Continuity. The bonding connection to the interior metal water piping system, as required by 250.104(A), must not be dependent on water meters, filtering devices, or similar equipment likely to be disconnected for repairs or replacement. When necessary, a bonding jumper must be installed around insulated joints and equipment likely to be disconnected for repairs or replacement to assist in clearing and removing dangerous voltage on metal parts due to a ground fault [250.68(B)]. Figure 250–46

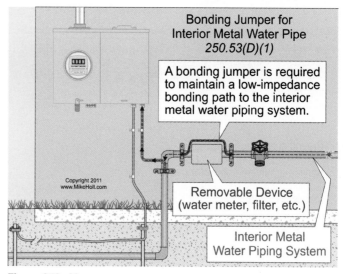

Bonding Jumper for
Interior Metal Water Pipe
250.53(D)(1)

A bonding jumper is required to maintain a low-impedance bonding path to the interior metal water piping system.

Copyright 2011
www.MikeHolt.com

Removable Device
(water meter, filter, etc.)

Interior Metal
Water Piping System

Figure 250–46

(2) Underground Metal Water Pipe Supplemental Electrode Required. When an underground metal water pipe grounding electrode is present [250.52(A)(1)], it must be supplemented by one of the following electrodes:

- Metal frame of the building/structure electrode [250.52(A)(2)]
- Concrete-encased electrode [250.52(A)(3)]
- Ground ring electrode [250.52(A)(4)]
- Ground rod electrode meeting the requirements of 250.52(A)(5)
- Other listed electrodes [250.52(A)(6)]
- Metal underground systems, piping systems, or underground tanks [250.52(A)(8)]

The termination of the supplemental grounding electrode conductor must be to one of the following locations: **Figure 250–47**

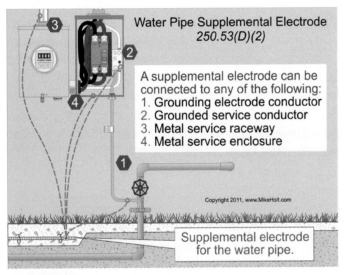

Water Pipe Supplemental Electrode
250.53(D)(2)

A supplemental electrode can be connected to any of the following:
1. Grounding electrode conductor
2. Grounded service conductor
3. Metal service raceway
4. Metal service enclosure

Supplemental electrode for the water pipe.

Copyright 2011, www.MikeHolt.com

Figure 250–47

(1) Grounding electrode conductor

(2) Service grounded conductor

(3) Metal service raceway

(4) Service equipment enclosure

Ex: The supplemental electrode is permitted to be bonded to interior metal water piping located not more than 5 ft from the point of entrance to the building/structure [250.68(C)(1)].

(E) Supplemental Ground Rod Electrode. The grounding electrode conductor to a ground rod that serves as a supplemental electrode isn't required to be larger than 6 AWG copper.

(F) Ground Ring. A ground ring encircling the building/structure, consisting of at least 20 ft of bare copper conductor not smaller than 2 AWG, must be buried not less than 30 in. [250.52(A)(4)]. **Figure 250–48**

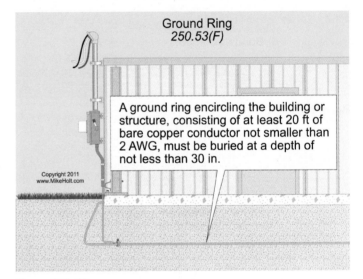

Ground Ring
250.53(F)

A ground ring encircling the building or structure, consisting of at least 20 ft of bare copper conductor not smaller than 2 AWG, must be buried at a depth of not less than 30 in.

Copyright 2011
www.MikeHolt.com

Figure 250–48

(G) Ground Rod Electrodes. Ground rod electrodes must be installed so that not less than 8 ft of length is in contact with the soil. If rock bottom is encountered, the ground rod must be driven at an angle not to exceed 45 degrees from vertical. If rock bottom is encountered at an angle up to 45 degrees from vertical, the ground rod can be buried in a minimum 30 in. deep trench. **Figure 250–49**

The upper end of the ground rod must be flush with or underground unless the grounding electrode conductor attachment is protected against physical damage as specified in 250.10.

Author's Comment: When the grounding electrode attachment fitting is located underground, it must be listed for direct soil burial [250.68(A) Ex 1 and 250.70].

250.60 Lightning Protection Electrode. Conductors and electrodes used for strike termination devices of a lightning protection system aren't permitted to be used in lieu of the grounding electrode system required by 250.50 for system and equipment grounding. **Figure 250–50**

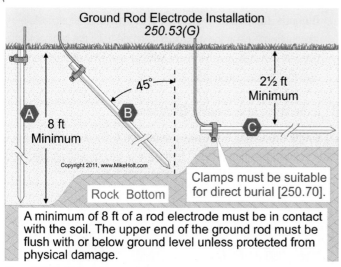

Figure 250–49

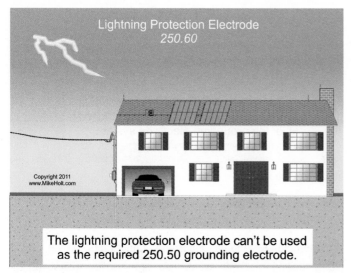

Figure 250–50

Note 2: If a lightning protection system is installed, the lightning protection system must be bonded to the building/structure grounding electrode system so as to limit potential difference between it and the electrical system wiring as per 250.106.

250.62 Grounding Electrode Conductor.
The grounding electrode conductor must be solid or stranded, insulated or bare, and it must be copper if within 18 in. of the earth [250.64(A)]. **Figure 250–51**

250.64 Grounding Electrode Conductor Installation.
Grounding electrode conductors must be installed as specified in (A) through (F).

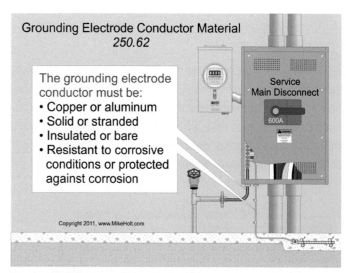

Figure 250–51

(A) Aluminum Conductors. Aluminum grounding electrode conductors must not be in contact with masonry, subject to corrosive conditions, or within 18 in. of the earth.

(B) Conductor Protection. Where installed exposed, grounding electrode conductors must be protected where subject to physical damage and are permitted to be installed on or through framing members. Grounding electrode conductors 6 AWG copper and larger can be installed exposed along the surface of the building if securely fastened and not subject to physical damage.

Grounding electrode conductors sized 8 AWG must be protected by installing them in rigid metal conduit, intermediate metal conduit, PVC conduit, electrical metallic tubing, or reinforced thermosetting resin conduit.

> **Author's Comment:** A ferrous metal raceway containing a grounding electrode conductor must be made electrically continuous by bonding each end of that type of raceway to the grounding electrode conductor [250.64(E)], so it's best to use PVC conduit.

(C) Continuous. Grounding electrode conductor(s) must be installed without a splice or joint except:

(1) By irreversible compression-type connectors or exothermic welding.

(2) Sections of busbars connected together to form a grounding electrode conductor.

(3) Bolted, riveted, or welded connections of structural metal frames of buildings or structures.

(4) Threaded, welded, brazed, soldered or bolted-flange connections of metal water piping.

(E) Ferrous Metal Enclosures Containing Grounding Electrode Conductor. To prevent inductive choking of grounding electrode conductors, ferrous raceways and enclosures containing grounding electrode conductors must have each end of the raceway or enclosure bonded to the grounding electrode conductor in accordance with 250.92(B)(2) through (B)(4). **Figure 250–52**

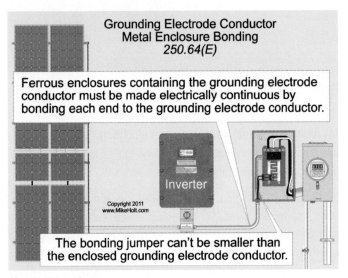

Figure 250– 52

Author's Comment: Nonferrous metal raceways, such as aluminum rigid metal conduit, enclosing the grounding electrode conductor aren't required to meet the "bonding each end of the raceway to the grounding electrode conductor" provisions of this section.

⚠️ **CAUTION:** *The effectiveness of a grounding electrode is significantly reduced if a ferrous metal raceway containing a grounding electrode conductor isn't bonded to the ferrous metal raceway at both ends. This is because a single conductor carrying high-frequency induced lightning current in a ferrous raceway causes the raceway to act as an inductor, which severely limits (chokes) the current flow through the grounding electrode conductor. ANSI/IEEE 142, Recommended Practice for Grounding of Industrial and Commercial Power Systems (Green Book) states: "An inductive choke can reduce the current flow by 97 percent."*

Author's Comment: To save a lot of time and effort, install the grounding electrode conductor exposed if it's not subject to physical damage [250.64(B)], or enclose it in PVC conduit suitable for the application [352.10(F)].

(F) Termination to Grounding Electrode.

(1) Single Grounding Electrode Conductor. A single grounding electrode conductor is permitted to terminate to any grounding electrode of the grounding electrode system. **Figure 250–53**

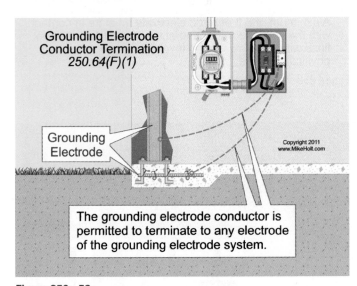

Figure 250– 53

(2) Multiple Grounding Electrode Conductors. When multiple grounding electrode conductors are installed [250.64(D)(2)], each grounding electrode conductor is permitted to terminate to any grounding electrode of the grounding electrode system. **Figure 250–54**

(3) Termination to Busbar. A grounding electrode conductor and grounding electrode bonding jumpers are permitted to terminate to a busbar sized not less than ¼ in. × 2 in. that's securely fastened at an accessible location. The terminations to the busbar must be made by a listed connector or by exothermic welding. **Figure 250–55**

250.66 Sizing Grounding Electrode Conductor. Except as permitted in (A) through (C), a grounding electrode conductor must be sized in accordance with Table 250.66.

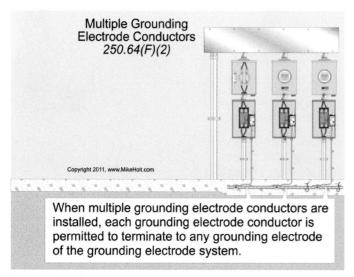

Figure 250-54

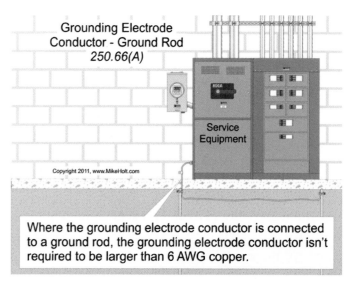

Figure 250-56

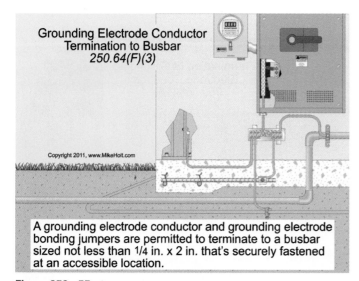

Figure 250- 55

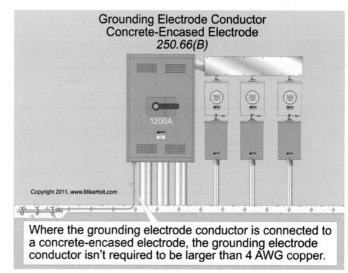

Figure 250-57

(A) Ground Rod. If the grounding electrode conductor is connected to a ground rod as permitted in 250.52(A)(5), that portion of the grounding electrode conductor that's the sole connection to the ground rod isn't required to be larger than 6 AWG copper. **Figure 250–56**

(B) Concrete-Encased Grounding Electrode. If the grounding electrode conductor is connected to a concrete-encased electrode, the portion of the grounding electrode conductor that's the sole connection to the concrete-encased electrode isn't required to be larger than 4 AWG copper. **Figure 250–57**

(C) Ground Ring. If the grounding electrode conductor is connected to a ground ring, the portion of the conductor that's the sole connection to the ground ring isn't required to be larger than the conductor used for the ground ring.

Author's Comments:

• A ground ring encircling the building/structure in direct contact with the earth must consist of at least 20 ft of bare copper conductor not smaller than 2 AWG [250.52(A)(4)]. See 250.53(F) for the installation requirements for a ground ring.

• Table 250.66 is used to size the grounding electrode conductor when the conditions of 250.66(A), (B), or (C) don't apply. **Figure 250–58**

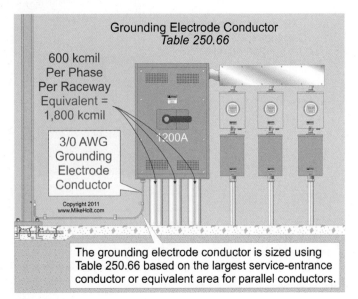

Figure 250–58

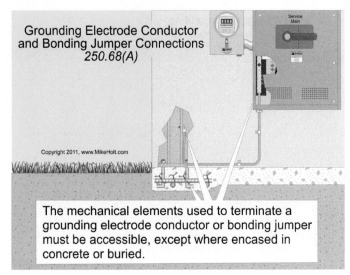

Figure 250–59

Table 250.66 Sizing Grounding Electrode Conductor	
Conductor or Area of Parallel Conductors	Copper Grounding Electrode Conductor
12 through 2 AWG	8 AWG
1 or 1/0 AWG	6 AWG
2/0 or 3/0 AWG	4 AWG
4/0 through 350 kcmil	2 AWG
400 through 600 kcmil	1/0 AWG
700 through 1,100 kcmil	2/0 AWG
1,200 kcmil and larger	3/0 AWG

250.68 Termination to the Grounding Electrode.

(A) Accessibility. The mechanical elements used to terminate a grounding electrode conductor or bonding jumper to a grounding electrode must be accessible. **Figure 250–59**

Ex 1: The termination isn't required to be accessible if the termination to the electrode is encased in concrete or buried in the earth. **Figure 250–60**

> **Author's Comment:** If the grounding electrode attachment fitting is encased in concrete or buried in the earth, it must be listed for direct soil burial or concrete encasement [250.70].

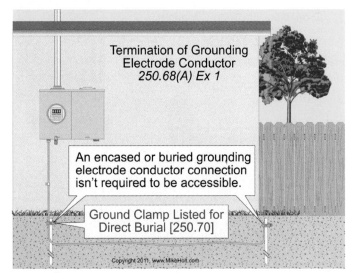

Figure 250–60

Ex 2: Exothermic or irreversible compression connections, together with the mechanical means used to attach to fireproofed structural metal, aren't required to be accessible.

250.70 Grounding Electrode Conductor Termination Fittings.
The grounding electrode conductor must terminate to the grounding electrode by exothermic welding, listed lugs, listed pressure connectors, listed clamps, or other listed means. In addition, fittings terminating to a grounding electrode must be listed for the materials of the grounding electrode.

When the termination to a grounding electrode is encased in concrete or buried in the earth, the termination fitting must be listed for direct soil burial or concrete encasement. No more than one conductor can terminate on a single clamp or fitting unless the clamp or fitting is listed for multiple connections. **Figure 250–61**

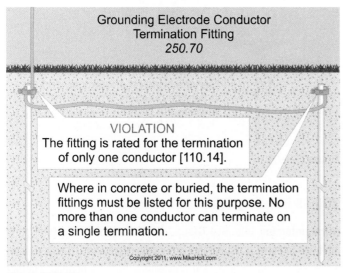

Figure 250–61

PART V. BONDING

250.90 General. Bonding must be provided to ensure electrical continuity and the capacity to conduct safely any fault current likely to be imposed.

250.92 Bonding Equipment for Services.

(A) Bonding Requirements for Equipment for Services. The metal parts of equipment indicated below must be bonded together in accordance with 250.92(B). **Figure 250–62**

(1) Metal raceways containing service conductors.

(2) Metal enclosures containing service conductors.

(B) Methods of Bonding. Electrical continuity at service equipment, service raceways, and service conductor enclosures must be ensured by one of the following methods:

(1) Grounded Conductor. By bonding the metal parts to the service grounded conductor. **Figure 250–63**

(4) Other listed devices, such as bonding-type locknuts, bushings, wedges, or bushings with bonding jumpers.

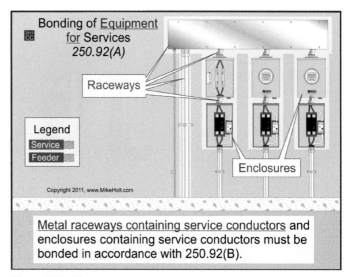

Metal raceways containing service conductors and enclosures containing service conductors must be bonded in accordance with 250.92(B).

Figure 250–62

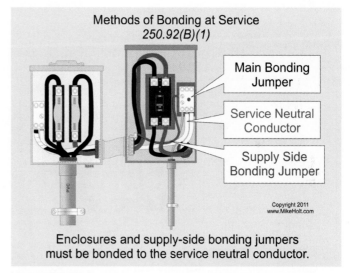

Enclosures and supply-side bonding jumpers must be bonded to the service neutral conductor.

Figure 250–63

Author's Comments:

- A listed bonding wedge or bushing with a bonding jumper must be used to bond one end of the service raceway to the service grounded conductor. The bonding jumper used for this purpose must be sized in accordance with Table 250.66, based on the area of the largest ungrounded service conductors within the raceway [250.102(C)]. **Figure 250–64**

- When a metal raceway containing service conductors terminates to an enclosure without a ringed knockout, a bonding-type locknut can be used. **Figure 250–65**

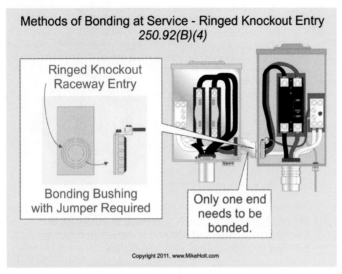

Figure 250–64

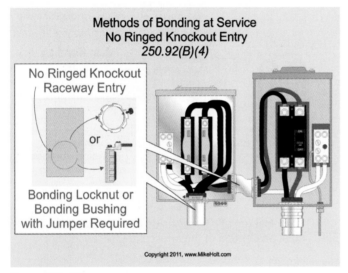

Figure 250–65

- A bonding locknut differs from a standard locknut in that it's a bonding screw with a sharp point that drives into the metal enclosure to ensure a solid connection.

- Bonding one end of a service raceway to the service grounded provides the low-impedance fault current path to the source. **Figure 250–66**

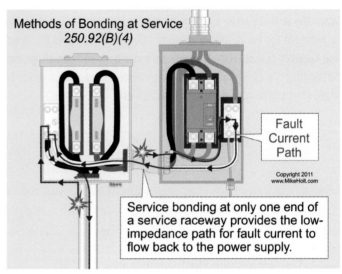

Figure 250–66

250.96 Bonding Other Enclosures.

(A) Maintaining Effective Ground-Fault Current Path. Metal parts intended to serve as equipment grounding conductors including raceways, cables, equipment, and enclosures must be bonded together to ensure they have the capacity to conduct safely any fault current likely to be imposed on them [110.10, 250.4(A)(5), and Note to Table 250.122]. **Figure 250–67**

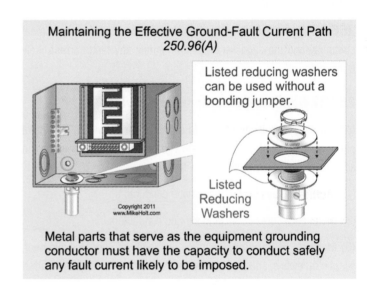

Figure 250–67

Nonconductive coatings such as paint, lacquer, and enamel on equipment must be removed to ensure an effective ground-fault current path, or the termination fittings must be designed so as to make such removal unnecessary [250.12].

Author's Comment: The practice of driving a locknut tight with a screwdriver and pliers is considered sufficient in removing paint and other nonconductive finishes to ensure an effective ground-fault current path.

250.97 Bonding Metal Parts for Circuits over 250V.

Metal raceways or cables terminating at ringed knockouts must be bonded to the metal enclosure with a bonding jumper sized in accordance with 250.122, based on the rating of the circuit overcurrent device. **Figure 250–68**

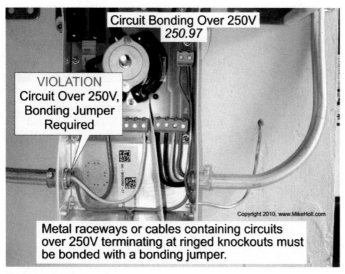

Figure 250–68

Author's Comments:

- Bonding jumpers for raceways and cables containing 277V or 480V circuits are required at ringed knockout terminations to ensure the ground-fault current path has the capacity to safely conduct the maximum ground-fault current likely to be imposed [110.10, 250.4(A)(5), and 250.96(A)].

- Ringed knockouts aren't listed to withstand the heat generated by a 277V ground fault, which generates five times as much heat as a 120V ground fault. **Figure 250–69**

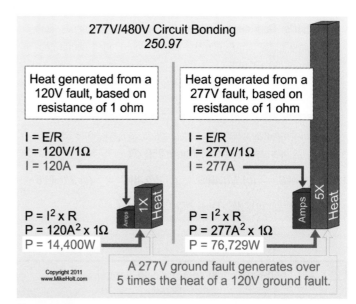

Figure 250–69

Ex: A bonding jumper isn't required where ringed knockouts aren't encountered, knockouts are totally punched out, or where the box is listed to provide a reliable bonding connection. **Figure 250–70**

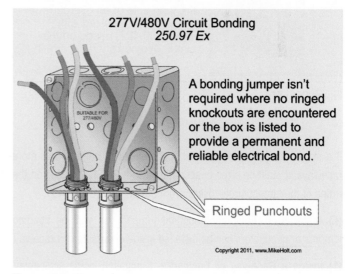

Figure 250–70

250.102 Bonding Conductors and Jumpers.

(D) Load Side Equipment Bonding Jumper Sizing. Bonding jumpers on the load side of feeder and branch-circuit overcurrent devices are sized in accordance with 250.122, based on the rating of the circuit overcurrent device.

Author's Comment: The equipment bonding jumper isn't required to be larger than the largest ungrounded circuit conductors [250.122(A)].

Question: What size equipment bonding jumper is required for a metal raceway where the circuit conductors are protected by a 1,200A overcurrent device? **Figure 250–71**

(a) 1 AWG   (b) 1/0 AWG   (c) 2/0 AWG   (d) 3/0 AWG

Answer: (d) 3/0 AWG [Table 250.122]

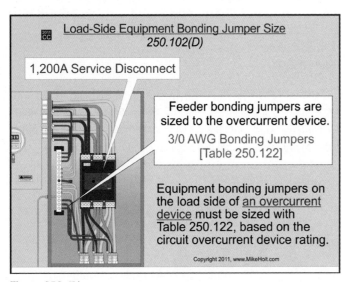

Figure 250–71

If a single equipment bonding jumper is used to bond two or more raceways, it must be sized in accordance with 250.122, based on the rating of the largest circuit overcurrent device. **Figure 250–72**

(E) Installation. Equipment bonding jumpers, as well as bonding jumpers or conductors can be installed inside or outside of a raceway.

(1) Inside a Raceway or Enclosure. If installed inside a raceway, the conductors must be identified in accordance with 250.119 and if circuit conductors are spliced or terminated on equipment within a metal box, the equipment grounding conductor associated with those circuits must be connected to the box in accordance with 250.148.

(2) Outside a Raceway. If the equipment bonding jumper is installed outside of a raceway, its length must not exceed 6 ft and it must be routed with the raceway. **Figure 250–73**

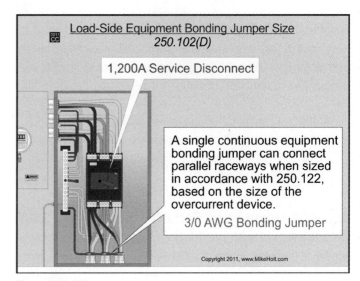

Figure 250–72

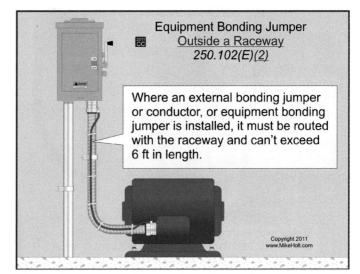

Figure 250–73

250.106 Lightning Protection System. If a lightning protection system is installed on a building/structure, it must be bonded to the building/structure grounding electrode system. **Figure 250–74**

Author's Comment: The grounding electrode for a lightning protection system must not be used as the required grounding electrode system for the buildings or structures [250.60]. **Figure 250–75**

Note 1: See NFPA 780, Standard for the Installation of Lightning Protection Systems, which contains detailed information on grounding, bonding, and side-flash distance from lightning protection systems.

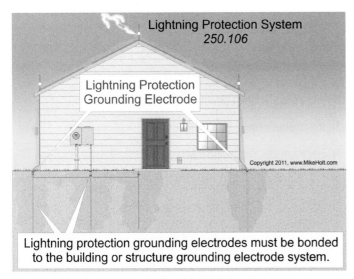

Figure 250–74

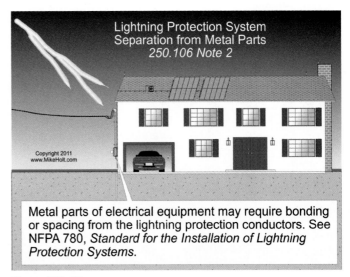

Figure 250–76

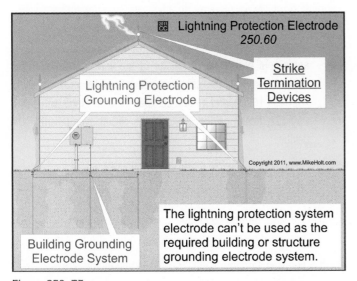

Figure 250–75

Note 2: To minimize the likelihood of arcing between metal parts because of induced voltage, metal raceways, enclosures, and other metal parts of electrical equipment may require bonding or spacing from the lightning protection conductors in accordance with NFPA 780, *Standard for the Installation of Lightning Protection Systems.* **Figure 250–76**

PART VI. EQUIPMENT GROUNDING AND EQUIPMENT GROUNDING CONDUCTORS

250.110 Fixed Equipment Connected by Permanent Wiring Methods—General.
Exposed metal parts of fixed equipment likely to become energized must be connected to the circuit equipment grounding conductor where the equipment is:

(1) Within 8 ft vertically or 5 ft horizontally of the earth or a grounded metal object

(2) Located in a wet or damp location

(3) In electrical contact with metal

(4) In a hazardous (classified) location [Articles 500 through 517]

(5) Supplied by a wiring method that provides an equipment grounding conductor

(6) Supplied by a 277V or 480V circuit

Ex 3: Listed double-insulated equipment isn't required to be connected to the circuit equipment grounding conductor.

250.118 Types of Equipment Grounding Conductors.
An equipment grounding conductor can be any one or a combination of the following: **Figure 250–77**

> **Note:** The equipment grounding conductor is intended to serve as the effective ground-fault current path. See 250.2.

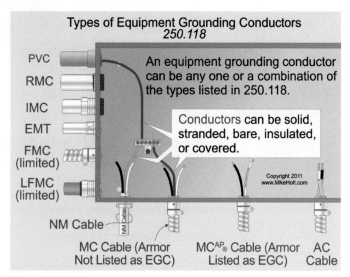

Figure 250–77

Author's Comment: The effective ground-fault path is an intentionally constructed low-impedance conductive path designed to carry fault current from the point of a ground fault on a wiring system to the electrical supply source. Its purpose is to quickly remove dangerous voltage from a ground fault by opening the circuit overcurrent device [250.2]. **Figure 250–78**

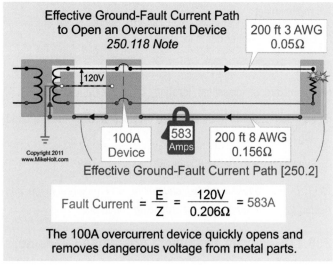

Figure 250–78

(1) A bare or insulated copper or aluminum conductor sized in accordance with 250.122.

Author's Comment: Examples include PVC conduit, Type NM cable, and Type MC cable with an equipment grounding conductor of the wire type.

(2) Rigid metal conduit (RMC).

(3) Intermediate metal conduit (IMC).

(4) Electrical metallic tubing (EMT).

(5) Listed flexible metal conduit (FMC) where:

    a. The raceway terminates in listed fittings.

    b. The circuit conductors are protected by an overcurrent device rated 20A or less.

    c. The combined length of the flexible conduit in the same ground-fault current path doesn't exceed 6 ft.

    d. If flexibility is required to minimize the transmission of vibration from equipment or to provide flexibility for equipment that requires movement after installation, an equipment grounding conductor of the wire type must be installed with the circuit conductors in accordance with 250.102(E), and it must be sized in accordance with 250.122, based on the rating of the circuit overcurrent device.

(6) Listed liquidtight flexible metal conduit (LFMC) where:

    a. The raceway terminates in listed fittings.

    b. For ⅜ in. through ½ in., the circuit conductors are protected by an overcurrent device rated 20A or less.

    c. For ¾ in. through 1¼ in., the circuit conductors are protected by an overcurrent device rated 60A or less.

    d. The combined length of the flexible conduit in the same ground-fault current path doesn't exceed 6 ft.

    e. If flexibility is required to minimize the transmission of vibration from equipment or to provide flexibility for equipment that requires movement after installation, an equipment grounding conductor of the wire type must be installed with the circuit conductors in accordance with 250.102(E), and it must be sized in accordance with 250.122, based on the rating of the circuit overcurrent device.

Author's Comments:

- The internal aluminum bonding strip isn't an equipment grounding conductor, but it allows the interlocked armor to serve as an equipment grounding conductor because it reduces the impedance of the armored spirals to ensure that a ground fault will be cleared. It's the aluminum bonding strip in combination with the cable armor that creates the circuit equipment grounding conductor. Once the bonding strip exits the cable, it can be cut off because it no longer serves any purpose.

- The effective ground-fault current path must be maintained by the use of fittings specifically listed for Type AC cable [320.40]. See 300.12, 300.15, and 320.100.

(9) The copper sheath of Type MI cable.

(10) Type MC cable that provides an effective ground-fault current path in accordance with one or more of the following:

(a) It contains an insulated or uninsulated equipment grounding conductor in compliance with 250.118(1). **Figure 250–79**

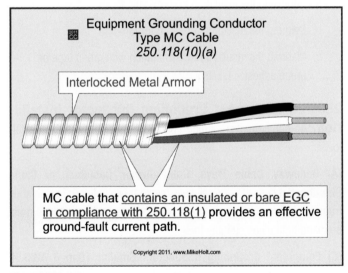

Figure 250–79

(b) The combined metallic sheath and uninsulated equipment grounding/bonding conductor of interlocked metal tape-type MC cable that's listed and identified as an equipment grounding conductor. **Figure 250–80**

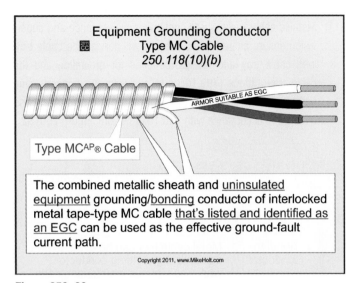

Figure 250–80

Author's Comment: Once the bare aluminum grounding/bonding conductor exits the cable, it can be cut off because it no longer serves any purpose. The effective ground-fault current path must be maintained by the use of fittings specifically listed for Type MCAP® cable [330.40]. See 300.12, 300.15, and 330.100. **Figure 250–81**

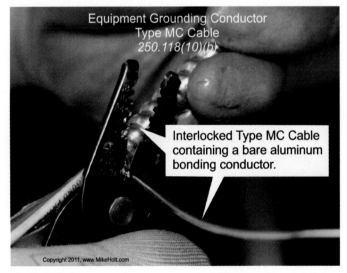

Figure 250–81

(c) The metallic sheath or the combined metallic sheath and equipment grounding conductors of the smooth or corrugated tube-type MC cable that's listed and identified as an equipment grounding conductor.

(11) Metallic cable trays where continuous maintenance and supervision ensure only qualified persons will service the cable tray, with cable tray and fittings identified for grounding and the cable tray, fittings [392.10], and raceways are bonded using bolted mechanical connectors or bonding jumpers sized and installed in accordance with 250.102 [392.60]. **Figure 250–82**

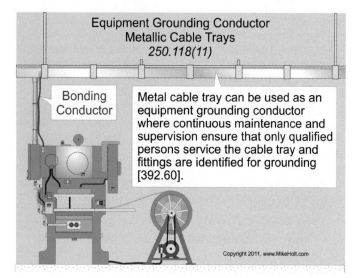

Figure 250–82

(13) Listed electrically continuous metal raceways, such as metal wireways [Article 376] or strut-type channel raceways [384.60].

(14) Surface metal raceways listed for grounding [Article 386].

250.119 Identification of Equipment Grounding Conductors.
Unless required to be insulated, equipment grounding conductors can be bare, covered, or insulated. Insulated equipment grounding conductors must have a continuous outer finish that's either green or green with one or more yellow stripes.

Conductors with insulation that's green, or green with one or more yellow stripes must not be used for an ungrounded or grounded conductor.

(A) Conductors Larger Than 6 AWG.

(1) Identified if Accessible. Insulated equipment grounding conductors larger than 6 AWG can be permanently reidentified at the time of installation at every point where the conductor is accessible.

Ex: Identification of equipment grounding conductors larger than 6 AWG in conduit bodies isn't required.

(2) Identification Method. Equipment grounding conductor identification must encircle the conductor by: **Figure 250–83**

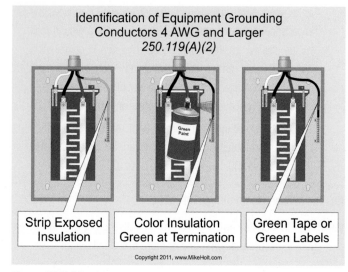

Figure 250–83

a. Removing the insulation at termination

b. Coloring the insulation green at termination

c. Marking the insulation at termination with green tape or green adhesive labels

250.120 Equipment Grounding Conductor Installation.
An equipment grounding conductor must be installed as follows:

(A) Raceway, Cable Trays, Cable Armor, Cablebus, or Cable Sheaths. If it consists of a raceway, cable tray, cable armor, cablebus framework, or cable sheath, fittings for joints and terminations must be made tight using suitable tools.

(C) Equipment Grounding Conductors Smaller Than 6 AWG. If not routed with circuit conductors as permitted in 250.130(C) and 250.134(B) Ex 2, equipment grounding conductors smaller than 6 AWG must be installed in a raceway or cable unless installed within hollow spaces of the framing members of buildings or structures and if not subject to physical damage.

250.122 Sizing Equipment Grounding Conductor.

(A) General. Equipment grounding conductors of the wire type must be sized not smaller than shown in Table 250.122 based on the rating of the circuit overcurrent device; however, the circuit equipment grounding conductor isn't required to be larger than the circuit conductors. **Figure 250–84**

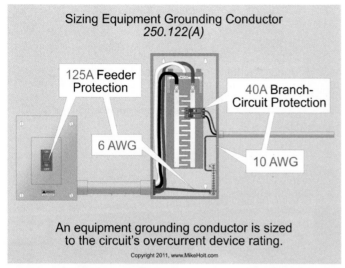

Figure 250–84

Equipment grounding conductors can be sectioned within a multiconductor cable, provided the combined circular mil area complies with Table 250.122.

Table 250.122 Sizing Equipment Grounding Conductor	
Overcurrent Device Rating	Copper Conductor
15A	14 AWG
20A	12 AWG
30A—60A	10 AWG
70A—100A	8 AWG
110A—200A	6 AWG
225A—300A	4 AWG
350A—400A	3 AWG
450A—500A	2 AWG
600A	1 AWG
700A—800A	1/0 AWG
1,000A	2/0 AWG
1,200A	3/0 AWG

(B) Increased in Size. If ungrounded conductors are increased in size from the minimum size, equipment grounding conductors must be proportionately increased in size according to the circular mil area of the ungrounded conductors.

> **Author's Comment:** Ungrounded conductors are often increased in size to accommodate conductor voltage drop, ampacity adjustment and correction, future capacity, or for a variety of other reasons.

PART VII. METHODS OF EQUIPMENT GROUNDING

250.136 Equipment Considered Grounded.

(A) Equipment Secured to Grounded Metal Supports. The structural metal frame of a building must not be used as the required equipment grounding conductor.

250.148 Continuity and Attachment of Equipment Grounding Conductors in Boxes. If circuit conductors are spliced or terminated on equipment within a metal box, the equipment grounding conductor associated with those circuits must be connected to the box in accordance with the following: **Figure 250–85**

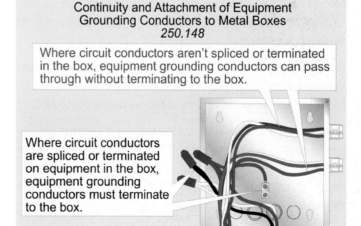

Figure 250–85

(A) Splicing. Equipment grounding conductors must be spliced together with a device listed for the purpose [110.14(B)].

Author's Comment: Wire connectors of any color can be used with equipment grounding conductor splices, but green wire connectors can only be used with equipment grounding conductors.

(B) Equipment Grounding Continuity. Equipment grounding conductors must terminate in a manner such that the disconnection or the removal of a receptacle, luminaire, or other device won't interrupt the grounding continuity.

(C) Metal Boxes. Equipment grounding conductors within metal boxes must be connected to the metal box with a grounding screw that's not used for any other purpose, an equipment fitting listed for grounding, or a listed grounding device such as a ground clip.

Author's Comment: Equipment grounding conductors aren't permitted to terminate to a screw that secures a plaster ring.

VIII. DIRECT-CURRENT SYSTEMS

250.166 Sizing Grounding Electrode Conductor.

Except as permitted in (C) through (E), the grounding electrode conductor must be sized in accordance with 250.166(A) or (B).

(A) Not Smaller Than the Neutral Conductor. Where the dc system consists of a 3-wire balancer set, the grounding electrode conductor is not permitted to be smaller than the neutral conductor and not smaller than 8 AWG.

(B) Not Smaller Than the Largest Conductor. The grounding electrode conductor must not be smaller than the largest ungrounded conductor supplied by the PV system, and not smaller than 8 AWG.

(C) Connection to Ground Rod. If the grounding electrode conductor is connected to a ground rod as in 250.52(A)(5), or (A)(7), that portion of the grounding electrode conductor that's the sole connection to the ground rod isn't required to be larger than 6 AWG copper. **Figure 250–86**

Author's Comment: This rule applies when there is one connection to the ground rod electrode, which only occurs for stand-alone dc systems grounded in accordance with 690.47(B).

(D) Connection to Concrete-Encased Grounding Electrode. If the grounding electrode conductor is connected to a concrete-encased electrode as in 250.52(A)(3), the portion of the grounding electrode conductor that's the sole connection to the concrete-encased electrode isn't required to be larger than 4 AWG copper. **Figure 250–87**

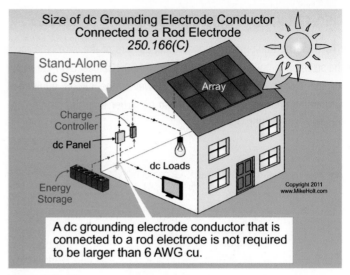

Figure 250–86

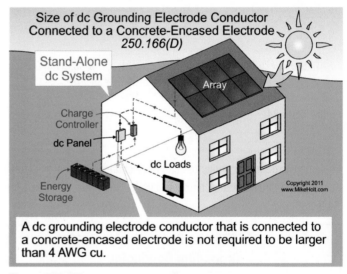

Figure 250–87

Author's Comment: This rule applies when there is one connection to the concrete-encased electrode, which only occurs for stand-alone dc systems grounded in accordance with 690.47(B).

250.169 Ungrounded Direct-Current Systems. Metal

enclosures, raceways, cables, and exposed noncurrent-carrying metal parts of equipment must have a grounding electrode conductor connected to an electrode that complies with Part III of this article. The grounding electrode conductor connection can be to the metal enclosure at any point on the PV system and it is sized in accordance with 250.166.

CHAPTER 2. WIRING AND PROTECTION — PRACTICE QUESTIONS

Article 200. Use and Identification of Grounded Conductors

1. Article 200 contains the requirements for _____.

   (a) identification of terminals
   (b) grounded conductors in premises wiring systems
   (c) identification of grounded conductors
   (d) all of these

2. An insulated grounded conductor of _____ or smaller shall be identified by a continuous white or gray outer finish, or by three continuous white stripes on other than green insulation along its entire length.

   (a) 8 AWG
   (b) 6 AWG
   (c) 4 AWG
   (d) 3 AWG

3. Grounded conductors _____ and larger can be identified by distinctive white or gray markings at their terminations.

   (a) 10 AWG
   (b) 8 AWG
   (c) 6 AWG
   (d) 4 AWG

Article 230. Services

1. Wiring methods permitted for service-entrance conductors include _____.

   (a) rigid metal conduit
   (b) electrical metallic tubing
   (c) PVC conduit
   (d) all of these

2. The service disconnecting means shall be marked as suitable for use as service equipment and shall be _____.

   (a) weatherproof
   (b) listed
   (c) approved
   (d) acceptable

3. Electrical equipment shall not be connected to the supply side of the service disconnecting means, except for a few specific exceptions such as _____.

   (a) Type 1 surge protective devices
   (b) taps used to supply legally required optional standby power systems, fire pump equipment, fire and sprinkler alarms, and load (energy) management devices
   (c) Solar photovoltaic systems
   (d) all of these

Article 240. Overcurrent Protection

1. Overcurrent protection for conductors and equipment is designed to _____ the circuit if the current reaches a value that will cause an excessive or dangerous temperature in conductors or conductor insulation.

   (a) open
   (b) close
   (c) monitor
   (d) record

2. Conductor overload protection shall not be required where the interruption of the _____ would create a hazard, such as in a material-handling magnet circuit or fire pump circuit. However, short-circuit protection is required.

   (a) circuit
   (b) line
   (c) phase
   (d) system

3. The next higher standard rating overcurrent device above the ampacity of the ungrounded conductors being protected shall be permitted to be used, provided all of the following conditions are met:

   (a) The conductors are not part of a branch circuit supplying more than one receptacle for cord-and-plug-connected portable loads.
   (b) The ampacity of the conductors doesn't correspond with the standard ampere rating of a fuse or circuit breaker.
   (c) The next higher standard rating selected doesn't exceed 800A.
   (d) all of these

4. If the circuit's overcurrent device exceeds _____, the conductor ampacity must have a rating not less than the rating of the overcurrent device.

   (a) 800A
   (b) 1,000A
   (c) 1,200A
   (d) 2,000A

5. Overcurrent protection shall not exceed _____.

   (a) 15A for 14 AWG copper
   (b) 20A for 12 AWG copper
   (c) 30A for 10 AWG copper
   (d) all of these

6. Which of the following is not standard size fuses or inverse time circuit breakers?

   (a) 45A
   (b) 70A
   (c) 75A
   (d) 80A

7. Overcurrent devices shall be readily accessible and installed so the center of the grip of the operating handle of the switch or circuit breaker, when in its highest position, is not more than _____ above the floor or working platform.

   (a) 2 ft
   (b) 4 ft 6 in.
   (c) 5 ft
   (d) 6 ft 7 in.

8. Overcurrent devices shall not be located _____.

   (a) where exposed to physical damage
   (b) near easily ignitible materials, such as in clothes closets
   (c) in bathrooms of dwelling units
   (d) all of these

9. Overcurrent devices aren't permitted to be located in the bathrooms of _____.

   (a) dwelling units
   (b) dormitories
   (c) guest rooms or guest suites of hotels or motels
   (d) all of these

10. _____ shall not be located over the steps of a stairway.

   (a) Disconnect switches
   (b) Overcurrent devices
   (c) Knife switches
   (d) Transformers

11. Enclosures for overcurrent devices shall be mounted in a _____ position unless impracticable.

   (a) vertical
   (b) horizontal
   (c) vertical or horizontal
   (d) there are no requirements

Article 250. Grounding and Bonding

Part I. General

1. An effective ground-fault current path is an intentionally constructed, permanent, low-impedance path designed and intended to carry fault current from the point of a ground fault on a wiring system to _____.

   (a) ground
   (b) earth
   (c) the electrical supply source
   (d) none of these

2. Equipment grounding conductors, grounding electrode conductors, and bonding jumpers shall be connected by _____.

   (a) listed pressure connectors
   (b) terminal bars
   (c) exothermic welding
   (d) any of these

3. Grounding and bonding connection devices shall not depend solely on _____.

   (a) pressure connections
   (b) solder
   (c) lugs
   (d) approved clamps

4. Ground clamps and fittings shall be protected from physical damage by being enclosed in _____ where there may be a possibility of physical damage.

   (a) metal
   (b) wood
   (c) the equivalent of a or b
   (d) none of these

5. _____ on equipment to be grounded shall be removed from contact surfaces to ensure good electrical continuity.

   (a) Paint
   (b) Lacquer
   (c) Enamel
   (d) any of these

Part II. System Grounding

1. For a grounded system, an unspliced _____ shall be used to connect the equipment grounding conductor(s) and the service disconnecting means to the grounded conductor of the system within the enclosure for each service disconnect.

   (a) grounding electrode
   (b) main bonding jumper
   (c) busbar
   (d) insulated copper conductor

2. Where an alternating-current system operating at less than 1,000V is grounded at any point, the _____ conductor(s) shall be routed with the ungrounded conductors to each service disconnecting means and shall be connected to each disconnecting means grounded conductor(s) terminal or bus.

   (a) ungrounded
   (b) grounded
   (c) grounding
   (d) none of these

3. The grounded conductor of an alternating-current system operating at less than 1,000V shall be routed with the ungrounded conductors and connected to each disconnecting means grounded conductor terminal or bus, which is then connected to the service disconnecting means enclosure via a(n) _____ that's installed between the service neutral conductor and the service disconnecting means enclosure.

   (a) equipment bonding conductor
   (b) main bonding jumper
   (c) grounding electrode
   (d) intersystem bonding terminal

4. The grounded conductor brought to service equipment shall be routed with the phase conductors and shall not be smaller than specified in Table _____ when the service-entrance conductors are 1,100 kcmil copper and smaller.

   (a) 250.66
   (b) 250.122
   (c) 310.16
   (d) 430.52

5. When service-entrance conductors exceed 1,100 kcmil for copper, the required grounded conductor for the service shall be sized not less than _____ percent of the circular mil area of the largest set of ungrounded service-entrance conductor(s).

(a) 9
(b) 11
(c) 12½
(d) 15

6. Where service-entrance phase conductors are installed in parallel in two or more raceways, the size of the grounded conductor in each raceway shall be based on the total circular mil area of the parallel ungrounded service-entrance conductor in the raceway, sized per 250.24(C)(1), but not smaller than _____.

(a) 1/0 AWG
(b) 2/0 AWG
(c) 3/0 AWG
(d) 4/0 AWG

Part III. Grounding Electrode System and Grounding Electrode Conductor

1. In order for a metal underground water pipe to be used as a grounding electrode, it shall be in direct contact with the earth for _____.

(a) 5 ft
(b) 10 ft or more
(c) less than 10 ft
(d) 20 ft or more

2. The metal frame of a building shall be considered a grounding electrode where one of the *NEC*-prescribed methods for connection of the metal frame to earth has been met:

(a) True
(b) False

3. A bare 4 AWG copper conductor installed horizontally near the bottom or vertically, and within that portion of a concrete foundation or footing that is in direct contact with the earth can be used as a grounding electrode when the conductor is at least _____ in length.

(a) 10 ft
(b) 15 ft
(c) 20 ft
(d) 25 ft

4. An electrode encased by at least 2 in. of concrete, located horizontally near the bottom or vertically and within that portion of a concrete foundation or footing that is in direct contact with the earth, shall be permitted as a grounding electrode when it consists of _____.

(a) at least 20 ft of ½ in. or larger steel reinforcing bars or rods
(b) at least 20 ft of bare copper conductor of 4 AWG or larger
(c) a or b
(d) none of these

5. Reinforcing bars for use as a concrete-encased electrode can be bonded together by the usual steel tie wires or other effective means.

(a) True
(b) False

6. Where more than one concrete-encased electrode is present at a building or structure, it shall be permitted to connect to only one of them.

(a) True
(b) False

7. A ground ring encircling the building or structure can be used as a grounding electrode when _____.

(a) the ring is in direct contact with the earth
(b) the ring consists of at least 20 ft of bare conductor
(c) the bare copper conductor is not smaller than 2 AWG
(d) all of these

8. Grounding electrodes that are driven rods require a minimum of _____ in contact with the soil.

   (a) 6 ft
   (b) 8 ft
   (c) 10 ft
   (d) 12 ft

9. Grounding electrodes of the rod type less than _____ in. in diameter shall be listed.

   (a) ½ in.
   (b) 5/8 in.
   (c) ¾ in.
   (d) none of these

10. A buried iron or steel plate used as a grounding electrode shall expose not less than _____ of surface area to exterior soil.

    (a) 2 sq ft
    (b) 4 sq ft
    (c) 9 sq ft
    (d) 10 sq ft

11. Local metal underground systems or structures such as _____ are permitted to serve as grounding electrodes.

    (a) piping systems
    (b) underground tanks
    (c) underground metal well casings
    (d) all of these

12. _____ shall not be used as grounding electrodes.

    (a) Underground gas piping systems
    (b) Aluminum
    (c) Metal well casings
    (d) a and b

13. Where practicable, rod, pipe, and plate electrodes shall be installed _____.

    (a) directly below the electrical meter
    (b) on the north side of the building
    (c) below permanent moisture level
    (d) all of these

14. Where the resistance-to-ground of 25 ohms or less is not achieved for a single rod electrode, _____.

    (a) other means besides electrodes shall be used in order to provide grounding
    (b) the single rod electrode shall be supplemented by one additional electrode
    (c) no additional electrodes are required
    (d) none of these

15. Two or more grounding electrodes bonded together are considered a single grounding electrode system.

    (a) True
    (b) False

16. Where a metal underground water pipe is used as a grounding electrode, the continuity of the grounding path or the bonding connection to interior piping shall not rely on _____ and similar equipment.

    (a) bonding jumpers
    (b) water meters or filtering devices
    (c) grounding clamps
    (d) all of these

17. Where the supplemental electrode is a rod, that portion of the bonding jumper that is the sole connection to the supplemental grounding electrode shall not be required to be larger than _____ AWG copper.

    (a) 8
    (b) 6
    (c) 4
    (d) 1

18. When a ground ring is used as a grounding electrode, it shall be buried at a depth below the earth's surface of not less than _____.

    (a) 18 in.
    (b) 24 in.
    (c) 30 in.
    (d) 8 ft

19. Ground rod electrodes shall be installed so that at least _____ of the length is in contact with the soil.

    (a) 5 ft
    (b) 8 ft
    (c) one-half
    (d) 80 percent

20. The upper end of a ground rod electrode shall be _____ ground level unless the aboveground end and the grounding electrode conductor attachment are protected against physical damage.

    (a) above
    (b) flush with
    (c) below
    (d) b or c

21. Where rock bottom is encountered when driving a ground rod at an angle up to 45 degrees, the electrode can be buried in a trench that is at least _____ deep.

    (a) 18 in.
    (b) 30 in.
    (c) 4 ft
    (d) 8 ft

22. Auxiliary grounding electrodes can be connected to the _____.

    (a) equipment grounding conductor
    (b) grounded conductor
    (c) a and b
    (d) none of these

23. When installing auxiliary electrodes, the earth shall not be used as an effective ground-fault current path.

    (a) True
    (b) False

24. Buildings or structures supplied by multiple services or feeders must use the same _____ to ground enclosures and equipment in or on that building.

    (a) service
    (b) disconnect
    (c) grounding electrode system
    (d) any of these

25. The grounding electrode used for grounding strike termination devices of a lightning protection system can be used as a grounding electrode system for the buildings or structures.

    (a) True
    (b) False

26. Grounding electrode conductors shall be made of _____ wire.

    (a) solid
    (b) stranded
    (c) insulated or bare
    (d) any of these

27. Where used outside, aluminum or copper-clad aluminum grounding electrode conductors shall not be terminated within _____ of the earth.

    (a) 6 in.
    (b) 12 in.
    (c) 15 in.
    (d) 18 in.

28. Bare aluminum or copper-clad aluminum grounding electrode conductors shall not be used where in direct contact with _____ or where subject to corrosive conditions.

    (a) masonry or the earth
    (b) bare copper conductors
    (c) wooden framing members
    (d) all of these

29. Grounding electrode conductors _____ and larger that are not subject to physical damage can be run exposed along the surface of the building construction if it is securely fastened to the construction.

    (a) 10 AWG
    (b) 8 AWG
    (c) 6 AWG
    (d) 4 AWG

30. Grounding electrode conductors smaller than _____ shall be in rigid metal conduit, IMC, PVC conduit, electrical metallic tubing, or cable armor.

    (a) 10 AWG
    (b) 8 AWG
    (c) 6 AWG
    (d) 4 AWG

31. Grounding electrode conductors shall be installed in one continuous length without a splice or joint, unless spliced _____.

    (a) by connecting together sections of a busbar
    (b) by irreversible compression-type connectors listed as grounding and bonding equipment
    (c) by the exothermic welding process
    (d) any of these

32. Where service equipment consists of more than one enclosure, grounding electrode connections shall be permitted to be _____.

    (a) multiple individual grounding electrode conductors
    (b) one grounding electrode conductor at a common location
    (c) common grounding electrode conductor and taps.
    (d) any of these

33. Ferrous metal enclosures for grounding electrode conductors shall be electrically continuous, from the point of attachment to cabinets or equipment, to the grounding electrode.

    (a) True
    (b) False

34. A grounding electrode conductor shall be permitted to be run to any convenient grounding electrode available in the grounding electrode system where the other electrodes, if any, are connected by bonding jumpers per 250.53(C).

    (a) True
    (b) False

35. A service consisting of 12 AWG service-entrance conductors requires a grounding electrode conductor sized no less than _____.

    (a) 10 AWG
    (b) 8 AWG
    (c) 6 AWG
    (d) 4 AWG

36. The largest size grounding electrode conductor required is _____ copper.

    (a) 6 AWG
    (b) 1/0 AWG
    (c) 3/0 AWG
    (d) 250 kcmil

37. What size copper grounding electrode conductor is required for a service that has three sets of 600 kcmil copper conductors per phase?

    (a) 1 AWG
    (b) 1/0 AWG
    (c) 2/0 AWG
    (d) 3/0 AWG

38. In an ac system, the size of the grounding electrode conductor to a concrete-encased electrode shall not be required to be larger than a(n) _____ copper conductor.

(a) 10 AWG
(b) 8 AWG
(c) 6 AWG
(d) 4 AWG

39. Mechanical elements used to terminate a grounding electrode conductor to a grounding electrode shall be accessible.

(a) True
(b) False

40. An encased or buried connection to a concrete-encased, driven, or buried grounding electrode shall be accessible.

(a) True
(b) False

41. The connection of the grounding electrode conductor to a buried grounding electrode (driven ground rod) shall be made with a listed terminal device that is accessible.

(a) True
(b) False

42. Exothermic or irreversible compression connections, together with the mechanical means used to attach to fireproofed structural metal, shall not be required to be accessible.

(a) True
(b) False

43. When an underground metal water piping system is used as a grounding electrode, bonding shall be provided around insulated joints and around any equipment that is likely to be disconnected for repairs or replacement.

(a) True
(b) False

44. Interior metal water piping located not more than _____ from the point of entrance to the building shall be permitted to be used as a conductor to interconnect electrodes that are part of the grounding electrode system.

(a) 2 ft
(b) 4 ft
(c) 5 ft
(d) 6 ft

45. Where conditions of maintenance and supervision ensure only qualified persons service the installation in _____ buildings, the entire length of the metal water piping system can be used for grounding purposes, provided the entire length, other than short sections passing through walls, floors, or ceilings, is exposed.

(a) industrial
(b) institutional
(c) commercial
(d) all of these

46. Grounding electrode conductors and grounding electrode bonding jumpers are permitted to terminate to the metal frame of a building/structure that's in direct contact with the earth for 10 ft or more [250.52(A)(2)] or connected to _____.

(a) a concrete-encased electrode] or ground ring
(b) a ground rod
(c) other approved earth connection
(d) any of these

47. The grounding conductor connection to the grounding electrode shall be made by _____.

(a) listed lugs
(b) exothermic welding
(c) listed pressure connectors
(d) any of these

Part V. Bonding

1. Bonding shall be provided where necessary to ensure _____ and the capacity to conduct safely any fault current likely to be imposed.

   (a) electrical continuity
   (b) fiduciary responsibility
   (c) listing requirements
   (d) electrical demand

2. The noncurrent-carrying metal parts of service equipment, such as _____, shall be bonded together.

   (a) service raceways or service cable armor
   (b) service equipment enclosures containing service conductors, including meter fittings, boxes, or the like, interposed in the service raceway or armor
   (c) service cable trays
   (d) all of these

3. Bonding jumpers for service raceways shall be used around impaired connections such as _____.

   (a) concentric knockouts
   (b) eccentric knockouts
   (c) reducing washers
   (d) any of these

4. Electrical continuity at service equipment, service raceways, and service conductor enclosures shall be ensured by _____.

   (a) bonding equipment to the grounded service conductor
   (b) connections utilizing threaded couplings on enclosures, if made up wrenchtight
   (c) by listed bonding devices, such as bonding-type locknuts, bushings, or bushings with bonding jumpers
   (d) any of these

5. Service raceways threaded into metal service equipment such as bosses (hubs) are considered to be effectively _____ to the service metal enclosure.

   (a) attached
   (b) bonded
   (c) grounded
   (d) none of these

6. Service metal raceways and metal-clad cables are considered effectively bonded when using threadless couplings and connectors that are _____.

   (a) nonmetallic
   (b) made up tight
   (c) sealed
   (d) classified

7. When bonding enclosures, metal raceways, frames, and fittings, any nonconductive paint, enamel, or similar coating shall be removed at _____.

   (a) contact surfaces
   (b) threads
   (c) contact points
   (d) all of these

8. Where installed to reduce electrical noise for electronic equipment, a metal raceway can terminate to a(n) _____ nonmetallic fitting(s) or spacer on the electronic equipment. The metal raceway shall be supplemented by an internal insulated equipment grounding conductor.

   (a) listed
   (b) labeled
   (c) identified
   (d) marked

9. For circuits over 250 volts-to-ground, electrical continuity can be maintained between a box or enclosure where no over-sized, concentric or eccentric knockouts are encountered, and a metal conduit by _____.

(a) threadless fittings for cables with metal sheath
(b) double locknuts on threaded conduit (one inside and one outside the box or enclosure)
(c) fittings that have shoulders that seat firmly against the box with a locknut on the inside or listed fittings
(d) all of these

10. Equipment bonding jumpers shall be of copper or other corrosion-resistant material.

(a) True
(b) False

11. Equipment bonding jumpers on the supply side of the service shall be no smaller than the sizes shown in _____.

(a) Table 250.66
(b) Table 250.122
(c) Table 310.15(B)(16)
(d) Table 310.15(B)(6)

12. The supply side bonding jumper on the supply side of services shall be sized according to the _____.

(a) overcurrent device rating
(b) ungrounded supply conductor size
(c) service-drop size
(d) load to be served

13. What is the minimum size copper supply side bonding jumper for a service raceway containing 4/0 THHN aluminum conductors?

(a) 6 AWG aluminum
(b) 4 AWG aluminum
(c) 4 AWG copper
(d) 3 AWG copper

14. Where ungrounded supply conductors are paralleled in two or more raceways or cables, the bonding jumper for each raceway or cable shall be based on the size of the _____ in each raceway or cable.

(a) overcurrent protection for conductors
(b) grounded conductors
(c) ungrounded supply conductors
(d) sum of all conductors

15. A service is supplied by three metal raceways, each containing 600 kcmil ungrounded conductors. Determine the copper supply side bonding jumper size for each service raceway.

(a) 1/0 AWG
(b) 3/0 AWG
(c) 250 kcmil
(d) 500 kcmil

16. What is the minimum size copper equipment bonding jumper for a 40A rated circuit?

(a) 14 AWG
(b) 12 AWG
(c) 10 AWG
(d) 8 AWG

17. An equipment bonding jumper can be installed on the outside of a raceway, providing the length of the equipment bonding jumper is not more than _____ and the equipment bonding jumper is routed with the raceway.

(a) 12 in.
(b) 24 in.
(c) 36 in.
(d) 72 in.

18. Lightning protection system ground terminals _____ be bonded to the building grounding electrode system.

(a) shall
(b) shall not
(c) shall be permitted to
(d) none of these

Part VI. Equipment Grounding and Equipment Grounding Conductors

1. Listed FMC can be used as the equipment grounding conductor if the length in any ground return path does not exceed 6 ft and the circuit conductors contained in the conduit are protected by overcurrent devices rated at _____ or less.

   (a) 15A
   (b) 20A
   (c) 30A
   (d) 60A

2. Listed FMC and LFMC shall contain an equipment grounding conductor if the raceway is installed for the reason of _____.

   (a) physical protection
   (b) flexibility after installation
   (c) minimizing transmission of vibration from equipment
   (d) b or c

3. The *Code* requires the installation of an equipment grounding conductor of the wire type in _____.

   (a) Rigid metal conduit (RMC).
   (b) Intermediate metal conduit (IMC).
   (c) Electrical metallic tubing (EMT).
   (d) Listed flexible metal conduit over 6 ft in length

4. Listed liquidtight flexible metal conduit (LFMC) is acceptable as an equipment grounding conductor when it terminates in listed fittings and is protected by an overcurrent device rated 60A or less for sizes 3/8 in. through ½ in.

   (a) True
   (b) False

5. The armor of Type AC cable containing an aluminum bonding strip is recognized by the *NEC* as an equipment grounding conductor.

   (a) True
   (b) False

6. Type MC cable provides an effective ground-fault current path and is recognized by the *NEC* as an equipment grounding conductor when _____.

   (a) It contains an insulated or uninsulated equipment grounding conductor in compliance with 250.118(1).
   (b) The combined metallic sheath and uninsulated equipment grounding/bonding conductor of interlocked metal tape–type MC cable is listed and identified as an equipment grounding conductor.
   (c) a or b
   (d) only when it is hospital grade Type MC cable

7. An equipment grounding conductor shall be identified by _____.

   (a) a continuous outer finish that is green
   (b) being bare
   (c) a continuous outer finish that is green with one or more yellow stripes
   (d) any of these

8. Conductors with the color _____ insulation shall not be used for ungrounded or grounded conductors.

   (a) green
   (b) green with one or more yellow stripes
   (c) a or b
   (d) white

9. The equipment grounding conductor shall not be required to be larger than the circuit conductors.

   (a) True
   (b) False

10. When ungrounded circuit conductors are increased in size, the equipment grounding conductor must be proportionately increased in size according to the _____ of the ungrounded conductors.

    (a) ampacity
    (b) circular mil area
    (c) diameter
    (d) none of these

11. When a single equipment grounding conductor is used for multiple circuits in the same raceway, cable or cable tray, the single equipment grounding conductor shall be sized according to _____.

    (a) combined rating of all the overcurrent devices
    (b) largest overcurrent device of the multiple circuits
    (c) combined rating of all the loads
    (d) any of these

12. Where conductors are run in parallel in multiple raceways or cables and include an EGC of the wire type, the equipment grounding conductor must be installed in parallel in each raceway or cable, sized in compliance with 250.122.

    (a) True
    (b) False

Part VII. Methods of Equipment Grounding

1. The structural metal frame of a building can be used as the required equipment grounding conductor for ac equipment.

    (a) True
    (b) False

2. Where circuit conductors are spliced or terminated on equipment within a box, any equipment grounding conductors associated with those circuit conductors shall be connected to the box with devices suitable for the use.

    (a) True
    (b) False

3. The arrangement of grounding connections shall be such that the disconnection or the removal of a receptacle, luminaire, or other device does not interrupt the grounding continuity.

    (a) True
    (b) False

4. A connection between equipment grounding conductors and a metal box shall be by _____.

    (a) a grounding screw used for no other purpose
    (b) equipment listed for grounding
    (c) a listed grounding device
    (d) any of these

INTRODUCTION TO CHAPTER 3—WIRING METHODS AND MATERIALS

Chapter 3 covers wiring methods and materials, and provides some very specific installation requirements for conductors, cables, boxes, raceways, and fittings. This chapter includes detailed information about the installation and restrictions involved with wiring methods.

It may be because of that detail that many people incorrectly apply the rules from this chapter. Be sure to pay careful attention to the details, and be sure that you make your installation in compliance with the rules in the *Code*, not just in the manner that's faster or easier to install. This is especially true when it comes to applying the Tables.

Violations of the rules for wiring methods found in Chapter 3 can result in problems with power quality and can lead to fire, shock, and other hazards.

The type of wiring method you'll use depends on several factors: Job specifications, *Code* requirements, the environment, need, and cost are among them.

Chapter 3 begins with rules that are common to most wiring methods [Article 300]. It then covers conductors [Article 310] and enclosures [Articles 312 and 314]. The articles that follow become more specific and deal more in-depth with individual wiring methods such as specific types of cables [Articles 320 through 340] and various raceways [Articles 342 through 390]. The chapter winds up with Article 392, a support system, and the final articles [Articles 394 through 398] for open wiring.

Notice as you read through the various wiring methods that the *Code* attempts to use similar subsection numbering for similar topics from one article to the next, using the same digits after the decimal point in the section number for the same topic. This makes it easier to locate specific requirements in a particular article. For example, the rules for securing and supporting can be found in the section that ends with .30 of each article. In addition to this, you'll find a "uses permitted" and "uses not permitted" section in nearly every article.

Wiring Method Articles

- **Article 300—Wiring Methods.** Article 300 contains the general requirements for all wiring methods included in the *NEC*, except for signaling and communications systems, which are covered in Chapters 7 and 8.

- **Article 310—Conductors for General Wiring.** This article contains the general requirements for conductors, such as insulation markings, ampacity ratings, and conductor use. Article 310 doesn't apply to conductors that are part of flexible cords, fixture wires, or conductors that are an integral part of equipment [90.6 and 300.1(B)].

- **Article 312—Cabinets, Cutout Boxes, and Meter Socket Enclosures.** Article 312 covers the installation and construction specifications for cabinets, cutout boxes, and meter socket enclosures.

- **Article 314—Outlet, Device, Pull and Junction Boxes, Conduit Bodies, Fittings, and Handhole Enclosures.** Installation requirements for outlet boxes, pull and junction boxes, as well as conduit bodies, and handhole enclosures are contained in this article.

Cable Articles

Articles 330 through 340 address specific types of cables. If you take the time to become familiar with the various types of cables, you'll:

- Understand what's available for doing the work.
- Recognize cable types that have special *NEC* requirements.
- Avoid buying cable that you can't install due to *Code* requirements you can't meet with that particular wiring method.

Here's a brief overview of each one:

- **Article 330—Metal-Clad Cable (Type MC).** Metal-clad cable encloses insulated conductors in a metal sheath of either corrugated or smooth copper or aluminum tubing, or spiral interlocked steel or aluminum. The physical characteristics of Type MC cable make it a versatile wiring method permitted in almost any location and for almost any application. The most commonly used Type MC cable is the interlocking kind, which looks similar to armored cable or flexible metal conduit.

- **Article 338—Service-Entrance Cable (Types SE and USE).** Service-entrance cable can be a single-conductor or a multiconductor assembly within an overall nonmetallic covering. This cable is used primarily for services not over 600V, but is also permitted for feeders and branch circuits.

Raceway Articles

Articles 342 through 392 address specific types of raceways. Refer to Article 100 for the definition of a raceway. If you take the time to become familiar with the various types of raceways, you'll:

- Understand what's available for doing the work.
- Recognize raceway types that have special *Code* requirements.
- Avoid buying a raceway that you can't install due to *NEC* requirements you can't meet with that particular wiring method.

Here's a brief overview of each one:

- **Article 342—Intermediate Metal Conduit (Type IMC).** Intermediate metal conduit is a circular metal raceway with the same outside diameter as rigid metal conduit. The wall thickness of intermediate metal conduit is less than that of rigid metal conduit, so it's a greater interior cross-sectional area for holding conductors. Intermediate metal conduit is lighter and less expensive than rigid metal conduit, but it's permitted in all the same locations as rigid metal conduit. Intermediate metal conduit also uses a different steel alloy, which makes it stronger than rigid metal conduit, even though the walls are thinner.

- **Article 344—Rigid Metal Conduit (Type RMC).** Rigid metal conduit is similar to intermediate metal conduit, except the wall thickness is greater, so it's a smaller interior cross-sectional area. Rigid metal conduit is heavier than intermediate metal conduit and it's permitted to be installed in any location, just like intermediate metal conduit.

- **Article 348—Flexible Metal Conduit (Type FMC).** Flexible metal conduit is a raceway of circular cross section made of a helically wound, interlocked metal strip of either steel or aluminum. It's commonly called "Greenfield" or "Flex."

- **Article 350—Liquidtight Flexible Metal Conduit (Type LFMC).** Liquidtight flexible metal conduit is a raceway of circular cross section with an outer liquidtight, non-metallic, sunlight-resistant jacket over an inner flexible metal core, with associated couplings, connectors, and fittings. It's listed for the installation of electric conductors. Liquidtight flexible metal conduit is commonly called "Sealtite®" or simply "liquidtight." Liquidtight flexible metal conduit is of similar construction to flexible metal conduit, but it's an outer thermoplastic covering.

- **Article 352—Rigid Polyvinyl Chloride Conduit (Type PVC).** Rigid polyvinyl chloride conduit is a nonmetallic raceway of circular cross section with integral or associated couplings, connectors, and fittings. It's listed for the installation of electrical conductors.

- **Article 356—Liquidtight Flexible Nonmetallic Conduit (Type LFNC).** Liquidtight flexible nonmetallic conduit is a raceway of circular cross section with an outer liquid-tight, nonmetallic, sunlight-resistant jacket over an inner flexible core, with associated couplings, connectors, and fittings. It's listed for the installation of electrical conductors. LFNC is available in three types:

  - Type LFNC-A (orange). A smooth seamless inner core and cover bonded together with reinforcement layers inserted between the core and covers.
  - Type LFNC-B (gray). A smooth inner surface with integral reinforcement within the conduit wall.
  - Type LFNC-C (black). A corrugated internal and external surface without integral reinforcement within the conduit wall.

- **Article 358—Electrical Metallic Tubing (EMT).** Electrical metallic tubing is a nonthreaded thinwall raceway of circular cross section designed for the physical protection and routing of conductors and cables. Compared to rigid metal conduit and intermediate metal conduit, electrical metallic tubing is relatively easy to bend, cut, and ream. EMT isn't threaded, so all connectors and couplings are of the threadless type. Today, it's available in a range of colors, such as red and blue.

- **Article 376—Metal Wireways.** A metal wireway is a sheet metal trough with hinged or removable covers for housing and protecting electrical conductors and cable, in which conductors are placed after the wireway has been installed as a complete system.

Cable Tray

- **Article 392—Cable Trays.** A cable tray system is a unit or assembly of units or sections with associated fittings that form a structural system used to securely fasten or support cables and raceways. A cable tray isn't a raceway; it's a support system for raceways, cables, and enclosures.

Notes

Wiring Methods

INTRODUCTION TO ARTICLE 300—WIRING METHODS

Article 300 contains the general requirements for all wiring methods included in the *NEC*. However, it article doesn't apply to communications systems, which are covered in Chapter 8, except when Article 300 is specifically referenced in Chapter 8.

This article is primarily concerned with how to install, route, splice, protect, and secure conductors and raceways. How well you conform to the requirements of Article 300 will generally be evident in the finished work, because many of the requirements tend to determine the appearance of the installation.

Because of this, it's often easy to spot Article 300 problems if you're looking for *Code* violations. For example, you can easily see when someone runs an equipment grounding conductor outside a raceway instead of grouping all conductors of a circuit together, as required by 300.3(B).

A good understanding of Article 300 will start you on the path to correctly installing the wiring methods included in Chapter 3. Be sure to carefully consider the accompanying illustrations, and refer to the definitions in Article 100 as needed.

PART I. GENERAL

300.1 Scope.

(A) Wiring Installations. Article 300 contains the general requirements for power and lighting wiring methods.

(B) Integral Parts of Equipment. The requirements contained in Article 300 don't apply to the internal parts of electrical equipment. **Figure 300–1**

(C) Trade Sizes. Designators for raceway trade sizes are given in Table 300.1(C).

> **Author's Comment:** Industry practice is to describe raceways using inch sizes, such as ½ in., 2 in., and so on; however, the proper reference (2005 *NEC* change) is to use "Trade Size ½," or "Trade Size 2." In this textbook we use the term "Trade Size."

300.3 Conductors.

(A) Conductors. Single conductors must be installed within a Chapter 3 wiring method, such as a raceway, cable, or enclosure.

Ex: Overhead conductors can be installed in accordance with 225.6.

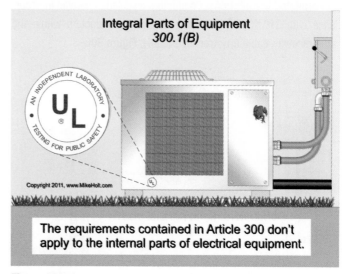

Integral Parts of Equipment
300.1(B)

Copyright 2011, www.MikeHolt.com

The requirements contained in Article 300 don't apply to the internal parts of electrical equipment.

Figure 300–1

(B) Circuit Conductors Grouped Together. All conductors of a circuit must be installed in the same raceway, cable, trench, cord, or cable tray, except as permitted by (1) through (4). **Figure 300–2**

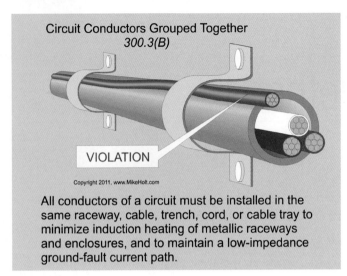

Circuit Conductors Grouped Together
300.3(B)

VIOLATION

Copyright 2011, www.MikeHolt.com

All conductors of a circuit must be installed in the same raceway, cable, trench, cord, or cable tray to minimize induction heating of metallic raceways and enclosures, and to maintain a low-impedance ground-fault current path.

Figure 300–2

Author's Comment: All conductors of a circuit must be installed in the same raceway, cable, trench, cord, or cable tray to minimize induction of the heating of ferrous metal raceways and enclosures, and to maintain a low-impedance ground-fault current path [250.4(A)(3)].

(1) Paralleled Installations. Conductors installed in parallel in accordance with 310.10(H) must have all circuit conductors within the same raceway, cable tray, trench, or cable. **Figure 300–3**

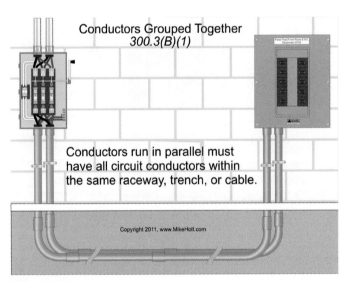

Conductors Grouped Together
300.3(B)(1)

Conductors run in parallel must have all circuit conductors within the same raceway, trench, or cable.

Copyright 2011, www.MikeHolt.com

Figure 300–3

Ex: Parallel conductors run underground can be installed in different raceways (Phase A in raceway 1, Phase B in raceway 2, and so forth) if, in order to reduce or eliminate inductive heating, the raceway is nonmetallic or nonmagnetic and the installation complies with 300.20(B). See 300.3(B)(3) and 300.5(I) Ex 2.

(2) Grounding and Bonding Conductors. Equipment grounding conductors can be installed outside of a raceway or cable assembly for certain existing installations. See 250.130(C). Equipment grounding jumpers can be located outside of a flexible raceway if the bonding jumper is installed in accordance with 250.102(E)(2).

Author's Comment: For PV systems, all conductors of a circuit, including the equipment grounding conductor, must be installed in the same raceway or cable, or otherwise run with the PV array circuit conductors when they leave the vicinity of the PV array [690.43(F)]. **Figure 300–4**

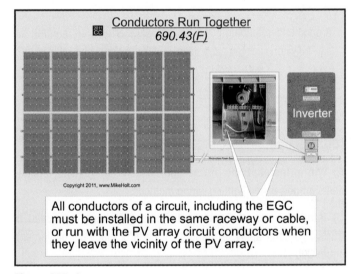

Conductors Run Together
690.43(F)

Inverter

Copyright 2011, www.MikeHolt.com

All conductors of a circuit, including the EGC must be installed in the same raceway or cable, or run with the PV array circuit conductors when they leave the vicinity of the PV array.

Figure 300–4

(3) Nonferrous Wiring Methods. Circuit conductors can be installed in different raceways (Phase A in raceway 1, Phase B in raceway 2, and so on) if, in order to reduce or eliminate inductive heating, the raceway is nonmetallic or nonmagnetic and the installation complies with 300.20(B). See 300.3(B)(1) and 300.5(I) Ex 2.

(C) Conductors of Different Systems.

(1) Mixing. Power conductors of alternating-current and direct-current systems rated 600V or less can occupy the same raceway, cable, or enclosure if all conductors have an insulation voltage rating not less than the maximum circuit voltage.

Note 2: PV system conductors, both direct current and alternating current, are permitted to be installed in the same raceways, outlet and junction boxes, or similar fittings with each other, but they must be kept entirely independent of all other non-PV system wiring [690.4(B)]. **Figure 300–5**

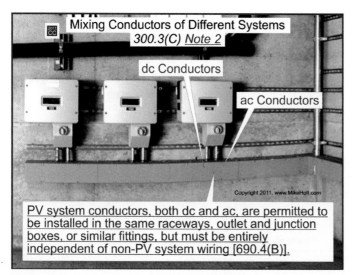

Figure 300–5

300.4 Protection Against Physical Damage. Conductors, raceways, and cables must be protected against physical damage [110.27(B)].

(A) Cables and Raceways Through Wood Members. When the following wiring methods are installed through wood members, they must comply with (1) and (2). **Figure 300–6**

- Armored Cable, Article 320
- Electrical Nonmetallic Tubing, Article 362
- Flexible Metal Conduit, Article 348
- Liquidtight Flexible Metal Conduit, Article 350
- Liquidtight Flexible Nonmetallic Conduit, Article 356
- Metal-Clad Cable, Article 330
- Nonmetallic-Sheathed Cable, Article 334
- Service-Entrance Cable, Article 338
- Underground Feeder and Branch-Circuit Cable, Article 340

(1) Holes in Wood Members. Holes through wood framing members for the above cables or raceways must be not less than 1¼ in. from the edge of the wood member. If the edge of the hole is less than 1¼ in. from the edge, a 1⁄16 in. thick steel plate of sufficient length and width must be installed to protect the wiring method from screws and nails.

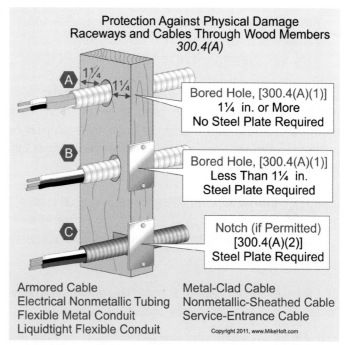

Figure 300–6

Ex 1: A steel plate isn't required to protect rigid metal conduit, intermediate metal conduit, PVC conduit, or electrical metallic tubing.

Ex 2: A listed and marked steel plate less than 1⁄16 in. thick that provides equal or better protection against nail or screw penetration is permitted. **Figure 300–7**

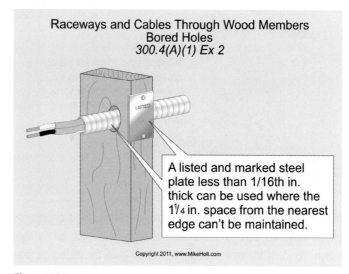

Figure 300–7

Author's Comment: Hardened steel plates thinner than 1/16 in. have been tested and found to provide better protection from screw and nail penetration than the thicker plates.

(2) Notches in Wood Members. If notching of wood framing members for cables and raceways are permitted by the building code, a 1/16 in. thick steel plate of sufficient length and width must be installed to protect the wiring method laid in these wood notches from screws and nails.

> **CAUTION:** When drilling or notching wood members, be sure to check with the building inspector to ensure you don't damage or weaken the structure and violate the building code.

Ex 1: A steel plate isn't required to protect rigid metal conduit, intermediate metal conduit, PVC conduit, or electrical metallic tubing.

Ex 2: A listed and marked steel plate less than ⅟₁₆ in. thick that provides equal or better protection against nail or screw penetration is permitted. **Figure 300–8**

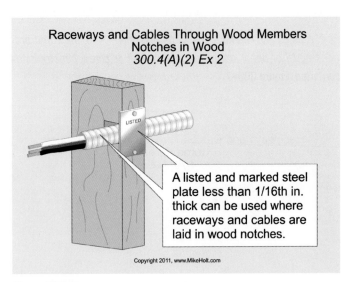

Raceways and Cables Through Wood Members
Notches in Wood
300.4(A)(2) Ex 2

A listed and marked steel plate less than 1/16th in. thick can be used where raceways and cables are laid in wood notches.

Copyright 2011, www.MikeHolt.com

Figure 300–8

(E) Wiring Under Roof Decking. Cables, raceways, and enclosures under metal-corrugated sheet roof decking must not be located within 1½ in. of the roof decking, measured from the lowest surface of the roof decking to the top of the cable, raceway, or box. In addition, cables, raceways, and enclosures aren't permitted in concealed locations of metal-corrugated sheet decking type roofing.

Note: Roof decking material will be repaired or replaced after the initial raceway or cabling which may be penetrated by the screws or other mechanical devices designed to provide "hold down" strength of the waterproof membrane or roof insulating material.

Ex: Spacing from roof decking doesn't apply to rigid metal conduit and intermediate metal conduit.

(G) Insulating Fittings. If raceways contain insulated circuit conductors 4 AWG and larger that enter an enclosure, the conductors must be protected from abrasion during and after installation by a fitting identified to provide a smooth, rounded insulating surface, such as an insulating bushing. **Figure 300–9**

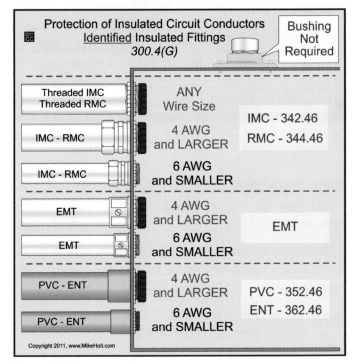

Protection of Insulated Circuit Conductors
Identified Insulated Fittings
300.4(G)

Bushing Not Required

Threaded IMC Threaded RMC	ANY Wire Size
IMC - RMC	4 AWG and LARGER
IMC - RMC	6 AWG and SMALLER
EMT	4 AWG and LARGER
EMT	6 AWG and SMALLER
PVC - ENT	4 AWG and LARGER
PVC - ENT	6 AWG and SMALLER

IMC - 342.46
RMC - 344.46

EMT

PVC - 352.46
ENT - 362.46

Copyright 2011, www.MikeHolt.com

Figure 300–9

Author's Comments:

• If IMC or RMC conduit enters an enclosure without a connector, a bushing must be provided, regardless of the conductor size [342.46 and 344.46].

• An insulated fitting isn't required for a grounding electrode.

Ex: Insulating bushings aren't required if a raceway terminates in a threaded raceway entry that provides a smooth, rounded, or flared surface for the conductors. An example would be a meter hub fitting or a Meyer's hub-type fitting.

(H) Structural Joints. A listed expansion/deflection fitting or other approved means must be used where a raceway crosses a structural joint intended for expansion, contraction or deflection.

300.5 Underground Installations.

(A) Minimum Burial Depths. When cables or raceways are installed underground, they must have a minimum "cover" in accordance with Table 300.5. **Figure 300–10**

Underground Installations - Minimum Cover Depths
Table 300.5

	UF or USE Cables or Conductors	RMC or IMC	PVC not Encased in Concrete	Residential 15A & 20A GFCI 120V Branch Ckts
Street Driveway Parking Lot	24 in.	24 in.	24 in.	24 in.
Driveways One - Two Family	18 in.	18 in.	18 in.	12 in.
Solid Rock With not Less than 2 in. of Concrete	Raceway Only			Raceway Only
All Other Applications	24 in.	6 in.	18 in.	12 in.

Copyright 2011, www.MikeHolt.com

Figure 300–10

Author's Comment: Note 1 to Table 300.5 defines "Cover" as the distance from the top of the underground cable or raceway to the top surface of finished grade. **Figure 300–11**

Table 300.5 Minimum Cover Requirements in Inches

Location	Buried Cables	Metal Raceway	Nonmetallic Raceway
Under Building	0	0	0
Dwelling Unit	24/12*	6	18
Dwelling Unit Driveway	18/12*	6	18/12*
Under Roadway	24	24	24
Other Locations	24	6	18

Residential branch circuits rated 120V or less with GFCI protection and maximum overcurrent protection of 20A. Note: This is a summary of the NEC's Table 300.5. See the table in the NEC for full details.

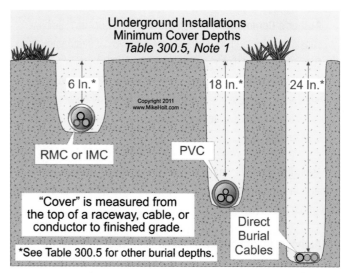

Figure 300–11

(B) Wet Locations. The interior of enclosures or raceways installed in an underground installation are considered to be a wet location. Cables and insulated conductors installed in underground enclosures or raceways must be listed for use in wet locations according to 310.10(C). Splices within an underground enclosure must be listed as suitable for wet locations [110.14(B)]. **Figure 300–12**

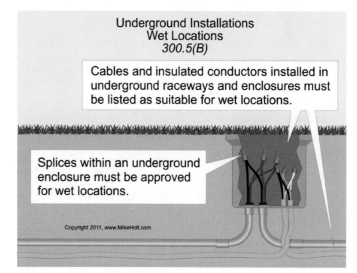

Figure 300–12

Author's Comment: The definition of a "Wet Location" as contained in Article 100 includes installations underground, in concrete slabs in direct contact with the earth, locations subject to saturation with water, and unprotected locations exposed to weather. If raceways are installed in wet locations above grade, the interior of these raceways is also considered to be a wet location [300.9].

(F) Backfill. Backfill material for underground wiring must not damage the underground cable or raceway, or contribute to the corrosion of the metal raceway.

Author's Comment: Large rocks, chunks of concrete, steel rods, mesh, and other sharp-edged objects must not be used for backfill material, because they can damage the underground conductors, cables, or raceways.

(G) Raceway Seals. If moisture could enter a raceway and contact energized live parts, a seal must be installed at one or both ends of the raceway.

Author's Comment: This is a common problem for equipment located downhill from the supply, or in underground equipment rooms. See 230.8 for service raceway seals and 300.7(A) for different temperature area seals.

Note: Hazardous explosive gases or vapors make it necessary to seal underground raceways that enter the building in accordance with 501.15.

Author's Comment: It isn't the intent of this Note to imply that sealing fittings of the types required in hazardous (classified) locations be installed in unclassified locations, except as required in Chapter 5. This also doesn't imply that the sealing material provides a watertight seal, but only that it prevents moisture from entering the raceways.

(H) Bushing. Raceways that terminate underground must have a bushing or fitting at the end of the raceway to protect emerging cables or conductors.

(I) Conductors Grouped Together. All conductors of the same circuit, including the equipment grounding conductor, must be inside the same raceway, or in close proximity to each other. See 300.3(B). Figure 300–13

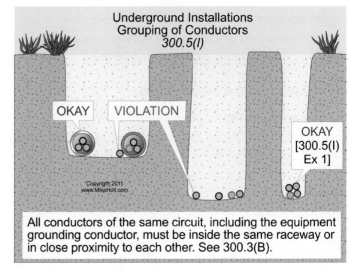

All conductors of the same circuit, including the equipment grounding conductor, must be inside the same raceway or in close proximity to each other. See 300.3(B).

Figure 300–13

Ex 1: Conductors can be installed in parallel in raceways, multiconductor cables, or direct-buried single-conductor cables. Each raceway or multiconductor cable must contain all conductors of the same circuit including the equipment grounding conductor. Each direct-buried single-conductor cable must be located in close proximity in the trench to the other single conductor cables in the same parallel set of conductors, including equipment grounding conductors.

Ex 2: Parallel circuit conductors installed in accordance with 310.10(H) of the same phase or grounded can be installed in underground PVC conduits, if inductive heating at raceway terminations is reduced by the use of aluminum locknuts and cutting a slot between the individual holes through which the conductors pass as required by 300.20(B). **Figure 300–14**

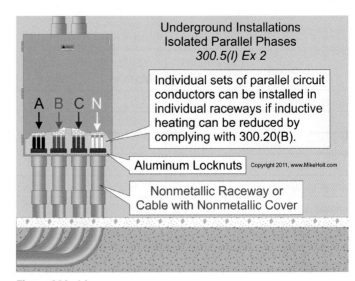

Underground Installations
Isolated Parallel Phases
300.5(I) Ex 2

Individual sets of parallel circuit conductors can be installed in individual raceways if inductive heating can be reduced by complying with 300.20(B).

Aluminum Locknuts

Nonmetallic Raceway or Cable with Nonmetallic Cover

Figure 300–14

Author's Comment: Installing ungrounded and grounded conductors in different PVC conduits makes it easier to terminate larger parallel sets of conductors, but it will result in higher levels of electromagnetic fields (EMF).

(J) Earth Movement. Direct-buried conductors, cables, or raceways that are subject to movement by settlement or frost must be arranged to prevent damage to conductors or equipment connected to the wiring.

(K) Directional Boring. Cables or raceways installed using directional boring equipment must be approved by the authority having jurisdiction for this purpose.

Author's Comment: Directional boring technology uses a directional drill, which is steered continuously from point "A" to point "B." When the drill head comes out of the earth at point "B," it's replaced with a back-reamer and the duct or raceway being installed is attached to it. The size of the boring rig (hp, torque, and pull-back power) comes into play, along with the types of soil, in determining the type of raceways required. For telecommunications work, multiple poly innerducts are pulled in at one time. At major crossings, such as expressways, railroads, or rivers, outerduct may be installed to create a permanent sleeve for the innerducts.

"Innerduct" and "outerduct" are terms usually associated with optical fiber cable installations, while "unitduct" comes with factory installed conductors. All of these come in various sizes. Galvanized rigid metal conduit, Schedule 40 and Schedule 80 PVC, HDPE conduit, and nonmetallic underground conduit with conductors (NUCC) are common wiring methods used with directional boring installations.

300.6 Protection Against Corrosion and Deterioration.

Raceways, cable trays, cablebus, cable armor, boxes, cable sheathing, cabinets, elbows, couplings, fittings, supports, and support hardware must be suitable for the environment. **Figure 300–15**

(A) Ferrous Metal Equipment. Ferrous metal raceways, enclosures, cables, cable trays, fittings, and support hardware must be protected against corrosion inside and outside by a coating of listed corrosion-resistant material. If corrosion protection is necessary, such as underground and in wet locations, and the conduit is threaded in the field, the threads must be coated with an approved electrically conductive, corrosion-resistant compound, such as cold zinc.

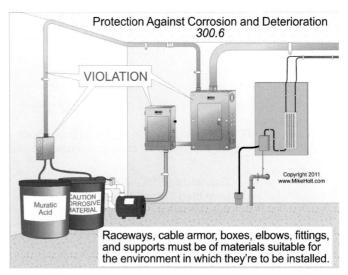

Figure 300–15

Author's Comment: Nonferrous metal raceways, such as aluminum rigid metal conduit, don't have to meet the provisions of this section.

(1) Protected from Corrosion Solely by Enamel. If ferrous metal parts are protected from corrosion solely by enamel, they must not be used outdoors or in wet locations as described in 300.6(D).

(2) Organic Coatings on Boxes or Cabinets. Boxes or cabinets having a system of organic coatings marked "Raintight," "Rainproof," or "Outdoor Type," can be installed outdoors.

(3) In Concrete or in Direct Contact with the Earth. Ferrous metal raceways, cable armor, boxes, cable sheathing, cabinets, elbows, couplings, nipples, fittings, supports, and support hardware can be installed in concrete or in direct contact with the earth, or in areas subject to severe corrosive influences if made of material approved for the condition, or if provided with corrosion protection approved for the condition.

Author's Comment: Galvanized steel electrical metallic tubing can be installed in concrete at grade level and in direct contact with the earth, but supplementary corrosion protection is usually required (UL White Book, Guide Information for Electrical Equipment, www.ul.com/regulators/2008_WhiteBook.pdf). Electrical metallic tubing can be installed in concrete above the ground floor slab generally without supplementary corrosion protection. **Figure 300–16**

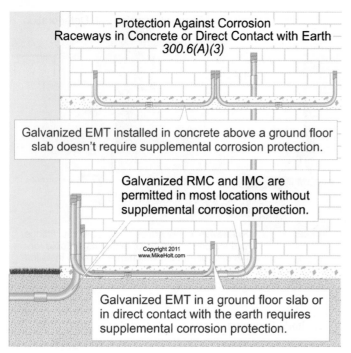

Figure 300–16

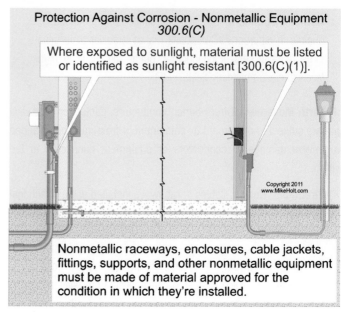

Figure 300–17

(B) Aluminum Equipment. Aluminum raceways, cable trays, cablebus, cable armor, boxes, cable sheathing, cabinets, elbows, couplings, nipples, fittings, supports, and support hardware embedded or encased in concrete or in direct contact with the earth must be provided with supplementary corrosion protection.

(C) Nonmetallic Equipment. Nonmetallic raceways, cable trays, cablebus, boxes, cables with a nonmetallic outer jacket and internal metal armor or jacket, cable sheathing, cabinets, elbows, couplings, nipples, fittings, supports, and support hardware must be made of material identified for the condition, and must comply with (1) and (2). **Figure 300–17**

(1) Exposed to Sunlight. If exposed to sunlight, the materials must be listed or identified as sunlight resistant.

(2) Chemical Exposure. If subject to exposure to chemical solvents, vapors, splashing, or immersion, materials or coatings must either be inherently resistant to chemicals based upon their listing, or be identified for the specific chemical.

(D) Indoor Wet Locations. In portions of dairy processing facilities, laundries, canneries, and other indoor wet locations, and in locations where walls are frequently washed or where there are surfaces of absorbent materials, such as damp paper or wood, the entire wiring system, where installed exposed, including all boxes, fittings, raceways, and cables, must be mounted so there's at least ¼ in. of airspace between it and the wall or supporting surface.

Author's Comment: See the definitions of "Exposed" and "Location, Wet" in Article 100.

Ex: Nonmetallic raceways, boxes, and fittings are permitted without the airspace on a concrete, masonry, tile, or similar surface.

Note: Areas where acids and alkali chemicals are handled and stored may present corrosive conditions, particularly when wet or damp. Severe corrosive conditions may also be present in portions of meatpacking plants, tanneries, glue houses, and some stables; in installations immediately adjacent to a seashore or swimming pool, spa, hot tub, and fountain areas; in areas where chemical deicers are used; and in storage cellars or rooms for hides, casings, fertilizer, salt, and bulk chemicals.

300.7 Raceways Exposed to Different Temperatures.

(A) Sealing. If a raceway is subjected to different temperatures, and where condensation is known to be a problem, the raceway must be filled with a material approved by the authority having jurisdiction that will prevent the circulation of warm air to a colder section of the raceway. An explosionproof seal isn't required for this purpose. **Figure 300–18**

(B) Expansion Fittings. Raceways must be provided with expansion fittings where necessary to compensate for thermal expansion and contraction. **Figure 300–19**

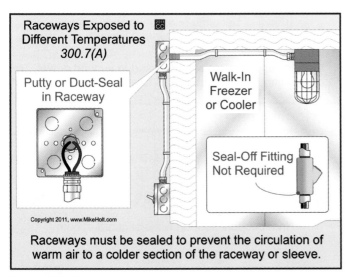

Figure 300–18

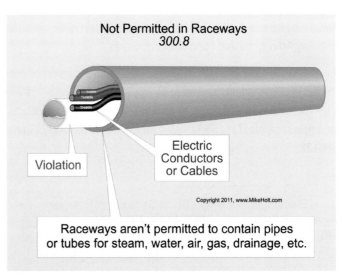

Figure 300–20

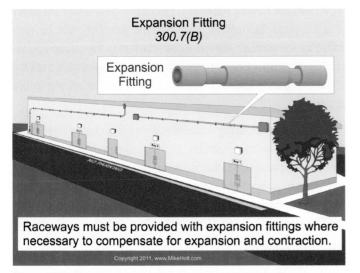

Figure 300–19

Note: Table 352.44 provides the expansion characteristics for PVC conduit. The expansion characteristics for metal raceways are determined by multiplying the values from Table 352.44 by 0.20, and the expansion characteristics for aluminum raceways are determined by multiplying the values from Table 352.44 by 0.40. Table 354.44 provides the expansion characteristics for reinforced thermosetting resin conduit (RTRC).

300.8 Not Permitted in Raceways. Raceways are designed for the exclusive use of electrical conductors and cables, and aren't permitted to contain nonelectrical components, such as pipes or tubes for steam, water, air, gas, drainage, and so forth. **Figure 300–20**

300.9 Raceways in Wet Locations Above Grade. Insulated conductors and cables installed in raceways in aboveground wet locations must be listed for use in wet locations according to 310.10(C).

300.10 Electrical Continuity. Metal raceways, cables, boxes, fittings, cabinets, and enclosures for conductors must be metallically joined together to form a continuous, low-impedance fault current path capable of carrying any fault current likely to be imposed on it [110.10, 250.4(A)(3), and 250.122]. **Figure 300–21**

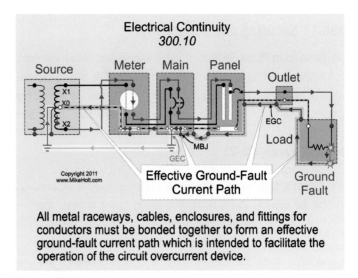

Figure 300–21

Metal raceways and cable assemblies must be mechanically secured to boxes, fittings, cabinets, and other enclosures.

Ex 1: Short lengths of metal raceways used for the support or protection of cables aren't required to be electrically continuous, nor are they required to be connected to an equipment grounding conductor of a type recognized in 250.118 [250.86 Ex 2 and 300.12 Ex]. **Figure 300–22**

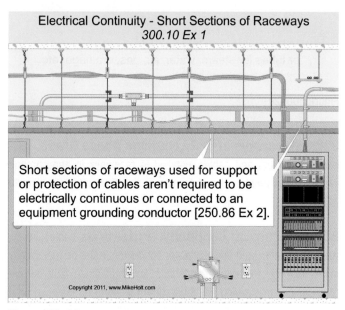

Figure 300–22

300.11 Securing and Supporting.

(A) Secured in Place. Raceways, cable assemblies, boxes, cabinets, and fittings must be securely fastened in place. The ceiling-support wires or ceiling grid must not be used to support raceways and cables (power, signaling, or communications). However, independent support wires that are secured at both ends and provide secure support are permitted. **Figure 300–23**

> **Author's Comment:** Outlet boxes [314.23(D)] and luminaires can be secured to the suspended-ceiling grid if securely fastened to the ceiling-framing members by mechanical means such as bolts, screws, or rivets, or by the use of clips or other securing means identified for use with the type of ceiling-framing member(s) used [410.36(B)].

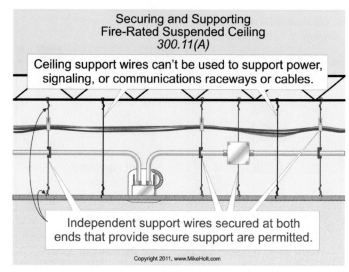

Figure 300–23

(1) Fire-Rated Ceiling Assembly. Electrical wiring within the cavity of a fire-rated floor-ceiling or roof-ceiling assembly can be supported by independent support wires attached to the ceiling assembly. The independent support wires must be distinguishable from the suspended-ceiling support wires by color, tagging, or other effective means.

(2) Nonfire-Rated Ceiling Assembly. Wiring in a nonfire-rated floor-ceiling or roof-ceiling assembly can be supported by independent support wires attached to the ceiling assembly. The independent support wires must be distinguishable from the suspended-ceiling support wires by color, tagging, or other effective means. **Figure 300–24**

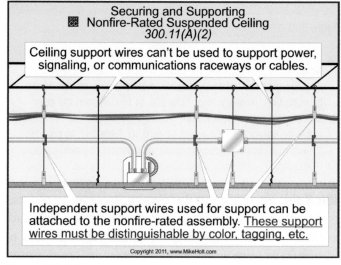

Figure 300–24

(B) Raceways Used for Support. Raceways must not be used as a means of support for other raceways, cables, or nonelectrical equipment, except as permitted in (1) through (3). **Figure 300–25**

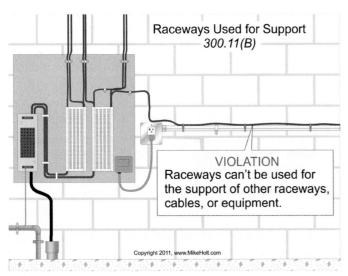

Figure 300–25

(1) Identified. If the raceway or means of support is identified for the purpose.(3) Boxes Supported by Raceways. Raceways are permitted as a means of support for threaded boxes and conduit bodies in accordance with 314.23(E) and (F), or to support luminaires in accordance with 410.36(E).300.12 Mechanical Continuity. Raceways and cable sheaths must be mechanically continuous between boxes, cabinets, and fittings. **Figure 300–26**

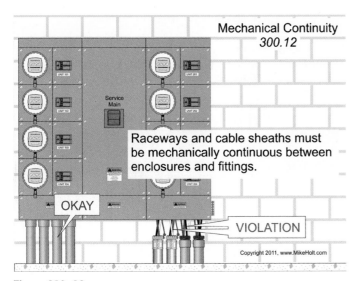

Figure 300–26

Ex 1: Short sections of raceways used to provide support or protection of cable from physical damage aren't required to be mechanically continuous [250.86 Ex 2 and 300.10 Ex 1]. **Figure 300–27**

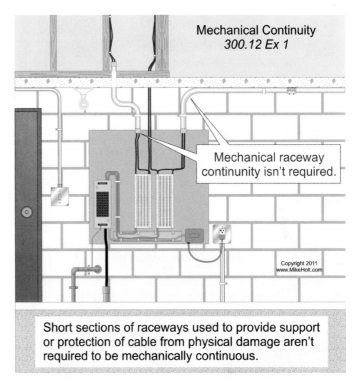

Short sections of raceways used to provide support or protection of cable from physical damage aren't required to be mechanically continuous.

Figure 300–27

300.13 Splices and Pigtails.

(A) Conductor Splices. Splices must be in enclosures in accordance with 300.15 and aren't permitted in raceways, except as permitted by 376.56, 384.56, 386.56, or 388.56. **Figure 300–28**

300.14 Length of Free Conductors. At least 6 in. of free conductor, measured from the point in the box where the conductors enter the enclosure, must be left at each outlet, junction, and switch point for splices or terminations of luminaires or devices. **Figure 300–29**

Boxes that have openings less than 8 in. in any dimension, must have at least 6 in. of free conductor, measured from the point where the conductors enter the box, and at least 3 in. of free conductor outside the box opening. **Figure 300–30**

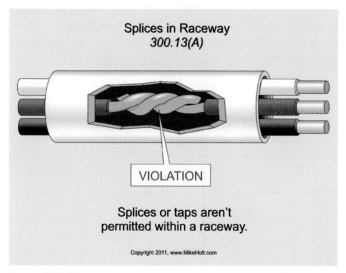

Figure 300–28

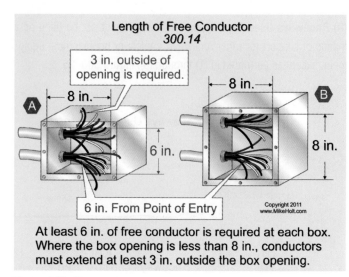

Figure 300–30

Ex: Six inches of free conductor isn't required for conductors that pass through a box without a splice or termination.

300.15 Boxes or Conduit Bodies. A box must be installed at each splice or termination point, except as permitted for: **Figure 300–31**

- Cabinet or Cutout Boxes, 312.8
- Conduit Bodies, 314.16(C) **Figure 300–32**
- Luminaires, 410.64
- Surface Raceways, 386.56 and 388.56
- Wireways, 376.56

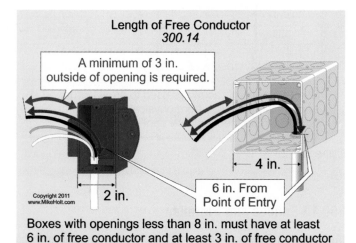

Figure 300–29

Author's Comment: The following text was the Panels' Statement when it rejected my proposal to require the free conductor length to be unspliced in the 2008 *NEC.* "The purpose of Section 300.14 is to permit access to the end of the conductor. Whether this conductor is spliced or unspliced does not affect the length of this free end of the conductor. Many conductors originate inside the box and are spliced to other conductors within the box but extend out of the box for connection to a device of some kind. Making this change would not permit this very common application. Even the exception to this section states that unspliced or unterminated conductors do not have to comply with 300.14."

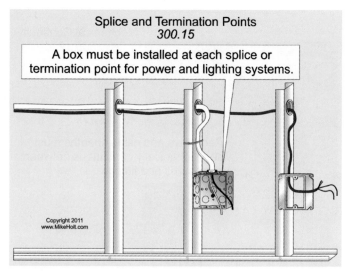

Figure 300–31

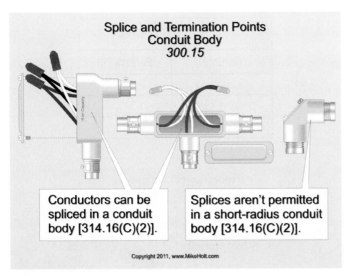

Figure 300–32

Fittings and Connectors. Fittings can only be used with the specific wiring methods for which they're listed and designed.

> **Author's Comment:** PVC conduit couplings and connectors are permitted with electrical nonmetallic tubing if the proper glue is used in accordance with manufacturer's instructions [110.3(B)]. See 362.48.

(C) Raceways for Support or Protection. When a raceway is used for the support or protection of cables, a fitting to reduce the potential for abrasion must be placed at the location the cables enter the raceway. **Figure 300–33**

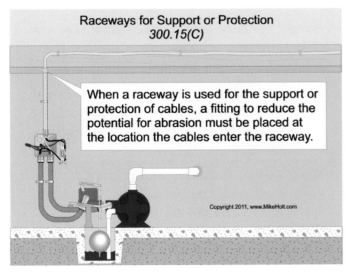

Figure 300–33

(F) Fitting. A fitting is permitted in lieu of a box or conduit body where conductors aren't spliced or terminated within the fitting if it's accessible after installation. **Figure 300–34**

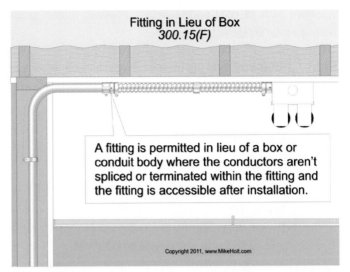

Figure 300–34

(L) Handhole Enclosures. A box or conduit body isn't required for conductors installed in a handhole enclosure. Splices must be made in accordance with 314.30. **Figure 300–35**

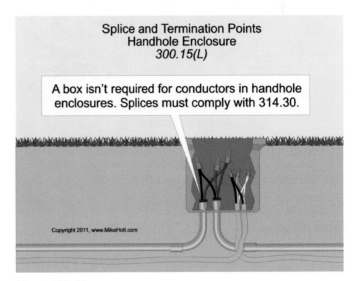

Figure 300–35

> **Author's Comment:** Splices or terminations within a handhole must be accomplished by the use of fittings listed as suitable for wet locations [110.14(B) and 314.30(C)].

300.16 Raceway or Cable to Open or Concealed Wiring.

(B) Bushing. A bushing is permitted in lieu of a box or terminal where the conductors emerge from a raceway and enter or terminate at equipment such as open switchboards, unenclosed control equipment, or similar equipment.

300.17 Raceway Sizing. Raceways must be large enough to permit the installation and removal of conductors without damaging the conductor's insulation.

Author's Comment: When all conductors in a raceway are the same size and of the same insulation type, the number of conductors permitted can be determined by Annex C.

Question: How many 12 THHN conductors can be installed in trade size ¾ electrical metallic tubing? **Figure 300–36**

(a) 12   (b) 13   (c) 14   (d) 16

Answer: (d) 16 conductors [Annex C, Table C1]

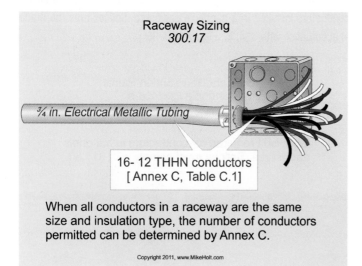

Figure 300–36

Author's Comment: When different size conductors are installed in a raceway, conductor fill is limited to the percentages in Table 1 of Chapter 9. **Figure 300–37**

Table 1, Chapter 9	
Number	Percent Fill
1 Conductor	53%
2 Conductors	31%
3 or more	40%

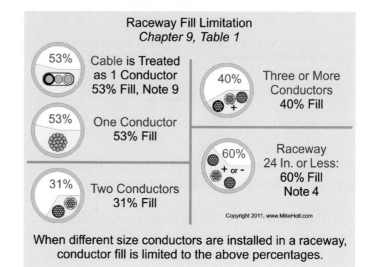

When different size conductors are installed in a raceway, conductor fill is limited to the above percentages.

Figure 300–37

The above percentages are based on conditions where the length of the conductor and number of raceway bends are within reasonable limits [Chapter 9, Table 1, Note 1].

Example: If a raceway has a maximum length of 24 in., it can be filled to 60 percent of its total cross-sectional area [Chapter 9, Table 1, Note 4]. **Figure 300–38**

Step 1: When sizing a raceway, first determine the total area of conductors (Chapter 9, Table 5 for insulated conductors and Chapter 9, Table 8 for bare conductors). **Figure 300–39**

Step 2: Select the raceway from Chapter 9, Table 4, in accordance with the percent fill listed in Chapter 9, Table 1. **Figure 300–40**

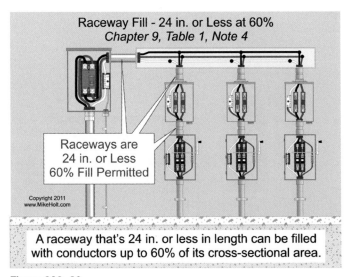

Raceway Fill - 24 in. or Less at 60%
Chapter 9, Table 1, Note 4

Raceways are 24 in. or Less 60% Fill Permitted

Copyright 2011
www.MikeHolt.com

A raceway that's 24 in. or less in length can be filled with conductors up to 60% of its cross-sectional area.

Figure 300–38

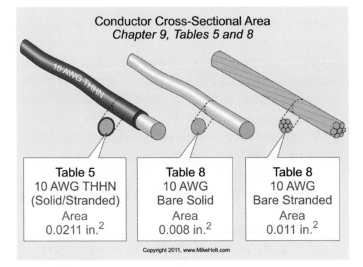

Conductor Cross-Sectional Area
Chapter 9, Tables 5 and 8

10 AWG THHN

Table 5	Table 8	Table 8
10 AWG THHN (Solid/Stranded) Area 0.0211 in.^{2}	10 AWG Bare Solid Area 0.008 in.^{2}	10 AWG Bare Stranded Area 0.011 in.^{2}

Copyright 2011, www.MikeHolt.com

Figure 300–39

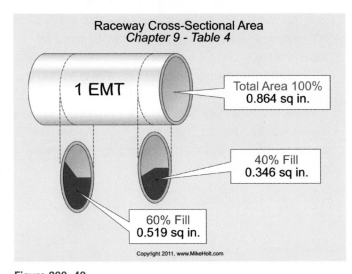

Raceway Cross-Sectional Area
Chapter 9 - Table 4

1 EMT

Total Area 100%
0.864 sq in.

40% Fill
0.346 sq in.

60% Fill
0.519 sq in.

Copyright 2011, www.MikeHolt.com

Figure 300–40

Question: What trade size Schedule 40 PVC conduit is required for the following conductors? **Figure 300–41**

    3—500 THHN

    1—250 THHN

    1—3 THHN

(a) 2   (b) 3   (c) 4   (d) 6

Answer: (b) 3

Step 1: Determine the total area of conductors [Chapter 9, Table 5]:

500 THHN	0.7073 x 3 =	2.1219 in.^{2}
250 THHN	0.3970 x 1 =	0.3970 in.^{2}
3 THHN	0.0973 x 1 =	+ 0.0973 in.^{2}
Total Area =		2.6162 in.^{2}

Step 2: Select the raceway at 40 percent fill [Chapter 9, Table 4]:

Trade size 3 Schedule 40 PVC = 2.907 sq in. of conductor fill at 40%.

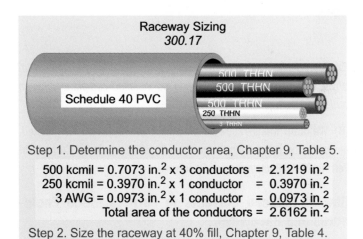

Raceway Sizing
300.17

Schedule 40 PVC

500 THHN
500 THHN
500 THHN
250 THHN
3 THHN

Step 1. Determine the conductor area, Chapter 9, Table 5.

500 kcmil = 0.7073 in.^{2} x 3 conductors = 2.1219 in.^{2}
250 kcmil = 0.3970 in.^{2} x 1 conductor = 0.3970 in.^{2}
3 AWG = 0.0973 in.^{2} x 1 conductor = 0.0973 in.^{2}
Total area of the conductors = 2.6162 in.^{2}

Step 2. Size the raceway at 40% fill, Chapter 9, Table 4.

Trade Size 3 PVC at 40 percent fill = 2.907 in.^{2} Copyright 2011 www.MikeHolt.com

Figure 300–41

300.18 Inserting Conductors in Raceways.

(A) Complete Runs. To protect conductor insulation from abrasion during installation, raceways must be mechanically completed between the pulling points before conductors are installed. See 300.10 and 300.12. **Figure 300–42**

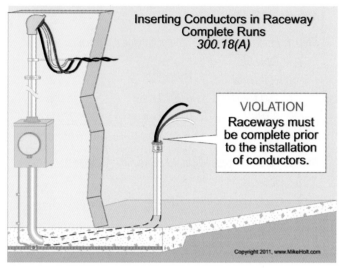

Figure 300–42

Ex: Short sections of raceways used for the protection of cables from physical damage aren't required to be installed complete between outlet, junction, or splicing points.

(B) Welding. Metal raceways must not be supported, terminated, or connected by welding to the raceway.300.20 Induced Currents in Ferrous Metal Enclosures and Raceways.

300.20 Induced Currents in Ferrous Metal Enclosures and Raceways.

(A) Conductors Grouped Together. To minimize induction heating of ferrous metal raceways and ferrous metal enclosures for alternating-current circuits, and to maintain an effective ground-fault current path, all conductors of a circuit must be installed in the same raceway, cable, trench, cord, or cable tray. See 250.102(E), 300.3(B), 300.5(I), and 392.8(D). **Figure 300–43**

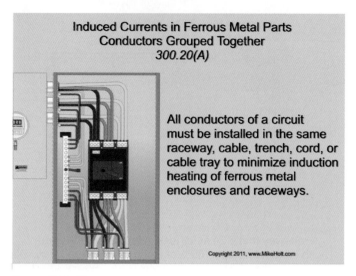

Figure 300–43

Author's Comment: When alternating current (ac) flows through a conductor, a pulsating or varying magnetic field is created around the conductor. This magnetic field is constantly expanding and contracting with the amplitude of the ac current. In the United States, the frequency is 60 cycles per second (Hz). Since ac reverses polarity 120 times per second, the magnetic field that surrounds the conductor also reverses its direction 120 times per second. This expanding and collapsing magnetic field induces eddy currents in the ferrous metal parts that surround the conductors, causing the metal parts to heat up from hysteresis heating.

Magnetic materials naturally resist the rapidly changing magnetic fields. The resulting friction produces its own additional heat—hysteresis heating—in addition to eddy current heating. A metal which offers high resistance is said to have high magnetic "permeability." Permeability can vary on a scale of 100 to 500 for magnetic materials; nonmagnetic materials have a permeability of one.

Simply put, the molecules of steel and iron align to the polarity of the magnetic field and when the magnetic field reverses, the molecules reverse their polarity as well. This back-and-forth alignment of the molecules heats up the metal, and the more the current flows, the greater the heat rises in the ferrous metal parts. **Figure 300–44**

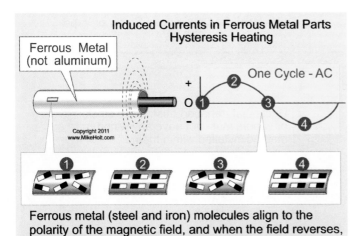

Induced Currents in Ferrous Metal Parts
Hysteresis Heating

One Cycle - AC

Ferrous metal (steel and iron) molecules align to the polarity of the magnetic field, and when the field reverses, the molecules reverse their polarity. This back-and-forth alignment of the molecules heats up ferrous metal parts.

Figure 300–44

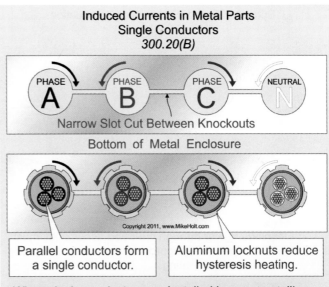

Induced Currents in Metal Parts
Single Conductors
300.20(B)

Narrow Slot Cut Between Knockouts

Bottom of Metal Enclosure

Parallel conductors form a single conductor.

Aluminum locknuts reduce hysteresis heating.

When single conductors are installed in a nonmetallic raceway, inductive heating of the metal enclosure can be minimized by cutting a slot between the individual holes through which the conductors pass.

Figure 300–45

When conductors of the same circuit are grouped together, the magnetic fields of the different conductors tend to cancel each other out, resulting in a reduced magnetic field around the conductors. The lower magnetic field reduces induced currents in the ferrous metal raceways or enclosures, which reduces the hysteresis heating of the surrounding metal enclosure.

⚠ **WARNING:** *There's been much discussion in the press on the effects of electromagnetic fields on humans. According to the Institute of Electrical and Electronics Engineers (IEEE), there's insufficient information at this time to define an unsafe electromagnetic field level.*

(B) Single Conductors. When single conductors are installed in non-metallic raceways as permitted in 300.5(I) Ex 2, the inductive heating of the metal enclosure must be minimized by the use of aluminum locknuts and by cutting a slot between the individual holes through which the conductors pass. **Figure 300–45**

> **Note:** Because aluminum is a nonmagnetic metal, aluminum parts don't heat up due to hysteresis heating.

> **Author's Comment:** Aluminum conduit, locknuts, and enclosures carry eddy currents, but because aluminum is nonferrous, it doesn't heat up [300.20(B) Note].

300.21 Spread of Fire or Products of Combustion.
Electrical circuits and equipment must be installed in such a way that the spread of fire or products of combustion won't be substantially increased. Openings <u>into or</u> through fire-rated walls, floors, and ceilings for electrical equipment must be fire-stopped using methods approved by the authority having jurisdiction to maintain the fire-resistance rating of the fire-rated assembly. **Figure 300–46**

> **Author's Comment:** Fire-stopping materials are listed for the specific types of wiring methods and the construction of the assembly that they penetrate.

> **Note:** Directories of electrical construction materials published by qualified testing laboratories contain listing and installation restrictions necessary to maintain the fire-resistive rating of assemblies. Outlet boxes must have a horizontal separation not less than 24 in. when installed in a fire-rated assembly, unless an outlet box is listed for closer spacing or protected by fire-resistant "putty pads" in accordance with manufacturer's instructions.

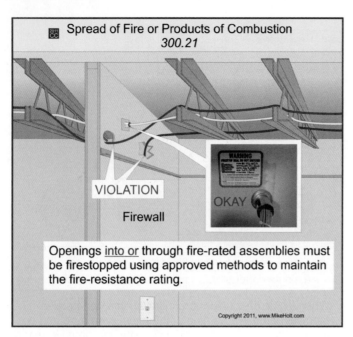

Figure 300–46

Figure 300–47

Author's Comment: Boxes installed in fire-resistance rated assemblies must be listed for the purpose. If steel boxes are used, they must be secured to the framing member, so cut-in type boxes aren't permitted (UL White Book, *Guide Information for Electrical Equipment,* www.ul.com/regulators/2008_WhiteBook.pdf).

300.22 Wiring in Ducts Not for Air Handling, Fabricated Ducts for Environmental Air, and Other Spaces For Environmental Air (Plenums). The provisions of this section apply to the installation and uses of electrical wiring and equipment in ducts used for dust, loose stock, or vapor removal; ducts specifically fabricated for environmental air, and spaces used for environmental air (plenums).

(A) Ducts Used for Dust, Loose Stock, or Vapor. Ducts that transport dust, loose stock, or vapors must not have any wiring method installed within them. **Figure 300–47**

(B) Ducts Specifically Fabricated for Environmental Air. If necessary for direct action upon, or sensing of, the contained air, Type MC cable that has a smooth or corrugated impervious metal sheath without an overall nonmetallic covering, electrical metallic tubing, flexible metallic tubing, intermediate metal conduit, or rigid metal conduit without an overall nonmetallic covering can be installed in ducts specifically fabricated to transport environmental air. Flexible metal conduit in lengths not exceeding 4 ft can be used to connect physically adjustable equipment and devices within the fabricated duct.

Equipment is only permitted within the duct specifically fabricated to transport environmental air if necessary for the direct action upon, or sensing of, the contained air. Equipment, devices, and/or illumination are only permitted to be installed in the duct if necessary to facilitate maintenance and repair. **Figure 300–48**

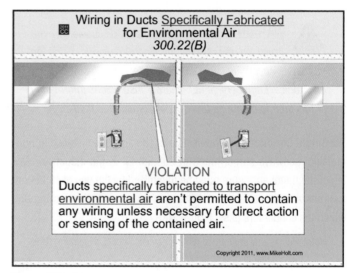

Figure 300–48

(C) Other Spaces Used for Environmental Air (Plenums). This section applies to wiring and equipment in spaces not specifically fabricated for environmental air-handling purposes (plenums) but used for air-handling purposes as a plenum. This requirement doesn't apply to habitable rooms or areas of buildings, the prime purpose of which isn't air handling.

Note 1: The spaces above a suspended ceiling or below a raised floor used for environmental air are examples of the type of space to which this section applies. **Figure 300–49**

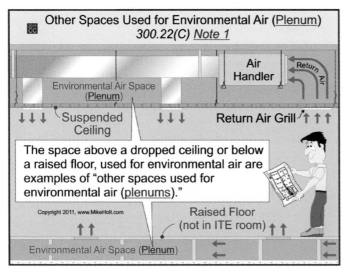

Figure 300–49

Note 2: The phrase "other space used for environmental air (plenum)" correlates with the term "plenum" in NFPA 90A, Standard for the Installation of Air-Conditioning and Ventilating Systems, and other mechanical codes where the plenum is used for return air purposes, as well as some other air-handling spaces.

Author's Comment: For the purpose of this textbook, when the *NEC* references "other space used for environmental air (plenum)," only the term "plenum" will be used.

(1) Wiring Methods. Electrical metallic tubing, rigid metal conduit, intermediate metal conduit, armored cable, metal-clad cable without a nonmetallic cover, and flexible metal conduit can be installed in plenums. If accessible, surface metal raceways or metal wireways with metal covers can be installed in plenums. **Figure 300–50**

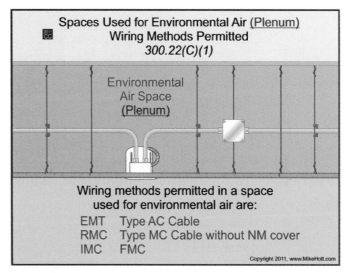

Figure 300–50

(3) Equipment. Electrical equipment with metal enclosures are permitted to be installed in plenum space.

Author's Comment: Examples of electrical equipment permitted in plenum space are air-handlers, junction boxes, and dry-type transformers.

Notes

INTRODUCTION TO ARTICLE 310—CONDUCTORS FOR GENERAL WIRING

This article contains the general requirements for conductors, such as insulation markings, ampacity ratings, and conditions of use. Article 310 doesn't apply to conductors that are part of flexible cords, fixture wires, or to conductors that are an integral part of equipment [90.7 and 300.1(B)].

People often make errors in applying the ampacity tables contained in Article 310. If you study the explanations carefully, you'll avoid common errors such as applying Table 310.15(B)(17) when you should be applying Table 310.15(B)(16).

Why so many tables? Why does Table 310.15(B)(17) list the ampacity of 6 THHN as 105 amperes, yet Table 310.15(B)(16) lists the same conductor as having an ampacity of only 75 amperes? To answer that, go back to Article 100 and review the definition of ampacity. Notice the phrase "conditions of use." These tables set a maximum current value at which premature failure of the conductor insulation shouldn't occur during normal use, under the conditions described in the tables.

The designations THHN, THHW, RHH, and so on, are insulation types. Every type of insulation has a limit to how much heat it can withstand. When current flows through a conductor, it creates heat. How well the insulation around a conductor can dissipate that heat depends on factors such as whether that conductor is in free air or not. Think about what happens when you put on a sweater, a jacket, and then a coat—all at the same time. You heat up. Your skin can't dissipate heat with all that clothing on nearly as well as it dissipates heat in free air. The same principal applies to conductors.

Conductor insulation also fails with age. That's why we conduct cable testing and take other measures to predict failure and replace certain conductors (for example, feeders or critical equipment conductors) while they're still within design specifications. But conductor insulation failure takes decades under normal use—and it's a maintenance issue. However, if a conductor is forced to exceed the ampacity listed in the appropriate table, and as a result its design temperature is exceeded, insulation failure happens much more rapidly—often catastrophically. Consequently, exceeding the allowable ampacity of a conductor is a serious safety issue.

PART I. GENERAL

310.1 Scope. Article 310 contains the general requirements for conductors, such as insulation markings, ampacity ratings, and their use. This article doesn't apply to conductors that are an integral part of equipment [90.7 and 300.1(B)].

PART II. INSTALLATION

310.10 Uses Permitted. Conductors described in 310.104 can be used in any of the wiring methods recognized in Chapter 3 as permitted in this *Code* [110.8].

(D) Locations Exposed to Direct Sunlight. Insulated conductors and cables exposed to the direct rays of the sun must be:

(1) Listed as sunlight resistant or marked as being sunlight resistant. **Figure 310–1**

> **Author's Comment:** SE cable and the conductors contained in the cable are listed as sunlight resistant. However, according to the UL listing standard, the conductors contained in SE cable aren't required to be marked as sunlight resistant.

(2) Covered with insulating material, such as tape or sleeving materials that are listed as being sunlight resistant or marked as being sunlight resistant.

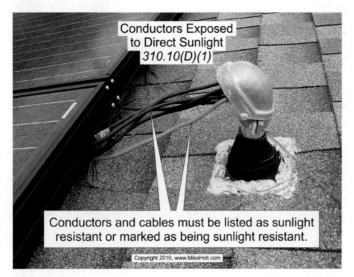

Figure 310–1

(G) Corrosive Conditions. Conductor insulation must be suitable for any substance to which it may be exposed that may have a detrimental effect on the conductor's insulation, such as oil, grease, vapor, gases, fumes, liquids, or other substances. See 110.11.

(H) Conductors in Parallel.

(1) General. Ungrounded and grounded conductors can be connected in parallel, <u>only in sizes</u> 1/0 AWG and larger.

(2) Conductor Characteristics. When circuit conductors are installed in parallel, the conductors must be connected so that the current will be evenly distributed between the individual parallel conductors by requiring all circuit conductors within each parallel set to: **Figure 310–2**

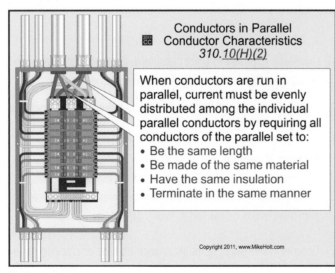

Figure 310–2

(1) Be the same length.

(2) Consist of the same conductor material (copper/aluminum).

(3) Be the same size in circular mil area (minimum 1/0 AWG).

(4) Have the same type of insulation (like THHN).

(5) Terminate in the same method (set screw versus compression).

> **Author's Comment:** Conductors aren't required to have the same physical characteristics as those of another ungrounded or grounded conductor to achieve balance.

(3) Separate Raceways or Cables. Raceways or cables containing parallel conductors must have the same electrical characteristics and the same number of conductors. **Figure 310–3**

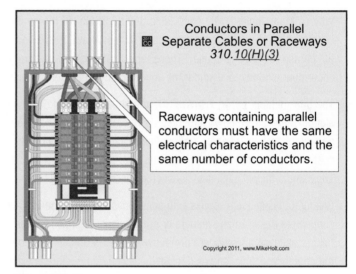

Figure 310–3

> **Author's Comment:** If one set of parallel conductors is installed in a metallic raceway and the other conductors are installed in PVC conduit, the conductors in the metallic raceway will have an increased opposition to current flow (impedance) as compared to the conductors in the nonmetallic raceway. This results in an unbalanced distribution of current between the parallel conductors.

Parallel sets of conductors aren't required to have the same physical characteristics as those of another set to achieve balance.

> **Author's Comment:** For example, a 400A feeder with a grounded load of 240A can be paralleled as follows: **Figure 310–4**

- Phase A, Two—250 kcmil THHN aluminum, 100 ft
- Phase B, Two—3/0 THHN copper, 104 ft

- Phase C, Two—3/0 THHN copper, 102 ft
- Grounded, Two—1/0 THHN aluminum, 103 ft
- Equipment Grounding Conductor, Two—3 AWG copper, 101 ft*

The minimum 1/0 AWG requirement doesn't apply to equipment grounding conductors [310.10(H)(5)].

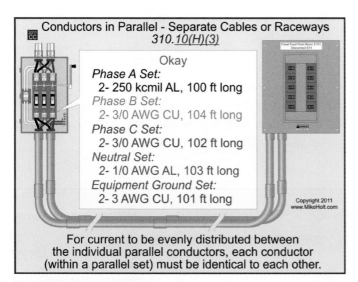

Figure 310–4

(4) Conductor Ampacity Adjustment. Each current-carrying conductor of a paralleled set of conductors must be counted as a current-carrying conductor for the purpose of conductor ampacity adjustment, in accordance with Table 310.15(B)(3)(a). **Figure 310–5**

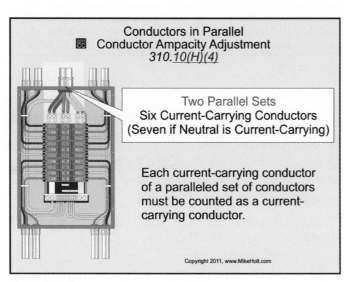

Figure 310–5

(5) Equipment Grounding Conductors. The equipment grounding conductors for circuits in parallel must be sized in accordance with 250.122(F). **Figure 310–6**

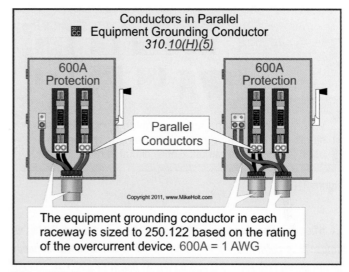

Figure 310–6

Author's Comment: The minimum 1/0 AWG parallel conductor size rule of 310.10(H) doesn't apply to equipment grounding conductors.

(6) Equipment Bonding Jumpers. Equipment bonding jumpers are sized in accordance with 250.102.

Author's Comment: The equipment bonding jumper isn't required to be larger than the largest ungrounded circuit conductors supplying the equipment.

310.15 Conductor Ampacity.

(A) General Requirements.

(1) Tables for Engineering Supervision. The ampacity of a conductor can be determined either by using the tables in accordance with 310.15(B), or under engineering supervision as provided in 310.15(C).

Note 1: Ampacities provided by this section don't take voltage drop into consideration. See 210.19(A) Note 4, for branch circuits and 215.2(D) Note 2, for feeders.

(2) Conductor Ampacity—Lower Rating. Where more than one ampacity applies for a given circuit length, the lowest value must be used. **Figure 310–7**

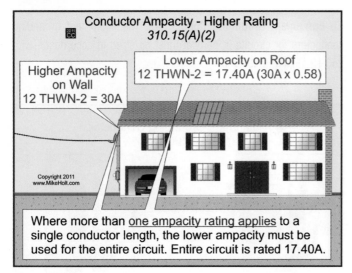

Figure 310–7

Ex: When different ampacities apply to a length of conductor, the higher ampacity is permitted for the entire circuit if the reduced ampacity length doesn't exceed 10 ft and its length doesn't exceed 10 percent of the length of the higher ampacity. **Figure 310–8**

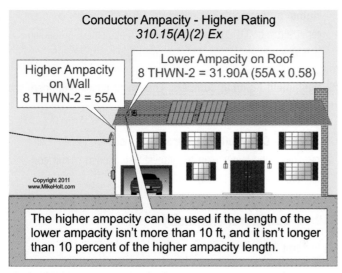

Figure 310–8

(3) Insulation Temperature Limitation. Conductors must not be used where the operating temperature exceeds that designated for the type of insulated conductor involved.

Note 1: The insulation temperature rating of a conductor is the maximum temperature a conductor [Table 310.104(A)] can withstand over a prolonged time period without serious degradation. The main factors to consider for conductor operating temperature include:

(1) Ambient temperature may vary along the conductor length as well as from time to time [Table 310.15(B)(2)(a)].

(2) Heat generated internally in the conductor—load current flow.

(3) The rate at which generated heat dissipates into the ambient medium.

(4) Adjacent load-carrying conductors have the effect of raising the ambient temperature and impeding heat dissipation [Table 310.15(B)(3)(a)].

Note 2: See 110.14(C) for the temperature limitation of terminations.

(B) Ampacity Table. The allowable conductor ampacities listed in Table 310.15(B)(16) are based on conditions where the ambient temperature isn't over 86°F, and no more than three current-carrying conductors are bundled together. **Figure 310–9**

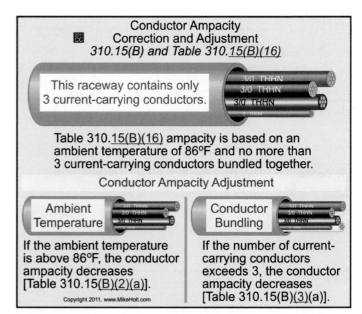

Figure 310–9

The temperature correction and adjustment factors apply to the ampacity for the temperature rating of the conductor.

(2) Ambient Temperature Correction Factors. When conductors are installed in an ambient temperature other than 78°F to 86°F, the ampacities listed in Table 310.15(B)(16) must be corrected in accordance with the multipliers listed in Table 310.15(B)(2)(a). **Figure 310–10**

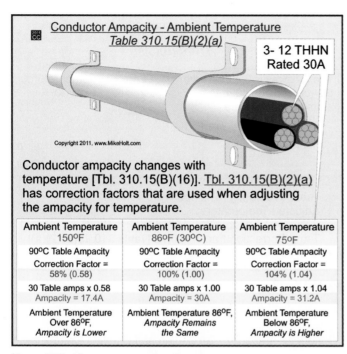

Conductor Ampacity - Ambient Temperature
Table 310.15(B)(2)(a)

3- 12 THHN
Rated 30A

Copyright 2011, www.MikeHolt.com

Conductor ampacity changes with temperature [Tbl. 310.15(B)(16)]. Tbl. 310.15(B)(2)(a) has correction factors that are used when adjusting the ampacity for temperature.

Ambient Temperature 150°F	Ambient Temperature 86°F (30°C)	Ambient Temperature 75°F
90°C Table Ampacity Correction Factor = 58% (0.58)	90°C Table Ampacity Correction Factor = 100% (1.00)	90°C Table Ampacity Correction Factor = 104% (1.04)
30 Table amps x 0.58 Ampacity = 17.4A	30 Table amps x 1.00 Ampacity = 30A	30 Table amps x 1.04 Ampacity = 31.2A
Ambient Temperature Over 86°F, Ampacity is Lower	Ambient Temperature 86°F, Ampacity Remains the Same	Ambient Temperature Below 86°F, Ampacity is Higher

Figure 310–10

Table 310.15(B)(2)(a) Ambient Temperature Correction

Ambient Temperature °F	Ambient Temperature °C	Correction Factor 75°C Conductors	Correction Factor 90°C Conductors
50 or less	10 or less	1.20	1.15
51–59°F	11–15°C	1.15	1.12
60–68°F	16–20°C	1.11	1.08
69–77°F	21–25°C	1.05	1.04
78–86°F	26–30°C	1.00	1.00
87–95°F	31–35°C	0.94	0.96
96–104°F	36–40°C	0.88	0.91
105–113°F	41–45°C	0.82	0.87
114–122°F	46–50°C	0.75	0.82
123–131°F	51–55°C	0.67	0.76
132–140°F	56–60°C	0.58	0.71
141–149°F	61–65°C	0.47	0.65
150–158°F	66–70°C	0.33	0.58
159–167°F	71–75°C	0.00	0.50
168–176°F	76–80°C	0.00	0.41
177–185°F	81–85°C	0.00	0.29

(3) Adjustment Factors.

(a) Conductor Bundle—Four or More Current-Carrying Conductors in a Raceway or Cable. Where four or more current-carrying power conductors are in a raceway longer than 24 in. [310.15(B)(3)(a)(3)], or where cables are bundled for a length longer than 24 in., the ampacity of each conductor must be reduced as shown in Table 310.15(B)(3)(a). Figure 310–11

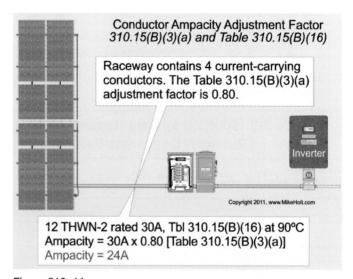

Conductor Ampacity Adjustment Factor
310.15(B)(3)(a) and Table 310.15(B)(16)

Raceway contains 4 current-carrying conductors. The Table 310.15(B)(3)(a) adjustment factor is 0.80.

Inverter

Copyright 2011, www.MikeHolt.com

12 THWN-2 rated 30A, Tbl 310.15(B)(16) at 90°C
Ampacity = 30A x 0.80 [Table 310.15(B)(3)(a)]
Ampacity = 24A

Figure 310–11

Table 310.15(B)(3)(a) Adjustment Factors for More Than Three Current-Carrying Conductors in a Raceway or Cable

Conductors[1]	Adjustment
4–6	.80 or 80%
7–9	.70 or 70%
10–20	.50 or 50%
21–30	.45 or 50%
31–40	.40 or 40%
41 and above	.35 or 35%

[1]Number of conductors is the total number of conductors in the raceway or cable adjusted in accordance with 310.15(B)(5) and (6).

(1) Adjustment factors don't apply to conductors installed in cable trays, the provisions of 392.80 apply.

(2) Adjustment factors don't apply to conductors in raceways having a length not exceeding 24 in. or cables bundled.

(c) <u>Circular Raceways</u> Exposed to Sunlight on Rooftops. When applying ampacity adjustment correction factors, the ambient temperature adjustment contained in Table 310.15(B)(3)(c) is added to the outdoor ambient temperature for conductors installed in <u>circular</u> raceways exposed to direct sunlight on or above rooftops to determine the applicable ambient temperature for ampacity correction factors in Table 310.15(B)(2)(a) or Table 310.15(B)(2)(b).

Note 1: See the ASHRAE *Handbook—Fundamentals* (www.ashrae.org) as a source for the average ambient temperatures in various locations.

Note 2: The temperature adders in Table 310.15(B)(<u>3</u>)(c) are based on the results of averaging the ambient temperatures.

Table 310.15(B)(<u>3</u>)(c) Ambient Temperature Adder for Raceways On or Above Rooftops

Distance of Raceway Above Roof	C°	F°
0 to ½ in.	33	60
Above ½ in. to 3½ in.	22	40
Above 3½ in. to 12 in.	17	30
Above 12 in. to 36 in.	14	25

Author's Comment: This rule requires the ambient temperature used for ampacity correction to be adjusted where conductors or cables are installed in a circular raceway on or above a rooftop and the raceway is exposed to direct sunlight. The reasoning is that the air inside circular raceways in direct sunlight is significantly hotter than the surrounding air, and appropriate ampacity corrections must be made in order to comply with 310.10.

For example, a conduit with three 8 THWN-2 conductors with direct sunlight exposure that's ¾ in. above the roof will require 40°F to be added to the correction factors on Table 310.15(B)(2)(a). Assuming an ambient temperature of 90°F, the temperature to use for conductor ampacity correction will be 130°F (90°F + 40°F), the 8 THWN-2 conductor ampacity after correction will be 41.80A (55A x 0.76). **Figure 310–12**

(**6**) **Grounding Conductors.** Grounding and bonding conductors aren't considered current carrying. **Figure 310–13**

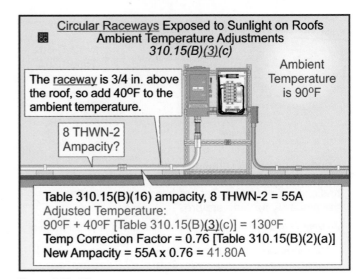

Circular Raceways Exposed to Sunlight on Roofs
Ambient Temperature Adjustments
310.15(B)(3)(c)

The <u>raceway</u> is 3/4 in. above the roof, so add 40°F to the ambient temperature.

Ambient Temperature is 90°F

8 THWN-2 Ampacity?

Table 310.15(B)(16) ampacity, 8 THWN-2 = 55A
Adjusted Temperature:
90°F + 40°F [Table 310.15(B)(<u>3</u>)(c)] = 130°F
Temp Correction Factor = 0.76 [Table 310.15(B)(2)(a)]
New Ampacity = 55A x 0.76 = 41.80A

Figure 310–12

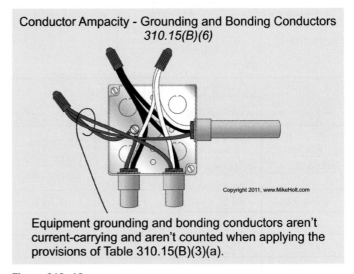

Conductor Ampacity - Grounding and Bonding Conductors
310.15(B)(6)

Copyright 2011, www.MikeHolt.com

Equipment grounding and bonding conductors aren't current-carrying and aren't counted when applying the provisions of Table 310.15(B)(3)(a).

Figure 310–13

Table 310.15(B)(16) Allowable Ampacities of Insulated Conductors Based on Not More Than Three Current-Carrying Conductors and Ambient Temperature of 30°C (86°F)*

Size	Temperature Rating of Conductor, See Table 310.13						Size
	60°C (140°F)	75°C (167°F)	90°C (194°F)	60°C (140°F)	75°C (167°F)	90°C (194°F)	
AWG kcmil	TW UF	THHW THW THWN XHHW	THHN THW-2 THWN-2 THHW XHHW XHHW-2 Dry Location	TW UF	THHN THW THWN XHHW	THHN THW-2 THWN-2 THHW XHHW XHHW-2	AWG kcmil
	Copper			Aluminum/Copper-Clad Aluminum			
14*	15	20	25				14*
12*	20	25	30	15	20	25	12*
10*	30	35	40	25	30	35	10*
8	40	50	55	35	40	45	8
6	55	65	75	40	50	55	6
4	70	85	95	55	65	75	4
3	85	100	115	65	75	85	3
2	95	115	130	75	90	100	2
1	110	130	145	85	100	115	1
1/0	125	150	170	100	120	135	1/0
2/0	145	175	195	115	135	150	2/0
3/0	165	200	225	130	155	175	3/0
4/0	195	230	260	150	180	205	4/0
250	215	255	290	170	205	230	250
300	240	285	320	195	230	260	300
350	260	310	350	210	250	280	350
400	280	335	380	225	270	305	400
500	320	380	430	260	310	350	500

*See 240.4(D)

PART III. CONSTRUCTION SPECIFICATIONS

310.104 Conductor Construction. Insulated conductors as permitted by the *Code* can be used in any of the wiring methods recognized in Chapter 3.

Author's Comment: The following explains the lettering on conductor insulation: **Figure 310–14**

- F   Fixture wires (solid or 7 strands) [Table 402.3]
- FF   Flexible fixture wire (19 strands) [Table 402.3]
- No H   60°C insulation rating [Table 310.104(A)]
- H   75°C insulation rating [Table 310.104(A)]
- HH   90°C insulation rating [Table 310.104(A)]
- N   Nylon outer cover [Table 310.104(A)]
- R   Thermoset insulation [Table 310.104(A)]
- T   Thermoplastic insulation [Table 310.104(A)]
- U   Underground [Table 310.104(A)]
- W   Wet or damp locations [Table 310.104(A)]
- X   Cross-linked polyethylene insulation [Table 310.104(A)]

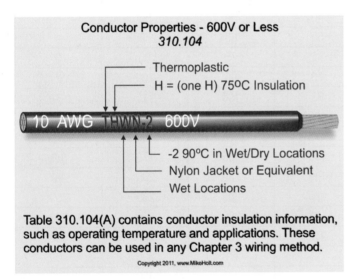

Conductor Properties - 600V or Less
310.104

Thermoplastic
H = (one H) 75ºC Insulation

10 AWG THWN-2 600V

-2 90°C in Wet/Dry Locations
Nylon Jacket or Equivalent
Wet Locations

Table 310.104(A) contains conductor insulation information, such as operating temperature and applications. These conductors can be used in any Chapter 3 wiring method.

Copyright 2011, www.MikeHolt.com

Figure 310–14

Equipment grounding conductors can be sectioned within a listed multiconductor cable, such as SE cable, provided the combined circular mil area complies with 250.122.

310.106 Conductors

(A) Minimum Size Conductors. The smallest conductor permitted for branch circuits for residential, commercial, and industrial locations is 14 AWG copper, except as permitted elsewhere in this *Code*.

Author's Comment: There's a misconception that 12 AWG copper is the smallest conductor permitted for commercial or industrial facilities. Although this isn't true based on *NEC* rules, it may be a local code requirement.

(C) Stranded Conductors. Conductors 8 AWG and larger must be stranded when installed in a raceway. **Figure 310–15**

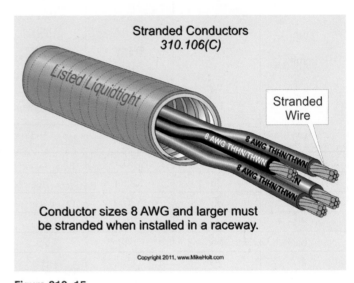

Stranded Conductors
310.106(C)

Listed Liquidtight

Stranded Wire

8 AWG THHN/THWN

Conductor sizes 8 AWG and larger must be stranded when installed in a raceway.

Copyright 2011, www.MikeHolt.com

Figure 310–15

Author's Comment: Solid conductors are often used for the grounding electrode conductor [250.62] and for the bonding of pools, spas, and outdoor hot tubs [680.26(C)]. Technically, the practice of installing 8 AWG and larger solid conductors in a raceway for the protection of grounding and bonding conductors is a violation of this rule.

310.110 Conductor Identification.

(A) Grounded Conductor. Grounded conductors must be identified in accordance with 200.6.

(B) Equipment Grounding Conductor. Equipment grounding conductors must be identified in accordance with 250.119.

(C) Ungrounded Conductors. Ungrounded conductors must be clearly distinguishable from grounded and equipment grounding conductors.Introduction to

Cabinets, Cutout Boxes, and Meter Socket Enclosures

ARTICLE 312—CABINETS AND CUTOUT BOXES

This article addresses the installation and construction specifications for the items mentioned in its title. In Article 310, we observed that the conditions of use have an effect on the ampacity of a conductor. Likewise, the conditions of use have an effect on the selection and application of cabinets, cutout boxes, and meter socket enclosures. For example, you can't use just any enclosure in a wet location or in a hazardous (classified) location. The conditions of use impose special requirements for these situations.

For all such enclosures, certain requirements apply—regardless of the use. For example, you must cover any openings, protect conductors from abrasion, and allow sufficient bending room for conductors.

Notice that Article 408 covers switchboards and panelboards, with primary emphasis on the interior, or "guts" while the cabinet that would be used to enclose a panelboard is covered here in Article 312. Therefore you'll find that some important considerations such as wire-bending space at terminals of panelboards are included in this article.

312.1 Scope. Article 312 covers the installation and construction specifications for cabinets, cutout boxes, and meter socket enclosures. **Figure 312–1**

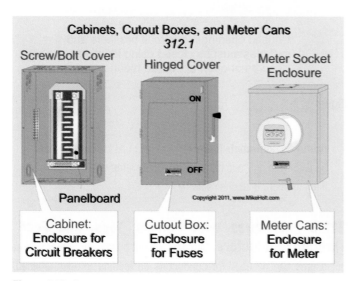

Cabinets, Cutout Boxes, and Meter Cans
312.1

Screw/Bolt Cover

Hinged Cover
ON
OFF

Meter Socket Enclosure

Panelboard

Copyright 2011, www.MikeHolt.com

| Cabinet: Enclosure for Circuit Breakers | Cutout Box: Enclosure for Fuses | Meter Cans: Enclosure for Meter |

Figure 312–1

Author's Comment: A cabinet is an enclosure for either surface mounting or flush mounting and provided with a frame in which a door may be hung. A cutout box is designed for surface mounting with a swinging door [Article 100]. The industry name for a meter socket enclosure is "meter can."

PART I. INSTALLATION

312.2 Damp or Wet Locations.

Enclosures in damp or wet locations must prevent moisture or water from entering or accumulating within the enclosure, and must be weatherproof. When the enclosure is surface mounted in a wet location, the enclosure must be mounted with not less than a ¼ in. air space between it and the mounting surface. See 300.6(D).

If raceways or cables enter above the level of uninsulated live parts of an enclosure in a wet location, a fitting listed for wet locations must be used for termination.

Author's Comment: A fitting listed for use in a wet location with a sealing locknut is suitable for this application.

Ex: The ¼ in. air space isn't required for nonmetallic equipment, raceways, or cables.

312.3 Installed in Walls. Cabinets or cutout boxes installed in walls of concrete, tile, or other noncombustible material must be installed so that the front edge of the enclosure is set back no more than ¼ in. from the finished surface. In walls constructed of wood or other combustible material, cabinets or cutout boxes must be flush with the finished surface or project outward.

312.4 Repairing Gaps. Gaps around cabinets and cutout boxes that are recessed in noncombustible surfaces (plaster, drywall, or plasterboard) having a flush-type cover, must be repaired so that there will be no gap more than a ⅛ in. at the edge of the cabinet or cutout box. **Figure 312–2**

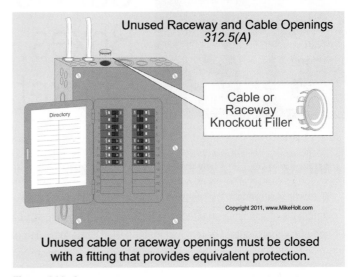

Unused Raceway and Cable Openings
312.5(A)

Cable or Raceway Knockout Filler

Unused cable or raceway openings must be closed with a fitting that provides equivalent protection.

Figure 312–3

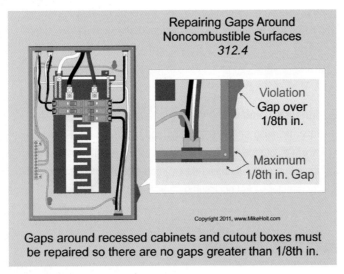

Repairing Gaps Around Noncombustible Surfaces
312.4

Violation
Gap over 1/8th in.

Maximum 1/8th in. Gap

Gaps around recessed cabinets and cutout boxes must be repaired so there are no gaps greater than 1/8th in.

Figure 312–2

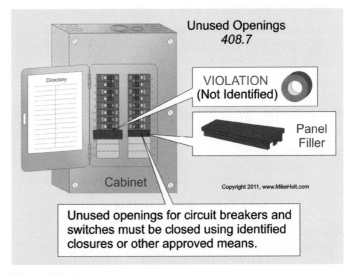

Unused Openings
408.7

VIOLATION (Not Identified)

Panel Filler

Cabinet

Unused openings for circuit breakers and switches must be closed using identified closures or other approved means.

Figure 312–4

312.5 Enclosures.

(A) Unused Openings. Openings intended to provide entry for conductors must be adequately closed. **Figure 312–3**

> **Author's Comment:** Unused openings for circuit breakers must be closed by means that provide protection substantially equivalent to the wall of the enclosure [408.7]. **Figure 312–4**

(C) Cable Termination. Cables must be secured to the enclosure with fittings designed and listed for the cable. **Figure 312–5**

> **Author's Comment:** Cable clamps or cable connectors must be used with only one cable, unless that clamp or fitting is identified for more than one cable.

312.8 Enclosures With Splices, Taps, and Feed-Through Conductors. Cabinets, cutout boxes, and meter socket enclosures can be used for conductors as feeding through, spliced, or tapping off to other enclosures, switches, or overcurrent devices where all of the following conditions are met:

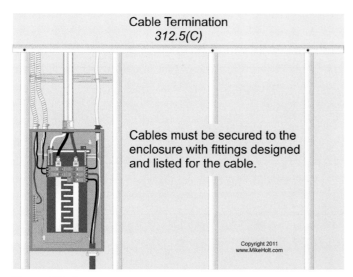

Figure 312–5

Cable Termination
312.5(C)

Cables must be secured to the enclosure with fittings designed and listed for the cable.

Copyright 2011
www.MikeHolt.com

(1) The total area of the conductors at any cross section doesn't exceed 40 percent of the cross-sectional area of the space. **Figure 312–6**

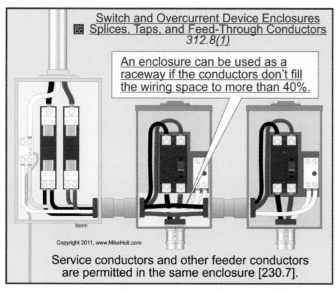

Switch and Overcurrent Device Enclosures
Splices, Taps, and Feed-Through Conductors
312.8(1)

An enclosure can be used as a raceway if the conductors don't fill the wiring space to more than 40%.

Copyright 2011, www.MikeHolt.com

Service conductors and other feeder conductors are permitted in the same enclosure [230.7].

Figure 312–6

(2) The total area of conductors, splices, and taps installed at any cross section doesn't exceed 75 percent of the cross-sectional area of that space. **Figure 312–7**

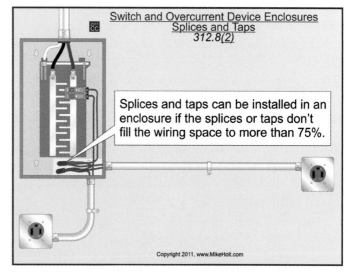

Switch and Overcurrent Device Enclosures
Splices and Taps
312.8(2)

Splices and taps can be installed in an enclosure if the splices or taps don't fill the wiring space to more than 75%.

Copyright 2011, www.MikeHolt.com

Figure 312–7

(3) A warning label on the enclosure identifies the disconnecting means for feed-through conductors. **Figure 312–8**

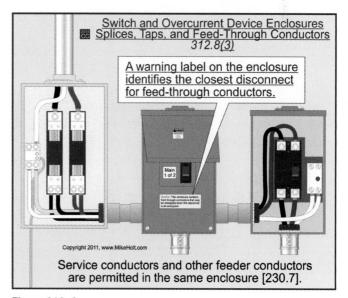

Switch and Overcurrent Device Enclosures
Splices, Taps, and Feed-Through Conductors
312.8(3)

A warning label on the enclosure identifies the closest disconnect for feed-through conductors.

Main
1 of 2

Copyright 2011, www.MikeHolt.com

Service conductors and other feeder conductors are permitted in the same enclosure [230.7].

Figure 312–8

Notes

Outlet, Device, Pull and Junction Boxes; Conduit Bodies; and Handhole Enclosures

INTRODUCTION TO ARTICLE 314—OUTLET, DEVICE, PULL AND JUNCTION BOXES; CONDUIT BODIES; AND HANDHOLE ENCLOSURES

Article 314 contains installation requirements for outlet boxes, pull and junction boxes, conduit bodies, and handhole enclosures. As with Article 312, the conditions of use have a bearing on the type of material and equipment selected for a particular installation. If a raceway is installed in a wet location, for example, the correct fittings and the proper installation methods must be used.

This article provides guidance for selecting and installing outlet and device boxes, pull and junction boxes, conduit bodies, and handhole enclosures. Information found here will help you size an outlet box using the proper cubic-inch capacity as well as calculating the minimum dimensions for larger pull boxes. There are limits on the amount of weight that can be supported by an outlet box and rules on how to support a device or outlet box to various surfaces. Article 314 will help you understand these types of rules so that your installation will be compliant with the *NEC*. As always, the clear illustrations in this unit will help you visualize the finished installation.

PART I. SCOPE AND GENERAL

314.1 Scope. Article 314 contains the installation requirements for outlet boxes, conduit bodies, pull and junction boxes, and handhole enclosures. **Figure 314–1**

Outlet Boxes, Conduit Bodies, Pull/Junction Boxes, and Handhole Enclosures
314.1

Outlet Boxes

Junction Box

Copyright 2011
www.MikeHolt.com

Conduit Body

Handhole Enclosure

Article 314 contains the installation requirements for outlet boxes, conduit bodies, pull and junction boxes, and handhole enclosures.

Figure 314–1

314.3 Nonmetallic Boxes. Nonmetallic boxes can only be used with nonmetallic cables and raceways.

Ex 1: Metal raceways and metal cables can be used with nonmetallic boxes if all raceways are bonded together in the nonmetallic box.

314.4 Metal Boxes. Metal boxes containing circuits that operate at 50V or more must be connected to an equipment grounding conductor of a type listed in 250.118 [250.112(I)]. **Figure 314–2**

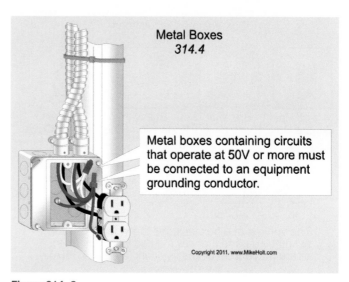

Metal Boxes
314.4

Metal boxes containing circuits that operate at 50V or more must be connected to an equipment grounding conductor.

Copyright 2011, www.MikeHolt.com

Figure 314–2

PART II. INSTALLATION

314.15 Damp or Wet Locations.
Boxes and conduit bodies in damp or wet locations must prevent moisture or water from entering or accumulating within the enclosure. Boxes, conduit bodies, and fittings installed in wet locations must be listed for use in wet locations.

> **Author's Comment:** If handhole enclosures without bottoms are installed, all enclosed conductors and any splices or terminations must be listed as suitable for wet locations [314.30(C)].

314.16 Number of 6 AWG and Smaller Conductors in Boxes and Conduit Bodies.
Boxes containing 6 AWG and smaller conductors must be sized to provide sufficient free space for all conductors, devices, and fittings. In no case can the volume of the box, as calculated in 314.16(A), be less than the volume requirement as calculated in 314.16(B).

Conduit bodies must be sized according to 314.16(C).

> **Author's Comment:** The requirements for sizing boxes and conduit bodies containing conductors 4 AWG and larger are contained in 314.28. The requirements for sizing handhole enclosures are contained in 314.30(A).

(A) Box Volume Calculations. The volume of a box includes the total volume of its assembled parts, including plaster rings, extension rings, and domed covers that are either marked with their volume in cubic inches (cu in.), or are made from boxes listed in Table 314.16(A). **Figure 314–3**

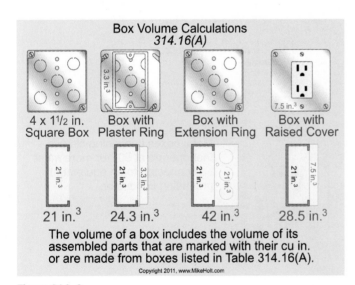

Figure 314–3

(B) Box Fill Calculations. The calculated conductor volume determined by (1) through (5) and Table 314.16(B) are added together to determine the total volume of the conductors, devices, and fittings. Raceway and cable fittings, including locknuts and bushings, aren't counted for box fill calculations. **Figure 314–4**

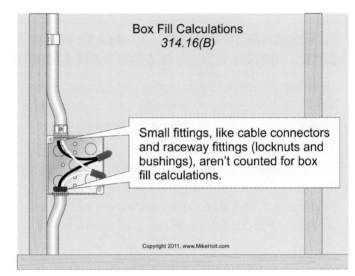

Figure 314–4

Table 314.16(B) Volume Allowance Required per Conductor	
Conductor AWG	Volume cu in.
18	1.50
16	1.75
14	2.00
12	2.25
10	2.50
8	3.00
6	5.00

(1) Conductor Volume. Each unbroken conductor that runs through a box, and each conductor that terminates in a box, is counted as a single conductor volume in accordance with Table 314.16(B). **Figure 314–5**

Each loop or coil of unbroken conductor having a length of at least twice the minimum length required for free conductors in 300.14 must be counted as two conductor volumes. Conductors that originate and terminate within the box, such as pigtails, aren't counted at all.

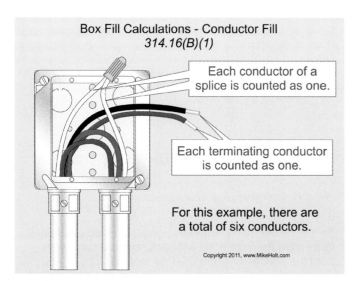

Figure 314–5

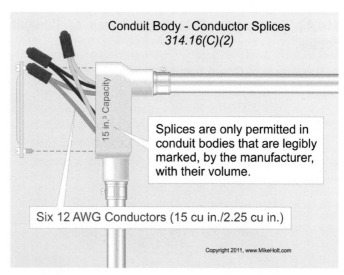

Figure 314–6

Author's Comment: According to 300.14, at least 6 in. of free conductor, measured from the point in the box where the conductors enter the enclosure, must be left at each outlet, junction, and switch point for splices or terminations of luminaires or devices.

(5) Equipment Grounding Conductor Volume. All equipment grounding conductors in a box count as a single conductor volume in accordance with Table 314.16(B), based on the largest equipment grounding conductor that enters the box. Insulated equipment grounding conductors for receptacles having insulated grounding terminals (isolated ground receptacles) [250.146(D)], count as a single conductor volume in accordance with Table 314.16(B).

(C) Conduit Bodies.

(2) Splices. Splices are permitted in conduit bodies that are legibly marked by the manufacturer with their volume and the maximum number of conductors permitted in a conduit body is limited in accordance with 314.16(B).

Question: How many 12 AWG conductors can be spliced in a 15 cu in. conduit body? **Figure 314–6**

(a) 4   *(b) 6*   *(c) 8*   *(d) 10*

Answer: (b) 6 conductors (15 cu in./2.25 cu in.)

   12 AWG = 2.25 cu in. [Table 314.16(B)]
   15 cu in./2.25 cu in. = 6

(3) Short-Radius Conduit Bodies. Capped elbows, handy ells, and service-entrance elbows aren't permitted to contain any splices. **Figure 314–7**

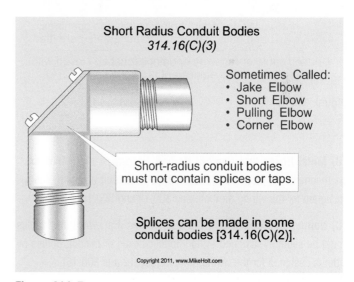

Figure 314–7

314.17 Conductors That Enter Boxes or Conduit Bodies.

(A) Openings to be Closed. Openings through which cables or raceways enter must be adequately closed.

> **Author's Comment:** Unused cable or raceway openings in electrical equipment must be effectively closed by fittings that provide protection substantially equivalent to the wall of the equipment [110.12(A)]. **Figure 314–8**

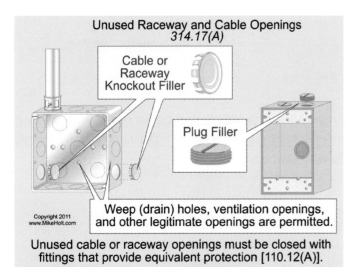

Unused cable or raceway openings must be closed with fittings that provide equivalent protection [110.12(A)].

Figure 314–8

(B) Metal Boxes and Conduit Bodies. Raceways and cables must be mechanically fastened to metal boxes or conduit bodies by fittings designed for the wiring method. See 300.12 and 300.15.

(C) Nonmetallic Boxes and Conduit Bodies. Raceways and cables must be securely fastened to nonmetallic boxes or conduit bodies by fittings designed for the wiring method [300.12 and 300.15].

314.20 Boxes Recessed in Walls or Ceilings. Boxes

having flush-type covers that are recessed in walls or ceilings of noncombustible material must have the front edge of the box, plaster ring, extension ring, or listed extender set back no more than ¼ in. from the finished surface. **Figure 314–9**

In walls or ceilings that are constructed of wood or other combustible material, boxes must be installed so the front edge of the enclosure, plaster ring, extension ring, or listed extender is flush with, or projects out from, the finished surface. **Figure 314–10**

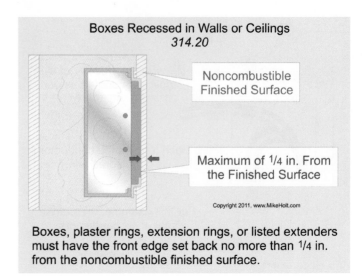

Boxes, plaster rings, extension rings, or listed extenders must have the front edge set back no more than ¼ in. from the noncombustible finished surface.

Figure 314–9

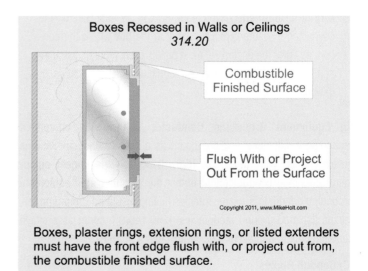

Boxes, plaster rings, extension rings, or listed extenders must have the front edge flush with, or project out from, the combustible finished surface.

Figure 314–10

> **Author's Comment:** Plaster rings and extension rings are available in a variety of depths to meet the above requirements.

314.21 Repairing Noncombustible Surfaces. Gaps

around boxes with flush-type covers that are recessed in noncombustible surfaces (such as plaster, drywall, or plasterboard) must be repaired so there will be no gap more than ⅛ in. at the edge of the box. **Figure 314–11**

314.23 Support of Boxes and Conduit Bodies. Boxes

must be securely supported by one of the following methods:

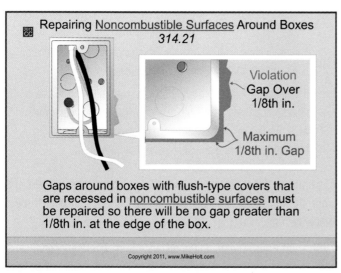

Figure 314–11

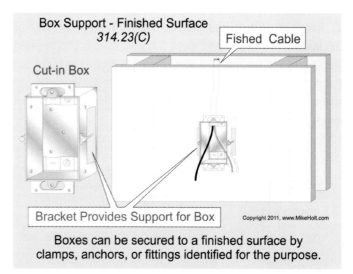

Figure 314–12

(A) Surface. Boxes can be fastened to any surface that provides adequate support.

(B) Structural Mounting. Boxes can be supported from a structural member of a building or supported from grade by a metal, plastic, or wood brace.

(1) Nails and Screws. Nails or screws can be used to fasten boxes, provided the exposed threads of screws are protected to prevent abrasion of conductor insulation.

(2) Braces. Metal braces no less than 0.020 in. thick and wood braces not less than a nominal 1 in. x 2 in. can support a box.

(C) Finished Surface Support. Boxes can be secured to a finished surface (drywall or plaster walls or ceilings) by clamps, anchors, or fittings identified for the purpose. **Figure 314–12**

(D) Suspended-Ceiling Support. Outlet boxes can be supported to the structural or supporting elements of a suspended ceiling, if securely fastened by one of the following methods:

(1) Ceiling-Framing Members. An outlet box can be secured to suspended-ceiling framing members by bolts, screws, rivets, clips, or other means identified for the suspended-ceiling framing member(s).

Author's Comment: If framing members of suspended-ceiling systems are used to support luminaires, they must be securely fastened to each other and must be securely attached to the building structure at appropriate intervals. In addition, luminaires must be attached to the suspended-ceiling framing members with screws, bolts, rivets, or clips listed and identified for such use [410.36(B)].

(2) Independent Support Wires. Outlet boxes can be secured, with fittings identified for the purpose, to the ceiling-support wires. If independent support wires are used for outlet box support, they must be taut and secured at both ends [300.11(A)]. **Figure 314–13**

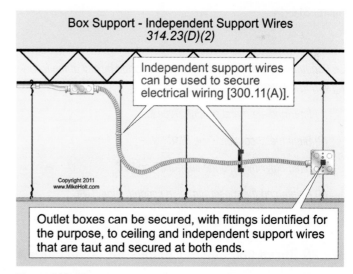

Figure 314–13

Author's Comment: See 300.11(A) on the use of independent support wires to support raceways and cables.

(E) Raceway—Boxes and Conduit Bodies Without Devices or Luminaires. Two intermediate metal or rigid metal conduits, threaded wrenchtight into the enclosure, can be used to support an outlet box that doesn't contain a device or luminaire, if each raceway is supported within 36 in. of the box or within 18 in. of the box if all conduit entries are on the same side. **Figure 314–14**

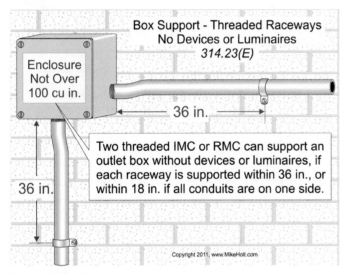

Figure 314–14

Ex: Conduit bodies are permitted to be supported by any of the following wiring methods:

    (1) Intermediate metal conduit, Type IMC

    (2) Rigid metal conduit, Type RMC

    (3) Rigid polyvinyl chloride conduit, Type PVC

    (4) Reinforced thermosetting resin conduit, Type RTRC

    (5) Electrical metallic tubing, Type EMT

314.28 Boxes and Conduit Bodies for Conductors 4 AWG and Larger. Boxes and conduit bodies containing conductors 4 AWG and larger that are required to be insulated must be sized so the conductor insulation won't be damaged.

Author's Comments:

- The requirements for sizing boxes and conduit bodies containing conductors 6 AWG and smaller are contained in 314.16.

- If conductors 4 AWG and larger enter a box or other enclosure, a fitting that provides a smooth, rounded, insulating surface, such as a bushing or adapter, is required to protect the conductors from abrasion during and after installation [300.4(G)].

(A) Minimum Size. For raceways containing conductors 4 AWG and larger, the minimum dimensions of boxes and conduit bodies must comply with the following:

(1) Straight Pulls. The minimum distance from where the conductors enter the box or conduit body to the opposite wall must not be less than eight times the trade size of the largest raceway. **Figure 314–15**

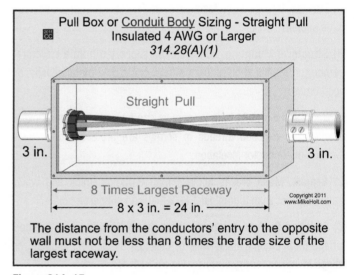

Figure 314–15

(2) Angle Pulls, U Pulls, or Splices.

Angle Pulls. The distance from the raceway entry of the box or conduit body to the opposite wall must not be less than six times the trade size of the largest raceway, plus the sum of the trade sizes of the remaining raceways on the same wall and row. **Figure 314–16**

U Pulls. When a conductor enters and leaves from the same wall of the box, the distance from where the raceways enter to the opposite wall must not be less than six times the trade size of the largest raceway, plus the sum of the trade sizes of the remaining raceways on the same wall and row. **Figure 314–17**

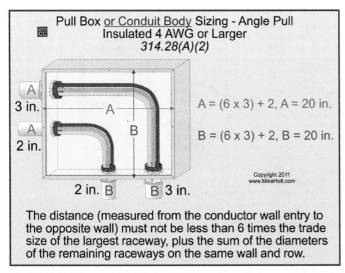

Pull Box or Conduit Body Sizing - Angle Pull
Insulated 4 AWG or Larger
314.28(A)(2)

A = (6 x 3) + 2, A = 20 in.

B = (6 x 3) + 2, B = 20 in.

Copyright 2011
www.MikeHolt.com

The distance (measured from the conductor wall entry to the opposite wall) must not be less than 6 times the trade size of the largest raceway, plus the sum of the diameters of the remaining raceways on the same wall and row.

Figure 314–16

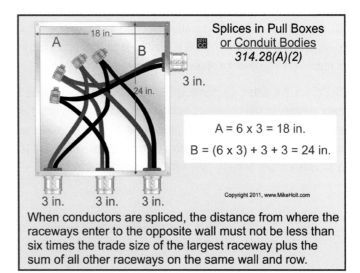

Splices in Pull Boxes or Conduit Bodies
314.28(A)(2)

A = 6 x 3 = 18 in.

B = (6 x 3) + 3 + 3 = 24 in.

Copyright 2011, www.MikeHolt.com

When conductors are spliced, the distance from where the raceways enter to the opposite wall must not be less than six times the trade size of the largest raceway plus the sum of all other raceways on the same wall and row.

Figure 314–18

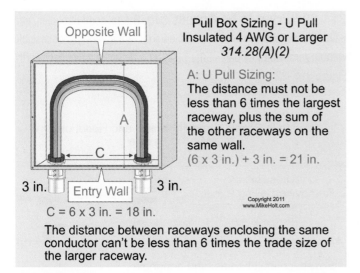

Pull Box Sizing - U Pull
Insulated 4 AWG or Larger
314.28(A)(2)

A: U Pull Sizing:
The distance must not be less than 6 times the largest raceway, plus the sum of the other raceways on the same wall.
(6 x 3 in.) + 3 in. = 21 in.

Copyright 2011
www.MikeHolt.com

C = 6 x 3 in. = 18 in.

The distance between raceways enclosing the same conductor can't be less than 6 times the trade size of the larger raceway.

Figure 314–17

Splices. When conductors are spliced, the distance from where the raceways enter to the opposite wall must not be less than six times the trade size of the largest raceway, plus the sum of the trade sizes of the remaining raceways on the same wall and row. **Figure 314–18**

Rows. If there are multiple rows of raceway entries, each row is calculated individually and the row with the largest distance must be used.

Distance Between Raceways. The distance between raceways enclosing the same conductor must not be less than six times the trade size of the largest raceway, measured from the raceways' nearest edge-to-nearest edge.

Ex: When conductors enter an enclosure with a removable cover, the distance from where the conductors enter to the removable cover must not be less than the bending distance as listed in Table 312.6(A) for one conductor per terminal. **Figure 314–19**

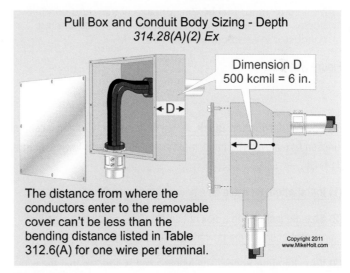

Pull Box and Conduit Body Sizing - Depth
314.28(A)(2) Ex

Dimension D
500 kcmil = 6 in.

The distance from where the conductors enter to the removable cover can't be less than the bending distance listed in Table 312.6(A) for one wire per terminal.

Copyright 2011
www.MikeHolt.com

Figure 314–19

(3) Smaller Dimensions. Boxes or conduit bodies smaller than those required in 314.28(A)(1) and 314.28(A)(2) are permitted, if the enclosure is permanently marked with the maximum number and maximum size of conductors.

(B) Conductors in Pull or Junction Boxes. Pull boxes or junction boxes with any dimension over 6 ft must have all conductors cabled or racked in an approved manner.

(C) Covers. Pull boxes, junction boxes, and conduit bodies must have a cover suitable for the conditions. Nonmetallic covers are permitted on any box, but metal covers are only permitted if they can be connected to an equipment grounding conductor of a type recognized in 250.118, in accordance with 250.110 [250.4(A)(3)]. **Figure 314–20**

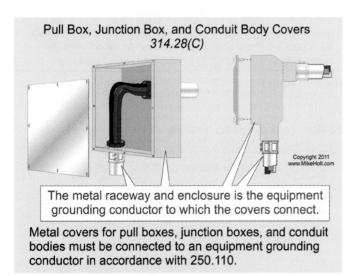

Pull Box, Junction Box, and Conduit Body Covers
314.28(C)

The metal raceway and enclosure is the equipment grounding conductor to which the covers connect.

Metal covers for pull boxes, junction boxes, and conduit bodies must be connected to an equipment grounding conductor in accordance with 250.110.

Copyright 2011
www.MikeHolt.com

Figure 314–20

(E) Power Distribution Block. Power distribution blocks installed in junction boxes over 100 cu in. must comply with the following: **Figure 314–21**

(1) Installation. Be listed as a power distribution block.

(2) Size. Be installed in a box not smaller than required by the installation instructions of the power distribution block.

(3) Wire-Bending Space. The junction box is sized so that the wire-bending space requirements of 312.6 can be met.

(4) Live Parts. Exposed live parts on the power distribution block aren't present when the junction box cover is removed.

(5) Through Conductors. Where the junction box has conductors that don't terminate on the power distribution block(s), the through conductors must be arranged so the power distribution block terminals are unobstructed following installation.

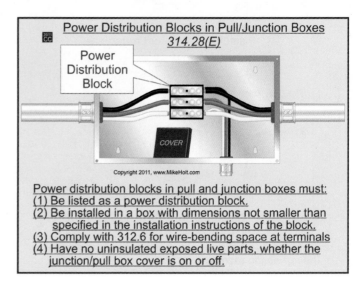

Power Distribution Blocks in Pull/Junction Boxes
314.28(E)

Power Distribution Block

COVER

Copyright 2011, www.MikeHolt.com

Power distribution blocks in pull and junction boxes must:
(1) Be listed as a power distribution block.
(2) Be installed in a box with dimensions not smaller than specified in the installation instructions of the block.
(3) Comply with 312.6 for wire-bending space at terminals
(4) Have no uninsulated exposed live parts, whether the junction/pull box cover is on or off.

Figure 314–21

314.29 Wiring to be Accessible. Boxes, conduit bodies, and handhole enclosures must be installed so that the wiring is accessible without removing any part of the building, sidewalks, paving, or earth. **Figure 314–22**

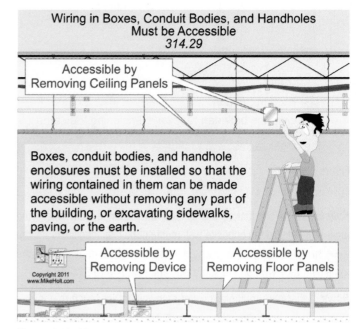

Wiring in Boxes, Conduit Bodies, and Handholes
Must be Accessible
314.29

Accessible by Removing Ceiling Panels

Boxes, conduit bodies, and handhole enclosures must be installed so that the wiring contained in them can be made accessible without removing any part of the building, or excavating sidewalks, paving, or the earth.

Copyright 2011
www.MikeHolt.com

Accessible by Removing Device

Accessible by Removing Floor Panels

Figure 314–22

Ex: Listed boxes and handhole enclosures can be buried if covered by gravel, light aggregate, or noncohesive granulated soil, and their location is effectively identified and accessible for excavation.

314.30 Handhole Enclosures. Handhole enclosures must be identified for underground use, and be designed and installed to withstand all loads likely to be imposed on them. **Figure 314–23**

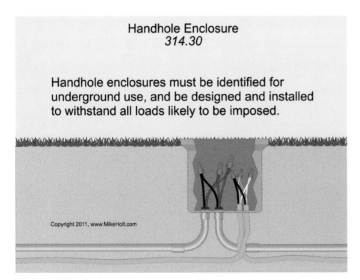

Handhole Enclosure
314.30

Handhole enclosures must be identified for underground use, and be designed and installed to withstand all loads likely to be imposed.

Copyright 2011, www.MikeHolt.com

Figure 314–23

(A) Size. Handhole enclosures must be sized in accordance with 314.28(A). For handhole enclosures without bottoms, the measurement to the removable cover is taken from the end of the raceway or cable assembly. When the measurement is taken from the end of the raceway or cable assembly, the values in Table 312.6(A) for one wire to terminal can be used [314.28(A)(2) Ex].

(B) Mechanical Raceway and Cable Connection. Underground raceways and cables entering a handhole enclosure aren't required to be mechanically connected to the handhole enclosure. **Figure 314–24**

(C) Enclosure Wiring. Splices or terminations within a handhole must be listed as suitable for wet locations [110.14(B)].

(D) Covers. Handhole enclosure covers must have an identifying mark or logo that prominently identifies the function of the enclosure, such as "electric." Handhole enclosure covers must require the use of tools to open, or they must weigh over 100 lb.

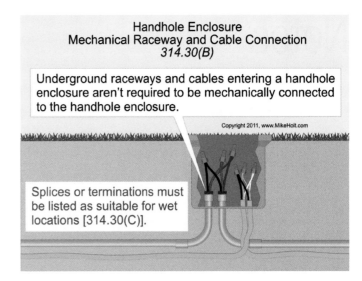

Handhole Enclosure
Mechanical Raceway and Cable Connection
314.30(B)

Underground raceways and cables entering a handhole enclosure aren't required to be mechanically connected to the handhole enclosure.

Copyright 2011, www.MikeHolt.com

Splices or terminations must be listed as suitable for wet locations [314.30(C)].

Figure 314–24

Metal covers and other exposed conductive surfaces of handhole enclosures must be connected to an equipment grounding conductor sized to the overcurrent device in accordance with 250.122. Metal covers of handhole enclosures containing service conductors must be connected to an equipment bonding jumper sized in accordance with Table 250.66 [250.92 and 250.102(C)]. **Figure 314–25**

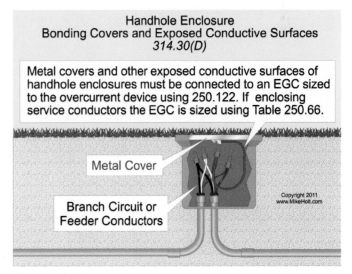

Handhole Enclosure
Bonding Covers and Exposed Conductive Surfaces
314.30(D)

Metal covers and other exposed conductive surfaces of handhole enclosures must be connected to an EGC sized to the overcurrent device using 250.122. If enclosing service conductors the EGC is sized using Table 250.66.

Metal Cover

Branch Circuit or Feeder Conductors

Copyright 2011, www.MikeHolt.com

Figure 314–25

Notes

ARTICLE 330

Metal-Clad Cable (Type MC)

INTRODUCTION TO ARTICLE 330—METAL-CLAD CABLE (TYPE MC)

Metal-clad cable encloses insulated conductors in a metal sheath of either corrugated or smooth copper or aluminum tubing, or spiral interlocked steel or aluminum. The physical characteristics of Type MC cable make it a versatile wiring method that you can use in almost any location, and for almost any application. The most commonly used Type MC cable is the interlocking kind, which looks similar to armored cable or flexible metal conduit. Traditional interlocked Type MC cable isn't permitted to serve as an equipment grounding conductor, therefore this cable must contain an insulated equipment grounding conductor in accordance with 250.118(1). There is a fairly new product called interlocked Type MCAP cable containing an aluminum grounding/bonding conductor running just below the metal armor, which allows the sheath to serve as an equipment grounding conductor [250.118(10)(b)].

PART I. GENERAL

330.1 Scope.
Article 330 covers the use, installation, and construction specifications of metal-clad cable.

330.2 Definition.

Metal-Clad Cable (Type MC). A factory assembly of insulated circuit conductors, with or without optical fiber members, enclosed in an armor of interlocking metal tape or a smooth or corrugated metallic sheath. Figure 330–1

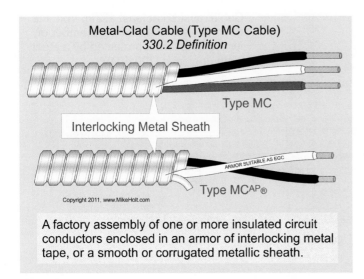

Figure 330–1

Author's Comment: Because the outer sheath of interlocked Type MC cable isn't listed as an equipment grounding conductor, it contains an equipment grounding conductor [330.108].

PART II. INSTALLATION

330.10 Uses Permitted.

(A) General Uses. Type MC cable is permitted only if not subject to physical damage, and in other locations and conditions not prohibited by 330.12, or elsewhere in the *Code*:

(1) In branch circuits, feeders and services.

(2) In power, lighting, control, and signal circuits.

(3) Indoors or outdoors.

(4) Exposed or concealed.

(5) Directly buried (if identified for the purpose).

(6) In a cable tray.

(7) In a raceway.

(8) As aerial cable on a messenger.

(9) In hazardous (classified) locations as permitted in 501.10(B), 502.10(B), and 503.10.

(10) Embedded in plaster or brick.

(11) In wet locations, if any of the following are met:

a. The metallic covering is impervious to moisture.

b. A moisture-impervious jacket is provided under the metal covering.

c. The insulated conductors under the metallic covering are listed for use in wet locations and a corrosion-resistant jacket is provided over the metallic sheath.

(12) If single-conductor cables are used, all circuit conductors must be grouped together to minimize induced voltage on the sheath [300.3(B)].

330.12 Uses Not Permitted. Type MC cable must not be used where:

(1) Subject to physical damage.

(2) Exposed to the destructive corrosive conditions in (a) or (b), unless the metallic sheath or armor is resistant or protected by material resistant to the conditions:

(a) Direct burial in the earth or embedded in concrete unless identified for the application.

(b) Exposed to cinder fills, strong chlorides, caustic alkalis, or vapors of chlorine or of hydrochloric acids.

330.17 Through or Parallel to Framing Members.
Type MC cable installed through or parallel to framing members or furring strips must be protected against physical damage from penetration of screws or nails by maintaining a 1¼ in. separation, or by installing a suitable metal plate in accordance with 300.4(A) and (D).

Author's Comments:

• 300.4(A)(1) Drilling Holes in Wood Members. When drilling holes through wood framing members for cables, the edge of the holes must be not less than 1¼ in. from the edge of the wood member. **Figure 330–2A**

   If the edge of the hole is less than 1¼ in. from the edge, a ¹⁄₁₆ in. thick steel plate of sufficient length and width must be installed to protect the wiring method from screws and nails. **Figure 330–2B**

• 300.4(A)(2) Notching Wood Members. If notching of wood framing members for cables is permitted by the building code, a ¹⁄₁₆ in. thick steel plate of sufficient length and width must be installed to protect the cables and raceways from screws and nails. **Figure 330–2C**

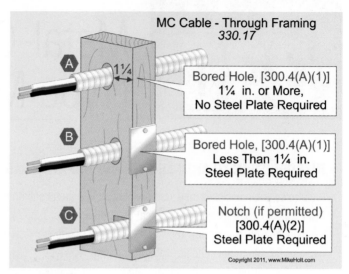

Figure 330–2

• 300.4(D) Cables Parallel to Framing Members and Furring Strips. Cables installed parallel to framing members or furring strips must be protected where likely to be penetrated by nails or screws. The wiring method must be installed so it's at least 1¼ in. from the nearest edge of the framing member or furring strips, or a ¹⁄₁₆ in. thick steel plate must protect it. **Figure 330–3**

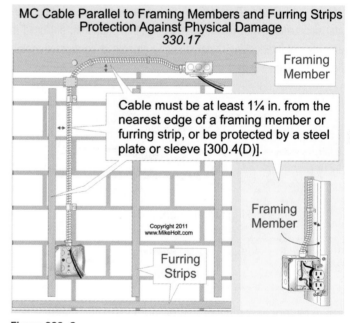

Figure 330–3

330.23 In Accessible Attics or Roof Spaces.

Type MC cable installed in accessible attics or roof spaces must comply with 320.23.

Author's Comments:

- On the Surface of Floor Joists, Rafters, or Studs. In attics and roof spaces that are accessible, substantial guards must protect cables installed across the top of floor joists, or across the face of rafters or studding within 7 ft of floor or floor joists. If this space isn't accessible by permanent stairs or ladders, protection is required only within 6 ft of the nearest edge of the scuttle hole or attic entrance [320.23(A)].

- Along the Side of Framing Members [320.23(B)]. When Type MC cable is installed on the side of rafters, studs, or floor joists, no protection is required if the cable is installed and supported so the nearest outside surface of the cable or raceway is at least 1¼ in. from the nearest edge of the framing member where nails or screws are likely to penetrate [300.4(D)].

330.24 Bends.

Bends must be made so that the cable won't be damaged, and the radius of the curve of any bend at the inner edge of the cable must not be less than what's dictated in each of the following instances:

(A) Smooth-Sheath Cables.

(1) Smooth-sheath Type MC cables must not be bent so the bending radius of the inner edge of the cable is less than 10 times the external diameter of the metallic sheath for cable up to ¾ in. in external diameter.

(B) Interlocked or Corrugated Sheath.

Interlocked- or corrugated-sheath Type MC cable must not be bent so the bending radius of the inner edge of the cable is less than seven times the external diameter of the cable. **Figure 330–4**

330.30 Securing and Supporting.

(A) General.

Type MC cable must be supported and secured by staples, cable ties, straps, hangers, or similar fittings, designed and installed so as not to damage the cable.

(B) Securing.

Type MC cable with four or less conductors sized no larger than 10 AWG, must be secured within 12 in. of every outlet box, junction box, cabinet, or fitting and at intervals not exceeding 6 ft. **Figure 330–5**

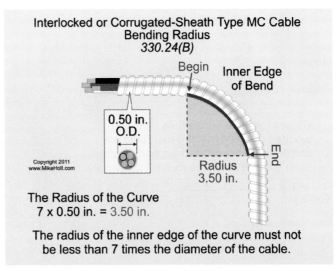

Interlocked or Corrugated-Sheath Type MC Cable Bending Radius
330.24(B)

Begin · Inner Edge of Bend

0.50 in. O.D.

Radius 3.50 in.

End

Copyright 2011 www.MikeHolt.com

The Radius of the Curve
7 x 0.50 in. = 3.50 in.

The radius of the inner edge of the curve must not be less than 7 times the diameter of the cable.

Figure 330–4

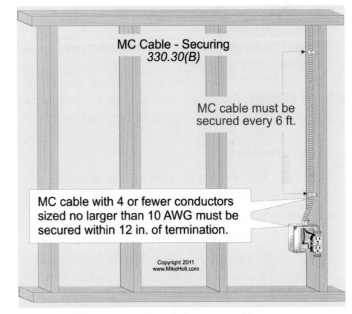

MC Cable - Securing
330.30(B)

MC cable must be secured every 6 ft.

MC cable with 4 or fewer conductors sized no larger than 10 AWG must be secured within 12 in. of termination.

Copyright 2011 www.MikeHolt.com

Figure 330–5

(C) Supporting.

Type MC cable must be supported at intervals not exceeding 6 ft. Cables installed horizontally through wooden or metal framing members are considered secured and supported if such support doesn't exceed 6 ft intervals. **Figure 330–6**

(D) Unsupported Cables.

Type MC cable can be unsupported if the cable is:

(1) Fished through concealed spaces in finished buildings or structures, if support is impracticable, or

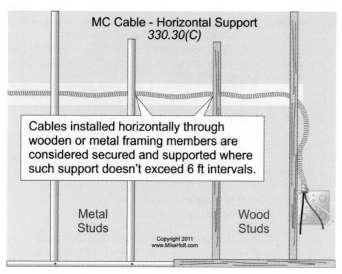

Figure 320–6

(2) Not more than 6 ft long from the last point of cable support to the point of connection to luminaires or other electrical equipment within an accessible ceiling. Type MC cable fittings are permitted as a means of cable support.

330.40 Fittings. Fittings used to secure Type MC cable to boxes or other enclosures must be listed and identified for such use [300.15].

Author's Comments:

• The *NEC* doesn't require anti-short bushings (red heads) at the termination of Type MC cable, but if they're supplied it's considered by many to be a good practice to use them.

• Conductors 4 AWG and larger that enter an enclosure must be protected from abrasion during and after installation by a fitting that provides a smooth, rounded, insulating surface, such as an insulating bushing unless the design of the box, fitting, or enclosure provides equivalent protection in accordance with 300.4(G).

330.80 Conductor Ampacities. Conductor ampacity is calculated in accordance with 310.15, based on the insulation rating of the conductors, provided the adjusted or corrected ampacity doesn't exceed the temperature ratings of terminations and equipment [110.14(C)].

PART III. CONSTRUCTION SPECIFICATIONS

330.108 Equipment Grounding Conductor. If Type MC cable is to serve as an equipment grounding conductor, it must comply with 250.118 and 250.122.

Author's Comment: The outer sheath of:

• Traditional interlocked Type MC cable isn't permitted to serve as an equipment grounding conductor, therefore this cable must contain an insulated equipment grounding conductor in accordance with 250.118(1). **Figure 330–7**

• Interlocked Type MC[AP] cable containing an aluminum grounding/bonding conductor running just below the metal armor is listed to serve as an equipment grounding conductor [250.118(10)(b)]. **Figure 330–8**

• Smooth or corrugated-tube Type MC cable is listed to serve as an equipment grounding conductor [250.118(10)(c)].

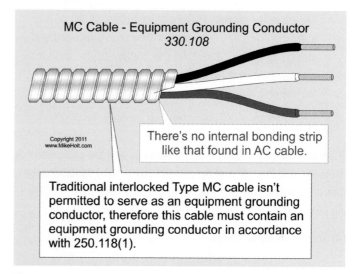

Figure 330–7

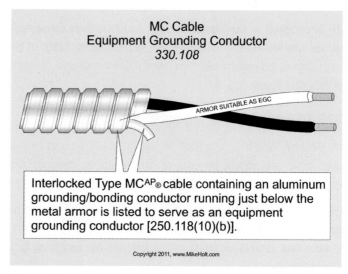

Figure 330–8

ARTICLE 338

Service-Entrance Cable (Types SE and USE)

IINTRODUCTION TO ARTICLE 338—SERVICE-ENTRANCE CABLE (TYPES SE AND USE)

Service-entrance cable is a single conductor or multiconductor assembly with or without an overall moisture-resistant covering. This cable is used primarily for services not over 600V, but can also be used for feeders and branch circuits when the limitations of this article are observed.

PART I. GENERAL

338.1 Scope. Article 338 covers the use, installation, and construction specifications of service-entrance cable, Types SE and USE.

338.2 Definitions.

Service-Entrance Cable. Service-entrance cable is a single or multiconductor assembly, with or without an overall covering, used primarily for services not over 600V.

Type SE. SE and SER cables have a flame-retardant, moisture-resistant covering and are permitted only in aboveground installations. These cables are permitted for branch circuits or feeders when installed in accordance with 338.10(B).

> **Author's Comment:** SER cable is SE cable with an insulated grounded, resulting in three insulated conductors with an uninsulated equipment grounding conductor. SER cable is round, while 2-wire SE cable is flat.

Type USE. USE cable is identified as a wiring method permitted for underground use; its covering is moisture resistant, but not flame retardant.

> **Author's Comment:** USE cable isn't permitted to be installed indoors [338.10(B)], except single-conductor USE dual rated as RHH/RHW.

PART II. INSTALLATION

338.10 Uses Permitted.

(A) Service-Entrance Conductors. Service-entrance cable used as service-entrance conductors must be installed in accordance with Article 230.

(B) Branch Circuits or Feeders.

(1) Insulated Conductor. Type SE service-entrance cable is permitted for branch circuits and feeders where the circuit conductors are insulated.

(2) Uninsulated Conductor. SE cable is permitted for branch circuits and feeders if the insulated conductors are used for circuit wiring, and the uninsulated conductor is only used for equipment grounding purposes.

(3) Temperature Limitations. SE cable must not be subjected to conductor temperatures exceeding its insulation rating.

(4) Installation Methods for Branch Circuits and Feeders. SE cable used for branch circuits or feeders must comply with (a) and (b).

(a) Interior Installations. SE cable used for interior branch circuit or feeder wiring must be installed in accordance with the same requirements as Type NM Cable—Article 334, excluding 334.80.

The maximum conductor temperature rating can be used [310.15(B)(2)] for ampacity adjustment and correction purposes, but when installed in thermal insulation the final corrected ampacity must not exceed that for a 60°C rated conductor.

⚠ **CAUTION:** *Underground service-entrance cable (USE) must not be used for interior wiring because it may not have flame-retardant insulation. It is permitted in interior wiring when listed with a building wire type such as RHW.*

338.12 Uses Not Permitted.

(A) Service-Entrance Cable. SE cable isn't permitted under the following conditions or locations:

(1) If subject to physical damage unless protected in accordance with 230.50(A).

(2) Underground with or without a raceway.

(B) Underground Service-Entrance Cable. USE cable isn't permitted:

(1) For interior wiring.

(2) Above ground, except where protected against physical damage in accordance with 300.5(D).

338.24 Bends. Bends in cable must be made so the protective coverings of the cable aren't damaged, and the radius of the curve of the inner edge is at least five times the diameter of the cable.

ARTICLE 342

Intermediate Metal Conduit (Type IMC)

INTRODUCTION TO ARTICLE 342—INTERMEDIATE METAL CONDUIT (TYPE IMC)

Intermediate metal conduit (IMC) is a circular metal raceway with an outside diameter equal to that of rigid metal conduit. The wall thickness of intermediate metal conduit is less than that of rigid metal conduit (RMC), so it has a greater interior cross-sectional area for containing conductors. Intermediate metal conduit is lighter and less expensive than rigid metal conduit, but it can be used in all of the same locations as rigid metal conduit. Intermediate metal conduit also uses a different steel alloy that makes it stronger than rigid metal conduit, even though the walls are thinner. Intermediate metal conduit is manufactured in both galvanized steel and aluminum; the steel type is much more common.

PART I. GENERAL

342.1 Scope.
Article 342 covers the use, installation, and construction specifications of intermediate metal conduit and associated fittings.

342.2 Definition.

Intermediate Metal Conduit (Type IMC). A listed steel raceway of circular cross section that can be threaded with integral or associated couplings. It's listed for the installation of electrical conductors, and is used with listed fittings to provide electrical continuity.

> **Author's Comment:** The type of steel from which intermediate metal conduit is manufactured, the process by which it's made, and the corrosion protection applied are all equal, or superior, to that of rigid metal conduit.

342.6 Listing Requirements.
Intermediate metal conduit and its associated fittings, such as elbows and couplings, must be listed.

PART II. INSTALLATION

342.10 Uses Permitted.

(A) All Atmospheric Conditions and Occupancies. Intermediate metal conduit is permitted in all atmospheric conditions and occupancies.

(B) Corrosion Environments. Intermediate metal conduit, elbows, couplings, and fittings can be installed in concrete, in direct contact with the earth, or in areas subject to severe corrosive influences if provided with corrosion protection and judged suitable for the condition in accordance with 300.6.

(C) Cinder Fill. IMC can be installed in or under cinder fill subject to permanent moisture when protected on all sides by 2 in. of non-cinder concrete; where the conduit isn't less than 18 in. under the fill; or where protected by corrosion protection judged suitable for the condition.

(D) Wet Locations. Support fittings, such as screws, straps, and so forth, installed in a wet location must be made of corrosion-resistant material, or be protected by corrosion-resistant coatings in accordance with 300.6.

> ⚠️ **CAUTION:** Supplementary coatings for corrosion protection haven't been investigated by a product testing and listing agency and these coatings are known to cause cancer in laboratory animals. There's a documented case where an electrician was taken to the hospital for lead poisoning after using a supplemental coating product (asphalted paint) in a poorly ventilated area. As with all products, be sure to read and follow all product instructions, including material data safety sheets, particularly when petroleum-based chemicals (volatile organic compounds) may be in the material.

342.14 Dissimilar Metals. If practical, contact with dissimilar metals should be avoided to prevent the deterioration of the metal because of galvanic action. Aluminum fittings and enclosures, however, are permitted with steel intermediate metal conduit.

342.20 Trade Size.

(A) Minimum. Intermediate metal conduit smaller than trade size ½ must not be used.

(B) Maximum. Intermediate metal conduit larger than trade size 4 must not be used.

342.22 Number of Conductors. The number of conductors in IMC isn't permitted to exceed the percentage fill specified in Table 1, Chapter 9. Raceways must be large enough to permit the installation and removal of conductors without damaging the conductor insulation. When all conductors in a raceway are the same size and insulation, the number of conductors permitted can be found in Annex C for the raceway type.

> **Question:** How many 10 THHN conductors can be installed in trade size 1 IMC?
>
> (a) 12   (b) 14   (c) 16   (d) 18
>
> **Answer:** (d) 18 conductors [Annex C, Table C4]

Author's Comment: See 300.17 for additional examples on how to size raceways when conductors aren't all the same size.

Cables can be installed in intermediate metal conduit, as long as the number of cables doesn't exceed the allowable percentage fill specified in Table 1, Chapter 9.

342.24 Bends. Raceway bends must not be made in any manner that would damage the raceway, or significantly change its internal diameter (no kinks). The radius of the curve of the inner edge of any field bend must not be less than shown in Table 2, Chapter 9.

Author's Comment: This is usually not a problem, because benders are made to comply with this table. However, when using a hickey bender (short-radius bender), be careful not to over-bend the raceway.

342.26 Number of Bends (360°). To reduce the stress and friction on conductor insulation, the maximum number of bends (including offsets) between pull points must not exceed 360°. Figure 342–1

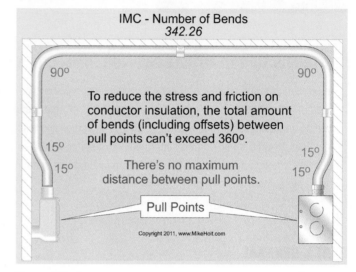

Figure 342–1

Author's Comment: There's no maximum distance between pull boxes because this is a design issue, not a safety issue.

342.28 Reaming. When the raceway is cut in the field, reaming is required to remove the burrs and rough edges.

Author's Comment: It's a commonly accepted practice to ream small raceways with a screwdriver or the backside of pliers. However, when the raceway is cut with a three-wheel pipe cutter, a reaming tool is required to remove the sharp edge of the indented raceway. When conduits are threaded in the field, the threads must be coated with an electrically conductive, corrosion-resistant compound approved by the authority having jurisdiction, in accordance with 300.6(A).

342.30 Securing and Supporting. Intermediate metal conduit must be installed as a complete system in accordance with 300.18 [300.10 and 300.12], and it must be securely fastened in place and supported in accordance with (A) and (B).

(A) Securely Fastened. IMC must be secured in accordance with one of the following:

(1) Fastened within 3 ft of each outlet box, junction box, device box, cabinet, conduit body, or other conduit termination. **Figure 342–2**

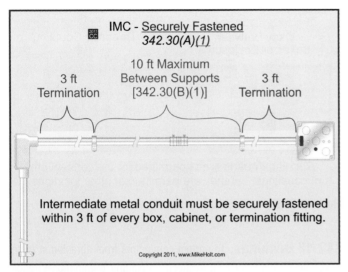

Figure 342–2

Author's Comment: Fastening is required within 3 ft of terminations, not within 3 ft of each coupling.

(2) When structural members don't permit the raceway to be secured within 3 ft of a box or termination fitting, the raceway must be secured within 5 ft of the termination. **Figure 342–3**

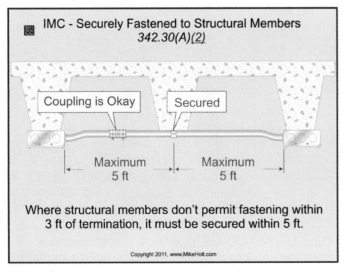

Figure 342–3

(3) Conduits aren't required to be securely fastened within 3 ft of the service head for an above-the-roof termination of a mast.

(B) Supports.

(1) General. Intermediate metal conduit must generally be supported at intervals not exceeding 10 ft.

(2) Straight Horizontal Runs. Straight horizontal runs made with threaded couplings can be supported in accordance with the distances listed in Table 344.30(B)(2). **Figure 342–4**

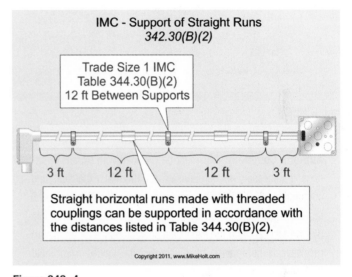

Figure 342–4

Table 344.30(B)(2)	
Trade Size	Support Spacing
½ – ¾	10 ft
1	12 ft
1¼ – 1½	14 ft
2 – 2½	16 ft
3 and larger	20 ft

(3) Vertical Risers. Exposed vertical risers for fixed equipment can be supported at intervals not exceeding 20 ft, if the conduit is made up with threaded couplings, firmly supported, securely fastened at the top and bottom of the riser, and if no other means of support is available. **Figure 342–5**

(4) Horizontal Runs. Conduits installed horizontally in bored or punched holes in wood or metal framing members, or notches in wooden members are considered supported, but the raceway must be secured within 3 ft of termination.

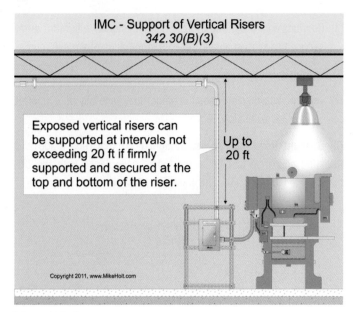

Figure 342–5

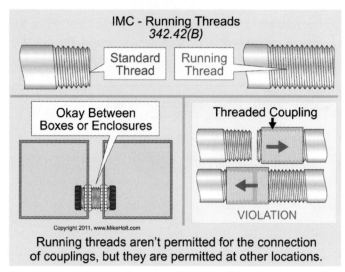

Running threads aren't permitted for the connection of couplings, but they are permitted at other locations.

Figure 342–6

Author's Comment: IMC must be provided with expansion fittings if necessary to compensate for thermal expansion and contraction [300.7(B)]. The expansion characteristics for metal raceways are determined by multiplying the values from Table 352.44 by 0.20, and the expansion characteristics for aluminum raceways is determined by multiplying the values from Table 352.44 by 0.40 [300.7 Note].

342.42 Couplings and Connectors.

(A) Installation. Threadless couplings and connectors must be made up tight to maintain an effective ground-fault current path to safely conduct fault current in accordance with 250.4(A)(5), 250.96(A), and 300.10.

> **Author's Comment:** Loose locknuts have been found to burn clear before a fault was cleared because loose termination fittings increase the impedance of the fault current path.

If buried in masonry or concrete, threadless fittings must be the concrete-tight type. If installed in wet locations, fittings must be listed for use in wet locations in accordance with 314.15(A).

Threadless couplings and connectors must not be used on threaded conduit ends unless listed for the purpose.

(B) Running Threads. Running threads aren't permitted for the connection of couplings, but they're permitted at other locations. **Figure 342–6**

342.46 Bushings.
To protect conductors from abrasion, a metal or plastic bushing must be installed on conduit termination threads, regardless of conductor size, unless the box, fitting, or enclosure is <u>designed to provide this</u> protection.

> **Note:** Conductors 4 AWG and larger that enter an enclosure must be protected from abrasion, during and after installation, by a fitting that provides a smooth, rounded, insulating surface, such as an insulating bushing, unless the design of the box, fitting, or enclosure provides equivalent protection, in accordance with 300.4(G). **Figure 342–7**

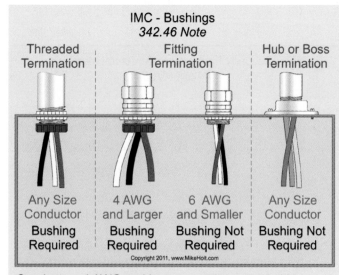

Conductors 4 AWG and larger must be protected by a fitting that provides a smooth, rounded, insulating surface, such as an insulating bushing [300.4(G)].

Figure 342–7

ARTICLE 344

Rigid Metal Conduit (Type RMC)

INTRODUCTION TO ARTICLE 344—RIGID METAL CONDUIT (TYPE RMC)

Rigid metal conduit, commonly called "rigid," has long been the standard raceway for providing protection from physical impact and from difficult environments. The outside diameter of rigid metal conduit is the same as intermediate metal conduit. However, the wall thickness of rigid metal conduit is greater than intermediate metal conduit; therefore it has a smaller interior cross-sectional area. Rigid metal conduit is heavier and more expensive than intermediate metal conduit, and it can be used in any location. Rigid metal conduit is manufactured in both galvanized steel and aluminum; the steel type is much more common.

PART I. GENERAL

344.1 Scope. Article 344 covers the use, installation, and construction specifications of rigid metal conduit and associated fittings.

344.2 Definition.

Rigid Metal Conduit (Type RMC). A listed metal raceway of circular cross section with integral or associated couplings, listed for the installation of electrical conductors, and used with listed fittings to provide electrical continuity.

> **Author's Comment:** When the mechanical and physical characteristics of rigid metal conduit are desired and a corrosive environment is anticipated, a PVC-coated raceway system is commonly used. This type of raceway is frequently used in the petrochemical industry. The common trade name of this coated raceway is "Plasti-bond®," and it's commonly referred to as "Rob Roy conduit." The benefits of the improved corrosion protection can be achieved only when the system is properly installed. Joints must be sealed in accordance with the manufacturer's instructions, and the coating must not be damaged with tools such as benders, pliers, and pipe wrenches. Couplings are available with an extended skirt that can be properly sealed after installation.

344.6 Listing Requirements. Rigid metal conduit, elbows, couplings, and associated fittings must be listed.

PART II. INSTALLATION

344.10 Uses Permitted.

(A) Atmospheric Conditions and Occupancies.

(1) Galvanized Steel and Stainless Steel. Galvanized steel and stainless steel rigid metal conduit is permitted in all atmospheric conditions and occupancies.

(2) Red Brass. Red brass rigid metal conduit is permitted for direct burial and swimming pool applications.

(3) Aluminum. Rigid aluminum conduit is permitted if judged suitable for the environment.

(B) Corrosion Environments.

(1) Galvanized Steel and Stainless Steel. Rigid metal conduit fittings, elbows, and couplings can be installed in concrete, in direct contact with the earth, or in areas subject to severe corrosive influences judged suitable for the condition.

(2) Aluminum. Rigid aluminum conduit must be provided with supplementary corrosion protection approved by the authority having jurisdiction if encased in concrete or in direct contact with the earth.

(C) Cinder Fill. Galvanized steel, stainless steel, and red brass RMC is permitted in or under cinder fill subject to permanent moisture, when protected on all sides by a layer of noncinder concrete not less than 2 in. thick; where the conduit isn't less than 18 in. under the fill; or where protected by corrosion protection judged suitable for the condition.

(D) Wet Locations. Support fittings, such as screws, straps, and so forth, installed in a wet location must be made of corrosion-resistant material or protected by corrosion-resistant coatings in accordance with 300.6.

> ⚠️ **CAUTION:** *Supplementary coatings (asphalted paint) for corrosion protection haven't been investigated by a product testing and listing agency and these coatings are known to cause cancer in laboratory animals.*

344.14 Dissimilar Metals. If practical, contact with dissimilar metals should be avoided to prevent the deterioration of the metal because of galvanic action. Aluminum fittings and enclosures are permitted, however, with rigid metal conduit.

344.20 Trade Size.

(A) Minimum. Rigid metal conduit smaller than trade size ½ must not be used.

(B) Maximum. Rigid metal conduit larger than trade size 6 must not be used.

344.22 Number of Conductors. Raceways must be large enough to permit the installation and removal of conductors without damaging the conductors' insulation. When all conductors in a raceway are the same size and insulation, the number of conductors permitted can be found in Annex C for the raceway type.

> *Question: How many 8 THHN conductors can be installed in trade size 1½ RMC?*
>
> *(a) 16   (b) 18   (c) 20   (d) 22*
>
> *Answer: 22 conductors [Annex C, Table C8]*

Author's Comment: See 300.17 for additional examples on how to size raceways when conductors aren't all the same size.

Cables can be installed in rigid metal conduit, as long as the number of cables doesn't exceed the allowable percentage fill specified in Table 1, Chapter 9.

344.24 Bends. Raceway bends must not be made in any manner that would damage the raceway, or significantly change its internal diameter (no kinks). The radius of the curve of the inner edge of any field bend must not be less than shown in Table 2, Chapter 9.

Author's Comment: This is usually not a problem because benders are made to comply with this table. However, when using a hickey bender (short-radius bender), be careful not to over-bend the raceway.

344.26 Number of Bends (360°). To reduce the stress and friction on conductor insulation, the maximum number of bends (including offsets) between pull points must not exceed 360°. Figure 344–1

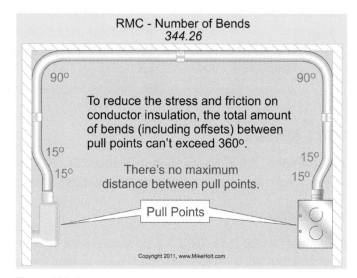

Figure 344–1

Author's Comment: There's no maximum distance between pull boxes because this is a design issue, not a safety issue.

344.28 Reaming. When the raceway is cut in the field, reaming is required to remove the burrs and rough edges.

Author's Comment: It's a commonly accepted practice to ream small raceways with a screwdriver or the backside of pliers. However, when the raceway is cut with a three-wheel pipe cutter, a reaming tool is required to remove the sharp edge of the indented raceway. When conduit is threaded in the field, the threads must be coated with an electrically conductive, corrosion-resistant compound approved by the authority having jurisdiction, in accordance with 300.6(A).

344.30 Securing and Supporting. Rigid metal conduit must be installed as a complete system in accordance with 300.18 [300.10 and 300.12], and it must be securely fastened in place and supported in accordance with (A) and (B).

(A) Securely Fastened. RMC must be secured in accordance with one of the following: Figure 344–2

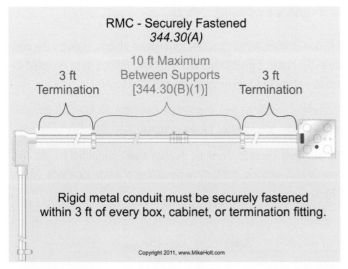

Figure 344–2

(1) Fastened within 3 ft of each outlet box, junction box, device box, cabinet, conduit body, or other conduit termination.

Author's Comment: Fastening is required within 3 ft of terminations, not within 3 ft of each coupling.

(2) When structural members don't permit the raceway to be secured within 3 ft of a box or termination fitting, the raceway must be secured within 5 ft of the termination. Figure 344–3

(3) Conduits aren't required to be securely fastened within 3 ft of the service head for an above-the-roof termination of a mast.

(B) Supports.

(1) General. Rigid metal conduit must be supported at intervals not exceeding 10 ft.

(2) Straight Horizontal Runs. Straight horizontal runs made with threaded couplings can be supported in accordance with the distances listed in Table 344.30(B)(2). Figure 344–4

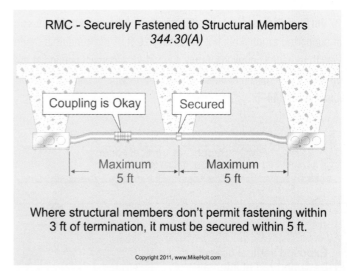

Figure 344–3

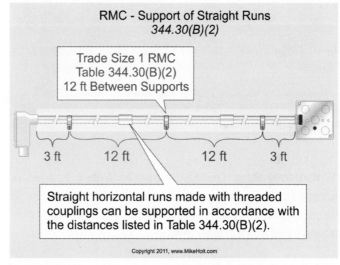

Figure 344–4

Table 344.30(B)(2)	
Trade Size	**Support Spacing**
½–¾	10 ft
1	12 ft
1¼–1½	14 ft
2–2½	16 ft
3 and larger	20 ft

(3) Vertical Risers. Exposed vertical risers for fixed equipment can be supported at intervals not exceeding 20 ft, if the conduit is made up with threaded couplings, firmly supported, securely fastened at the top and bottom of the riser, and if no other means of support is available. **Figure 344–5**

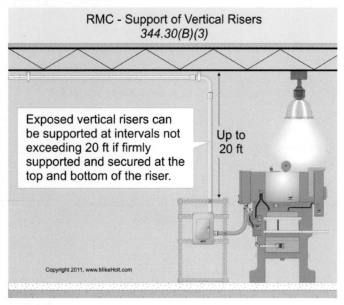

Figure 344–5

(4) Horizontal Runs. Conduits installed horizontally in bored or punched holes in wood or metal framing members, or notches in wooden members, are considered supported, but the raceway must be secured within 3 ft of termination.

> **Author's Comment:** Rigid metal conduit must be provided with expansion fittings if necessary to compensate for thermal expansion and contraction [300.7(B)]. The expansion characteristics for metal raceways are determined by multiplying the values from Table 352.44 by 0.20, and the expansion characteristics for aluminum raceways is determined by multiplying the values from Table 352.44 by 0.40 [300.7 Note].

344.42 Couplings and Connectors.

(A) Installation. Threadless couplings and connectors must be made up tight to maintain an effective ground-fault current path to safely conduct fault current in accordance with 250.4(A)(5), 250.96(A), and 300.10.

> **Author's Comment:** Loose locknuts have been found to burn clear before a fault was cleared because loose connections increase the impedance of the fault current path.

If buried in masonry or concrete, threadless fittings must be the concrete-tight type. If installed in wet locations, fittings must be listed for use in wet locations, in accordance with 314.15(A).

Threadless couplings and connectors must not be used on threaded conduit ends, unless listed for the purpose.

(B) Running Threads. Running threads aren't permitted for the connection of couplings, but they're permitted at other locations. **Figure 344–6**

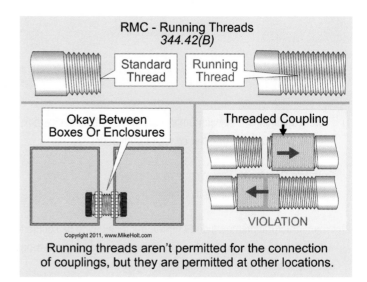

Running threads aren't permitted for the connection of couplings, but they are permitted at other locations.

Figure 344–6

344.46 Bushings. To protect conductors from abrasion, a metal or plastic bushing must be installed on conduit threads at terminations, regardless of conductor size, unless the box, fitting, or enclosure is <u>designed to provide this</u> protection.

> **Note:** Conductors 4 AWG and larger that enter an enclosure must be protected from abrasion, during and after installation, by a fitting that provides a smooth, rounded, insulating surface, such as an insulating bushing, unless the design of the box, fitting, or enclosure provides equivalent protection, in accordance with 300.4(G). **Figure 344–7**

PART III. CONSTRUCTION SPECIFICATIONS

344.130 Standard Lengths. The standard length of RMC is 10 ft including an attached coupling, and each end must be threaded. Longer or shorter lengths with or without a coupling and threaded or unthreaded are permitted.

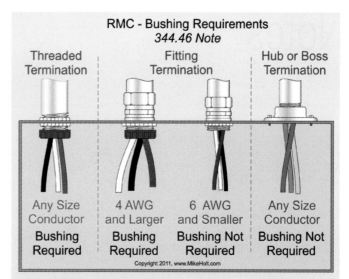

Conductors 4 AWG and larger must be protected by a fitting that provides a smooth, rounded, insulating surface, such as an insulating bushing [300.4(G)].

Figure 344–7

Notes

ARTICLE 348

Flexible Metal Conduit (Type FMC)

INTRODUCTION TO ARTICLE 348—FLEXIBLE METAL CONDUIT (TYPE FMC)

Flexible metal conduit (FMC), commonly called "Greenfield" or "flex," is a raceway of an interlocked metal strip of either steel or aluminum. It's primarily used for the final 6 ft or less of raceways between a more rigid raceway system and equipment that moves, shakes, or vibrates. Examples of such equipment include pump motors and industrial machinery.

PART I. GENERAL

348.1 Scope. Article 348 covers the use, installation, and construction specifications for flexible metal conduit and associated fittings.

348.2 Definition.

Flexible Metal Conduit (Type FMC). A raceway of circular cross section made of a helically wound, formed, interlocked metal strip.

348.6 Listing Requirements. Flexible metal conduit and associated fittings must be listed.

PART II. INSTALLATION

348.10 Uses Permitted. Flexible metal conduit is permitted exposed or concealed.

348.12 Uses Not Permitted.

(1) In wet locations.

(2) In hoistways, other than as permitted in 620.21(A)(1).

(3) In storage battery rooms.

(4) In any hazardous (classified) location, except as permitted by 501.10(B).

(5) Exposed to material having a deteriorating effect on the installed conductors.

(6) Underground or embedded in poured concrete.

(7) If subject to physical damage.

348.22 Number of Conductors.

Trade Size ½ and Larger. Flexible metal conduit must be large enough to permit the installation and removal of conductors without damaging the conductors' insulation. When all conductors in a raceway are the same size and insulation, the number of conductors permitted can be found in Annex C for the raceway type.

> **Question:** How many 6 THHN conductors can be installed in trade size 1 flexible metal conduit?
>
> (a) 2   (b) 4   (c) 6   (d) 8
>
> **Answer:** (c) 6 conductors [Annex C, Table C3]

Author's Comment: See 300.17 for additional examples on how to size raceways when conductors aren't all the same size.

Trade Size ⅜. The number and size of conductors in trade size ⅜ flexible metal conduit must comply with Table 348.22.

> **Question:** How many 12 THHN conductors can be installed in trade size ⅜ flexible metal conduit that uses outside fittings?
>
> (a) 1   (b) 3   (c) 5   (d) 7
>
> **Answer:** (b) 3 conductors [Table 348.22]

One insulated, covered, or bare equipment grounding conductor of the same size is permitted with the circuit conductors. See the "*" note at the bottom of Table 348.22.

Cables can be installed in flexible metal conduit as long as the number of cables doesn't exceed the allowable percentage fill specified in Table 1, Chapter 9.

348.24 Bends. Bends must be made so that the conduit won't be damaged, and its internal diameter won't be effectively reduced. The radius of the curve of the inner edge of any field bend must not be less than shown in Table 2, Chapter 9 using the column "Other Bends."

348.26 Number of Bends (360°). To reduce the stress and friction on conductor insulation, the maximum number of bends (including offsets) between pull points must not exceed 360°.

Author's Comment: There's no maximum distance between pull boxes because this is a design issue, not a safety issue.

348.28 Trimming. The cut ends of flexible metal conduit must be trimmed to remove the rough edges, but this isn't necessary if fittings are threaded into the convolutions.

348.30 Securing and Supporting.

(A) Securely Fastened. Flexible metal conduit must be securely fastened by a means approved by the authority having jurisdiction within 1 ft of termination, and it must be secured and supported at intervals not exceeding 4½ ft. **Figure 348–1**

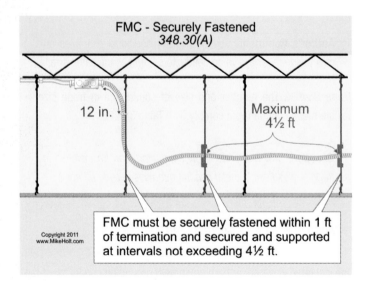

Figure 348–1

Ex 1: Flexible metal conduit isn't required to be securely fastened or supported where fished between access points through concealed spaces and supporting is impracticable.

Ex 2: If flexibility is necessary after installation, unsecured lengths from the last point the raceway is securely fastened must not exceed:

(1) 3 ft for trade sizes ½ through 1¼

(2) 4 ft for trade sizes 1½ through 2

(3) 5 ft for trade sizes 2½ and larger

(B) Horizontal Runs. Flexible metal conduit installed horizontally in bored or punched holes in wood or metal framing members, or notches in wooden members, is considered supported, but the raceway must be secured within 1 ft of terminations. **Figure 348–2**

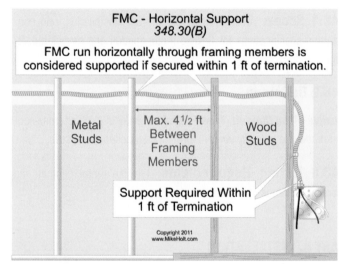

Figure 348–2

348.42 Fittings. Angle connectors must not be concealed.

348.60 Grounding and Bonding. If flexibility is necessary to minimize the transmission of vibration from equipment or to provide flexibility for equipment that requires movement after installation, an equipment grounding conductor of the wire type must be installed with the circuit conductors in accordance with 250.118(5), based on the rating of the circuit overcurrent device in accordance with 250.122. **Figure 348–3**

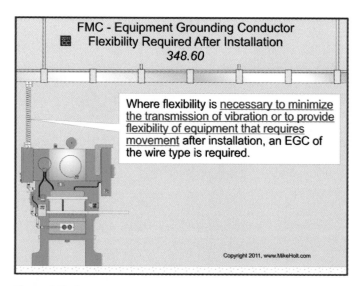

FMC - Equipment Grounding Conductor
Flexibility Required After Installation
348.60

Where flexibility is <u>necessary to minimize the transmission of vibration or to provide flexibility of equipment that requires movement</u> after installation, an EGC of the wire type is required.

Copyright 2011, www.MikeHolt.com

Figure 348–3

If flexibility isn't <u>necessary</u> after installation, <u>and vibration isn't a concern,</u> the metal armor of flexible metal conduit can serve as an equipment grounding conductor if the circuit conductors contained in the raceway are protected by an overcurrent device rated 20A or less, and the combined length of the flexible metal raceway in the same ground-fault return path doesn't exceed 6 ft [250.118(5)].

If an equipment bonding jumper is installed outside of a raceway, the length of the equipment bonding jumper must not exceed 6 ft, and it must be routed with the raceway or enclosure in accordance with 250.102(E)(2).

Notes

ARTICLE 350

Liquidtight Flexible Metal Conduit (Type LFMC)

INTRODUCTION TO ARTICLE 350—LIQUIDTIGHT FLEXIBLE METAL CONDUIT (TYPE LFMC)

Liquidtight flexible metal conduit (LFMC), with its associated connectors and fittings, is a flexible raceway commonly used for connections to equipment that vibrate or are required to move occasionally. Liquidtight flexible metal conduit is commonly called "Sealtight®" or "liquid-tight." Liquidtight flexible metal conduit is of similar construction to flexible metal conduit, but it also has an outer liquidtight thermoplastic covering. It has the same primary purpose as flexible metal conduit, but it also provides protection from moisture and some corrosive effects.

PART I. GENERAL

350.1 Scope.
Article 350 covers the use, installation, and construction specifications of liquidtight flexible metal conduit and associated fittings.

350.2 Definition.

Liquidtight Flexible Metal Conduit (Type LFMC). A raceway of circular cross section, having an outer liquidtight, nonmetallic, sunlight-resistant jacket over an inner flexible metal core, with associated connectors and fittings for the installation of electric conductors.

350.6 Listing Requirements.
Liquidtight flexible metal conduit and its associated fittings must be listed. **Figure 350–1**

LFMC - Listing Required
350.6

Listed Liquidtight

LFMC and associated fittings
must be listed for the purpose.

Copyright 2011, www.MikeHolt.com

Figure 350–1

PART II. INSTALLATION

350.10 Uses Permitted.

(A) Permitted Use. Listed liquidtight flexible metal conduit is permitted, either exposed or concealed, at any of the following locations:

(1) If flexibility or protection from liquids, vapors, or solids is required.

(2) In hazardous (classified) locations, as permitted in 501.10(B), 502.10(A)(2), 502.10(B)(2), or 503.10(A)(2).

(3) For direct burial, if listed and marked for this purpose.

350.12 Uses Not Permitted.

(1) If subject to physical damage.

(2) If the combination of the ambient and conductor operating temperatures exceeds the rating of the raceway.

350.20 Trade Size.

(A) Minimum. Liquidtight flexible metal conduit smaller than trade size ½ must not be used.

Ex: Liquidtight flexible metal conduit can be smaller than trade size ½ if installed in accordance with 348.20(A).

> **Author's Comment:** According to 348.20(A), LFMC smaller than trade size ½ is permitted for the following:
>
> (1) For enclosing the leads of motors.
> (2) Not exceeding 6 ft in length:
>   a. For utilization equipment,
>   b. As part of a listed assembly, or
>   c. For tap connections to luminaires as permitted by 410.117(C).
> (3) In manufactured wiring systems, 604.6(A).
> (4) In hoistways, 620.21(A)(1).
> (5) As part of a listed assembly to connect wired luminaire sections, 410.137(C).

(B) Maximum. Liquidtight flexible metal conduit larger than trade size 4 must not be used.

350.22 Number of Conductors.

(A) Raceway Trade Size ½ and Larger. Raceways must be large enough to permit the installation and removal of conductors without damaging the insulation. When all conductors in a raceway are the same size and insulation, the number of conductors permitted can be found in Annex C for the raceway type.

> *Question: How many 6 THHN conductors can be installed in trade size 1 LFMC?* **Figure 350–2**
>
> *(a) 3   (b) 5   (c) 7   (d) 9*
>
> *Answer: (c) 7 conductors [Annex C, Table C.7]*

> **Author's Comment:** See 300.17 for additional examples on how to size raceways when conductors aren't all the same size.

Cables can be installed in liquidtight flexible metal conduit as long as the number of cables doesn't exceed the allowable percentage fill specified in Table 1, Chapter 9.

(B) Raceway Trade Size 3⁄8. The number and size of conductors in a trade size 3⁄8 liquidtight flexible metal conduit must comply with Table 348.22.

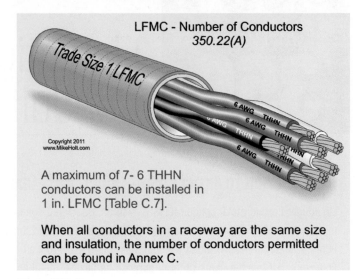

LFMC - Number of Conductors
350.22(A)

Trade Size 1 LFMC

6 AWG THHN

Copyright 2011
www.MikeHolt.com

A maximum of 7- 6 THHN conductors can be installed in 1 in. LFMC [Table C.7].

When all conductors in a raceway are the same size and insulation, the number of conductors permitted can be found in Annex C.

Figure 350–2

> *Question: How many 12 THHN conductors can be installed in trade size 3⁄8 LFMC that uses outside fittings?*
>
> *(a) 1   (b) 3   (c) 5   (d) 7*
>
> *Answer: (b) 3 conductors [Table 348.22]*

One insulated, covered, or bare equipment grounding conductor of the same size is permitted with the circuit conductors. See the "*" note at the bottom of Table 348.22.

350.24 Bends. Bends must be made so that the conduit won't be damaged and the internal diameter of the conduit won't be effectively reduced. The radius of the curve of the inner edge of any field bend must not be less than shown in Table 2, Chapter 9 using the column "Other Bends."

350.26 Number of Bends (360°). To reduce the stress and friction on conductor insulation, the maximum number of bends (including offsets) between pull points must not exceed 360°.

> **Author's Comment:** There's no maximum distance between pull boxes because this is a design issue, not a safety issue.

350.30 Securing and Supporting. Liquidtight flexible metal conduit must be securely fastened in place and supported in accordance with (A) and (B).

(A) Securely Fastened. Liquidtight flexible metal conduit must be securely fastened by a means approved by the authority having jurisdiction within 1 ft of termination, and must be secured and supported at intervals not exceeding 4½ ft. **Figure 350–3**

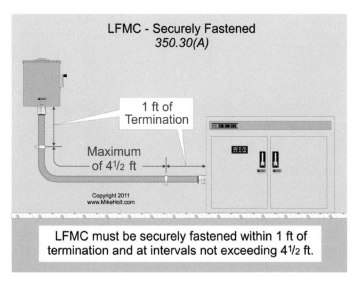

Figure 350–3

Ex 1: Liquidtight flexible metal conduit isn't required to be securely fastened or supported where fished between access points through concealed spaces and supporting is <u>impracticable.</u>

Ex 2: If flexibility is necessary after installation, unsecured lengths <u>from the last point where the raceway is securely fastened</u> must not exceed:

    (1) 3 ft for trade sizes ½ through 1¼
    (2) 4 ft for trade sizes 1½ through 2
    (3) 5 ft for trade sizes 2½ and larger

(B) Horizontal Runs. Liquidtight flexible metal conduit installed horizontally in bored or punched holes in wood or metal framing members, or notches in wooden members, is considered supported, but the raceway must be secured within 1 ft of termination.

350.42 Fittings. Angle connectors must not be <u>concealed.</u>

350.60 Grounding and Bonding. If flexibility is <u>necessary to minimize the transmission of vibration from equipment or to provide flexibility for equipment that requires movement</u> after installation, an equipment grounding conductor of the wire type must be installed with the circuit conductors in accordance with 250.118(6), based on the rating of the circuit overcurrent device in accordance with 250.122. **Figure 350–4**

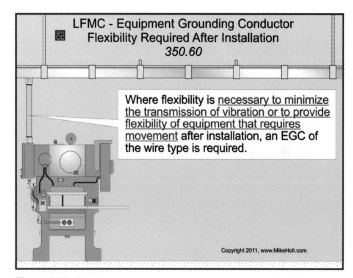

Figure 350–4

If flexibility isn't <u>necessary</u> after installation, <u>and vibration isn't a concern</u>, the metal armor of flexible metal conduit can serve as an equipment grounding conductor if the circuit conductors contained in the raceway are protected by an overcurrent device rated 20A or less, and the combined length of the flexible metal raceway in the same ground-fault return path doesn't exceed 6 ft [250.118(6)].

If an equipment bonding jumper is installed outside of a raceway, the length of the equipment bonding jumper must not exceed 6 ft, and it must be routed with the raceway or enclosure in accordance with 250.102(E)(2).

Notes

ARTICLE 352

Rigid Polyvinyl Chloride Conduit (TYPE PVC)

INTRODUCTION TO ARTICLE 352—RIGID POLYVINYL CHLORIDE CONDUIT (TYPE PVC)

Rigid polyvinyl chloride conduit (PVC) is a rigid nonmetallic conduit that provides many of the advantages of rigid metal conduit, while allowing installation in areas that are wet or corrosive. It's an inexpensive raceway, and easily installed. It's lightweight, easily cut, glued together, and relatively strong. However, conduits manufactured from polyvinyl chloride (PVC) are brittle when cold, and they sag when hot. This type of conduit is commonly used as an underground raceway because of its low cost, ease of installation, and resistance to corrosion and decay.

PART I. GENERAL

352.1 Scope. Article 352 covers the use, installation, and construction specifications of PVC conduit and associated fittings.

352.2 Definition.

Rigid Polyvinyl Chloride Conduit (PVC). A rigid nonmetallic <u>conduit</u> of circular cross section with integral or associated couplings, listed for the installation of electrical conductors and cables. **Figure 352–1**

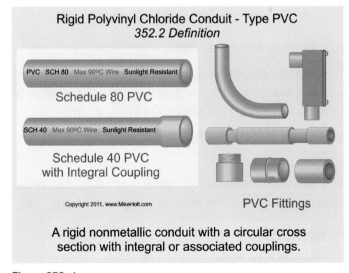

Figure 352–1

PART II. INSTALLATION

352.10 Uses Permitted.

> **Note:** In extreme cold, PVC conduit can become brittle, and is more susceptible to physical damage.

(A) Concealed. PVC conduit can be concealed within walls, floors, or ceilings, directly buried or embedded in concrete in buildings of any height.

(B) Corrosive Influences. PVC conduit is permitted in areas subject to severe corrosion for which the material is specifically approved by the authority having jurisdiction.

> **Author's Comment:** If subject to exposure to chemical solvents, vapors, splashing, or immersion, materials or coatings must either be inherently resistant to chemicals based upon their listing, or be identified for the specific chemical reagent [300.6(C)(2)].

(D) Wet Locations. PVC conduit is permitted in wet locations such as dairies, laundries, canneries, car washes, and other areas frequently washed or in outdoor locations. Support fittings such as straps, screws, and bolts must be made of corrosion-resistant materials, or must be protected with a corrosion-resistant coating, in accordance with 300.6(A).

(E) Dry and Damp Locations. PVC conduit is permitted in dry and damp locations, except where limited in 352.12.

(F) Exposed. Schedule 40 PVC conduit is permitted for exposed locations where not subject to physical damage. **Figure 352–2**

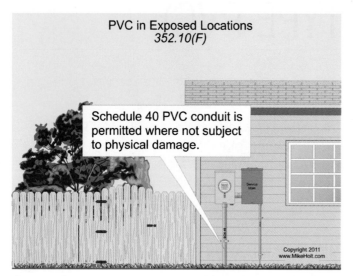

Figure 352–2

If PVC conduit is exposed to physical damage, the raceway must be identified for the application.

> **Note:** PVC Schedule 80 conduit is identified for use in areas subject to physical damage. **Figure 352–3**

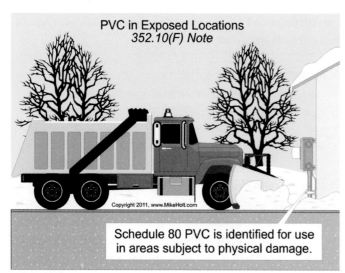

Figure 352–3

(G) Underground. PVC conduit installed underground must comply with the burial requirements of 300.5.

(H) Support of Conduit Bodies. PVC conduit is permitted to support nonmetallic conduit bodies that aren't larger than the largest trade size of an entering raceway. These conduit bodies can't support luminaires or other equipment, and aren't permitted to contain devices, other than splicing devices permitted by 110.14(B) and 314.16(C)(2).

(I) Insulation Temperature Limitations. Conductors rated at a temperature higher than the listed temperature rating of PVC conduit must not be operated at a temperature above the raceway's listed temperature rating. **Figure 352–4**

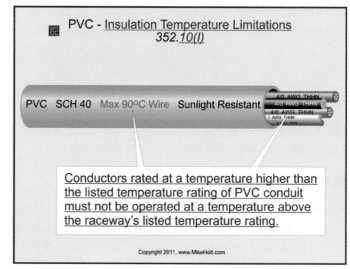

Figure 352–4

352.12 Uses Not Permitted.

(A) Hazardous (Classified) Locations. PVC conduit isn't permitted to be used in hazardous (classified) locations except as permitted by 501.10(A)(1)(a) Ex, 503.10(A), 504.20, 514.8 Ex 2, and 515.8.

(2) In Class I, Division 2 locations, except as permitted in 501.10(B) (7).

(B) Support of Luminaires. PVC conduit must not be used for the support of luminaires or other equipment not described in 352.10(H).

> **Author's Comment:** PVC conduit is permitted to support conduit bodies in accordance with 314.23(E) Ex.

(C) Physical Damage. Schedule 40 PVC conduit must not be installed if subject to physical damage, unless identified for the application.

Author's Comment: PVC Schedule 80 conduit is identified for use in areas subject to physical damage [352.10(F) Note].

(D) Ambient Temperature. PVC conduit must not be installed if the ambient temperature exceeds 50°C (122°F).

352.20 Trade Size.

(A) Minimum. PVC conduit smaller than trade size ½ must not be used.

(B) Maximum. PVC conduit larger than trade size 6 must not be used.

352.22 Number of Conductors. Raceways must be large enough to permit the installation and removal of conductors without damaging the conductors' insulation, and the number of conductors must not exceed that permitted by the percentage fill specified in Table 1, Chapter 9.

When all conductors in a raceway are the same size and insulation, the number of conductors permitted can be found in Annex C for the raceway type.

> *Question: How many 4/0 THHN conductors can be installed in trade size 2 Schedule 40 PVC?*
>
> *(a) 2 (b) 4 (c) 6 (d) 8*
>
> ***Answer:** (b) 4 conductors [Annex C, Table C10]*

Author's Comment: Schedule 80 PVC conduit has the same outside diameter as Schedule 40 PVC conduit, but the wall thickness of Schedule 80 PVC conduit is greater, which results in a reduced interior area for conductor fill.

> *Question: How many 4/0 THHN conductors can be installed in trade size 2 Schedule 80 PVC conduit?*
>
> *(a) 3   (b) 4   (c) 7 (d) 9*
>
> ***Answer:** (a) 3 conductors [Annex C, Table C9]*

Author's Comment: See 300.17 for additional examples on how to size raceways when conductors aren't all the same size.

Cables can be installed in PVC conduit, as long as the number of cables doesn't exceed the allowable percentage fill specified in Table 1, Chapter 9.

352.24 Bends. Raceway bends must not be made in any manner that would damage the raceway, or significantly change its internal diameter (no kinks). The radius of the curve of the inner edge of any field bend must not be less than shown in Table 2, Chapter 9.

Author's Comment: Be sure to use equipment designed for heating the nonmetallic raceway so it's pliable for bending (for example, a "hot box"). Don't use open-flame torches.

352.26 Number of Bends (360°). To reduce the stress and friction on conductor insulation, the maximum number of bends (including offsets) between pull points must not exceed 360°. **Figure 352–5**

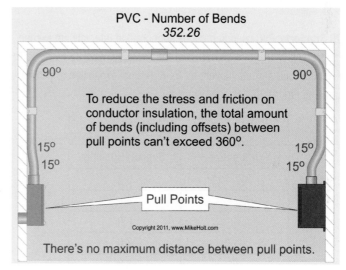

Figure 352–5

352.28 Trimming. The cut ends of PVC conduit must be trimmed (inside and out) to remove the burrs and rough edges.

Author's Comment: Trimming PVC conduit is very easy; most of the burrs will rub off with fingers, and a knife will smooth the rough edges.

352.30 Securing and Supporting. PVC conduit must be securely fastened and supported in accordance with (A) and (B).

(A) Secured. PVC conduit must be secured within 3 ft of every box, cabinet, or termination fitting, such as a conduit body. **Figure 352–6**

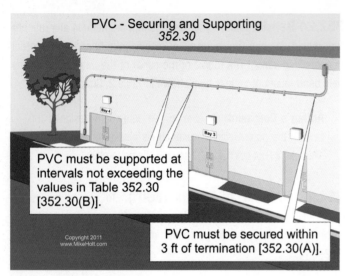

Figure 352–6

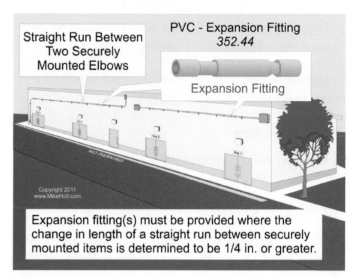

Figure 352–7

(B) Supports. PVC conduit must be supported at intervals not exceeding the values in Table 352.30, and the raceway must be fastened in a manner that permits movement from thermal expansion or contraction. See **Figure 352–6**.

Table 352.30	
Trade Size	Support Spacing
½–1	3 ft
1¼–2	5 ft
2½–3	6 ft
3½–5	7 ft
6	8 ft

PVC conduit installed horizontally in bored or punched holes in wood or metal framing members, or notches in wooden members, is considered supported, but the raceway must be secured within 3 ft of termination.

352.44 Expansion Fittings. If PVC conduit is installed in a straight run between securely mounted items, such as boxes, cabinets, elbows, or other conduit terminations, expansion fittings must be provided to compensate for thermal expansion and contraction of the raceway in accordance with Table 352.44, if the length change is determined to be ¼ in. or greater. **Figure 352–7**

Author's Comment: Table 352.44 in the *NEC* was created based on the following formula: **Figure 352–8**

Expansion/Contraction Inches =
Raceway Length/100 x [(Temp Change/100) x 4.00]

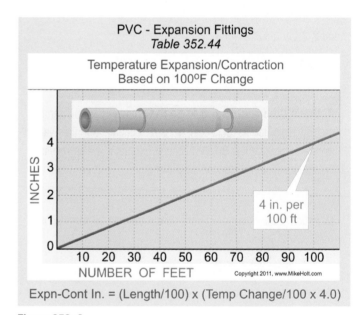

Expn-Cont In. = (Length/100) x (Temp Change/100 x 4.0)

Figure 352–8

Example: *How much will a 25 ft run of PVC conduit contract when it's located in an ambient temperature change of 25°F?*

(a) 1 in.   (b) 2 in.   (c) 3 in.   (d) 4 in.

Answer: *(a) 1 in.*

Expansion/Contraction Inches =
Raceway Length/100 x ((Temp °F Change/100) x 4.00)
Expansion/Contraction Inches = (25/100) x ((25/100) x 4.00)
Expansion/Contraction Inches = 0.25 in.

352.46 Bushings.
Conductors 4 AWG and larger that enter an enclosure must be protected from abrasion, during and after installation, by a fitting that provides a smooth, rounded insulating surface, such as an insulating bushing, unless the design of the box, fitting, or enclosure provides equivalent protection, in accordance with 300.4(G). PVC bell-ends provide the conductor protection required in this section. Figure 352–9

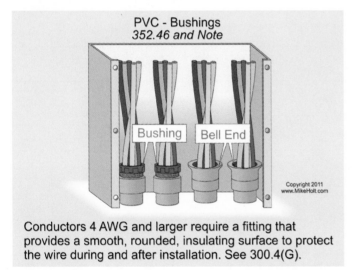

PVC - Bushings
352.46 and Note

Bushing   Bell End

Copyright 2011
www.MikeHolt.com

Conductors 4 AWG and larger require a fitting that provides a smooth, rounded, insulating surface to protect the wire during and after installation. See 300.4(G).

Figure 352–9

Author's Comment: When PVC conduit is stubbed into an open-bottom switchboard, the raceway, including the end fitting (bell-end), must not rise more than 3 in. above the bottom of the switchboard enclosure [300.16(B) and 408.5].

352.48 Joints.
Joints, such as couplings and connectors, must be made in a manner approved by the authority having jurisdiction.

Author's Comment: Follow the manufacturer's instructions for the raceway, fittings, and glue. Some glue requires the raceway surface to be cleaned with a solvent before it's applied. After applying glue to both surfaces, a quarter turn of the fitting is required.

352.60 Equipment Grounding Conductor.
If equipment grounding is required, a separate equipment grounding conductor of the wire type must be installed within the conduit [300.2(B)]. **Figure 352–10**

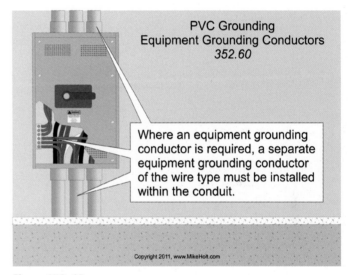

PVC Grounding
Equipment Grounding Conductors
352.60

Where an equipment grounding conductor is required, a separate equipment grounding conductor of the wire type must be installed within the conduit.

Copyright 2011, www.MikeHolt.com

Figure 352–10

Notes

Liquidtight Flexible Nonmetallic Conduit (Type LFNC)

INTRODUCTION TO ARTICLE 356—LIQUIDTIGHT FLEXIBLE NONMETALLIC CONDUIT (TYPE LFNC)

Liquidtight flexible nonmetallic conduit (LFNC) is a listed raceway of circular cross section having an outer liquidtight, nonmetallic, sunlight-resistant jacket over an inner flexible core with associated couplings, connectors, and fittings.

PART I. GENERAL

356.1 Scope. Article 356 covers the use, installation, and construction specifications of liquidtight flexible nonmetallic conduit and associated fittings.

356.2 Definition.

Liquidtight Flexible Nonmetallic Conduit (Type LFNC). A listed raceway of circular cross section, having an outer liquidtight, nonmetallic, sunlight-resistant jacket over a flexible inner core, with associated couplings, connectors, and fittings, li'sted for the installation of electrical conductors.

(1) Type LFNC-A (orange color). A smooth seamless inner core and cover having reinforcement layers between the core and cover.

(2) Type LFNC-B (gray color). A smooth inner surface with integral reinforcement within the conduit wall.

(3) Type LFNC-C (black color). A corrugated internal and external surface without integral reinforcement.

356.6 Listing Requirement. Liquidtight flexible nonmetallic conduit, and its associated fittings, must be listed. **Figure 356–1**

PART II. INSTALLATION

356.10 Uses Permitted. Listed liquidtight flexible nonmetallic conduit is permitted, either exposed or concealed, at any of the following locations:

(1) If flexibility is required.

(2) If protection from liquids, vapors, or solids is required.

(3) Outdoors, if listed and marked for this purpose.

LFNC - Listing Required
356.6

Listed Liquidtight

LFNC and associated fittings
must be listed for the purpose.

Copyright 2011, www.MikeHolt.com

Figure 356–1

(4) Directly buried in the earth, if listed and marked for this purpose.

(5) LFNC-B (gray color) is permitted in lengths over 6 ft if secured according to 356.30.

(6) LFNC-B (black color) as a listed manufactured prewired assembly.

(7) Encasement in concrete if listed for direct burial.

356.12 Uses Not Permitted.

(1) If subject to physical damage.

(2) If the combination of ambient and conductor temperature will produce an operating temperature above the rating of the raceway.

(3) Longer than 6 ft, except if approved by the authority having jurisdiction as essential for a required degree of flexibility.

---

(4) If the operating voltage of the contained conductors exceeds 600 volts, nominal.

(5) In any hazardous (classified) location, except as permitted by 501.10(B), 502.10(A) and (B), and 504.20.

356.20 Trade Size.

(A) Minimum. Liquidtight flexible nonmetallic conduit smaller than trade size ½ isn't permitted, except as permitted in the following:

(1) Enclosing the leads of motors, 430.245(B).

(2) For tap connections to lighting fixtures as permitted by 410.117(C).

(B) Maximum. Liquidtight flexible nonmetallic conduit larger than trade size 4 isn't permitted.

356.22 Number of Conductors.
Raceways must be large enough to permit the installation and removal of conductors without damaging the insulation. When all conductors in a raceway are the same size and insulation, the number of conductors permitted can be found in Annex C for the raceway type. **Figure 356–2**

> **Question:** How many 8 THHN conductors can be installed in trade size ¾ LFNC-B?
>
> **Answer:** Six conductors [Annex C, Table C5]

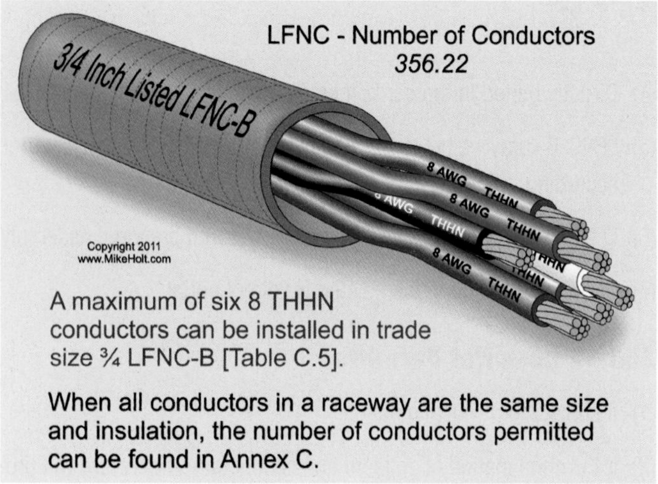

A maximum of six 8 THHN conductors can be installed in trade size ¾ LFNC-B [Table C.5].

When all conductors in a raceway are the same size and insulation, the number of conductors permitted can be found in Annex C.

Figure 356–2

Author's Comment: See 300.17 for additional examples on how to size raceways when conductors aren't all the same size.

Cables can be installed in liquidtight flexible nonmetallic conduit, as long as the number of cables doesn't exceed the allowable percentage fill specified in Table 1, Chapter 9.

356.24 Bends.
Raceway bends must not be made in any manner that would damage the raceway or significantly change its internal diameter (no kinks). The radius of the curve of the inner edge of any field bend must not be less than shown in Table 2, Chapter 9 using the column "Other Bends."

356.26 Number of Bends (360°).
To reduce the stress and friction on conductor insulation, the maximum number of bends (including offsets) between pull points must not exceed 360°.

Author's Comment: There's no maximum distance between pull boxes because this is a design issue, not a safety issue.

356.30 Securing and Supporting.
LFNC-B (gray color) must be securely fastened and supported in accordance with one of the following: **Figure 356–3**

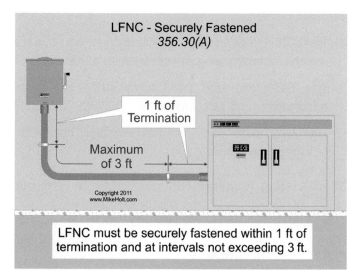

LFNC must be securely fastened within 1 ft of termination and at intervals not exceeding 3 ft.

Figure 356–3

(1) The conduit must be securely fastened at intervals not exceeding 3 ft, and within 1 ft of termination when installed longer than 6 ft.

(2) Securing or supporting isn't required if it's fished, installed in lengths not exceeding 3 ft at terminals if flexibility is required, or installed in lengths not exceeding 6 ft for tap conductors to luminaires, as permitted in 410.117(C).

(3) Horizontal runs of liquidtight flexible nonmetallic conduit installed horizontally in bored or punched holes in wood or metal framing members, or notches in wooden members, are considered supported, but the raceway must be secured within 1 ft of termination.

(4) Securing or supporting of LFNC-B (gray color) isn't required if installed in lengths not exceeding 6 ft from the last point where the raceway is securely fastened for connections within an accessible ceiling to luminaire(s) or other equipment.

356.42 Fittings. Only fittings listed for use with liquidtight flexible nonmetallic conduit can be used [300.15]. Angle connector fittings must not be used in concealed raceway installations. Straight liquidtight flexible nonmetallic conduit fittings are permitted for direct burial or encasement in concrete.

Author's Comment: Conductors 4 AWG and larger that enter an enclosure must be protected from abrasion, during and after installation, by a fitting that provides a smooth, rounded, insulating surface, such as an insulating bushing, unless the design of the box, fitting, or enclosure provides equivalent protection, in accordance with 300.4(G).

356.60 Equipment Grounding Conductor. If equipment grounding is required, a separate equipment grounding conductor of the wire type must be installed within the conduit [300.2(B)]. **Figure 356–4**

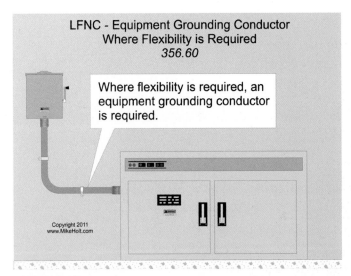

Figure 356–4

If an equipment bonding jumper is installed outside of a raceway, the length of the equipment bonding jumper must not exceed 6 ft, and it must be routed with the raceway or enclosure in accordance with 250.102(E)(2).

Notes

Electrical Metallic Tubing (Type EMT)

INTRODUCTION TO ARTICLE 358—ELECTRICAL METALLIC TUBING (TYPE EMT)

Electrical metallic tubing (EMT) is a lightweight raceway that's relatively easy to bend, cut, and ream. Because it isn't threaded, all connectors and couplings are of the threadless type and provide quick, easy, and inexpensive installation when compared to other metallic conduit systems, which makes it very popular. Electrical metallic tubing is manufactured in both galvanized steel and aluminum; the steel type is the most common type used.

PART I. GENERAL

358.1 Scope. Article 358 covers the use, installation, and construction specifications of electrical metallic tubing.

358.2 Definition.

Electrical Metallic Tubing (Type EMT). A metallic tubing of circular cross section used for the installation and physical protection of electrical conductors when joined together with fittings.

358.6 Listing Requirement. Electrical metallic tubing, elbows, and associated fittings must be listed.

PART II. INSTALLATION

358.10 Uses Permitted.

(A) Exposed and Concealed. Electrical metallic tubing is permitted exposed or concealed.

(B) Corrosion Protection. Electrical metallic tubing, elbows, couplings, and fittings can be installed in concrete, in direct contact with the earth, or in areas subject to severe corrosive influences if protected by corrosion protection and <u>approved as</u> suitable for the condition. Figure 358–1

> ⚠️ **CAUTION:** *Supplementary coatings for corrosion protection (asphalted paint) haven't been investigated by a product testing and listing agency and these coatings are known to cause cancer in laboratory animals.*

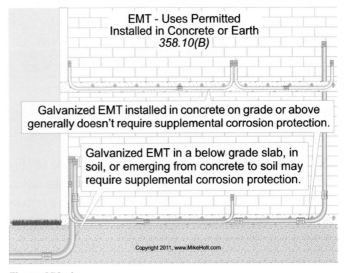

EMT - Uses Permitted
Installed in Concrete or Earth
358.10(B)

Galvanized EMT installed in concrete on grade or above generally doesn't require supplemental corrosion protection.

Galvanized EMT in a below grade slab, in soil, or emerging from concrete to soil may require supplemental corrosion protection.

Copyright 2011, www.MikeHolt.com

Figure 358–1

(C) Wet Locations. Support fittings, such as screws, straps, and so on, installed in a wet location must be made of corrosion-resistant material, or a corrosion-resistant coating must protect them in accordance with 300.6.

> **Author's Comment:** Fittings used in wet locations must be listed for the application (wet location) [314.15]. For more information, visit http://www.etpfittings.com/.

358.12 Uses Not Permitted. EMT must not be used under the following conditions:

(1) Where, during installation or afterward, it will be subject to severe physical damage.

(2) If protected from corrosion solely by enamel.

(3) In cinder concrete or cinder fill where subject to permanent moisture, unless encased in not less than 2 in. of concrete.

(4) In any hazardous (classified) location, except as permitted by 502.10, 503.10, and 504.20.

(5) For the support of luminaires or other equipment (like boxes), except conduit bodies no larger than the largest trade size of the tubing that can be supported by the raceway.

(6) If practical, contact with dissimilar metals must be avoided to prevent the deterioration of the metal because of galvanic action.

Ex: Aluminum fittings are permitted on steel electrical metallic tubing, and steel fittings are permitted on aluminum EMT.

358.20 Trade Size.

(A) Minimum. Electrical metallic tubing smaller than trade size ½ isn't permitted.

(B) Maximum. Electrical metallic tubing larger than trade size 4 isn't permitted.

358.22 Number of Conductors.
Raceways must be large enough to permit the installation and removal of conductors without damaging the conductor insulation. When all conductors in a raceway are the same size and insulation, the number of conductors permitted can be found in Annex C for the raceway type.

> *Question: How many 12 THHN conductors can be installed in trade size 1 EMT?* **Figure 358–2**
>
> (a) 26   (b) 28   (c) 30   (d) 32
>
> *Answer: (a) 26 conductors [Annex C, Table C.1]*

Author's Comment: See 300.17 for additional examples on how to size raceways when conductors aren't all the same size.

Cables can be installed in electrical metallic tubing, as long as the number of cables doesn't exceed the allowable percentage fill specified in Table 1, Chapter 9.

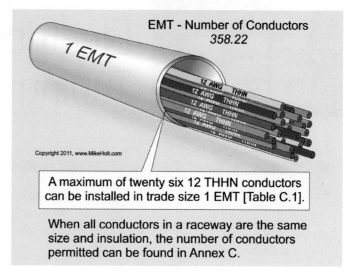

A maximum of twenty six 12 THHN conductors can be installed in trade size 1 EMT [Table C.1].

When all conductors in a raceway are the same size and insulation, the number of conductors permitted can be found in Annex C.

Figure Figure 358–2

358.24 Bends.
Raceway bends must not be made in any manner that would damage the raceway, or significantly change its internal diameter (no kinks). The radius of the curve of the inner edge of any field bend must not be less than shown in Chapter 9, Table 2 for one-shot and full shoe benders.

Author's Comment: This typically isn't a problem, because most benders are made to comply with this table.

358.26 Number of Bends (360°).
To reduce the stress and friction on conductor insulation, the maximum number of bends (including offsets) between pull points can't exceed 360°. **Figure 358–3**

Author's Comment: There's no maximum distance between pull boxes because this is a design issue, not a safety issue.

358.28 Reaming and Threading.

(A) Reaming. Reaming to remove the burrs and rough edges is required when the raceway is cut.

Author's Comment: It's considered an accepted practice to ream small raceways with a screwdriver or the backside of pliers.

(B) Threading. Electrical metallic tubing must not be threaded.

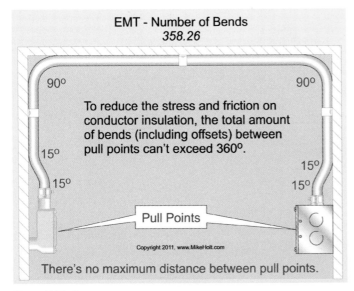

Figure 358–3

Ex 1: *When structural members don't permit the raceway to be secured within 3 ft of a box or termination fitting, an unbroken raceway can be secured within 5 ft of a box or termination fitting.* **Figure 358–5**

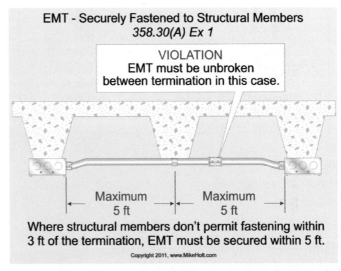

Figure 358–5

358.30 Securing and Supporting.

Electrical metallic tubing must be installed as a complete system in accordance with 300.18 [300.10 and 300.12], and it must be securely fastened in place and supported in accordance with (A) and (B).

(A) Securely Fastened. Electrical metallic tubing must generally be securely fastened within 3 ft of every box, cabinet, or termination fitting, and at intervals not exceeding 10 ft. **Figure 358–4**

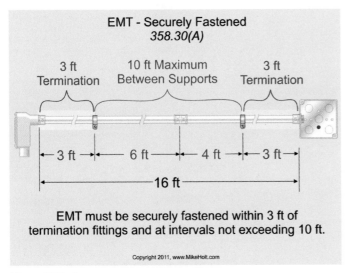

Figure 358–4

Author's Comment: Fastening is required within 3 ft of termination, not within 3 ft of a coupling.

(B) Horizontal Runs. Electrical metallic tubing installed horizontally in bored or punched holes in wood or metal framing members, or notches in wooden members, is considered supported, but the raceway must be secured within 3 ft of termination.

358.42 Couplings and Connectors.

Couplings and connectors must be made up tight to maintain an effective ground-fault current path to safely conduct fault current in accordance with 250.4(A)(5), 250.96(A), and 300.10.

If buried in masonry or concrete, threadless electrical metallic tubing fittings must be of the concrete-tight type. If installed in wet locations, fittings must be listed for use in wet locations in accordance with 314.15(A).

Author's Comment: Conductors 4 AWG and larger that enter an enclosure must be protected from abrasion, during and after installation, by a fitting that provides a smooth, rounded, insulating surface, such as an insulating bushing, unless the design of the box, fitting, or enclosure provides equivalent protection, in accordance with 300.4(G). **Figure 358–6**

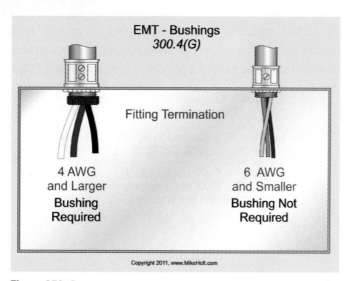

Figure 358–6

INTRODUCTION TO ARTICLE 376—METAL WIREWAYS

Metal wireways are commonly used where access to the conductors within the raceway is required to make terminations, splices, or taps to several devices at a single location. High cost precludes their use for other than short distances except in some commercial or industrial occupancies where the wiring is frequently revised.

Author's Comment: Both metal wireways and nonmetallic wireways are often called "troughs" or "gutters" in the field.

PART I. GENERAL

376.1 Scope. Article 376 covers the use, installation, and construction specifications of metal wireways and associated fittings.

376.2 Definition.

Metal Wireway. A sheet metal raceway with hinged or removable covers for housing and protecting electric conductors and cable, and in which conductors are placed after the wireway has been installed. Figure 376–1

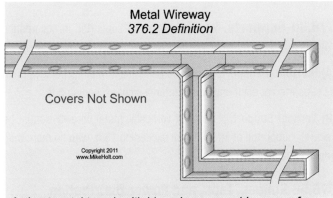

Metal Wireway
376.2 Definition

Covers Not Shown

Copyright 2011
www.MikeHolt.com

A sheet metal trough with hinged or removable covers for housing and protecting electric wires and cable, and in which conductors are placed after the wireway has been installed.

Figure 376–1

PART II. INSTALLATION

376.10 Uses Permitted.

(1) Exposed.

(2) In any hazardous (classified) locations, as permitted by <u>other articles in the *Code*.</u>

(3) <u>Wet locations where listed for the purpose.</u>

(4) Unbroken through walls, partitions, and floors.

Author's Comment: See 501.10(B), 502.10(B), and 504.20 for metal wireways used in hazardous locations.

376.12 Uses Not Permitted.

(1) Where subject to severe physical damage.

(2) Where subject to corrosive environments.

376.21 Conductors—Maximum Size. The maximum size conductor permitted in a wireway must not be larger than that for which the wireway is designed.

376.22 Number of Conductors and Ampacity. The number of conductors and their ampacity must comply with 376.22(A) and (B).

(A) Number of Conductors. The maximum number of conductors permitted in a wireway is limited to 20 percent of the cross-sectional area of the wireway. Figure 376–2

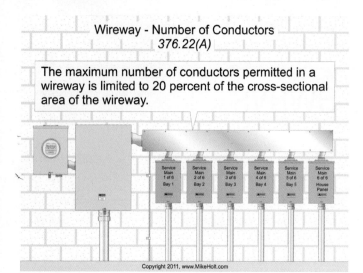

Wireway - Number of Conductors
376.22(A)

The maximum number of conductors permitted in a wireway is limited to 20 percent of the cross-sectional area of the wireway.

Copyright 2011, www.MikeHolt.com

Figure 376–2

Author's Comment: Splices and taps must not fill more than 75 percent of the wiring space at any cross section [376.56].

Conductors for signaling circuits or controller conductors between a motor and its starter and used only for starting duty are not to be considered as current-carrying conductors.

(B) Conductor Ampacity Adjustment Factors. When more than 30 current-carrying conductors are installed in any cross-sectional area of the wireway, the conductor ampacity, as listed in Table 310.15(B)(16), must be adjusted in accordance with Table 310.15(B)(3)(a). Figure 376–3

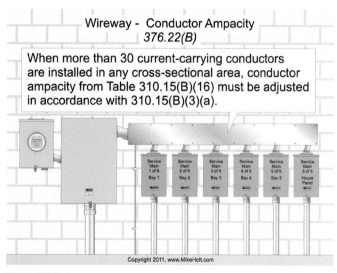

Wireway - Conductor Ampacity
376.22(B)

When more than 30 current-carrying conductors are installed in any cross-sectional area, conductor ampacity from Table 310.15(B)(16) must be adjusted in accordance with 310.15(B)(3)(a).

Copyright 2011, www.MikeHolt.com

Figure 376–3

Signaling and motor control conductors between a motor and its starter used only for starting duty aren't considered current carrying for conductor ampacity adjustment.

376.23 Wireway Sizing.

(A) Sizing for Conductor Bending Radius. If conductors are bent within a metal wireway, the wireway must be sized to meet the bending radius requirements contained in Table 312.6(A), based on one wire per terminal. Figure 376–4

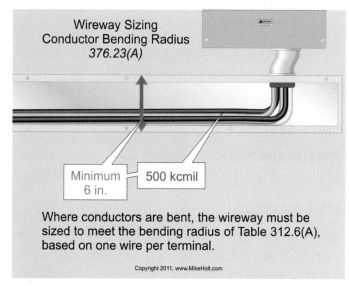

Wireway Sizing
Conductor Bending Radius
376.23(A)

Minimum 6 in.   500 kcmil

Where conductors are bent, the wireway must be sized to meet the bending radius of Table 312.6(A), based on one wire per terminal.

Copyright 2011, www.MikeHolt.com

Figure 376–4

376.30 Supports. Wireways must be supported in accordance with (A) and (B).

(A) Horizontal Support. If installed horizontally, metal wireways must be supported at each end and at intervals not exceeding 5 ft.

(B) Vertical Support. If installed vertically, metal wireways must be securely supported at intervals not exceeding 15 ft, with no more than one joint between supports.

376.56 Splices, Taps, and Power Distribution Blocks.

(A) Splices and Taps. Splices and taps in metal wireways must be accessible, and they must not fill the wireway to more than 75 percent of its cross-sectional area. Figure 376–5

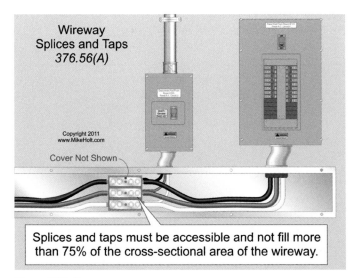

Figure 376–5

Author's Comment: The maximum number of conductors permitted in a metal wireway is limited to 20 percent of its cross-sectional area at any point [376.22(A)].

(B) Power Distribution Blocks.

(1) Installation. Power distribution blocks installed in wireways must be listed.

(2) Size of Enclosure. In addition to the wiring space requirements [376.56(A)], the power distribution block must be installed in a metal wireway not smaller than specified in the installation instructions of the power distribution block.

(3) Wire-Bending Space. Wire-bending space at the terminals of power distribution blocks must comply with 312.6(B).

(4) Live Parts. Power distribution blocks must not have uninsulated exposed live parts in the metal wireway after installation, whether or not the wireway cover is installed. **Figure 376–6**

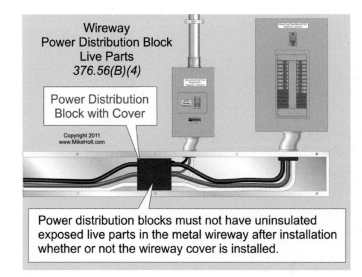

Figure 376–6

Notes

ARTICLE 392

Cable Trays

INTRODUCTION TO ARTICLE 392—CABLE TRAYS

A cable tray system is a unit or an assembly of units or sections with associated fittings that forms a structural system used to securely fasten or support cables and raceways. Cable tray systems include ladder, ventilated trough, ventilated channel, solid bottom, and other similar structures. Cable trays are manufactured in many forms, from a simple hanger or wire mesh to a substantial, rigid, steel support system. Cable trays are designed and manufactured to support specific wiring methods, as identified in 392.10(A).

PART I. GENERAL

392.1 Scope. Article 392 covers cable tray systems, including ladder, ventilated trough, ventilated channel, solid bottom, and other similar structures.

392.2 Definition.

Cable Tray System. A unit or assembly of units or sections with associated fittings forming a rigid structural system used to securely fasten or support cables, raceways, and boxes.

> **Author's Comment:** Cable tray isn't a type of raceway. It's a support system for cables and raceways.

PART II. INSTALLATION

392.10 Uses Permitted. Cable trays can be used as a support system for service, feeder, or branch-circuit conductors, as well as communications circuits, control circuits, and signaling circuits. Figure 392–1

> **Author's Comments:**
>
> - Cable trays used to support service-entrance conductors must contain only service-entrance conductors unless a solid fixed barrier separates the service-entrance conductors from other conductors [230.44].
>
> - Cable tray installations aren't limited to industrial establishments.

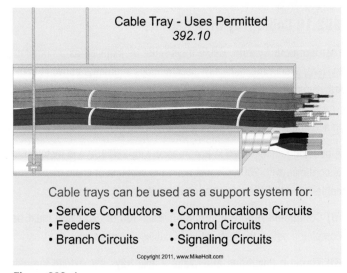

Figure 392–1

- If exposed to the direct rays of the sun, insulated conductors and jacketed cables must be identified as being sunlight resistant. The manufacturer must identify cable trays and associated fittings for their intended use.

(A) Wiring Methods. Any wiring methods listed in Table 392.10(A) can be installed in a cable tray.

(B) In Industrial Establishments.

(1) Where conditions of maintenance and supervision ensure that only qualified persons service the installed cable tray system, single conductor cables can be installed in accordance with the following:

(a) 1/0 AWG and larger listed and marked for use in cable trays.

(c) Equipment grounding conductors must be 4 AWG and larger.

(C) Hazardous (Classified) Locations. Cable trays in hazardous (classified) locations must contain only the cable types and raceways permitted by the *Code* for the application

> **Author's Comment:** For permitted cable types, see 501.10, 502.10, 503.10, 504.20, and 505.15.

(D) Nonmetallic Cable Trays. In addition to the uses permitted elsewhere in Article 392, nonmetallic cable trays can be installed in corrosive areas, and in areas requiring voltage isolation.

392.12 Uses Not Permitted. Cable tray systems aren't permitted in hoistways, or where subject to severe physical damage.

392.18 Cable Tray Installations

(A) Complete System. Cable trays must be installed as a complete system, except mechanically discontinuous segments between cable tray runs, or between cable tray runs and equipment are permitted. The system must provide for the support of the cables and raceways in accordance with their corresponding articles.

A bonding jumper, sized in accordance with 250.102 and installed in accordance with 250.96, must bond the sections of cable tray, or the cable tray and the raceway or equipment.

(B) Completed Before Installation. Each run of cable tray must be completed before the installation of cables or conductors.

(D) Through Partitions and Walls. Cable trays can extend through partitions and walls, or vertically through platforms and floors if the installation is made in accordance with the firestopping requirements of 300.21.

(E) Exposed and Accessible. Cable trays must be exposed and accessible, except as permitted by 392.10(H).

(F) Adequate Access. Sufficient space must be provided and maintained about cable trays to permit adequate access for installing and maintaining the cables.

(G) Raceways, Cables, and Boxes Supported from Cable Trays. In industrial facilities where conditions of maintenance and supervision ensure only qualified persons will service the installation, and if the cable tray system is designed and installed to support the load, cable tray systems can support raceways, cables, boxes, and conduit bodies. **Figure 392–2**

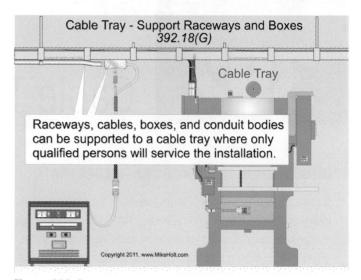

Figure 392–2

For raceways terminating at the tray, a listed cable tray clamp or adapter must be used to securely fasten the raceway to the cable tray system. The raceway must be supported in accordance with the appropriate raceway article.

Raceways or cables running parallel to the cable tray system can be attached to the bottom or side of a cable tray system. The raceway or cable must be fastened and supported in accordance with the appropriate raceway or cable's *Code* article.

Boxes and conduit bodies attached to the bottom or side of a cable tray system must be fastened and supported in accordance with 314.23.

392.20 Cable and Conductor Installation

(C) Connected in Parallel. To prevent unbalanced current in the parallel conductors due to inductive reactance, all circuit conductors of a parallel set [310.10(H)] must be bundled together and secured to prevent excessive movement due to fault current magnetic forces.

(D) Single Conductors. Single conductors of a circuit not connected in parallel must be installed in a single layer, unless the conductors are bound together.

392.22 Number of Conductors or Cables.

(A) Number of Multiconductor Cables in Cable Trays. The number of multiconductor cables, rated 2,000 volts or less, permitted in a single cable tray must not exceed the requirements of this section. The conductor sizes herein apply to both aluminum and copper conductors.

(1) Any Mixture of Cables. If ladder or ventilated trough cable trays contain multiconductor power or lighting cables, the maximum number of cables must conform to the following:

(a) If all of the cables are 4/0 AWG and larger, the sum of the diameters of all cables must not exceed the cable tray width, and the cables must be installed in a single layer.

392.30 Securing and Supporting.

(A) Fastened Securely. Cables installed vertically must be securely fastened to transverse members of the cable tray.

(B) Support. Supports for cable trays must be provided to prevent stress on cables where they enter raceways or other enclosures from cable tray systems. Cable trays must be supported in accordance with the manufacturer's installation instructions.

392.46 Bushed Raceway. A box isn't required where cables or conductors exit a bushed raceway used for the support or protection of the conductors.

392.56 Cable Splices. Splices are permitted in a cable tray if the splice is accessible and insulated by a method approved by the authority having jurisdiction. Splices can project above the side rails of the cable tray if not subject to physical damage. Figure 392–3

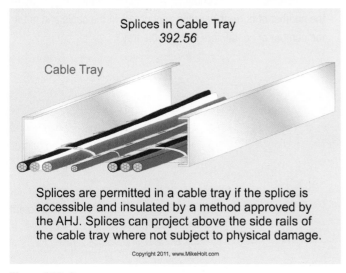

Splices in Cable Tray
392.56

Cable Tray

Splices are permitted in a cable tray if the splice is accessible and insulated by a method approved by the AHJ. Splices can project above the side rails of the cable tray where not subject to physical damage.

Copyright 2011, www.MikeHolt.com

Figure 392–3

392.60 Equipment Grounding Conductor.

(A) Metallic Cable Trays. Metallic cable trays can be used as equipment grounding conductors where continuous maintenance and supervision ensure that qualified persons service the installed cable tray system. **Figure 392–4**. The metallic cable trays that support conductors must be bonded together to ensure that they have the capacity to conduct safely any fault current likely to be imposed in accordance with 250.96(A).

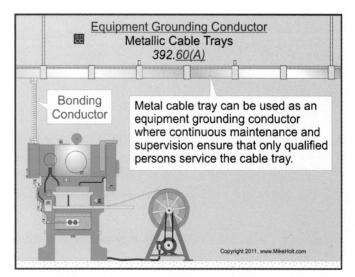

Equipment Grounding Conductor
Metallic Cable Trays
392.60(A)

Bonding Conductor

Metal cable tray can be used as an equipment grounding conductor where continuous maintenance and supervision ensure that only qualified persons service the cable tray.

Copyright 2011, www.MikeHolt.com

Figure 392–4

Metal cable trays containing communications, data, and signaling conductors and cables must be electrically continuous through listed connections or the use of an insulated stranded bonding jumper not smaller than 10 AWG. **Figure 392–5**

Author's Comment: Nonconductive coatings such as paint, lacquer, and enamel on equipment must be removed to ensure an effective ground-fault current path, or the termination fittings must be designed so as to make such removal unnecessary [250.12].

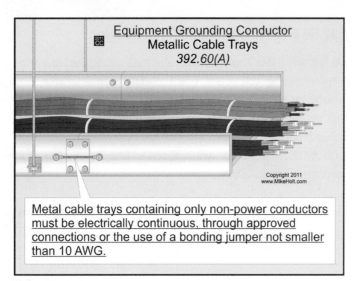

Figure 392–5

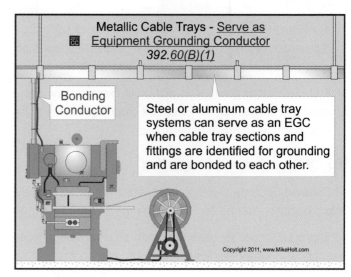

Figure 392–6

(B) Serve as Equipment Grounding Conductor. Metal cable trays can serve as equipment grounding conductors where maintenance and supervision ensure that qualified persons service the installed cable tray system, and the following requirements have been met [392.10(C)]:

(1) Cable tray sections and fittings are identified for grounding. **Figure 392–6**

> **Author's Comment:** Identification will be marked on each cable tray section.

(4) Cable tray sections, fittings, and connected raceways are effectively bonded to each other to ensure electrical continuity and the capacity to conduct safely any fault current likely to be imposed on them [250.96(A)]. This is accomplished by using bolted mechanical connectors or bonding jumpers sized in accordance with 250.102.

392.80 Ampacity of Conductors.

(A) Ampacity in Cable Trays.

(1) The allowable ampacity of multiconductor cables installed in accordance with the requirements of 392.22(A) must be as given in Table 310.15(B)(16) and Table 310.15(B)(18).

(a) The conductor ampacity adjustment factors of 310.15(B)(3)(a) apply to a given cable if it contains more than three current-carrying conductors. The conductor adjustment factors only apply to the number of current-carrying conductors in the cable and not to the number of conductors in the cable tray.

CHAPTER 3. WIRING METHODS AND MATERIALS — PRACTICE QUESTIONS

Article 300. Wiring Methods

1. Conductors shall be installed within a raceway, cable, or enclosure.

   (a) True
   (b) False

2. All conductors of a circuit, including the grounded and equipment grounding conductors, shall be contained within the same _____, unless otherwise permitted elsewhere in the *Code*.

   (a) raceway
   (b) cable
   (c) trench
   (d) all of these

3. Conductors of ac and dc circuits, rated 600V or less, shall be permitted to occupy the same _____ provided that all conductors have an insulation rating equal to the maximum voltage applied to any conductor.

   (a) enclosure
   (b) cable
   (c) raceway
   (d) all of these

4. Where cables or nonmetallic raceways are installed through bored holes in joists, rafters, or wood members, holes shall be bored so that the edge of the hole is _____ the nearest edge of the wood member.

   (a) not less than 1¼ in. from
   (b) immediately adjacent to
   (c) not less than ¹⁄₁₆ in. from
   (d) 90° away from

5. Cables laid in wood notches require protection against nails or screws by using a steel plate at least _____ thick, installed before the building finish is applied.

   (a) ¹⁄₁₆ in.
   (b) 1/8 in.
   (c) ¼ in.
   (d) ½ in.

6. A cable, raceway, or box installed under metal-corrugated sheet roof decking shall be supported so the top of the cable, raceway, or box is not less than _____ from the lowest surface of the roof decking to the top of the cable, raceway, or box.

   (a) ½ in.
   (b) 1 in.
   (c) 1½ in.
   (d) 2 in.

7. When installed under metal-corrugated sheet roof decking, cables, raceways, and enclosures are permitted in concealed locations of metal-corrugated sheet decking type roofing if they are at least 2 in. away from a structural support member.

   (a) True
   (b) False

8. When installed under metal-corrugated sheet roof decking, the rules for spacing from roof decking apply equally to rigid metal conduit and intermediate metal conduit.

   (a) True
   (b) False

9. Where raceways contain insulated circuit conductors _____ AWG and larger, the conductors shall be protected from abrasion during and after installation by a fitting that provides a smooth, rounded insulating surface.

    (a) 8
    (b) 6
    (c) 4
    (d) 2

10. A listed expansion/deflection fitting or other approved means must be used where a raceway crosses a _____ intended for expansion, contraction or deflection used in buildings, bridges, parking garages, or other structures.

    (a) junction box
    (b) structural joint
    (c) cable tray
    (d) unistrut hanger

11. What is the minimum cover requirement for direct burial Type UF cable installed outdoors that supplies a 120V, 30A circuit?

    (a) 6 in.
    (b) 12 in.
    (c) 18 in.
    (d) 24 in.

12. Rigid metal conduit that is directly buried outdoors shall have at least _____ of cover.

    (a) 6 in.
    (b) 12 in.
    (c) 18 in.
    (d) 24 in.

13. When installing PVC conduit underground without concrete cover, there shall be a minimum of _____ of cover.

    (a) 6 in.
    (b) 12 in.
    (c) 18 in.
    (d) 22 in.

14. _____ is defined as the area between the top of direct-burial cable and the top surface of the finished grade.

    (a) Notch
    (b) Cover
    (c) Gap
    (d) none of these

15. The interior of underground raceways shall be considered a _____ location.

    (a) wet
    (b) dry
    (c) damp
    (d) corrosive

16. Backfill used for underground wiring shall not _____.

    (a) damage the wiring method
    (b) prevent compaction of the fill
    (c) contribute to the corrosion of the raceway
    (d) all of these

17. Conduits or raceways through which moisture may contact live parts shall be _____ at either or both ends.

    (a) sealed
    (b) plugged
    (c) bushed
    (d) a or b

18. When installing direct-buried cables, a _____ shall be used at the end of a conduit that terminates underground.

    (a) splice kit
    (b) terminal fitting
    (c) bushing
    (d) b or c

19. All conductors of the same circuit shall be _____, unless otherwise specifically permitted in the *Code*.

    (a) in the same raceway or cable
    (b) in close proximity in the same trench
    (c) the same size
    (d) a or b

20. Each direct-buried single conductor cable must be located _____ in the trench to the other single conductor cables in the same parallel set of conductors, including equipment grounding conductors.

    (a) perpendicular
    (b) bundled together
    (c) in close proximity
    (d) spaced apart

21. Direct-buried conductors, cables, or raceways, which are subject to movement by settlement or frost, shall be arranged to prevent damage to the _____ or to equipment connected to the raceways.

    (a) siding of the building mounted on
    (b) landscaping around the cable or raceway
    (c) the enclosed conductors
    (d) expansion fitting

22. Cables or raceways installed using directional boring equipment shall be _____ for this purpose.

    (a) marked
    (b) listed
    (c) labeled
    (d) approved

23. Raceways, cable trays, cablebus, auxiliary gutters, cable armor, boxes, cable sheathing, cabinets, elbows, couplings, fittings, supports, and support hardware shall be of materials suitable for _____.

    (a) corrosive locations
    (b) wet locations
    (c) the environment in which they are to be installed
    (d) none of these

24. Where corrosion protection is necessary for ferrous metal equipment and the conduit is threaded in the field, the threads shall be coated with a(n) _____, electrically conductive, corrosion-resistant compound.

    (a) marked
    (b) listed
    (c) labeled
    (d) approved

25. Which of the following metal parts shall be protected from corrosion?

    (a) ferrous metal raceways
    (b) ferrous metal elbows
    (c) ferrous boxes
    (d) all of these

26. Ferrous metal raceways, boxes, fittings, supports, and support hardware can be installed in concrete or in direct contact with the earth or other areas subject to severe corrosive influences, where _____ approved for the conditions.

    (a) the soil is
    (b) made of material
    (c) the qualified installer is
    (d) none of these

27. Aluminum raceways, cable trays, cablebus, auxiliary gutters, cable armor, boxes, cable sheathing, cabinets, elbows, couplings, nipples, fittings, supports, and support hardware _____ shall be provided with supplementary corrosion protection.

    (a) embedded or encased in concrete
    (b) in direct contact with the earth
    (c) likely to become energized
    (d) a or b

28. Where exposed to sunlight, nonmetallic raceways, cable trays, boxes, cables with a nonmetallic outer jacket, fittings, and support hardware shall be _____.

    (a) listed as sunlight resistant
    (b) identified as sunlight resistant
    (c) a and b
    (d) a or b

29. Where nonmetallic wiring methods are subject to exposure to chemical solvents or vapors, they shall be inherently resistant to chemicals based upon their being _____.

    (a) listed for the chemical
    (b) identified for the chemical
    (c) a and b
    (d) a or b

30. An exposed wiring system for indoor wet locations where walls are frequently washed shall be mounted so that there is at least a _____ between the mounting surface and the electrical equipment.

    (a) ¼ in. airspace
    (b) separation by insulated bushings
    (c) separation by noncombustible tubing
    (d) none of these

31. In general, areas where acids and alkali chemicals are handled and stored may present corrosive conditions, particularly when wet or damp.

    (a) True
    (b) False

32. Where portions of a cable raceway or sleeve are subjected to different temperatures and condensation is known to be a problem, the _____ shall be filled with an approved material to prevent the circulation of warm air to a colder section of the raceway or sleeve.

    (a) raceway
    (b) sleeve
    (c) a or b
    (d) none of these

33. Raceways shall be provided with expansion fittings where necessary to compensate for thermal expansion and contraction.

    (a) True
    (b) False

34. Raceways or cable trays containing electric conductors shall not contain any pipe or tube for steam, water, air, gas, drainage, or any service other than _____.

    (a) as permitted by the authority having jurisdiction
    (b) electrical
    (c) pneumatic
    (d) as designed by the engineer

35. Where raceways are installed in wet locations above grade, the interior of these raceways shall be considered a _____ location.

    (a) wet
    (b) dry
    (c) damp
    (d) corrosive

36. Metal raceways, cable armors, and other metal enclosures shall be _____ joined together into a continuous electric conductor so as to provide effective electrical continuity.

    (a) electrically
    (b) permanently
    (c) metallically
    (d) none of these

37. Raceways, cable assemblies, boxes, cabinets, and fittings shall be securely fastened in place.

    (a) True
    (b) False

38. Where independent support wires of a ceiling assembly are used to support raceways, cable assemblies, or boxes above a ceiling, they shall be secured at _____ ends.

    (a) one
    (b) both
    (c) a or b
    (d) none of these

39. Electrical wiring within the cavity of a fire-rated floor-ceiling or roof-ceiling assembly shall not be supported by the ceiling assembly or ceiling support wires.

    (a) True
    (b) False

40. The independent support wires for supporting electrical wiring methods in a fire-rated ceiling assembly shall be distinguishable from fire-rated suspended-ceiling framing support wires by _____.

    (a) color
    (b) tagging
    (c) other effective means
    (d) any of these

41. Ceiling-support wires used for the support of electrical raceways and cables within nonfire-rated assemblies shall be distinguishable from the suspended-ceiling framing support wires.

    (a) True
    (b) False

42. Raceways can be used as a means of support of Class 2 circuit conductors or cables that connect to the same equipment.

    (a) True
    (b) False

43. Metal or nonmetallic raceways, cable armors, and cable sheaths _____ between cabinets, boxes, fittings or other enclosures or outlets.

    (a) can be attached with electrical tape
    (b) are allowed gaps for expansion
    (c) shall be continuous
    (d) none of these

44. Conductors in raceways shall be _____ between outlets, boxes, devices, and so forth.

    (a) continuous
    (b) installed
    (c) copper
    (d) in conduit

45. When the opening to an outlet, junction, or switch point is less than 8 in. in any dimension, each conductor shall be long enough to extend at least _____ outside the opening of the enclosure.

    (a) 0 in.
    (b) 3 in.
    (c) 6 in.
    (d) 12 in.

46. Fittings and connectors shall be used only with the specific wiring methods for which they are designed and listed.

    (a) True
    (b) False

47. A box or conduit body shall not be required where cables enter or exit from conduit or tubing that is used to provide cable support or protection against physical damage.

    (a) True
    (b) False

48. A box or conduit body shall not be required for conductors in handhole enclosures, except where connected to electrical equipment.

    (a) True
    (b) False

49. A bushing shall be permitted in lieu of a box or terminal where the conductors emerge from a raceway and enter or terminate at equipment such as open switchboards, unenclosed control equipment, or similar equipment.

    (a) True
    (b) False

50. The number and size of conductors permitted in a raceway is limited to _____.

    (a) permit heat to dissipate
    (b) prevent damage to insulation during installation
    (c) prevent damage to insulation during removal of conductors
    (d) all of these

51. Raceways shall be _____ between outlet, junction, or splicing points prior to the installation of conductors.

    (a) installed complete
    (b) tested for ground faults
    (c) a minimum of 80 percent complete
    (d) none of these

52. Prewired raceway assemblies shall be used only where specifically permitted in the *NEC* for the applicable wiring method.

    (a) True
    (b) False

53. Short sections of raceways used for _____ shall not be required to be installed complete between outlet, junction, or splicing points.

    (a) meter to service enclosure connection
    (b) protection of cables from physical damage
    (c) nipples
    (d) separately derived systems

54. Metal raceways shall not be _____ by welding to the raceway.

    (a) supported
    (b) terminated
    (c) connected
    (d) all of these

55. Conductors in ferrous metal raceways and enclosures shall be arranged so as to avoid heating the surrounding ferrous metal by alternating-current induction. To accomplish this, the _____ conductor(s) shall be grouped together.

    (a) phase
    (b) grounded
    (c) equipment grounding
    (d) all of these

56. _____ is a nonferrous, nonmagnetic metal that has no heating due to hysteresis heating.

    (a) Steel
    (b) Iron
    (c) Aluminum
    (d) all of these

57. Electrical installations in hollow spaces, vertical shafts, and ventilation or air-handling ducts shall be made so that the possible spread of fire or products of combustion is not _____.

    (a) substantially increased
    (b) allowed
    (c) inherent
    (d) possible

58. Openings around electrical penetrations into or through fire-resistant-rated walls, partitions, floors, or ceilings shall _____ to maintain the fire-resistance rating.

    (a) be documented
    (b) not be permitted
    (c) be firestopped using approved methods
    (d) be enlarged

59. No wiring of any type shall be installed in ducts used to transport _____.

    (a) dust
    (b) flammable vapors
    (c) loose stock
    (d) all of these

60. Equipment and devices shall only be permitted within ducts or plenum chambers specifically fabricated to transport environmental air if necessary for their direct action upon, or sensing of, the _____.

    (a) contained air
    (b) air quality
    (c) air temperature
    (d) none of these

61. The space above a hung ceiling used for environmental air-handling purposes is an example of _____, and the wiring limitations of _____ apply.

    (a) a specifically fabricated duct used for environmental air, 300.22(B)
    (b) other space used for environmental air (plenum), 300.22(C)
    (c) a supply duct used for environmental air, 300.22(B)
    (d) none of these

62. Wiring methods permitted in the ceiling areas used for environmental air include _____.

    (a) electrical metallic tubing
    (b) FMC of any length
    (c) RMC without an overall nonmetallic covering
    (d) all of these

63. _____ shall be permitted to support the wiring methods and equipment permitted to be used in other spaces used for environmental air (plenum).

    (a) Metal cable tray system
    (b) Nonmetallic wireways
    (c) PVC conduit
    (d) Surface nonmetallic raceways

64. Electrical equipment with _____ and having adequate fire-resistant and low-smoke-producing characteristics can be installed within an air-handling space (plenum).

    (a) a metal enclosure
    (b) a nonmetallic enclosures listed for use within an air-handling (plenum) space
    (c) any type of enclosure
    (d) a or b

Article 310. Conductors for General Wiring

1. Conductors shall be permitted for use in any of the wiring methods recognized in Chapter 3 and as permitted in the *NEC*.

    (a) True
    (b) False

2. In general, the minimum size conductor permitted for use in parallel installations is _____ AWG.

    (a) 10
    (b) 4
    (c) 1
    (d) 1/0

3. Conductors smaller than 1/0 AWG can be connected in parallel to supply control power, provided _____.

    (a) they are all contained within the same raceway or cable
    (b) each parallel conductor has an ampacity sufficient to carry the entire load
    (c) the circuit overcurrent device rating does not exceed the ampacity of any individual parallel conductor
    (d) all of these

4. Parallel conductors shall have the same _____.

    (a) length
    (b) material
    (c) size in circular mil area
    (d) all of these

5. Where conductors in parallel are run in separate raceways, the raceways shall have the same electrical characteristics.

(a) True
(b) False

6. No conductor shall be used where its operating temperature exceeds that designated for the type of insulated conductor involved.

(a) True
(b) False

7. The _____ rating of a conductor is the maximum temperature, at any location along its length, which the conductor can withstand over a prolonged period of time without serious degradation.

(a) ambient
(b) temperature
(c) maximum withstand
(d) short-circuit

8. There are four principal determinants of conductor operating temperature, one of which is _____ generated internally in the conductor as the result of load current flow, including fundamental and harmonic currents.

(a) friction
(b) magnetism
(c) heat
(d) none of these

9. The ampacities listed in the Tables of Article 310.15(B)(16) do not take _____ into consideration.

(a) continuous loads
(b) voltage drop
(c) insulation
(d) wet locations

10. The ampacity of a conductor can be different along the length of the conductor. The higher ampacity can be used beyond the point of transition for a distance of no more than _____ ft, or no more than _____ percent of the circuit length figured at the higher ampacity, whichever is less.

(a) 10, 10
(b) 10, 20
(c) 15, 15
(d) 20, 10

11. Each current-carrying conductor of a paralleled set of conductors shall be counted as a current-carrying conductor for the purpose of applying the adjustment factors of 310.15(B)(3)(a).

(a) True
(b) False

12. Where six current-carrying conductors are run in the same conduit or cable, the ampacity of each conductor shall be adjusted by a factor of _____ percent.

(a) 40
(b) 60
(c) 80
(d) 90

13. Conductor derating factors shall not apply to conductors in raceways having a length not exceeding _____.

(a) 12 in.
(b) 24 in.
(c) 36 in.
(d) 48 in.

14. Where conductors or cables are installed in circular conduits exposed to direct sunlight on or above rooftops, the ambient temperature shall be increased by _____ where the conduits are less than ½ in. from the rooftop.

(a) 30°F
(b) 40°F
(c) 50°F
(d) 60°F

15. When bare conductors are installed with insulated conductors, their ampacities shall be limited to _____.

    (a) 60°C
    (b) 75°C
    (c) 90°C
    (d) the lowest temperature rating for any of the insulated conductors

16. When determining the number of current-carrying conductors, a grounding or bonding conductor shall not be counted when applying the provisions of 310.15(B)(3)(a) _____.

    (a) True
    (b) False

17. Where installed in raceways, conductors _____ AWG and larger shall be stranded.

    (a) 10
    (b) 8
    (c) 6
    (d) 4

Article 312. Cabinets, Cutout Boxes, and Meter Socket Enclosures

1. Surface-type cabinets, cutout boxes, and meter socket enclosures in damp or wet locations shall be mounted so there is at least _____ airspace between the enclosure and the wall or supporting surface.

    (a) $\frac{1}{16}$ in.
    (b) $\frac{1}{4}$ in.
    (c) $1\frac{1}{4}$ in.
    (d) 6 in.

2. Cabinets, cutout boxes, and meter socket enclosures installed in wet locations shall be _____.

    (a) waterproof
    (b) raintight
    (c) weatherproof
    (d) watertight

3. Where raceways or cables enter above the level of uninsulated live parts of cabinets, cutout boxes, and meter socket enclosures in a wet location, a(n) _____ shall be used.

    (a) fitting listed for wet locations
    (b) explosionproof seal
    (c) fitting listed for damp locations
    (d) insulated fitting

4. In walls constructed of wood or other _____ material, electrical cabinets shall be flush with the finished surface or project there from.

    (a) nonconductive
    (b) porous
    (c) fibrous
    (d) combustible

5. Noncombustible surfaces that are broken or incomplete shall be repaired so there will be no gaps or open spaces greater than _____ at the edge of a cabinet or cutout box employing a flush-type cover.

    (a) $\frac{1}{32}$ in.
    (b) $\frac{1}{16}$ in.
    (c) $\frac{1}{8}$ in.
    (d) $\frac{1}{4}$ in.

6. Openings in cabinets, cutout boxes, and meter socket enclosures through which conductors enter shall be _____.

    (a) adequately closed
    (b) made using concentric knockouts only
    (c) centered in the cabinet wall
    (d) identified

7. Each cable entering a cutout box _____.

    (a) shall be secured to the cutout box
    (b) can be sleeved through a chase
    (c) shall have a maximum of two cables per connector
    (d) all of these

8. Nonmetallic cables can enter the top of surface-mounted cabinets, cutout boxes, and meter socket enclosures through nonflexible raceways not less than 18 in. or more than _____ ft in length if all of the required conditions are met.

(a) 3
(b) 10
(c) 25
(d) 100

9. Enclosures for switches or overcurrent devices are allowed to have conductors feeding through where the wiring space at any cross section is not filled to more than _____ percent of the cross-sectional area of the space.

(a) 20
(b) 30
(c) 40
(d) 60

10. Cabinets, cutout boxes, and meter socket enclosures can be used for conductors feeding through, spliced, or tapping off to other enclosures, switches, or overcurrent devices where _____.

(a) the total area of the conductors at any cross section doesn't exceed 40 percent of the cross-sectional area of the space
(b) the total area of conductors, splices, and taps installed at any cross section doesn't exceed 75 percent of the cross-sectional area of that space
(c) a warning label on the enclosure identifies the disconnecting means for feed-through conductors
(d) all of these

Article 314. Outlet, Device, Pull and Junction Boxes; Conduit Bodies; Fittings; and Handhole Enclosures

1. Nonmetallic boxes can be used with _____.

(a) nonmetallic cables
(b) nonmetallic raceways
(c) flexible cords
(d) all of these

2. Metal boxes shall be _____ in accordance with Article 250.

(a) grounded
(b) bonded
(c) a and b
(d) none of these

3. Boxes, conduit bodies, and fittings installed in wet locations shall be required to be listed for use in wet locations.

(a) True
(b) False

4. According to the *NEC*, the volume of a 3 x 2 x 2 in. device box is _____.

(a) 8 cu in.
(b) 10 cu in.
(c) 12 cu in.
(d) 14 cu in.

5. When counting the number of conductors in a box, a conductor running through the box with an unbroken loop or coil not less than twice the minimum length required for free conductors shall be counted as _____ conductor(s).

(a) one
(b) two
(c) three
(d) four

6. Where one or more equipment grounding conductors enter a box, a _____ volume allowance in accordance with Table 314.16(b) shall be made, based on the largest equipment grounding conductor.

(a) single
(b) double
(c) triple
(d) none of these

7. Conduit bodies containing conductors larger than 6 AWG shall have a cross-sectional area at least twice that of the largest conduit to which they can be attached.

   (a) True
   (b) False

8. Conduit bodies that are durably and legibly marked by the manufacturer with their volume can contain splices, taps, or devices

   (a) True
   (b) False

9. Short-radius conduit bodies such as capped elbows, and service-entrance elbows that enclose conductors 6 AWG and smaller shall not contain _____.

   (a) splices
   (b) taps
   (c) devices
   (d) any of these

10. In noncombustible walls or ceilings, the front edge of a box, plaster ring, extension ring, or listed extender employing a flush-type cover, shall be set back not more than _____ from the finished surface.

    (a) ⅛ in.
    (b) ¼ in.
    (c) ⅜ in.
    (d) ½ in.

11. In walls or ceilings constructed of wood or other combustible surface material, boxes, plaster rings, extension rings, or listed extenders shall _____.

    (a) be flush with the surface
    (b) project from the surface
    (c) a or b
    (d) be set back no more than ¼ in.

12. Noncombustible surfaces that are broken or incomplete around boxes employing a flush-type cover or faceplate shall be repaired so there will be no gaps or open spaces larger than _____ at the edge of the box.

    (a) ¹⁄₁₆ in.
    (b) ⅛ in.
    (c) ¼ in.
    (d) ½ in.

13. Surface-mounted outlet boxes shall be _____.

    (a) rigidly and securely fastened in place
    (b) supported by cables that protrude from the box
    (c) supported by cable entries from the top and permitted to rest against the supporting surface
    (d) none of these

14. _____ can be used to fasten boxes to structural members of a building using brackets on the outside of the enclosure.

    (a) Nails
    (b) Screws
    (c) Bolts
    (d) a and b

15. A wood brace used for supporting a box for structural mounting shall have a cross-section not less than nominal _____.

    (a) 1 in. x 2 in.
    (b) 2 in. x 2 in.
    (c) 2 in. x 3 in.
    (d) 2 in. x 4 in.

16. When mounting an enclosure in a finished surface, the enclosure shall be _____ secured to the surface by clamps, anchors, or fittings identified for the application.

    (a) temporarily
    (b) partially
    (c) never
    (d) rigidly

17. Outlet boxes can be secured to suspended-ceiling framing members by mechanical means such as _____, or by other means identified for the suspended-ceiling framing member(s).

    (a) bolts
    (b) screws
    (c) rivets
    (d) all of these

18. Enclosures not over 100 cu in. having threaded entries and not containing a device shall be considered to be adequately supported where _____ or more conduits are threaded wrenchtight into the enclosure and each conduit is secured within 3 ft of the enclosure.

    (a) one
    (b) two
    (c) three
    (d) none of these

19. Utilization equipment weighing less than 6 lb can be supported to any box or plaster ring secured to a box, provided the equipment is secured with at least two _____ or larger screws.

    (a) No. 6
    (b) No. 8
    (c) No. 10
    (d) self tapping

20. In straight pulls, the length of the box or conduit body shall not be less than _____ times the trade size of the largest raceway.

    (a) six
    (b) eight
    (c) twelve
    (d) none of these

21. Where angle or U pulls are made, the distance between each raceway entry inside the box or conduit body and the opposite wall of the box or conduit body shall not be less than _____ times the trade size of the largest raceway in a row plus the sum of the trade sizes of the remaining raceways in the same wall and row .

    (a) six
    (b) eight
    (c) twelve
    (d) none of these

22. Pull boxes or junction boxes with any dimension over _____ shall have all conductors cabled or racked in an approved manner.

    (a) 3 ft
    (b) 6 ft
    (c) 9 ft
    (d) 12 ft

23. Power distribution blocks shall be permitted in pull and junction boxes over 100 cubic inches when they comply with the provisions of 314.28(E).

    (a) True
    (b) False

24. Power distribution blocks shall be permitted in pull and junction boxes over 100 cubic inches when _____.

    (a) they are listed as a power distribution block.
    (b) they are installed in a box not smaller than required by the installation instructions of the power distribution block.
    (c) the junction box is sized so that the wire-bending space requirements of 312.6 can be met.
    (d) all of these

25. Exposed live parts on the power distribution block are allowed when the junction box cover is removed.

    (a) True
    (b) False

26. Where the junction box contains a power distribution block, and it has conductors that don't terminate on the power distribution block(s), the through conductors must be arranged so the power distribution block terminals are _____ following installation.

    (a) unobstructed
    (b) above the through conductors
    (c) visible
    (d) labeled

27. _____ shall be installed so that the wiring contained can be rendered accessible without removing any part of the building or, in underground circuits, without excavating sidewalks, paving, or earth.

    (a) Boxes
    (b) Conduit bodies
    (c) Handhole enclosures
    (d) all of these

28. Listed boxes and handhole enclosures designed for underground installation can be directly buried when covered by _____, if their location is effectively identified and accessible.

    (a) concrete
    (b) gravel
    (c) noncohesive granulated soil
    (d) b or c

29. Handhole enclosures shall be designed and installed to withstand _____.

    (a) 600 lb
    (b) 3,000 lb
    (c) 6,000 lb
    (d) all loads likely to be imposed

30. Underground raceways and cable assemblies entering a handhole enclosure shall extend into the enclosure, but they are not required to be _____.

    (a) bonded
    (b) insulated
    (c) mechanically connected to the handhole enclosure
    (d) below minimum cover requirements after leaving the handhole

31. Conductors, splices or terminations in a handhole enclosure shall be listed as _____.

    (a) suitable for wet locations
    (b) suitable for damp locations
    (c) suitable for direct burial in the earth
    (d) none of these

32. Handhole enclosure covers shall have an identifying _____ that prominently identifies the function of the enclosure, such as electric.

    (a) mark
    (b) logo
    (c) a or b
    (d) manual

33. Handhole enclosure covers shall require the use of tools to open, or they shall weigh over _____.

    (a) 45 lb
    (b) 70 lb
    (c) 100 lb
    (d) 200 lb

Article 330. Metal-Clad Cable (Type MC)

1. Type _____ is a factory assembly of insulated circuit conductors within an armor of interlocking metal tape, or a smooth or corrugated metallic sheath.

    (a) AC
    (b) MC
    (c) NM
    (d) b and c

2. Type MC cable shall not be _____ unless the metallic sheath or armor is resistant to the conditions, or is protected by material resistant to the conditions.

(a) used for direct burial in the earth
(b) embedded in concrete
(c) exposed to cinder fill
(d) all of these

3. Type MC cable installed through, or parallel to, framing members shall be protected against physical damage from penetration by screws or nails by 1¼ in. separation or protected by a suitable metal plate.

(a) True
(b) False

4. Smooth-sheath Type MC cable with an external diameter not greater than ¾ in. shall have a bending radius not more than _____ times the cable external diameter.

(a) five
(b) 10
(c) 12
(d) 13

5. Bends made in interlocked or corrugated sheath Type MC cable shall have a radius of at least _____ times the external diameter of the metallic sheath.

(a) 5
(b) 7
(c) 10
(d) 12

6. Type MC cable containing four or fewer conductors, sized no larger than 10 AWG, shall be secured within _____ of every box, cabinet, fitting, or other cable termination.

(a) 8 in.
(b) 12 in.
(c) 18 in.
(d) 24 in.

7. Type MC cable shall be secured at intervals not exceeding _____.

(a) 3 ft
(b) 4 ft
(c) 6 ft
(d) 8 ft

8. Type MC cable installed horizontally through wooden or metal framing members are considered secured and supported where such support doesn't exceed _____ intervals.

(a) 3 ft
(b) 4 ft
(c) 6 ft
(d) 8 ft

9. Type MC cable can be unsupported where _____.

(a) fished between concealed access points in finished buildings or structures and support is impracticable
(b) not more than 2 ft in length at terminals where flexibility is necessary
(c) not more than 6 ft from the last point of support within an accessible ceiling for the connection of luminaires or other electrical equipment
(d) a or c

10. Fittings used for connecting Type MC cable to boxes, cabinets, or other equipment shall _____.

(a) be nonmetallic only
(b) be listed and identified for such use
(c) be listed and identified as weatherproof
(d) include anti-shorting bushings

Article 338. Service-Entrance Cable (Types SE and USE)

1. Type _____ cable is an assembly primarily for services.

(a) NM
(b) TC
(c) SE
(d) none of these

2. Type _____ is a multiconductor cable identified for use as underground service-entrance cable.

   (a) SE
   (b) NM
   (c) UF
   (d) USE

3. Type SE cable shall be permitted to be used as _____ in wiring systems where all of the circuit conductors of the cable are of the thermoset or thermoplastic type.

   (a) branch circuits
   (b) feeders
   (c) a or b
   (d) neither a or b

4. Type SE cables shall be permitted to be used for branch circuits or feeders where the insulated conductors are used for circuit wiring and the uninsulated conductor is used only for _____ purposes.

   (a) grounded connection
   (b) equipment grounding
   (c) remote control and signaling
   (d) none of these

5. Type SE cable can be used for interior wiring as long as it complies with the installation requirements of Part II of Article 334, excluding 334.80.

   (a) True
   (b) False

6. Type USE cable is not permitted for _____ wiring.

   (a) underground
   (b) interior
   (c) a or b
   (d) a and b

7. Type USE cable used for service laterals shall be permitted to emerge from the ground if terminated in an enclosure at an outside location and protected in accordance with 300.5(D).

   (a) True
   (b) False

8. The radius of the curve of the inner edge of any bend, during or after installation, shall not be less than _____ times the diameter of Type USE or SE cable.

   (a) five
   (b) seven
   (c) 10
   (d) 12

Article 342. Intermediate Metal Conduit (Type IMC)

1. IMC can be installed in or under cinder fill subject to permanent moisture _____.

   (a) where the conduit is not less than 18 in. under the fill
   (b) when protected on all sides by 2 in. of noncinder concrete
   (c) where protected by corrosion protection judged suitable for the condition
   (d) any of these

2. Materials such as straps, bolts, screws, and so forth, that are associated with the installation of IMC in wet locations shall be _____.

   (a) weatherproof
   (b) weathertight
   (c) corrosion resistant
   (d) none of these

3. Where practicable, contact of dissimilar metals shall be avoided in an IMC raceway installation to prevent _____.

   (a) corrosion
   (b) galvanic action
   (c) shorts
   (d) none of these

4. A run of IMC shall not contain more than the equivalent of _____ quarter bends between pull points such as conduit bodies and boxes.

   (a) one
   (b) two
   (c) three
   (d) four

5. When IMC is cut in the field, reaming is required to remove the burrs and rough edges.

   (a) True
   (b) False

6. IMC must be secured _____.

   (a) by fastening within 3 ft of each outlet box, junction box, device box, cabinet, conduit body, or other conduit termination
   (b) within 5 ft of a box or termination fitting when structural members don't permit the raceway to be secured within 3 ft of the termination
   (c) except when the IMC is within 3 ft of the service head for an above-the-roof termination of a mast
   (d) a, b, or c

7. Trade size 1 IMC shall be supported at intervals not exceeding _____.

   (a) 8 ft
   (b) 10 ft
   (c) 12 ft
   (d) 14 ft

8. Horizontal runs of IMC supported by openings through framing members at intervals not exceeding 10 ft and securely fastened within 3 ft of terminations shall be permitted.

   (a) True
   (b) False

9. Threadless couplings and connectors used on threaded IMC ends shall be listed for the purpose.

   (a) True
   (b) False

10. Threadless couplings approved for use with IMC in wet locations shall be _____.

    (a) rainproof
    (b) listed for wet locations
    (c) moistureproof
    (d) concrete-tight

11. Running threads shall not be used on IMC for connection at couplings.

    (a) True
    (b) False

12. Where IMC enters a box, fitting, or other enclosure, _____ shall be provided to protect the wire from abrasion, unless the design of the box, fitting, or enclosure affords equivalent protection.

    (a) a bushing
    (b) duct seal
    (c) electrical tape
    (d) seal fittings

Article 344. Rigid Metal Conduit (Type RMC)

1. Galvanized steel, stainless steel and red brass RMC can be installed in concrete, in direct contact with the earth, or in areas subject to severe corrosive influences when protected by _____ and judged suitable for the condition.

   (a) ceramic
   (b) corrosion protection
   (c) backfill
   (d) a natural barrier

2. Galvanized steel, stainless steel, and red brass RMC shall be permitted in or under cinder fill subject to permanent moisture, when protected on all sides by a layer of noncinder concrete not less than _____ thick.

    (a) 2 in.
    (b) 4 in.
    (c) 6 in.
    (d) 18 in.

3. Materials such as straps, bolts, and so forth., associated with the installation of RMC in wet locations shall be _____.

    (a) weatherproof
    (b) weathertight
    (c) corrosion resistant
    (d) none of these

4. Aluminum fittings and enclosures can be used with _____ conduit where not subject to severe corrosive influences.

    (a) steel rigid metal
    (b) aluminum rigid metal
    (c) PVC-coated rigid conduit only
    (d) a and b

5. The minimum radius of a field bend on trade size 1¼ RMC is _____.

    (a) 7 in.
    (b) 8 in.
    (c) 10 in.
    (d) 14 in.

6. A run of RMC shall not contain more than the equivalent of _____ quarter bends between pull points such as conduit bodies and boxes.

    (a) one
    (b) two
    (c) three
    (d) four

7. Cut ends of RMC shall be _____ or otherwise finished to remove rough edges.

    (a) threaded
    (b) reamed
    (c) painted
    (d) galvanized

8. Horizontal runs of RMC supported by openings through _____ at intervals not exceeding 10 ft and securely fastened within 3 ft of termination points shall be permitted.

    (a) walls
    (b) trusses
    (c) rafters
    (d) framing members

9. Threadless couplings and connectors used with RMC in wet locations shall be _____.

    (a) listed for wet locations
    (b) listed for damp locations
    (c) nonabsorbent
    (d) weatherproof

10. Threadless couplings and connectors used with RMC buried in masonry or concrete shall be the _____ type.

    (a) raintight
    (b) wet and damp location
    (c) nonabsorbent
    (d) concrete-tight

11. Running threads shall not be used on RMC for connection at _____.

    (a) boxes
    (b) cabinets
    (c) couplings
    (d) meter sockets

12. Where RMC enters a box, fitting, or other enclosure, _____ shall be provided to protect the wire from abrasion, unless the design of the box, fitting, or enclosure affords equivalent protection.

(a) a bushing
(b) duct seal
(c) electrical tape
(d) seal fittings

13. Each length of RMC shall be clearly and durably identified in every _____.

(a) 3 ft
(b) 5 ft
(c) 10 ft
(d) 20 ft

14. The standard length of RMC shall _____.

(a) be 10 ft
(b) include a coupling on each length
(c) be threaded on each end
(d) all of these

Article 348. Flexible Metal Conduit (Type FMC)

1. _____ is a raceway of circular cross section made of a helically wound, formed, interlocked metal strip.

(a) Type MC cable
(b) Type AC Cable
(c) LFMC
(d) FMC

2. FMC shall not be installed _____.

(a) in wet locations
(b) embedded in poured concrete
(c) where subject to physical damage
(d) all of these

3. FMC can be installed exposed or concealed where not subject to physical damage.

(a) True
(b) False

4. Bends in FMC shall be made so that the conduit is not damaged and the internal diameter of the conduit is _____.

(a) larger than ⅜ in.
(b) not effectively reduced
(c) increased
(d) larger than 1 in.

5. Bends in FMC _____ between pull points.

(a) shall not be made
(b) need not be limited (in degrees)
(c) shall not exceed 360 degrees
(d) shall not exceed 180 degrees

6. Cut ends of FMC shall be trimmed or otherwise finished to remove rough edges, except where fittings _____.

(a) are the crimp-on type
(b) thread into the convolutions
(c) contain insulated throats
(d) are listed for grounding

7. FMC shall be supported and secured _____.

(a) at intervals not exceeding 4½ ft
(b) within 8 in. on each side of a box where fished
(c) where fished
(d) at intervals not exceeding 6 ft

8. Flexible metal conduit must be securely fastened by a means approved by the authority having jurisdiction within _____ of termination.

(a) 6 in.
(b) 10 in.
(c) 1 ft
(d) 10 ft

9. Flexible metal conduit shall not be required to be _____ where fished between access points through concealed spaces in finished buildings or structures and supporting is impracticable.

    (a) secured
    (b) supported
    (c) complete
    (d) (a) and (b)

10. For flexible metal conduit, if flexibility is necessary after installation, unsecured lengths from the last point the raceway is securely fastened must not exceed _____.

    (a) 3 ft for trade sizes ½ through 1 ¼
    (b) 4 ft for trade sizes 1 ½ through 2
    (c) 5 ft for trade sizes 2 ½ and larger
    (d) all of these

11. FMC to a luminaire or electrical equipment within an accessible ceiling is permitted to be unsupported for not more than 6 ft from the last point where the raceway is securely fastened.

    (a) True
    (b) False

12. In an FMC installation, _____ connectors shall not be concealed.

    (a) straight
    (b) angle
    (c) grounding-type
    (d) none of these

13. When FMC is used where flexibility is necessary to minimize the transmission of vibration from equipment or to provide flexibility for equipment that requires movement after installation, _____ shall be installed.

    (a) an equipment grounding conductor
    (b) an expansion fitting
    (c) flexible nonmetallic connectors
    (d) none of these

Article 350. Liquidtight Flexible Metal Conduit (Type LFMC)

1. _____ is a raceway of circular cross section having an outer liquidtight, nonmetallic, sunlight-resistant jacket over an inner flexible metal core.

    (a) FMC
    (b) LFNMC
    (c) LFMC
    (d) none of these

2. The use of LFMC shall be permitted for _____.

    (a) direct burial where listed and marked for the purpose
    (b) exposed work
    (c) concealed work
    (d) all of these

3. Liquidtight flexible metal conduit must be securely fastened by a means approved by the authority having jurisdiction within _____ of termination.

    (a) 6 in.
    (b) 10 in.
    (c) 1 ft
    (d) 10 ft

4. LFMC shall be supported and secured _____.

    (a) at intervals not exceeding 4½ ft
    (b) within 8 in. on each side of a box where fished
    (c) where fished
    (d) at intervals not exceeding 6 ft

5. LFMC shall not be required to be secured or supported where fished between access points through _____ spaces in finished buildings or structures and supporting is impractical.

    (a) concealed
    (b) exposed
    (c) hazardous
    (d) completed

6. For liquidtight flexible metal conduit, if flexibility is necessary after installation, unsecured lengths from the last point the raceway is securely fastened must not exceed _____.

(a) 3 ft for trade sizes ½ through 1 ¼
(b) 4 ft for trade sizes 1 ½ through 2
(c) 5 ft for trade sizes 2 ½ and larger
(d) all of these

7. _____ connectors shall not be concealed when used in installations of LFMC.

(a) Straight
(b) Angle
(c) Grounding-type
(d) none of these

8. When LFMC is used to connect equipment where flexibility is necessary to minimize the transmission of vibration from equipment of for equipment requiring movement after installation, a(n) _____ conductor shall be installed.

(a) main bonding
(b) grounded
(c) equipment grounding
(d) none of these

9. Where flexibility _____, liquidtight flexible metal conduit shall be permitted to be used as an equipment grounding conductor when installed in accordance with 250.118(6).

(a) is required after installation
(b) is not required after installation
(c) either a or d
(d) is optional

Article 352. Rigid Polyvinyl Chloride Conduit (Type PVC)

1. Extreme _____ may cause PVC conduit to become brittle, and therefore more susceptible to damage from physical contact.

(a) sunlight
(b) corrosive conditions
(c) heat
(d) cold

2. PVC conduit shall be permitted for exposed work where subject to physical damage if identified for such use.

(a) True
(b) False

3. PVC conduit can support nonmetallic conduit bodies not larger than the largest entering raceway, but the conduit bodies shall not contain devices, luminaires, or other equipment.

(a) True
(b) False

4. Conductors rated at a temperature _____ than the listed temperature rating of PVC conduit shall not be installed in PVC conduit, unless the conductors are not operated at a temperature above the raceways listed temperature rating of the PVC conduit.

(a) lower
(b) the same as
(c) higher
(d) a or b

5. PVC conduit shall not be used _____, unless specifically permitted.

(a) in hazardous (classified) locations
(b) for the support of luminaires or other equipment
(c) where subject to physical damage unless identified for such use
(d) all of these

6. The number of conductors permitted in PVC conduit shall not exceed the percentage fill specified in _____.

(a) Chapter 9, Table 1
(b) Table 250.66
(c) Table 310.15(B)(16)
(d) 240.6

7. Bends in PVC conduit shall be made only _____.

   (a) by hand forming the bend
   (b) with bending equipment identified for the purpose
   (c) with a truck exhaust pipe
   (d) by use of an open flame torch

8. Bends in PVC conduit shall _____ between pull points.

   (a) not be made
   (b) not be limited in degrees
   (c) be limited to 360 degrees
   (d) be limited to 180 degrees

9. The cut ends of PVC conduit must be trimmed to remove the burrs and rough edges.

   (a) True
   (b) False

10. PVC conduit shall be securely fastened within _____ of each box.

    (a) 6 in.
    (b) 12 in.
    (c) 24 in.
    (d) 36 in.

11. Where PVC conduit enters a box, fitting, or other enclosure, a bushing or adapter shall be provided to protect the conductor from abrasion unless the design of the box, fitting, or enclosure affords equivalent protection.

    (a) True
    (b) False

12. Joints between PVC conduit, couplings, fittings, and boxes shall be made by _____.

    (a) the authority having jurisdiction
    (b) set screw fittings
    (c) an approved method
    (d) expansion fittings

13. PVC conduit and fittings for use above ground shall have the following characteristics _____.

    (a) flame retardant
    (b) resistance to low temperatures and sunlight
    (c) resistance to distortion from heat
    (d) all of these

Article 356—Liquidtight Flexible Nonmetallic Conduit (Type LFNC

1. LFNC shall be permitted for _____.

   (a) direct burial where listed and marked for the purpose
   (b) exposed work
   (c) outdoors where listed and marked for this purpose
   (d) all of these

2. The number of conductors permitted in LFNC shall not exceed the percentage fill specified in _____.

   (a) Chapter 9, Table 1
   (b) Table 250.66
   (c) Table 310.15(B)(16)
   (d) 240.6

3. Bends in LFNC shall be made so that the conduit will not be damaged and the internal diameter of the conduit will not be effectively reduced. Bends can be made _____.

   (a) manually without auxiliary equipment
   (b) with bending equipment identified for the purpose
   (c) with any kind of conduit bending tool that will work
   (d) by the use of an open flame torch

4. Bends in LFNC shall _____ between pull points.

   (a) not be made
   (b) not be limited in degrees
   (c) be limited to 360 degrees
   (d) be limited to 180 degrees

5. When LFNC is used to connect equipment requiring flexibility after installation, a separate _____ shall be installed.

    (a) equipment grounding conductor
    (b) expansion fitting
    (c) flexible nonmetallic connector
    (d) none of these

Article 358. Electrical Metallic Tubing (Type EMT)

1. _____ is a listed thin-wall, metallic tubing of circular cross section used for the installation and physical protection of electrical conductors when joined together with listed fittings.

    (a) LFNC
    (b) EMT
    (c) NUCC
    (d) RTRC

2. EMT, elbows, couplings, and fittings can be installed in concrete, in direct contact with the earth, or in areas subject to severe corrosive influences if _____.

    (a) protected by corrosion protection
    (b) approved as suitable for the condition
    (c) a and b
    (d) list for wet locations

3. When EMT is installed in wet locations, all supports, bolts, straps, and screws shall be _____.

    (a) of corrosion-resistant materials
    (b) protected against corrosion
    (c) a or b
    (d) of nonmetallic materials only

4. EMT shall not be used where _____.

    (a) subject to severe physical damage
    (b) protected from corrosion only by enamel
    (c) used for the support of luminaires
    (d) any of these

5. EMT shall not be threaded.

    (a) True
    (b) False

6. EMT couplings and connectors shall be made up _____.

    (a) of metal
    (b) in accordance with industry standards
    (c) tight
    (d) none of these

Article 376. Metal Wireways

1. Metal wireways are sheet metal troughs with _____ for housing and protecting electric conductors and cable.

    (a) removable covers
    (b) hinged covers
    (c) a or b
    (d) none of these

2. Wireways shall be permitted for _____.

    (a) exposed work
    (b) totally concealed work
    (c) wet locations if listed for the purpose
    (d) a and c

3. Wireways can pass transversely through a wall _____.

    (a) if the length passing through the wall is unbroken
    (b) if the wall is of fire-rated construction
    (c) in hazardous (classified) locations
    (d) if the wall is not of fire-rated construction

4. Conductors larger than that for which the wireway is designed can be installed in any wireway.

    (a) True
    (b) False

5. The sum of the cross-sectional areas of all contained conductors at any cross-section of a metal wireway shall not exceed _____.

(a) 50 percent
(b) 20 percent
(c) 25 percent
(d) 80 percent

6. The derating factors in 310.15(B)(3)(a) shall be applied to a metal wireway only where the number of current-carrying conductors in the wireway exceeds _____.

(a) 30
(b) 40
(c) 50
(d) 60

7. Where insulated conductors are deflected within a metal wireway, the wireway shall be sized to meet the bending requirements corresponding to _____ wire per terminal in Table 312.6(A).

(a) one
(b) two
(c) three
(d) four

8. Power distribution blocks installed in metal wireways shall be listed.

(a) True
(b) False

9. Power distribution blocks installed in metal wireways shall _____.

(a) allow for sufficient wire-bending space at terminals
(b) not have uninsulated exposed live parts
(c) a or b
(d) a and b

Article 392. Cable Trays

1. A cable tray is a unit or assembly of units or sections and associated fittings forming a _____ system used to securely fasten or support cables and raceways.

(a) structural
(b) flexible
(c) movable
(d) secure

2. Cable trays can be used as a support system for _____.

(a) service conductors, feeders, and branch circuits
(b) communications circuits
(c) control and signaling circuits
(d) all of these

3. Where exposed to the direct rays of the sun, insulated conductors and jacketed cables installed in cable trays shall be _____ as being sunlight resistant.

(a) listed
(b) approved
(c) identified
(d) none of these

4. Cable trays and their associated fittings shall be _____ for the intended use.

(a) listed
(b) approved
(c) identified
(d) none of these

5. Any of the following wiring methods can be installed in a cable tray:

(a) metal raceways
(b) nonmetallic raceways
(c) cables
(d) all of these

6. Cable tray systems shall not be used _____.

   (a) in hoistways
   (b) where subject to severe physical damage
   (c) in hazardous (classified) locations
   (d) a or b

7. Each run of cable tray shall be _____ before the installation of cables.

   (a) tested for 25 ohms resistance
   (b) insulated
   (c) completed
   (d) all of these

8. Cable trays shall be _____ except as permitted by 392.10(D).

   (a) exposed
   (b) accessible
   (c) concealed
   (d) a and b

9. In industrial facilities where conditions of maintenance and supervision ensure that only qualified persons will service the installation, cable tray systems can be used to support _____.

   (a) raceways
   (b) cables
   (c) boxes and conduit bodies
   (d) all of these

10. For raceways terminating at a cable tray, a(n) _____ cable tray clamp or adapter shall be used to securely fasten the raceway to the cable tray system.

   (a) listed
   (b) approved
   (c) identified
   (d) none of these

11. Where single conductor cables comprising each phase, neutral, or grounded conductor of a circuit are connected in parallel in a cable tray, the conductors shall be installed _____, to prevent current unbalance in the paralleled conductors due to inductive reactance.

   (a) in groups consisting of not more than three conductors per phase or neutral
   (b) in groups consisting of not more than one conductor per phase or neutral
   (c) as individual conductors securely bound to the cable tray
   (d) in separate groups

12. Cable trays shall be supported at intervals in accordance with the installation instructions.

   (a) True
   (b) False

13. A box shall not be required where cables or conductors from cable trays are installed in bushed conduit and tubing used as support or for protection against _____.

   (a) abuse
   (b) unauthorized access
   (c) physical damage
   (d) tampering

14. Cable _____ made and insulated by approved methods can be located within a cable tray provided they are accessible, and do not project above the side rails where the splices are subject to physical damage.

   (a) connections
   (b) jumpers
   (c) splices
   (d) conductors

15. Metal cable trays containing only non-power conductors such as communication, data, signal, conductors and cables must be electrically continuous, through listed connections or the use of an insulated stranded bonding jumper not smaller than _____.

    (a) 12 AWG
    (b) 10 AWG
    (c) 6 AWG
    (d) 4 AWG

16. Steel or aluminum cable tray systems shall be permitted to be used as an equipment grounding conductor, provided the cable tray sections and fittings are identified as _____, among other requirements.

    (a) an equipment grounding conductor
    (b) special
    (c) industrial
    (d) all of these

17. The conductor ampacity adjustment factors only apply to the number of current-carrying conductors in the cable and not to the number of conductors in the cable tray.

    (a) True
    (b) False

18. The messenger of messenger-supported wiring shall be supported at dead ends and at intermediate locations so as to eliminate _____ on the circuit conductors.

    (a) static
    (b) magnetism
    (c) tension
    (d) induction

Notes

EQUIPMENT FOR GENERAL USE

INTRODUCTION TO CHAPTER 4—EQUIPMENT FOR GENERAL USE

With the first three chapters behind you, the final chapter in the *NEC* for building a solid foundation in general work is Chapter 4. This chapter helps you apply the first three chapters to installations involving general equipment. These first four chapters follow a natural sequential progression. Each of the next four *NEC* Chapters—5, 6, 7, and 8—build upon the first four, but in no particular order. You need to understand all of the first four chapters to properly apply any of the next four.

- **Article 400.—Flexible Cords and Flexible Cables.** Article 400 covers the general requirements, applications, and construction specifications for flexible cords and flexible cables.

- **Article 404—Switches.** The requirements of Article 404 apply to switches of all types. These include snap (toggle) switches, dimmer switches, fan switches, knife switches, circuit breakers used as switches, and automatic switches such as time clocks, timers, and switches and circuit breakers used for disconnecting means.

- **Article 408—Switchboards and Panelboards.** Article 408 covers specific requirements for switchboards, panelboards, and distribution boards that supply lighting and power circuits.

- **Article 480—Batteries.** Article 480 covers stationary installations of storage batteries.

Notes

Flexible Cords and Flexible Cables

INTRODUCTION TO ARTICLE 400—FLEXIBLE CORDS AND FLEXIBLE CABLES

This article covers the general requirements, applications, and construction specifications for flexible cords and flexible cables. The *NEC* doesn't consider flexible cords to be wiring methods like those defined in Chapter 3.

Always use a cord (and fittings) identified for the application. Table 400.4 will help you in that regard. For example, use cords listed for a wet location if you're using them outdoors. The jacket material of any cord is tested to maintain its insulation properties and other characteristics in the environments for which it has been listed. Tables 400.5(A)(1) and 400.5(A)(2) are also important tables to turn to when looking for the ampacity of flexible cords and cables.

400.1 Scope. Article 400 covers the general requirements, applications, and construction specifications for flexible cords and flexible cables as contained in Table 400.4.

> **Author's Comment:** Extension cords must not be used as a substitute for fixed wiring [400.8(1)], but they can be used for temporary wiring if approved by the authority having jurisdiction in accordance with 590.2(B).

400.3 Suitability. Flexible cords and flexible cables, as well as their fittings must be suitable for the use and location.

400.4 Types of Flexible Cords and Flexible Cables. The use of flexible cords and flexible cables must conform to the descriptions contained in Table 400.4.

> **Author's Comment:** The suffix "W" at the end of a cord type designates that the cord is water and sunlight resistant [Table 400.4, Note 15].

400.7 Uses Permitted.

(A) Uses Permitted. Flexible cords and flexible cables within the scope of this article can be used for the following applications:

(1) Pendants [210.50(A) and 314.23(H)].

> **Author's Comment:** Only cords identified for use as pendants in Table 400.4 may be used for pendants.

(2) Wiring of luminaires [410.24(A) and 410.62(B)].

(3) Connection of portable luminaires, portable and mobile signs, or appliances [422.16].

(4) Elevator cables.

(5) Wiring of cranes and hoists.

(6) Connection of utilization equipment to facilitate frequent interchange [422.16]. **Figure 400–1**

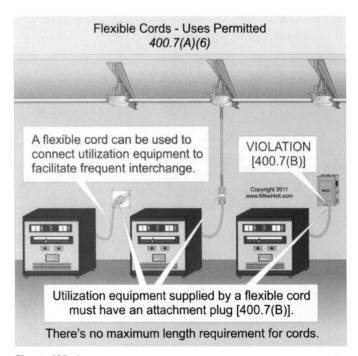

Flexible Cords - Uses Permitted
400.7(A)(6)

A flexible cord can be used to connect utilization equipment to facilitate frequent interchange.

VIOLATION
[400.7(B)]

Copyright 2011
www.MikeHolt.com

Utilization equipment supplied by a flexible cord must have an attachment plug [400.7(B)].

There's no maximum length requirement for cords.

Figure 400–1

(7) Prevention of the transmission of noise or vibration [422.16].

(8) Appliances where the fastening means and mechanical connections are specifically designed to permit ready removal for maintenance and repair, and the appliance is intended or identified for flexible cord connections [422.16].

(9) Connection of moving parts.

(10) If specifically permitted elsewhere in this *Code*.

(B) Attachment Plugs. Attachment plugs are required for flexible cords used in any of the following applications:

- Portable luminaires, portable and mobile signs, or appliances [400.7(A)(3)].
- Stationary equipment to facilitate its frequent interchange [400.7(A)(6) and 422.16].
- Appliances specifically designed to permit ready removal for maintenance and repair, and identified for flexible cord connection [400.7(A)(8)].

Author's Comment: An attachment plug can serve as the disconnecting means for stationary appliances [422.33] and room air conditioners [440.63].

400.8 Uses Not Permitted. Unless specifically permitted in 400.7, flexible cords must not be:

(1) Used as a substitute for the fixed wiring of a structure.

(2) Run through holes in walls, structural ceilings, suspended or dropped ceilings, or floors. **Figure 400–2**

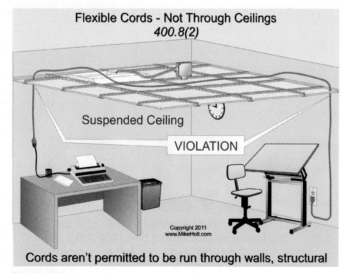

Figure 400–2

Author's Comment: According to an article in the *International Association of Electrical Inspectors* magazine *(IAEI News)*, a flexible cord installed through a cabinet for an appliance isn't considered as being installed through a wall.

(3) Run through doorways, windows, or similar openings.

(4) Attached to building surfaces.

(5) Concealed by walls, floors, or ceilings, or located above suspended or dropped ceilings.

(6) Installed in raceways, except as permitted elsewhere in the *Code*.

(7) If subject to physical damage.

400.10 Pull at Joints and Terminals. Flexible cords must be installed so tension won't be transmitted to the conductor terminals.

> **Note:** This can be accomplished by knotting the cord, winding the cord with tape, or by using fittings designed for the purpose, such as strain-relief fittings. **Figure 400–3**

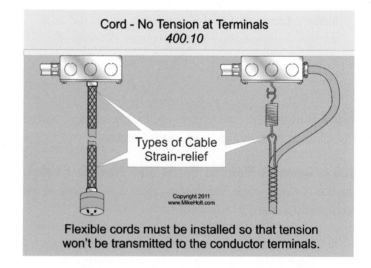

Figure 400–3

Author's Comment: When critical health and economic activities are dependent on flexible cord-supplied equipment, the best method is a factory-made, stress-relieving, listed device, not an old-timer's knot.

400.14 Protection from Damage. Flexible cords must be protected by bushings or fittings where passing through holes in covers, outlet boxes, or similar enclosures.

In industrial establishments where the conditions of maintenance and supervision ensure that only qualified persons will service the installation, flexible cords or flexible cables not exceeding 50 ft can be installed in aboveground raceways.

400.23 Equipment Grounding Conductor Identification. A conductor intended to be used as an equipment grounding conductor must have a continuous green color or a continuous identifying marker distinguishing it from the other conductor(s). Conductors with green insulation, or green with one or more yellow stripes must not be used for an ungrounded or neutral conductor [250.119].

Notes

Switches

INTRODUCTION TO ARTICLE 404—SWITCHES

The requirements of Article 404 apply to switches of all types, including snap (toggle) switches, dimmer switches, fan switches, knife switches, circuit breakers used as switches, and automatic switches, such as time clocks and timers.

404.1 Scope. The requirements of Article 404 apply to all types of switches, switching devices, and circuit breakers used as switches. Figure 404–1

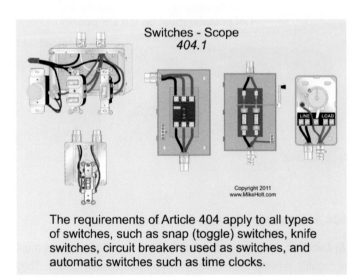

The requirements of Article 404 apply to all types of switches, such as snap (toggle) switches, knife switches, circuit breakers used as switches, and automatic switches such as time clocks.

Figure 404–1

404.2 Switch Connections.

(B) Switching Neutral Conductors. Only the ungrounded conductor is permitted to be used for switching, and the grounded conductor must not be disconnected by switches or circuit breakers.

Ex: A switch or circuit breaker is permitted to disconnect a grounded circuit conductor where it disconnects all circuit conductors simultaneously.

404.3 Switch Enclosures.

(A) General. Switches and circuit breakers used as switches must be of the externally operable type mounted in an enclosure listed for the intended use.

(B) Used for Raceways or Splices. Switch or circuit-breaker enclosures can contain splices and taps if the splices and/or taps don't fill the wiring space at any cross section to more than 75 percent.

Switch or circuit-breaker enclosures can have conductors feed through them if the wiring doesn't fill the wiring space at any cross section to more than 40 percent [312.8].

404.4 Damp or Wet Locations.

(A) Surface-Mounted Switches or Circuit Breakers. Surface-mounted switches and circuit breakers in a damp or wet location must be installed in a weatherproof enclosure. The enclosure must be installed so not less than ¼ in. of airspace is provided between the enclosure and the wall or other supporting surface [312.2]. **Figure 404–2**

(B) Flush-Mounted Switches or Circuit Breakers. A flush-mounted switch or circuit breaker in a damp or wet location must have a weatherproof cover. Figure 404–3

(C) Switches in Bathtub or Shower Spaces. Switches can be located next to but not within a bathtub, hydromassage bathtub, or shower space unless installed as part of a listed tub or shower assembly.

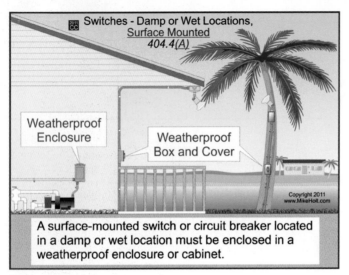

Figure 404–2

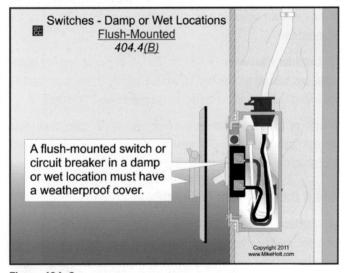

Figure 404–3

404.6 Position of Knife Switches.

(A) Single-Throw Knife Switch. Single-throw knife switches must be installed so gravity won't tend to close them.

(C) Connection of Switches. Single-throw knife switches, molded case switches, and circuit breakers used as switches must have the the terminals supplying the load deenergize when the switch is in the open position.

Exception: The blades and terminals supplying the load can be energized when the switch is in the open position. For such installations, a permanent sign must on the switch enclosure or immediately adjacent to open switch is required to read:

⚠ WARNING — LOAD SIDE TERMINALS MAY BE ENERGIZED BY BACKFEED.

404.7 Indicating. Switches, motor circuit switches, and circuit breakers used as switches must be marked to indicate whether they're in the "on" or "off" position. When the switch is operated vertically, it must be installed so the "up" position is the "on" position [240.81]. **Figure 404–4**

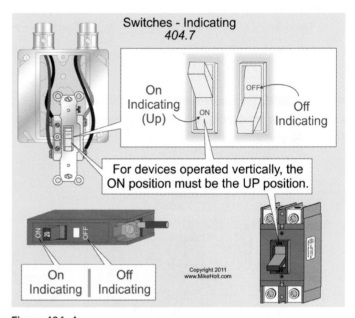

Figure 404–4

404.8 Accessibility and Grouping.

(A) Location. Switches and circuit breakers used as switches must be capable of being operated from a readily accessible location. They must also be installed so the center of the grip of the operating handle of the switch or circuit breaker, when in its highest position, isn't more than 6 ft 7 in. above the floor or working platform [240.24(A)]. **Figure 404–5**

Ex 2: Switches and circuit breakers used as switches can be mounted above 6 ft 7 in. if they're next to the equipment they supply, and are accessible by portable means [240.24(A)(4)]. **Figure 404–6**

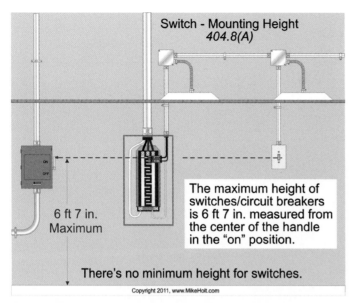

Switch - Mounting Height
404.8(A)

6 ft 7 in.
Maximum

The maximum height of switches/circuit breakers is 6 ft 7 in. measured from the center of the handle in the "on" position.

There's no minimum height for switches.

Copyright 2011, www.MikeHolt.com

Figure 404–5

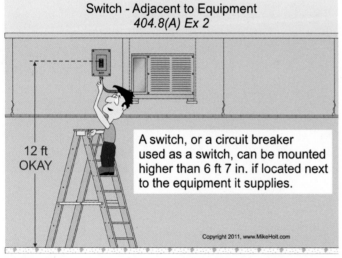

Switch - Adjacent to Equipment
404.8(A) Ex 2

12 ft
OKAY

A switch, or a circuit breaker used as a switch, can be mounted higher than 6 ft 7 in. if located next to the equipment it supplies.

Copyright 2011, www.MikeHolt.com

Figure 404–6

404.11 Circuit Breakers Used as Switches. A manually operable circuit breaker used as a switch must show when it's in the "on" (closed) or "off" (open) position [404.7].

404.12 Grounding of Enclosures. Metal enclosures for switches and circuit breakers used as switches must be connected to an equipment grounding conductor of a type recognized in 250.118 [250.4(A)(3)]. Nonmetallic boxes for switches must be installed using a wiring method that includes an equipment grounding conductor.

404.15 Switch Marking.

(A) Markings. Switches must be marked with the current, voltage, and if horsepower rated, the maximum rating for which they're designed.

(B) Off Indication. If in the off position, a switching device with a marked "off" position must completely disconnect all ungrounded conductors of the load it controls.

Notes

ARTICLE 408

Switchboards and Panelboards

INTRODUCTION TO ARTICLE 408—SWITCHBOARDS AND PANELBOARDS

Article 408 covers the specific requirements for switchboards and panelboards that control power and lighting circuits. Some key points to remember:

- One objective of Article 408 is that the installation prevents contact between current-carrying conductors and people or equipment.
- The circuit directory of a panelboard must clearly identify the purpose or use of each circuit that originates in the panelboard.
- You must understand the detailed grounding and overcurrent protection requirements for panelboards.

PART I. GENERAL

408.1 Scope. Article 408 covers the specific requirements for switchboards, and panelboards that control power and lighting circuits. Figure 408–1

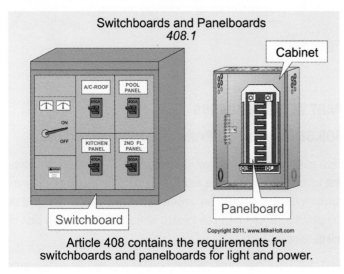

Switchboards and Panelboards
408.1

Article 408 contains the requirements for switchboards and panelboards for light and power.

Figure 408–1

Author's Comment: For the purposes of this textbook, we'll only cover the requirements for panelboards.

408.4 Field Identification.

(A) Circuit Directory or Circuit Identification. All circuits, and circuit modifications, must be legibly identified as to their clear, evident, and specific purpose. Spare positions that contain unused overcurrent devices must also be identified. Identification must include sufficient detail to allow each circuit to be distinguished from all others, and the identification must be on a circuit directory located on the face or inside of the door of the panelboard. See 110.22. Figure 408–2

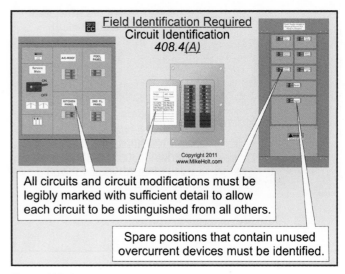

Field Identification Required
Circuit Identification
408.4(A)

All circuits and circuit modifications must be legibly marked with sufficient detail to allow each circuit to be distinguished from all others.

Spare positions that contain unused overcurrent devices must be identified.

Figure 408–2

Author's Comment: Circuit identification must not be based on transient conditions of occupancy, such as Steven's, or Brittney's bedroom. **Figure 408–3**

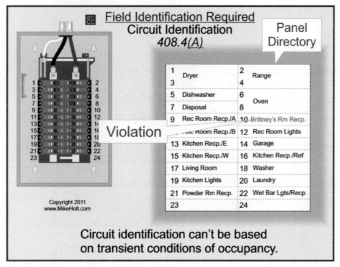

Figure 408–3

(B) Source of Supply. All switchboards and panelboards supplied by a feeder in other than one- or two-family dwellings must be marked as to the device or equipment where the power supply originates. **Figure 408–4**

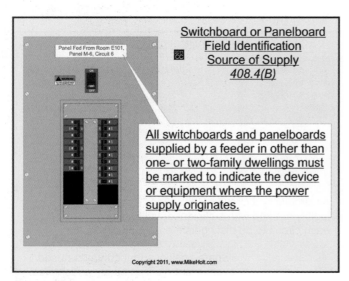

Figure 408–4

408.5 Clearance for Conductors Entering Bus Enclosures. If raceways enter a switchboard, floor-standing panelboard, or similar enclosure, the raceways, including end fittings, must not rise more than 3 in. above the bottom of the enclosure.

408.7 Unused Openings. Unused openings for circuit breakers and switches must be closed using identified closures, or other means approved by the authority having jurisdiction, that provide protection substantially equivalent to the wall of the enclosure. **Figure 408–5**

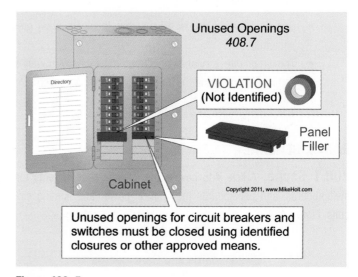

Figure 408–5

PART III. PANELBOARDS

408.36 Overcurrent Protection of Panelboards.

Each panelboard must be provided with a single overcurrent protection located within, or on the supply side of the panelboard. The overcurrent device must have an ampere rating not greater than that of the panelboard, and it can be located within or on the supply side of the panelboard.

Ex 1: Individual overcurrent protection isn't required for panelboards used as service equipment with up to six disconnecting means in accordance with 230.71.

(D) Back-Fed Devices. Plug-in circuit breakers that are back-fed from field-installed ac conductors must be secured in place by an additional fastener that requires other than a pull to release the breaker from the panelboard. **Figure 408–6**

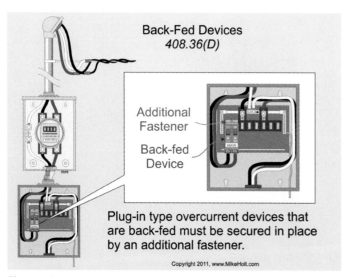

Back-Fed Devices
408.36(D)

Additional Fastener

Back-fed Device

Plug-in type overcurrent devices that are back-fed must be secured in place by an additional fastener.

Copyright 2011, www.MikeHolt.com

Figure 408–6

Author's Comment: The purpose of the breaker fastener is to prevent the circuit breaker from being accidentally removed from the panelboard while energized, thereby exposing someone to dangerous voltage.

⚠️ **CAUTION:** *Circuit breakers marked "Line" and "Load" must be installed in accordance with listing or labeling instructions [110.3(B)]; therefore, these types of devices must not be back-fed.* **Figure 408–7**

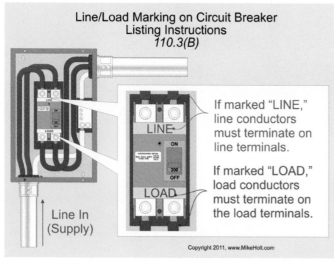

Line/Load Marking on Circuit Breaker Listing Instructions
110.3(B)

LINE

ON

200 OFF

LOAD

If marked "LINE," line conductors must terminate on line terminals.

If marked "LOAD," load conductors must terminate on the load terminals.

Line In (Supply)

Copyright 2011, www.MikeHolt.com

Figure 408–7

408.40 Equipment Grounding Conductor. Metal panelboard cabinets and frames must be connected to an equipment grounding conductor of a type recognized in 250.118 [215.6 and 250.4(A)(3)].

If the panelboard cabinet is used with nonmetallic raceways or cables, or where separate equipment grounding conductors are provided, a terminal bar for the circuit equipment grounding conductors must be bonded to the metal cabinet. **Figure 408–8**

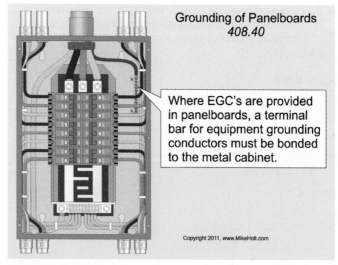

Grounding of Panelboards
408.40

Where EGC's are provided in panelboards, a terminal bar for equipment grounding conductors must be bonded to the metal cabinet.

Copyright 2011, www.MikeHolt.com

Figure 408–8

Equipment grounding conductors must not terminate on the neutral terminal bar, and neutral conductors must not terminate on the equipment grounding terminal bar, except as permitted by 250.142 for services and separately derived systems. **Figure 408–9**

Author's Comment: See the definition of "Separately Derived System" in Article 100.

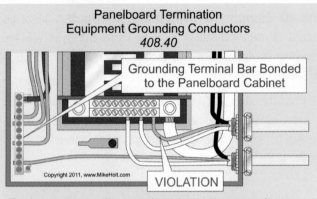

Panelboard Termination
Equipment Grounding Conductors
408.40

Grounding Terminal Bar Bonded
to the Panelboard Cabinet

Copyright 2011, www.MikeHolt.com

VIOLATION

Equipment grounding conductors must not terminate on
the same terminal bar with the neutral conductor, except
as permitted by 250.142 for services and separately
derived systems.

Figure 408–9

ARTICLE 480

Storage Batteries

INTRODUCTION TO ARTICLE 480—STORAGE BATTERIES

The stationary battery is the heart of any uninterruptible power supply. Article 480 addresses stationary batteries for commercial and industrial grade power supplies, not the small, "point of use" UPS boxes.

Stationary batteries are also used in other applications, such as emergency power systems. Regardless of the application, if it uses stationary batteries then Article 480 applies.

Lead-acid stationary batteries fall into two general categories: flooded, and valve regulated (VRLA). These differ markedly in such ways as maintainability, total cost of ownership, and scalability. The *NEC* doesn't address these differences, as they're engineering issues and not fire safety or electrical safety issues [90.1].

The *Code* doesn't address such design issues as optimum tier height, distance between tiers, determination of charging voltage, or string configuration. Nor does it address battery testing, monitoring, or maintenance. All of these involve highly specialized areas of knowledge, and are required for optimizing operational efficiency. Standards other than the *NEC* address these issues.

What the *Code* does address, in Article 480, are issues related to preventing electrocution and the ignition of the gases that all stationary batteries (even "sealed" ones) emit.

480.1 Scope. The provisions of Article 480 apply to stationary storage battery installations.

480.2 Definitions.

Battery System. Storage batteries, battery chargers, inverters, converters, and associated electrical equipment.

Nominal Battery Voltage. The voltage of a battery based on 2V per cell for lead-acid type, 1.50V per cell for alkali type, and 4V per cell for lithium-ion types. Figure 480–1

Sealed Cell or Battery. A cell or battery with no provision for the routine addition of water or electrolyte.

Storage Battery. Battery consisting of one or more rechargeable cells.

480.3 Wiring and Equipment Supplied from Batteries.
Wiring and equipment supplied from storage batteries must be in accordance with Chapters 1 through 4.

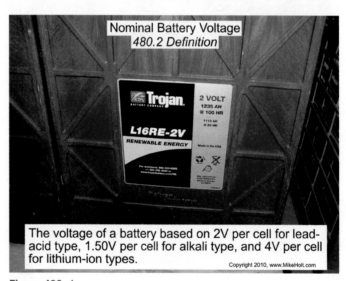

The voltage of a battery based on 2V per cell for lead-acid type, 1.50V per cell for alkali type, and 4V per cell for lithium-ion types.

Copyright 2010, www.MikeHolt.com

Figure 480–1

480.4 Overcurrent Protection for Prime Movers.
Overcurrent protection for ungrounded battery conductors is required and the overcurrent protection device must be located as close as practical to the storage battery terminals [240.21(H)].

The requirement contained in 300.3 that single conductors be installed where part of a recognized wiring method of Chapter 3 and all conductors of the circuit be contained within the same raceway or cable doesn't apply.

480.5 Disconnecting Means.
A readily accessible disconnecting means is required within sight of the storage battery for all ungrounded battery system conductors operating at over 50V nominal.

> **Author's Comment:** According to Article 100, within sight means that it's visible and not more than 50 ft from one to the other.

> **Note:** Overcurrent protection for ungrounded battery conductors must be located as close as practical to the storage battery terminals [240.21(H)].

480.8 Racks and Trays.
Racks and trays must be:

(A) Racks. Racks (rigid frames designed to support battery cells or trays) must be made of one of the following: **Figure 480-2**

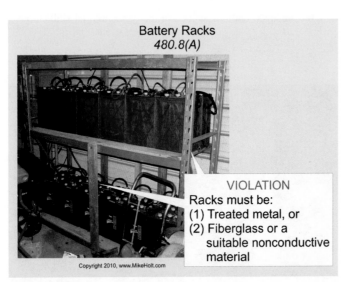

Battery Racks
480.8(A)

VIOLATION
Racks must be:
(1) Treated metal, or
(2) Fiberglass or a suitable nonconductive material

Copyright 2010, www.MikeHolt.com

Figure 480–2

(1) Metal, treated to be resistant to deteriorating action by the electrolyte and provided with nonconducting or continuous insulating material members directly supporting the cells.

(2) Fiberglass or other suitable nonconductive materials.

(B) Trays. Trays (boxes of nonconductive material) must be constructed or treated so as to be resistant to deteriorating action by the electrolyte. **Figure 480-3**

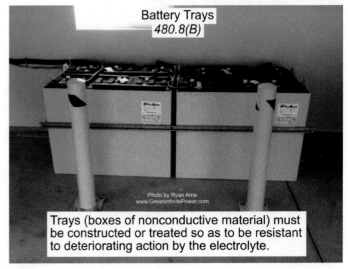

Battery Trays
480.8(B)

Photo by Ryan Arne
www.GreenInfinitePower.com

Trays (boxes of nonconductive material) must be constructed or treated so as to be resistant to deteriorating action by the electrolyte.

Figure 480–3

480.9 Battery Locations.

(A) Ventilation. Provisions must permit sufficient diffusion and ventilation of battery gases to prevent the accumulation of an explosive mixture. **Figure 480-4**

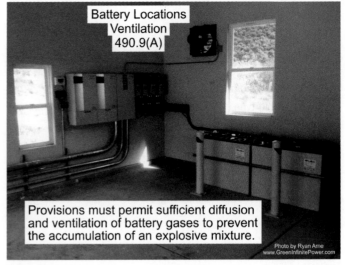

Battery Locations
Ventilation
490.9(A)

Provisions must permit sufficient diffusion and ventilation of battery gases to prevent the accumulation of an explosive mixture.

Photo by Ryan Arne
www.GreenInfinitePower.com

Figure 480–4

(B) Live Parts. Live parts of battery systems must be protected in accordance with 110.27.

> **Author's Comment:** According to 110.27, electrical equipment must not be installed where subject to physical damage, unless en closures or guards are arranged and of such strength as to prevent damage [110.27(B)]. In addition, entrances to rooms and other guarded locations containing exposed live parts must be marked with conspicuous signs forbidding unqualified persons to enter [110.27(C)].

(C) Working Space. The required working space requirements of 110.26 are measured from the edge of the battery rack.

Notes

CHAPTER 4. EQUIPMENT FOR GENERAL USE — PRACTICE QUESTIONS

Article 400. Flexible Cords and Cables

1. HPD cord shall be permitted for _____.

   (a) not hard usage
   (b) hard usage
   (c) extra-hard usage
   (d) all of these

2. TPT and TST cords shall be permitted in lengths not exceeding _____ when attached directly to a portable appliance rated 50W or less.

   (a) 8 ft
   (b) 10 ft
   (c) 15 ft
   (d) 20 ft

3. Flexible cords and cables can be used for _____.

   (a) wiring of luminaires
   (b) connection of portable luminaires or appliances
   (c) connection of utilization equipment to facilitate frequent interchange
   (d) all of these

4. Flexible cords shall not be used as a substitute for _____ wiring.

   (a) temporary
   (b) fixed
   (c) overhead
   (d) none of these

5. Flexible cords and cables shall not be used where _____.

   (a) run through holes in walls, ceilings, or floors
   (b) run through doorways, windows, or similar openings
   (c) attached to building surfaces, unless permitted by 368.56(B)
   (d) all of these

6. Flexible cords and cables shall not be concealed behind building _____, or run through doorways, windows, or similar openings.

   (a) structural ceilings
   (b) suspended or dropped ceilings
   (c) floors or walls
   (d) all of these

7. Flexible cords and cables shall be connected to fittings so that tension will not be transmitted to joints or terminal screws by _____.

   (a) knotting the cord
   (b) winding the cord with tape
   (c) fittings designed for the purpose
   (d) any of these

8. Flexible cords and cables shall be protected by _____ where passing through holes in covers, outlet boxes, or similar enclosures.

   (a) bushings
   (b) fittings
   (c) a or b
   (d) none of these

9. In industrial establishments where conditions of maintenance and supervision ensure that only qualified persons service the installation, flexible cords and cables can be installed in aboveground raceways that are no longer than _____, to protect the flexible cord or cable from physical damage.

(a) 25 ft
(b) 50 ft
(c) 100 ft
(d) no limit

10. A flexible cord conductor intended to be used as a(n) _____ conductor shall have a continuous identifying marker readily distinguishing it from the other conductor or conductors. One means of identification is a braid finished to show a continuous green color or a green color with one or more yellow stripes on one conductor.

(a) ungrounded
(b) equipment grounding
(c) service
(d) high-leg

Article 404. Switches

1. Switches or circuit breakers shall not disconnect the grounded conductor of a circuit unless the switch or circuit breaker _____.

(a) can be opened and closed by hand levers only
(b) simultaneously disconnects all conductors of the circuit
(c) opens the grounded conductor before it disconnects the ungrounded conductors
(d) none of these

2. Surface-mounted switches or circuit breakers in a damp or wet location shall be enclosed in a _____ enclosure or cabinet that complies with 312.2.

(a) weatherproof
(b) rainproof
(c) watertight
(d) raintight

3. Single-throw knife switches shall be installed so that gravity will tend to close the switch.

(a) True
(b) False

4 Which of the following switches must indicate whether they are in the open (off) or closed (on) position?

(a) General-use switches
(b) Motor-circuit switches
(c) Circuit breakers
(d) all of these

5. Switches and circuit breakers used as switches shall be installed so that they may be operated from a readily accessible place.

(a) True
(b) False

6. Switches and circuit breakers used as switches can be mounted _____ if they are installed adjacent to motors, appliances, or other equipment that they supply and are accessible by portable means.

(a) not higher than 6 ft 7 in.
(b) higher than 6 ft 7 in.
(c) in the mechanical equipment room
(d) up to 8 ft high

7. Metal enclosures for switches or circuit breakers shall be connected to the circuit _____.

(a) grounded conductor
(b) grounding conductor
(c) equipment grounding conductor
(d) any of these

8. Switches shall be marked with _____.

(a) current
(b) voltage
(c) maximum horsepower, if horsepower rated
(d) all of these

9. A switching device with a marked OFF position shall completely disconnect all _____ conductors of the load it controls.

(a) grounded
(b) ungrounded
(c) grounding
(d) all of these

Article 408. Switchboards and Panelboards

1. Circuit directories can include labels that depend on transient conditions of occupancy.

(a) True
(b) False

2. The purpose or use of panelboard circuits and circuit _____, including spare positions, shall be legibly identified on a circuit directory located on the face or inside of the door of a panelboard, and at each switch or circuit breaker on a switchboard.

(a) manufacturers
(b) conductors
(c) feeders
(d) modifications

3. All switchboards and panelboards supplied by a feeder in _____ shall be marked as to the device or equipment where the power supply originates.

(a) other than one- or two-family dwellings
(b) all dwelling units
(c) all non dwelling units
(d) b and c

4. Unused openings for circuit breakers and switches in switchboards and panelboards shall be closed using _____ or other approved means that provide protection substantially equivalent to the wall of the enclosure.

(a) duct seal and tape
(b) identified closures
(c) exothermic welding
(d) sheet metal

5. A panelboard shall be protected by an overcurrent device within the panelboard, or at any point on the _____ side of the panelboard.

(a) load
(b) supply
(c) a or b
(d) none of these

6. Panelboards equipped with snap switches rated at 30A or less shall have overcurrent protection not exceeding _____.

(a) 30A
(b) 50A
(c) 100A
(d) 200A

7. Plug-in-type circuit breakers that are back-fed shall be _____ by an additional fastener that requires more than a pull to release.

(a) grounded
(b) secured in place
(c) shunt tripped
(d) none of these

8. When equipment grounding conductors are installed in panelboards, a _____ shall be secured inside the cabinet.

(a) grounded conductor
(b) terminal lug
(c) terminal bar
(d) none of these

Article 480. Storage Batteries

1. The provisions of Article _____ apply to stationary storage battery installations.

(a) 450
(b) 460
(c) 470
(d) 480

2. A battery system includes storage batteries, battery chargers, and can include inverters, converters, and associated electrical equipment.

    (a) True
    (b) False

3. Nominal battery voltage, as it relates to storage batteries, is defined as the voltage of a battery based on the _____ of cells in the battery.

    (a) number
    (b) type
    (c) a and b
    (d) a or b

4. Nominal battery voltage is typically _____.

    (a) 2V per cell for lead-acid systems
    (b) 1.2V for per cell for alkali systems
    (c) 4V per cell for lithium-ion systems
    (d) all of these

5. Wiring and equipment supplied from storage batteries must be in accordance with Chapters 1 through 4 of the *NEC* unless otherwise permitted by 480.4.

    (a) True
    (b) False

6. A disconnecting means is required within sight of the storage battery for all ungrounded battery system conductors operating at over _____ nominal.

    (a) 20V
    (b) 30V
    (c) 40V
    (d) 50V

7. A _____ disconnecting means is required within sight of the storage battery for all ungrounded battery system conductors operating at over 50V nominal.

    (a) accessible
    (b) readily accessible
    (c) safety
    (d) all of these

8. A vented alkaline-type battery, as it relates to storage batteries, operating at less than 250V shall be installed with not more than _____ cells in the series circuit of any one tray.

    (a) 10
    (b) 12
    (c) 18
    (d) 20

9. Racks (rigid frames designed to support battery cells or trays) must be made of one of the following:

    (a) Metal, treated to be resistant to deteriorating action by the electrolyte and provided with nonconducting or continuous insulating material members directly supporting the cells
    (b) Fiberglass
    (c) Other suitable nonconductive materials
    (d) Any of these

10. Provisions shall be made for sufficient diffusion and ventilation of the gases from a storage battery to prevent the accumulation of a(n) _____ mixture.

    (a) corrosive
    (b) explosive
    (c) toxic
    (d) all of these

11. The required working space requirements of 110.26 are measured from the edge of the battery _____.

    (a) terminals
    (b) enclosure
    (c) rack
    (d) any of these

12. Each vented cell of a battery, as it relates to storage batteries, shall be equipped with _____ that is(are) designed to prevent destruction of the cell due to ignition of gases within the cell by an external spark or flame under normal operating conditions.

    (a) pressure relief
    (b) a flame arrester
    (c) fluid level indicators
    (d) none of these

CHAPTER 6

SPECIAL EQUIPMENT

INTRODUCTION TO CHAPTER 6—SPECIAL EQUIPMENT

Chapter 6, which covers special equipment, is the second of three *NEC* chapters that deal with special topics. Remember, the first four chapters of the *Code* are sequential and form a foundation for each of the subsequent three.

What exactly is "Special Equipment?" Equipment that, by the nature of its use, construction, or by its unique nature creates a need for additional measures to ensure the "safeguarding of people and property" mission of the *NEC*, as stated in Article 90.

- **Article 690—Solar Photovoltaic Systems.** Article 690 focuses on reducing the electrical hazards that may arise from installing and operating a solar photovoltaic system, to the point where it can be considered safe for property and people. The requirements of the *NEC* Chapters 1 through 4 apply to these installations, except as specifically modified by Article 690.

Notes

ARTICLE 690

Solar Photovoltaic (PV) Systems

INTRODUCTION TO ARTICLE 690—SOLAR PHOTOVOLTAIC (PV) SYSTEMS

You've seen, or maybe own, photocell-powered devices such as night lights, car coolers, and toys. These generally consist of a small solar panel and a small light or motor. Typically, these run on less than 10V dc and draw only a fraction of an ampere. These kinds of devices are very different from a system that can power a house or interconnect with a utility to offset a building's energy consumption.

Consider the sheer size and weight of solar modules for providing electrical power to a building. You're looking at mechanical and site selection issues that may require specialized expertise. The value of these modules also means there are security issues to consider, which may require more than just installing locks. There are also civil and architectural issues to address.

In summary, these installations are complicated and require expertise in several non-electrical areas, which the *NEC* doesn't address.

Article 690 focuses on reducing the electrical hazards that may arise from installing and operating a solar photovoltaic system, to the point where it can be considered safe for property and people.

This article consists of eight Parts, but the general requirements of Chapters 1 through 4 apply to these installations, except as specifically modified by Article 690.

PART I. GENERAL

690.1 Scope.

Article 690 applies to photovoltaic (PV) electrical energy systems, array circuit(s), inverter(s), and charge controller(s) for PV systems, which may be interactive with other electrical power sources (electric utility) or stand-alone with or without energy storage (batteries). Figures 690–1 and 690–2

690.2 Definitions.

Alternating-Current PV Module. A PV module unit consisting of solar cells, inverter, and components necessary to generate alternating-current (ac) power when exposed to sunlight. Figure 690–3

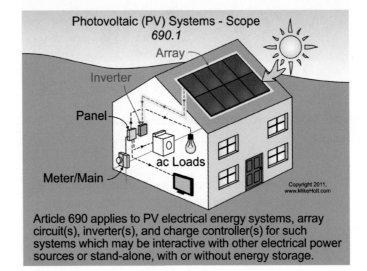

Photovoltaic (PV) Systems - Scope
690.1

Array
Inverter
Panel
ac Loads
Meter/Main

Copyright 2011,
www.MikeHolt.com

Article 690 applies to PV electrical energy systems, array circuit(s), inverter(s), and charge controller(s) for such systems which may be interactive with other electrical power sources or stand-alone, with or without energy storage.

Figure 690–1

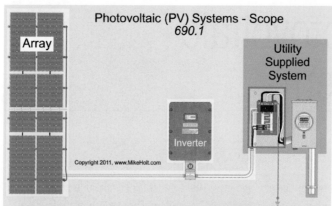

Figure 690–2

Article 690 applies to PV electrical energy systems, array circuit(s), inverter(s), and charge controller(s) for such systems which may be interactive with other electrical power sources or stand-alone, with or without energy storage.

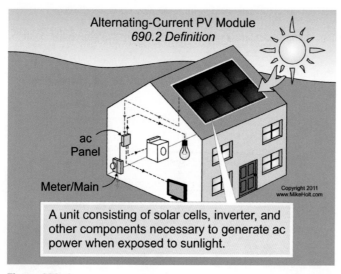

A unit consisting of solar cells, inverter, and other components necessary to generate ac power when exposed to sunlight.

Figure 690–3

Author's Comment: According to the UL White Book, ac modules provide single-phase power at 50/60 Hz when exposed to sunlight. An ac module consists of a photovoltaic module and an integral static inverter that changes direct-current power to ac power. Alternating-current modules may be connected in parallel and are intended for operation interactive with an electric utility supply. They've been evaluated to de-energize their output upon loss of utility power.

Alternating-current modules are marked with the maximum size of the dedicated branch circuit on which they may be installed and the maximum number of modules which may be connected in parallel.

Array. An electrical assembly of PV modules that convert sunlight to direct current (dc), support structure and foundation, tracker, and other components that form a dc power-producing unit. **Figure 690–4**

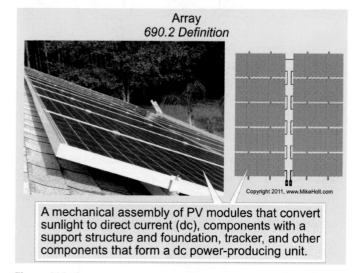

A mechanical assembly of PV modules that convert sunlight to direct current (dc), components with a support structure and foundation, tracker, and other components that form a dc power-producing unit.

Figure 690–4

Building Integrated Photovoltaics. PV cells integrated into the outer surface or structure of a building. **Figure 690–5**

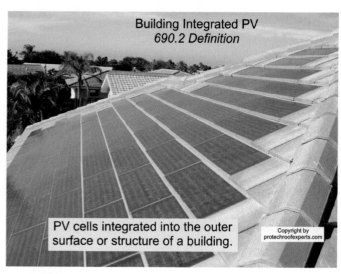

PV cells integrated into the outer surface or structure of a building.

Figure 690–5

Charge Controller. A device that regulates voltage and current from the array to the batteries to protect the batteries from overcharge, overdischarge, and sometimes load control functions. **Figures 690–6 and 690–7**

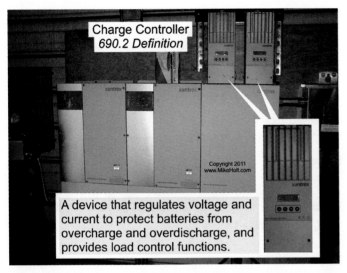

Figure 690–6

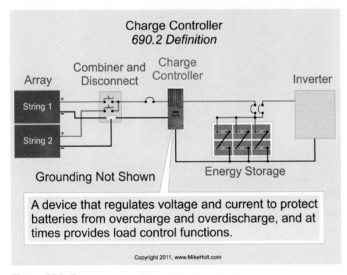

Figure 690–7

Electrical Production and Distribution Network (Utility Power System). The ac wiring system of a building/structured energized by the electric utility that is external to and not controlled by the photovoltaic power system. **Figure 690–8**

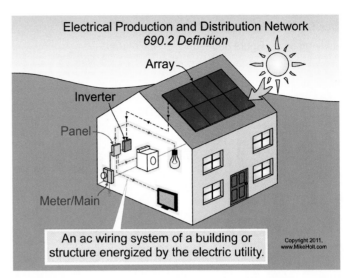

Figure 690–8

Interactive System. PV system that operates in parallel (interactive) with electrical utility power through a utility-interactive inverter. **Figure 690–9**

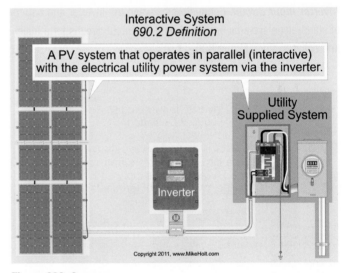

Figure 690–9

Author's Comment: A listed utility-interactive inverter automatically ceases exporting power upon loss of utility source power and will automatically resume exporting power to the utility source once the utility source has been restored [705.40 Ex].

Inverter. Electrical equipment that changes dc from the PV system to utility-grade ac. **Figure 690–10**

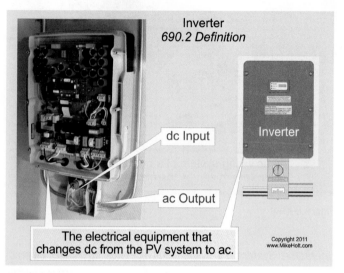

Figure 690–10

Inverter Input Circuit. Conductors between the inverter and battery of stand-alone systems or inverter and PV output circuits for a utility-interactive system. **Figure 690–11**

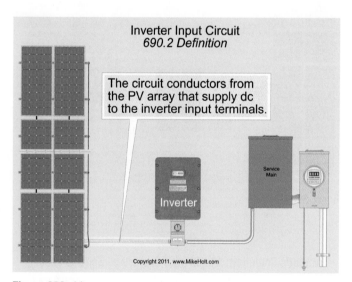

Figure 690–11

Inverter Output Circuit. The circuit conductors from the inverter output terminals that supply ac power to ac premises wiring, including the conductors from ac modules [690.6(B)]. **Figure 690–12**

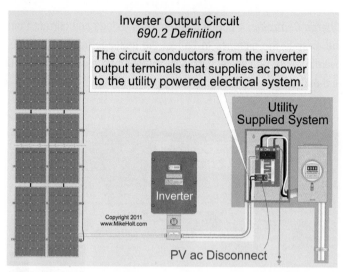

Figure 690–12

Module. PV unit designed to generate dc power when exposed to sunlight. **Figure 690–13**

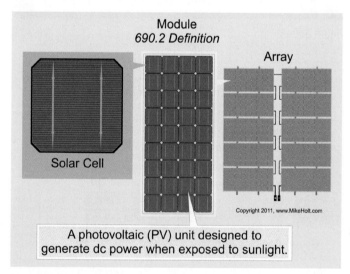

Figure 690–13

PV Output Circuit. Circuit conductors between the PV source circuit (combiner) and the dc input terminals of the inverter or dc disconnect. **Figure 690–14**

PV Power Source. The array of PV modules that generates dc power. **Figure 690–15**

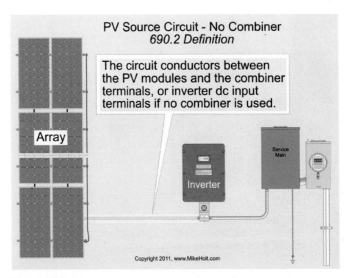

Figure 690–14

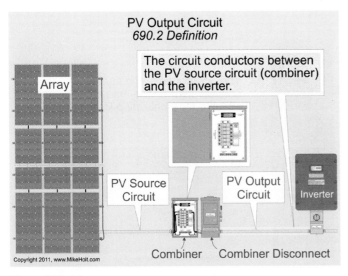

Figure 690–16

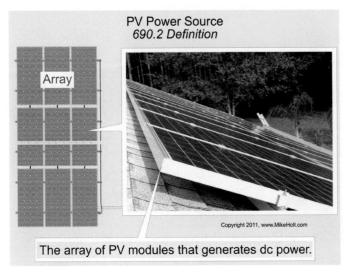

Figure 690–15

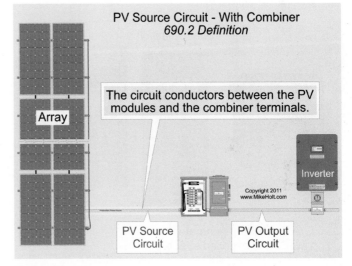

Figure 690–17

PV Source Circuit. The circuit conductors between the PV modules and the terminals of the combiner or inverter dc input terminals if no combiner is used. **Figures 690–16 and 690–17**

PV System Voltage. The output voltage of the PV power source measured between two dc conductors after the PV modules have been connected in series. **Figure 690–18**

Solar Cell. The basic building block of PV modules that generates dc power when exposed to sunlight. **Figure 690–19**

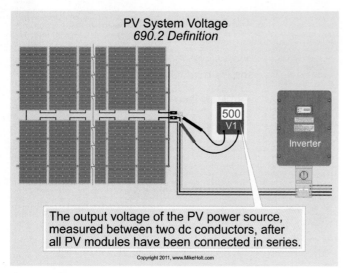

Figure 690–18

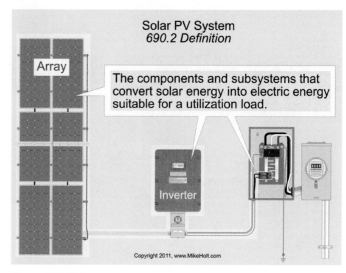

Figure 690–20

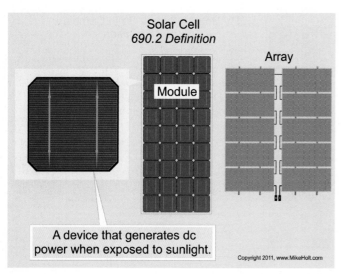

Figure 690–19

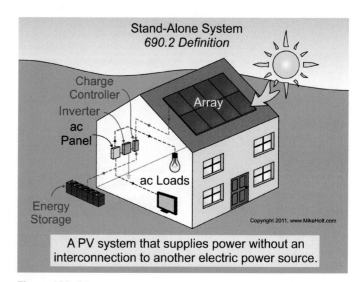

Figure 690–21

Solar Photovoltaic System. The components and subsystems that convert solar energy into electric energy suitable for connection to utilization equipment. **Figure 690–20**

> **Author's Comment:** For ease of use, the term "Solar Photovoltaic System" will be commonly referred to as PV System.

Stand-Alone System. A PV system that supplies power without an interconnection to another electric power source. **Figure 690–21**

690.3 Other Articles. All of the requirements contained in Chapters 1, 2, 3, and 4 apply to PV installations, except where supplemented or modified by this article.

690.4 Installation.

(A) Solar Photovoltaic System. A PV system is permitted to supply power to a building/structure in addition to any other electricity supply system(s).

(B) Identification and Grouping. PV system conductors, both dc and ac, can be installed in the same raceways, outlet and junction boxes, or similar fittings with each other, but must be kept entirely independent of non-PV system wiring conductors. **Figure 690–22**

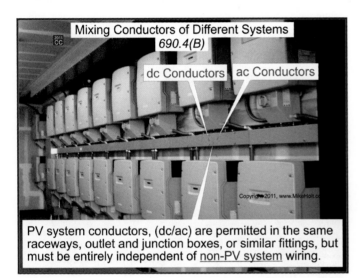

Mixing Conductors of Different Systems
690.4(B)

dc Conductors   ac Conductors

PV system conductors, (dc/ac) are permitted in the same raceways, outlet and junction boxes, or similar fittings, but must be entirely independent of non-PV system wiring.

Figure 690–22

PV system conductors must be identified by separate color coding, marking tape, tagging, or other approved means and grouped as follows:

(1) PV Source Circuits. Identified at points of termination, connection, and splices.

(2) PV Output and Inverter Circuits. Identified at points of termination, connection, and splices.

(3) Multiple Systems. Conductors of each system must be identified at termination, connection, and splice points. **Figure 690–23**

Ex: Identification of different systems isn't required where conductor identification is evident by spacing or arrangement.

(4) Grouping. Where the conductors of more than one PV system occupy the same junction box or raceway with removable cover, the ac and dc conductors of each system must be grouped together by cable ties and at intervals not to exceed 6 ft. **Figure 690–24**

Installation - Multiple Systems
690.4(B)(3)

Conductors of each system must be identified at each termination, connection, and splice point.

Figure 690–23

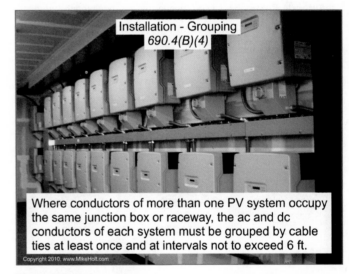

Installation - Grouping
690.4(B)(4)

Where conductors of more than one PV system occupy the same junction box or raceway, the ac and dc conductors of each system must be grouped by cable ties at least once and at intervals not to exceed 6 ft.

Figure 690–24

Ex: Grouping isn't required if the PV circuit enters from a cable or raceway unique to the circuit that makes the grouping obvious.

(C) Module Connection. Module connections must be arranged so that the removal of a module doesn't interrupt the grounded conductor to other PV source circuits.

(D) Equipment. Equipment for PV systems such as inverters, photovoltaic modules, source-circuit combiners, and charge controllers must be identified and listed for the application. **Figure 690–25**

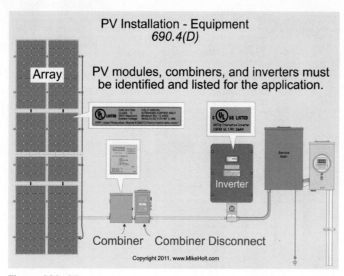

PV Installation - Equipment
690.4(D)

PV modules, combiners, and inverters must be identified and listed for the application.

Array

Combiner   Combiner Disconnect

Copyright 2011, www.MikeHolt.com

Figure 690–25

Author's Comment: Listing means that the equipment is in a list published by a testing laboratory acceptable to the authority having jurisdiction [Article 100].

(E) Qualified Persons. PV systems, associated wiring, and interconnections must be installed by a qualified person. **Figure 690–26**

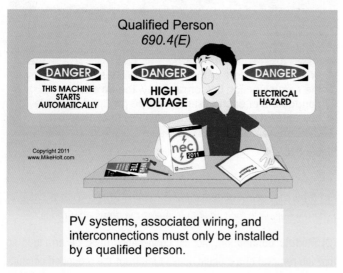

Qualified Person
690.4(E)

DANGER
THIS MACHINE
STARTS
AUTOMATICALLY

DANGER
HIGH
VOLTAGE

DANGER
ELECTRICAL
HAZARD

Copyright 2011
www.MikeHolt.com

PV systems, associated wiring, and interconnections must only be installed by a qualified person.

Figure 690–26

Note: A qualified person has the knowledge related to construction and operation of PV equipment and installations; along with safety training to recognize and avoid hazards to persons and property [Article 100].

(F) Circuit Routing. PV source and output conductors must be routed along building structural members (beams, rafters, trusses, and columns) where the location of those structural members can be determined by observation.

The location of PV source and output conductors imbedded in built-up, laminate, or membrane roofing materials in areas not covered by PV modules and associated equipment must be clearly marked.

(H) Multiple Inverters. Where multiple utility-interactive inverters are located remote from each other, a directory is required at each dc PV system disconnecting means, at each ac disconnecting means, and at the main service disconnecting means showing the location of all ac and dc PV system disconnecting means in the building/structure.

Ex: A directory isn't required where all PV system disconnecting means are grouped at the service disconnecting means.

690.5 Ground-Fault Protection. PV systems must have ground-fault protection to reduce fire hazards. **Figure 690–27**

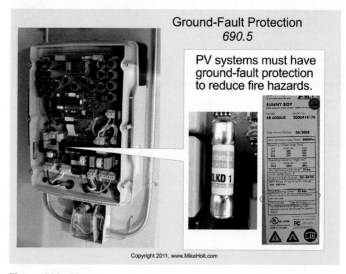

Ground-Fault Protection
690.5

PV systems must have ground-fault protection to reduce fire hazards.

Copyright 2011, www.MikeHolt.com

Figure 690–27

(C) Labels and Markings. A warning label must be on the utility-interactive inverter stating the following: **Figure 690–28**

⚠️ **WARNING ELECTRIC SHOCK HAZARD—IF A GROUND FAULT IS INDICATED, NORMALLY GROUNDED CONDUCTORS MAY BE UNGROUNDED AND ENERGIZED**

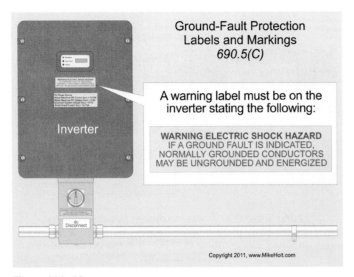

Figure 690–28

⚠️ **CAUTION:** *The label must resist the environment for 25 to 40 years of system use and be suitable for the environment and be installed so as not to void equipment listing [110.3(B)]. When plastic is used, it should not be placed in direct sunlight, unless specifically manufactured as sunlight resistant; a metallic engraved sign would be best.*

690.6 Alternating-Current Modules.

(A) PV Source Circuits. Article 690 requirements pertaining to dc PV circuits don't apply to ac PV modules since ac PV modules have no dc output. Figure 690–29

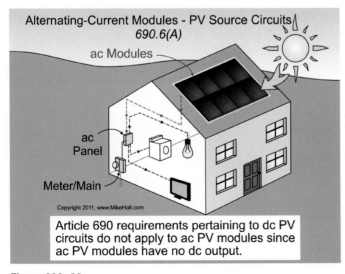

Figure 690–29

(B) Inverter Output Circuit. The output circuit conductors of an ac module are considered an "Inverter Output Circuit" as defined in 690.2. Figure 690–30

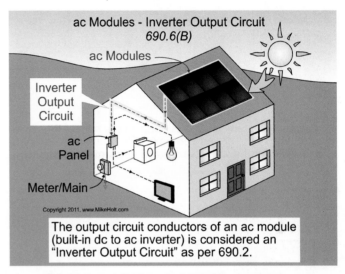

Figure 690–30

PART II. CIRCUIT REQUIREMENTS

690.7 Maximum Voltage

(A) Maximum PV System Voltage. Maximum PV system voltage is equal to the sum of the rated open-circuit voltage (Voc) of the series-connected PV modules as corrected for the lowest-expected ambient temperature in accordance with Table 690.7.

Open-circuit voltage temperature coefficients supplied in the instructions for PV modules must be used to calculate the maximum PV system voltage instead of Table 690.7. Figure 690–31

> **Note:** One source for lowest-expected ambient temperature is the Extreme Annual Mean Minimum Design Dry Bulb Temperature found in the *ASHRAE Handbook—Fundamentals.* See http://www.solarabcs.org/permitting/map/.

Author's Comment: PV module voltage has an inverse relationship with temperature, which means that at lower temperatures, PV modules' voltage raises and at higher temperatures, PV modules' voltage falls from its nameplate rating.

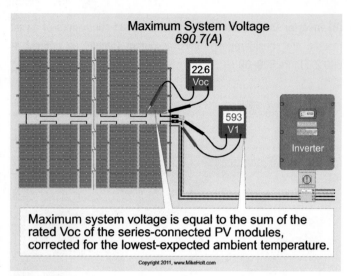

Figure 690–31

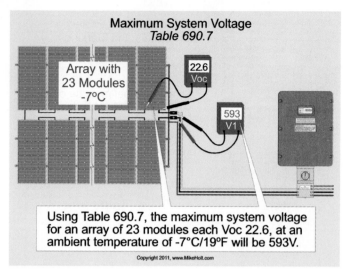

Figure 690–32

Table 690.7 Voltage Correction Factors		
Lowest-Expected Ambient Temperature °C °F		Temperature Correction Factor
0 to 4	32 to 40	1.10
-1 to -5	23 to 31	1.12
-6 to -10	14 to 22	1.14
-11 to -15	5 to 13	1.16
-16 to -20	4 to -4	1.18
-21 to -25	-5 to -13	1.20
-26 to -30	-14 to -22	1.21
-31 to -35	-23 to -31	1.23
-36 to -40	-32 to -40	1.25

Example: Using Table 690.7, what's the maximum PV source circuit voltage for twenty-three modules each rated Voc 22.60, at an ambient temperature of -7°C? **Figure 690–32**

PV Voc Table 690.7 = Module Voc × Table 690.7 Correction Factor × # Modules per Series String
PV Voc = 22.60 Voc × 1.14 × 23 modules
PV Voc = 593V

PV System Voltage Based on Manufacturer Temperature Coefficient %/°C

Example: Using the manufacturer's temperature coefficient -0.31%/°C, what's the maximum PV source circuit voltage for twenty-three modules each rated Voc 22.60, at a cell temperature of -7°C? **Figure 690–33**

PV Voc = Rated Voc × {1 + [(Min. Temp. °C - 25°C) × Module Coefficient %/°C]} × # Modules per Series String
PV Voc = 22.60 Voc × {1+ [(-7°C - 25°C) × -0.31%/°C]} × 23 modules
PV Voc = 22.60 Voc × {1 + [-32°C × -0.31%/°C]}) × 23 modules
PV Voc = 22.60 Voc × {1 + 9.92%} × 23 modules
PV Voc = 22.60 Voc × 1.0992 × 23 modules
PV Voc = 571V

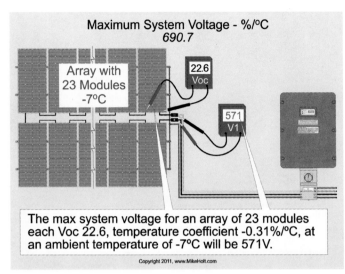

The max system voltage for an array of 23 modules each Voc 22.6, temperature coefficient -0.31%/°C, at an ambient temperature of -7°C will be 571V.

Copyright 2011, www.MikeHolt.com

Figure 690–33

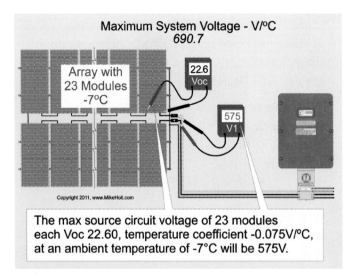

The max source circuit voltage of 23 modules each Voc 22.60, temperature coefficient -0.075V/°C, at an ambient temperature of -7°C will be 575V.

Copyright 2011, www.MikeHolt.com

Figure 690–34

PV System Voltage Based on Manufacturer Temperature Coefficient V/°C

Example: *Using the manufacturer's temperature coefficient -0.075V/°C, what's the maximum PV source circuit voltage for twenty-three modules each rated Voc 22.60, at an ambient temperature of -7°C?* **Figure 690–34**

PV Voc (V/°C) = {Rated Voc + [(Min. Temp. °C - 25°C) ×
Module Coefficient V/°C]} × # Modules per Series String

PV Voc = {22.60V + [(-7°C - 25°C) × -0.075V/°C]} × 23

PV Voc = {22.60V + [-32°C × -0.075V/°C)) × 23

PV Voc *= (22.60V + 2.40V) × 23*

PV Voc = 25V × 23

PV Voc = 575V

Author's Comment: Inverters require a minimum dc voltage to start; therefore PV voltage calculations should be performed to ensure the modules can produce sufficient voltage to start the system [110.3(B)]. **Figure 690–35**

Installation and Use
110.3(B)

	SB 5000US
Recommended Max. PV Power (Module STC)	6250 W
Max. DC Voltage	600 V
Peak Power Tracking Voltage	250 - 480 V
DC Max. Input Current	21 A
DC Voltage Ripple	< 5%
Number of Fused String Inputs	3 (inverter), 4 × 15 A (DC disconnect)
PV Start Voltage	300 V
AC Nominal Power	5000 W
AC Maximum Output Power	5000 W
AC Maximum Output Current (@ 208, 240, 277 V)	24 A, 21 A, 18 A
AC Nominal Voltage / Range	183 - 229 V @ 208 V
	211 - 264 V @ 240 V
	244 - 305 V @ 277 V

Inverters require a minimum dc voltage to operate in accordance with manufacturer's instructions.

Copyright 2011, www.MikeHolt.com

Figure 690–35

Example: *Using the manufacturer's temperature coefficient -0.31%/°C, what's the maximum PV source circuit voltage for twenty-three modules each rated Voc 22.60, at a cell temperature of 67.8°C?* **Figure 690–36**

PV Voc = Rated Voc × {1 + [(Min. Temp. °C - 25°C) × Module Coefficient %/°C]} × # Modules per Series String

PV Voc = 22.60 Voc × {1+ [(67.8°C - 25°C) × -0.31%/°C]} × 23 modules

PV Voc = 22.60 Voc × {1 + [42.8°C × -0.31%/°C]}) × 23 modules

PV Voc = 22.60 Voc × {1 + (-13.27%)} × 23 modules

PV Voc = 22.60 Voc × 0.8673 × 23 modules

PV Voc = 451V

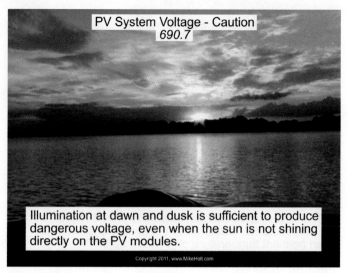

PV System Voltage - Caution
690.7

Illumination at dawn and dusk is sufficient to produce dangerous voltage, even when the sun is not shining directly on the PV modules.

Copyright 2011, www.MikeHolt.com

Figure 690–37

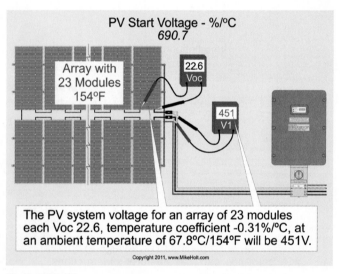

PV Start Voltage - %/°C
690.7

Array with 23 Modules 154°F

22.6 Voc

451 V1

The PV system voltage for an array of 23 modules each Voc 22.6, temperature coefficient -0.31%/°C, at an ambient temperature of 67.8°C/154°F will be 451V.

Copyright 2011, www.MikeHolt.com

Figure 690–36

⚠ **CAUTION:** *Illumination at dawn and dusk is sufficient to produce dangerous voltage, even when the sun isn't shining directly on the PV modules. Although moonlight may not generate lethal voltages, a shock hazard may still exist [690.18 Note].* **Figure 690–37**

(C) Maximum PV System Voltage. For one- and two-family dwellings, the maximum PV system voltage is limited to 600V, which is the standard voltage of electrical building wiring. **Figure 690–38**

(D) Accessible. In one- and two-family dwellings, live parts over 150V to ground must only be accessible to qualified persons. **Figure 690–39**

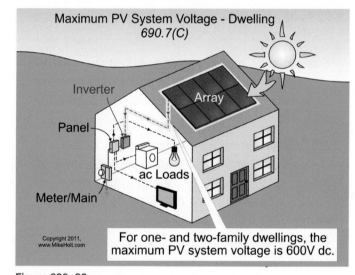

Maximum PV System Voltage - Dwelling
690.7(C)

Inverter

Panel

ac Loads

Meter/Main

Array

Copyright 2011, www.MikeHolt.com

For one- and two-family dwellings, the maximum PV system voltage is 600V dc.

Figure 690–38

(E) Bipolar Source and Output Circuits. For 2-wire circuits connected to bipolar systems, the maximum system voltage is the highest voltage between the conductors of the 2-wire circuit if all of the following conditions apply:

(1) One conductor of each circuit of a bipolar subarray is solidly grounded.

Exception: The operation of ground-fault or arc-fault devices (abnormal operation) shall be permitted to interrupt this connection to ground when the entire bipolar array becomes two distinct arrays isolated from each other and the utilization equipment.

(2) Each circuit is connected to a separate subarray.

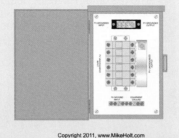

Maximum Voltage - Accessible
690.7(D)

Copyright 2011, www.MikeHolt.com

For one- and two-family dwellings, live parts over 150V to ground must not be accessible to other than qualified persons while energized.

Figure 690–39

(3) The equipment is clearly marked with a label as follows:

⚠ **WARNING — BIPOLAR PHOTOVOLTAIC ARRAY DISCONNECTION OF NEUTRAL OR GROUNDED CONDUCTORS MAY RESULT IN OVERVOLTAGE ON ARRAY OR INVERTER.**

690.8 Circuit Sizing and Protection.

(A) Maximum Circuit Current.

(1) Maximum PV Source Circuit Current. The maximum PV source circuit current is calculated by multiplying the module nameplate short-circuit current rating (Isc) by 125 percent. **Figure 690–40**

Maximum PV Source Circuit Current (Isc)
690.8(A)(1)

Electrical Characteristics

Standard Test Conditions (STC)[1]

	ES-A-200 -fa3*	ES-A-205 -fa3*	ES-A-210 -fa3*	
P_{mp}[2]	200	205	210	W
$P_{tolerance}$	-0/+4.99	-0/+4.99	-0/+4.99	W
$P_{mp, max}$	204.99	209.99	214.99	W
$P_{mp, min}$	200.00	205.00	210.00	W
η_{min}	12.7	13.1	13.4	%
P_{ptc}[3]	180.6	185.2	189.8	W
V_{mp}	18.10	18.20	18.30	V
I_{mp}	11.05	11.27	11.48	A
V_{oc}	22.60	22.70	22.80	V
I_{sc}	11.80	11.93	12.11	A

Copyright 2011, www.MikeHolt.com

Maximum PV source circuit current is calculated by multiplying the module nameplate Isc by 125 percent.

Figure 690–40

Author's Comments:

- The 125% current multiplier is due to the module's ability to produce more current than its rated value based on the intensity of the sunlight.

- The PV source circuit consists of the circuit conductors between the PV modules and the terminals of the combiner or inverter dc input terminals if no combiner is used. [690.2].

Example: *What's the maximum PV source circuit current for twenty-three series connected dc modules having a nameplate Isc of 11.80A?* **Figure 690–41**

Maximum PV Source Circuit Current = Module Isc × 1.25
Maximum PV Source Circuit Current = 11.80A × 1.25
Maximum PV Source Circuit Current = 14.75A

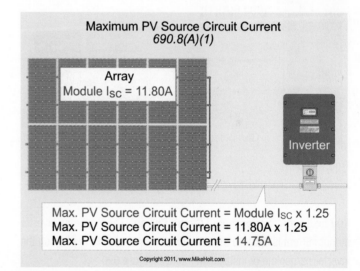

Maximum PV Source Circuit Current
690.8(A)(1)

Array
Module I_{SC} = 11.80A

Inverter

Max. PV Source Circuit Current = Module I_{SC} x 1.25
Max. PV Source Circuit Current = 11.80A x 1.25
Max. PV Source Circuit Current = 14.75A

Copyright 2011, www.MikeHolt.com

Figure 690–41

(2) Maximum PV Output Circuit Current. The maximum PV output circuit current is equal to the sum of parallel PV source circuit currents as calculated in 690.8(A)(1).

Author's Comment: The PV output circuit consists of circuit conductors between the PV source circuit (combiner) and the dc input terminals of the inverter or dc disconnect.

Example: *What's the maximum PV output circuit current for two strings, each containing twenty-three dc modules having a nameplate Isc of 11.80A?* **Figure 690–42**

Maximum PV Output Circuit Current = (Module Isc × 1.25)* × Number of Strings

Maximum PV Output Circuit Current = (11.80A × 1.25)* × 2

Maximum PV Output Circuit Current = (14.75A)* × 2

Maximum PV Output Circuit Current = 29.50A

*690.8(A)(1)

Maximum Output Circuit Current
690.8(A)(2)

Max Output Ckt Current = (Module I$_{SC}$ x 1.25)* x # of Strings

Max Output Ckt Current = (11.80A x 1.25)* x 2
Max Output Ckt Current = 14.75A* x 2 strings
Max Output Ckt Current = 29.5A
*[690.8(A)(1)]

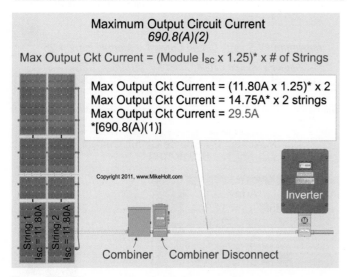

Figure 690–42

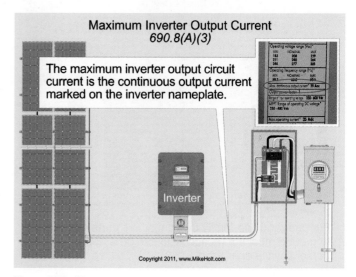

Figure 690–43

Example—PV Source Circuit: *Where required, size the OCPD for a single PV source circuit having a nameplate Isc of 11.80A?* **Figure 690–44**

OCPD = (Module Isc × 1.25)* × 1.25

OCPD = (11.80A × 1.25)* × 1.25

OCPD = (14.75A)* × 1.25

OCPD = 18.44A

OCPD = 20A [240.6(A)]

*690.8(A)(1)

(3) Maximum Inverter Output Circuit Current. The maximum inverter output current is equal to the continuous output current marked on the inverter nameplate or installation manual. **Figure 690–43**

Author's Comment: The inverter output circuit consists of the circuit conductors from the inverter output terminals or ac modules [690.6(B)] to ac premises wiring.

(B) Ampacity and Overcurrent Protection Device (OCPD) Ratings.

(1) Overcurrent Devices. Where conductor overcurrent protection Is required [690.9], It must be:

(a) Overcurrent devices must be sized not less than 125 percent of 690.8(A) circuit current.

Author's Comment: The 125% current multiplier is because the modules are expected to provide continuous current for more than three hours.

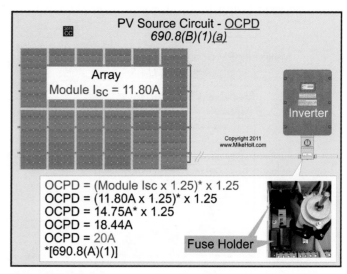

PV Source Circuit - OCPD
690.8(B)(1)(a)

Array
Module I$_{SC}$ = 11.80A

OCPD = (Module Isc x 1.25)* x 1.25
OCPD = (11.80A x 1.25)* x 1.25
OCPD = 14.75A* x 1.25
OCPD = 18.44A
OCPD = 20A
*[690.8(A)(1)]

Fuse Holder

Figure 690–44

Author's Comment: The PV source circuit OCPD isn't permitted to exceed the maximum overcurrent rating marked on the PV module nameplate [110.3(B)]. **Figure 690–45**

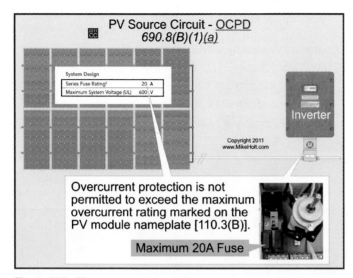

Figure 690–45

Example—PV Output Circuit: *Where required, size the OCPD for a PV output circuit supplied by two PV source circuits, each having nameplate Isc of 11.80A?* **Figure 690–46**

OCPD = (Module Isc × 1.25 × Number of Strings)* × 1.25

OCPD = (11.80A × 1.25 × 2 strings)* × 1.25

OCPD = (29.50A)* × 1.25

OCPD = 36.88A

OCPD = 40A [240.6(A)]

*690.8(A)(2)

Example—Inverter Output Circuit: *What size OCPD is required for an inverter output circuit having a maximum inverter continuous ac output nameplate current rating of 24A?* **Figure 690–47**

OCPD = Inverter ac Output Current Rating* × 1.25

OCPD = 24A* × 1.25

OCPD = 30A

OCPD = 30A circuit breaker [240.6(A)]

*690.8(A)(3)

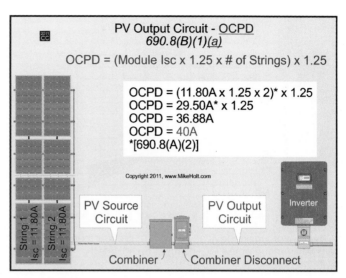

Figure 690–46

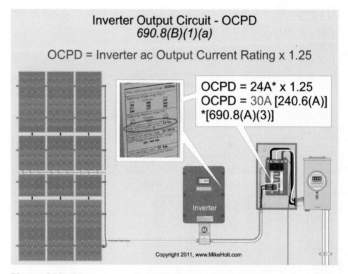

Figure 690–47

(c) Where overcurrent devices operate at greater than 40°C, the ampacity rating of the OCPD must be adjusted in accordance with manufacturer's temperature correction factors. **Figure 690–48**

Author's Comment: Single element fuses are insignificantly impacted by elevated ambient temperature.

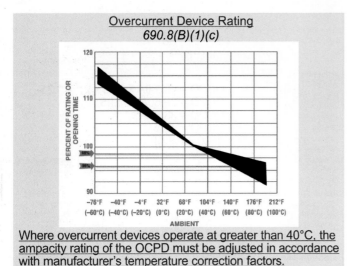

Where overcurrent devices operate at greater than 40°C, the ampacity rating of the OCPD must be adjusted in accordance with manufacturer's temperature correction factors.

Figure 690–48

(2) Conductor Ampacity. PV circuit conductors must be sized to the larger of 690.8(B)(2)(a) or 690.8(B)(2)(b).

(a) PV circuit conductors must be sized to carry not less than 125 percent of 690.8(A) current before the application of conductor ampacity correction [310.15(B)(2)(a) and 310.15(B)(3)(c)] and adjustment [310.15(B)(3)(a)]. **Figure 690–49**

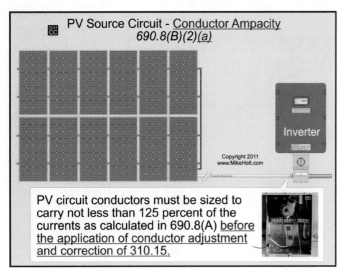

PV circuit conductors must be sized to carry not less than 125 percent of the currents as calculated in 690.8(A) before the application of conductor adjustment and correction of 310.15.

Figure 690–49

Example—PV Source Circuit: *What's the minimum PV source circuit conductor ampacity before the application of conductor correction or adjustment for a string having a short-circuit current rating of 11.80A; assuming all terminals are rated 75°C?* **Figure 690–50**

Conductor Ampacity = (Module Isc × 1.25)* × 1.25

Conductor Ampacity = (11.80A × 1.25)* × 1.25

Conductor Ampacity = (14.75A)* × 1.25

Conductor Ampacity = 18.44A

Conductor Ampacity = 14 AWG rated 20A at 75°C [Table 310.15(B)(16)]

*690.8(A)(1)

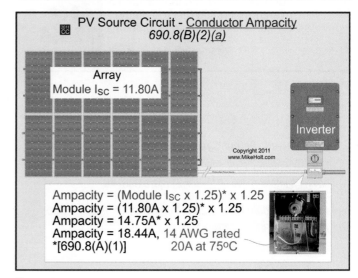

Figure 690–50

Author's Comment: Conductors terminating on terminals rated 75°C are sized in accordance with the ampacities listed in the 75°C temperature column of Table 310.15(B)(16) [110.14(C)(1)(a)(3)].

Example—PV Output Circuit: *What's the minimum PV output circuit conductor ampacity, before the application of conductor correction or adjustment, supplied by two PV source circuits, each having a short-circuit current rating of 11.80A; assuming all terminals are rated 75°C?* **Figure 690–51**

Conductor Ampacity = (Module Isc × 1.25 × Number of Source Circuits)* × 1.25

Conductor Ampacity = (11.80A × 1.25 × 2 strings)* × 1.25

Conductor Ampacity = 29.5A* × 1.25

Conductor Ampacity = 36.88A

Conductor Ampacity = 8 AWG rated 50A at 75°C [Table 310.15(B)(16)]

*690.8(A)(2)

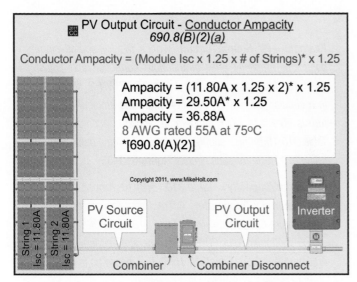

Figure 690–51

Example—Inverter Output Circuit: *What's the minimum inverter ac output circuit conductor ampacity, before the application of conductor correction or adjustment, if the maximum continuous nameplate ac rating of the inverter is 24A; assuming all terminals are rated 75°C?* **Figure 690–52**

Conductor Ampacity = Inverter Nameplate Rating* × 1.25

Conductor Ampacity = 24A* × 1.25

Conductor Ampacity = 30A

Conductor Ampacity = 10 AWG rated 35A at 75°C [310.15(B)(16)]

*690.8(A)(3)

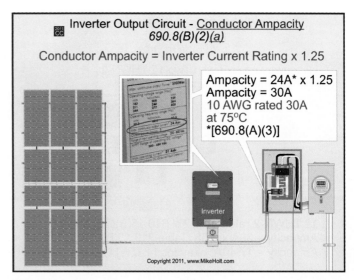

Figure 690–52

(b) Circuit conductors must be sized to carry 100% of 690.8(A) current after the application of conductor ampacity correction [310.15(B)(2)(a) and 310.15(B)(3)(c)] and adjustment [310.15(B)(3)(a)].

Author's Comment: When performing conductor ampacity correction and adjustment calculations, use the conductor ampacity listed in the 90°C column of Table 310.15(B)(16) for THWN-2 insulated conductors [310.15(B)].

Example—PV Source Circuit: *What's the PV source circuit conductor ampacity after temperature correction for two current-carrying size 12 THWN-2 conductors in a circular raceway on the roof, ambient temperature is 90°F with 60°F temperature added in accordance with Table 310.15(B)(3)(c), supplying modules having a nameplate Isc rating of 11.80A?* **Figure 690–53**

Conductor Ampacity = Table 310.15(B)(16) Ampacity at 90°C Column x Temperature Correction[

Temperature Correction = 0.58, Table 310.15(B)(2)(a) based on 150°F (ambient plus 60°F roof temperature adder)

Conductor Ampacity = 30A x 0.58

Conductor Ampacity = 17.40A, which has sufficient ampacity after correction and adjustment to supply 690.8(A)(1) calculated current of 14.75A (11.80A x 1.25).

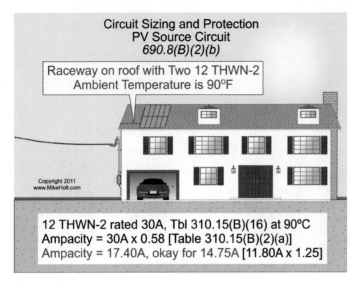

Figure 690–53

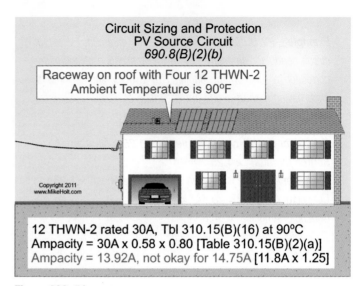

Figure 690–54

Example—PV Source Circuit: *What's the PV source circuit conductor ampacity after temperature correction and adjustment for four current-carrying size 12 THWN-2 conductors in a circular raceway on the roof, ambient temperature is 90°F with 60°F temperature added in accordance with Table 310.15(B)(3)(c), supplying modules having a nameplate Isc rating of 11.80A for each circuit?* **Figure 690–54**

Conductor Ampacity = Table 310.15(B)(16) Ampacity at 90°C Column x Temperature Correction x Adjustment

Temperature Correction = 0.58, Table 310.15(B)(2)(a) based on 150°F (ambient plus 60°F roof temperature adder)

Adjustment = 0.80, Table 310.15(B)(3)(a), based on four current-carrying conductors in a raceway

Conductor Ampacity = 30A x 0.58 x 0.80

Conductor Ampacity = 13.92A, which does not have sufficient ampacity to supply carry 690.8(A)(2) calculated current of 14.75A [11.80A x 1.25], therefore a 10 AWG THWN-2 conductor would be required.

Example—PV Source Circuit: *What's the PV source circuit conductor ampacity after temperature correction and adjustment for four current-carrying size 10 THWN-2 conductors in a circular raceway on the roof where the ambient temperature is 90°F with 60°F temperature added in accordance with Table 310.15(B)(3)(c), supplying modules having a nameplate Isc rating of 11.80A for each circuit?* **Figure 690–55**

Conductor Ampacity = Table 310.15(B)(16) Ampacity at 90°C Column x Temperature Correction x Adjustment

Temperature Correction = 0.58, Table 310.15(B)(2)(a) based on 150°F (ambient plus 60°F roof temperature adder)

Adjustment = 0.80, Table 310.15(B)(3)(a), based on four current-carrying conductors in a raceway

Conductor Ampacity = 40A x 0.58 x 0.80 [Tables 310.15(B)(2)(a), 310.15(B)(3)(c), and 310.15(B)(3)(a)]

Conductor Ampacity = 18.56A, which has sufficient ampacity after correction and adjustment to supply 690.8(A)(1) calculated current of 14.75A (11.80A x 1.25)

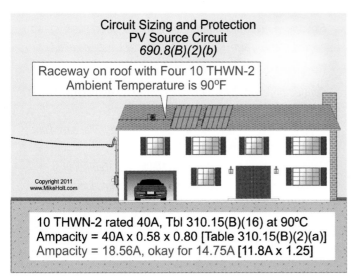

Circuit Sizing and Protection PV Source Circuit *690.8(B)(2)(b)*

Raceway on roof with Four 10 THWN-2 Ambient Temperature is 90°F

10 THWN-2 rated 40A, Tbl 310.15(B)(16) at 90°C
Ampacity = 40A x 0.58 x 0.80 [Table 310.15(B)(2)(a)]
Ampacity = 18.56A, okay for 14.75A [11.8A x 1.25]

Figure 690–55

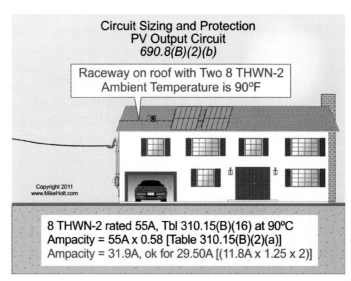

Circuit Sizing and Protection PV Output Circuit *690.8(B)(2)(b)*

Raceway on roof with Two 8 THWN-2 Ambient Temperature is 90°F

8 THWN-2 rated 55A, Tbl 310.15(B)(16) at 90°C
Ampacity = 55A x 0.58 [Table 310.15(B)(2)(a)]
Ampacity = 31.9A, ok for 29.50A [(11.8A x 1.25 x 2)]

Figure 690–56

Example—PV Output Circuit: *What's the PV output current ampacity after temperature correction for two current-carrying 8 size THWN-2 conductors in a circular raceway on the roof where the ambient temperature is 90°F supplied by two parallel PV source circuits, each having a Isc rating 11.80A?* **Figure 690–56**

Conductor Ampacity = Table 310.15(B)(16) Ampacity at 90°C Column x Temperature Correction

Temperature Correction = 0.58, Table 310.15(B)(2)(a) based on 150°F (ambient plus 60°F roof temperature adder)

Conductor Ampacity = 55A x 0.58 [Tables 310.15(B)(2)(a) and 310.15(B)(3)(c)]

Conductor Ampacity = 31.90A, which has sufficient ampacity after correction and adjustment to supply 690.8(A)(2) calculated current of 29.5A (11.80A x 1.25 x 2)

Example—Inverter Output Circuit: *What's the ampacity of two current-carrying size 10 THWN-2 conductors installed at a location where the ambient temperature is 90°F?*

Conductor Ampacity = Table 310.15(B)(16) Ampacity at 90°C Column x Temperature Correction

Temperature Correction = 0.58, Table 310.15(B)(2)(a) based on 90°F ambient temperature

Conductor Ampacity = 30A x 0.96 [Table 310.15(B)(2)(a)]

Conductor Ampacity = 28.80A

(c) The overcurrent protection device is sized to protect the conductor after the application of conductor ampacity correction and adjustment of 310.15 in accordance with 240.4. **Figure 690–57**

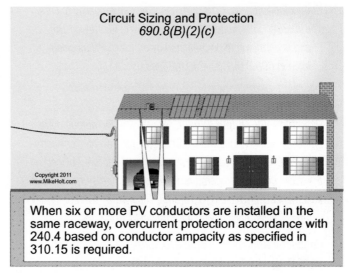

Circuit Sizing and Protection *690.8(B)(2)(c)*

When six or more PV conductors are installed in the same raceway, overcurrent protection accordance with 240.4 based on conductor ampacity as specified in 310.15 is required.

Figure 690–57

Author's Comments:

- Overcurrent protection is only required when six or more PV conductors are installed in the same raceway [690.9(A) Ex].

- When the ampacity of a conductor doesn't correspond with the standard size OCPD of 250.6(A), the next higher standard rating of overcurrent device is permitted, as long as the next size doesn't exceed 800A [240.4(B)].

Example—PV Source Circuit: *PV source circuit supplies six current-carrying size 10 THWN-2 conductors in a circular raceway placed on the roof, ambient temperature 90°F with 60°F temperature added in accordance with Table 310.15(B)(3)(c), and modules nameplate Isc rating of 11.80A?*

Conductor Ampacity = Table 310.15(B)(16) Ampacity at 90°C Column x Temperature Correction x Adjustment

Temperature Correction = 0.58, Table 310.15(B)(2)(a) based on 150°F (ambient plus 60°F roof temperature adder)

Adjustment = 0.80, Table 310.15(B)(3)(a), based on six current-carrying conductors in a raceway

Conductor Ampacity = 40A x 0.58 x 0.80

Conductor Ampacity = 18.56A, has sufficient ampacity to carry 690.8(A)(1) calculated current of 14.75A [11.80A x 1.25], and is permitted to be protected by a 20A OCPD as calculated in 690.8(B)(1)(a) [240.4(B) and 690.8(C)].

Example—PV Output Circuit: *What's the PV output current ampacity after temperature correction for two current-carrying size 6 THWN-2 conductors in a circular raceway placed on the roof, ambient temperature 90°F with temperature added in accordance with Table 310.15(B)(3), supplied by two parallel PV source circuits, each having a Isc rating 11.80A?*

Conductor Ampacity = Table 310.15(B)(16) Ampacity at 90°C Column x Temperature Correction

Temperature Correction = 0.58, Table 310.15(B)(2)(a) based on 150°F (ambient plus 60°F roof temperature adder)

Conductor Ampacity = 75A x 0.58 [Tables 310.15(B)(2)(a) and 310.15(B)(3)(c)]

Conductor Ampacity = 43.50A, has sufficient ampacity to carry 690.8(A)(2) calculated current of 29.5A [11.80A x 1.25 x 2], and is permitted to be protected by a 40A OCPD as calculated in 690.8(B)(1)(a) [240.4 and 690.8(C)].

Example—Inverter Output Circuit: *What's the ampacity of two current-carrying size 10 THWN-2 conductors installed at a location where the ambient temperature is 90°F?*

Conductor Ampacity = Table 310.15(B)(16) Ampacity at 90°C Column x Temperature Correction

Temperature Correction = 0.58, Table 310.15(B)(2)(a) based on 90°F ambient temperature

Conductor Ampacity = 30A x 0.96 [Table 310.15(B)(2)(a)]

Conductor Ampacity = 28.80A, has sufficient ampacity to carry 690.8(A)(3) calculated current of 24A and is permitted to be protected by a 30A OCPD as calculated in 690.8(B)(1)(a) [240.4(B) and 690.8(B)].

690.9 Overcurrent Protection.

(A) Circuits and Equipment. PV source circuits, PV output circuits, inverter output circuits, and equipment must have overcurrent protection in accordance with Article 240. **Figure 690–58**

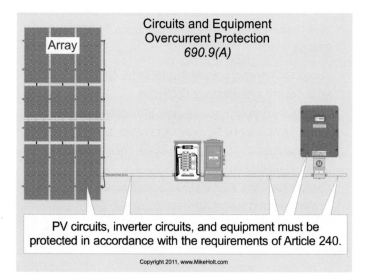

Figure 690–58

Author's Comment: For an ungrounded system [690.35], both positive and negative conductors require overcurrent protection; for grounded systems, only one conductor requires overcurrent protection, typically the positive conductor [240.15].

Ex: Overcurrent protection isn't required for PV dc circuits where the short-circuit currents (Isc) from all sources can't exceed the ampacity of the PV circuit conductors *or the maximum overcurrent device size specified on the PV module nameplate.* **Figure 690–59**

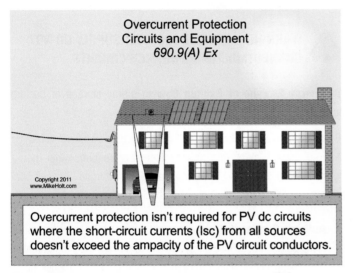

Figure 690–59

Author's Comment: This occurs when the PV source or PV output circuits consist of no more than four conductors. **Figures 690–60 and 690–61**

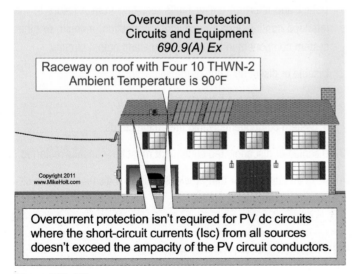

Figure 690–60

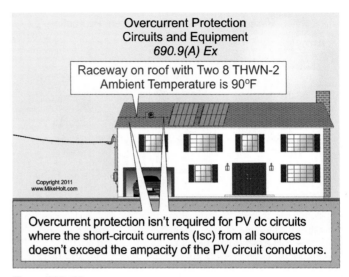

Figure 690–61

(C) PV Source Circuits. Overcurrent protection devices for PV source circuits are not required to be readily accessible. **Figure 690–62**

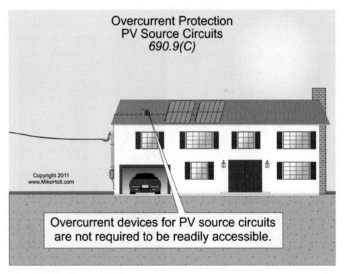

Figure 690–62

Supplementary overcurrent devices come in one ampere size increments up to and including 15A; higher standard values are in accordance with 240.6(A). **Figure 690–63**

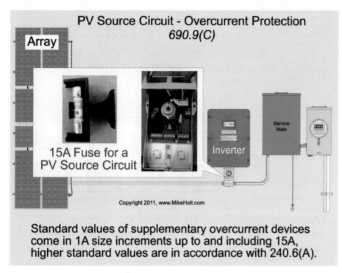

PV Source Circuit - Overcurrent Protection
690.9(C)

Array

15A Fuse for a
PV Source Circuit

Inverter

Copyright 2011, www.MikeHolt.com

Standard values of supplementary overcurrent devices come in 1A size increments up to and including 15A, higher standard values are in accordance with 240.6(A).

Figure 690–63

(D) Direct-Current Rating. OCPD for PV dc circuits must be listed for dc circuits and the voltage and current for the applied circuit. **Figure 690–64**

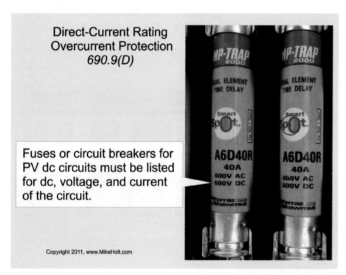

Direct-Current Rating
Overcurrent Protection
690.9(D)

Fuses or circuit breakers for PV dc circuits must be listed for dc, voltage, and current of the circuit.

Copyright 2011, www.MikeHolt.com

Figure 690–64

(E) Series Overcurrent Protection. A single OCPD can be used to protect PV modules and interconnecting PV source circuit conductors.

690.10 Stand-Alone Systems.

(A) Inverter Output. The ac current output from a stand-alone battery based inverter(s) is not permitted to be less than the largest single utilization equipment connected to the system.

(B) Sizing and Protection. Inverter ac output circuit conductors must have overcurrent protection in accordance with Article 240.

(C) Single 120V Supply. The battery based inverter output is permitted to supply a 120V single-phase, 3-wire, 120/240V distribution panel marked with the following words or equivalent:

 WARNING — SINGLE 120-VOLT SUPPLY DO NOT CONNECTMULTIWIRE BRANCH CIRCUITS

(D) Energy Storage or Backup Power. Energy storage or backup power supplies aren't required.

(E) Backfed Circuit Breakers. Plug-in circuit breakers must be secured in place by an additional fastener that requires other than a pull to release the breaker from the panelboard. Circuit breakers that are marked line and load must not be backfed.

> **Author's Comment:** The purpose of the breaker fastener for stand-alone battery based inverter systems is to prevent the circuit breaker from being accidentally removed from the panelboard while energized, thereby exposing persons to dangerous voltage.

690.11 Arc-Fault Circuit Protection (Direct Current).

Photovoltaic dc circuit conductors operating at 80V or greater within a building must be protected by a listed PV type dc arc-fault circuit interrupter. The AFCI protection device must:

(1) Detect and interrupt arcing faults resulting from a failure in the intended continuity of a conductor, connection, module, or other system component in the dc PV source and output circuits.

(2) Disable or disconnect one of the following:

    a. Inverters or charge controllers

    b. System components within the arcing circuit

(3) Disabled or disconnected equipment must be manually restarted.

(4) Have an annunciator that provides a visual indication that the circuit interrupter has operated.

PART III. DISCONNECTING MEANS

690.13 Disconnecting Means for Conductors. A disconnecting means is required to open all ungrounded dc circuit conductors, typically the positive conductor for grounded systems and the positive and negative conductor for ungrounded systems.

A switch, circuit breaker, or other device isn't permitted to open the grounded dc conductor. **Figure 690–65**

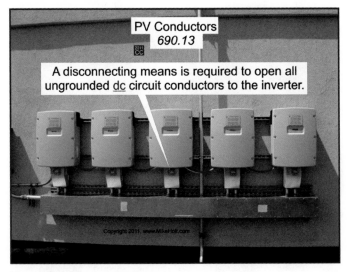

Figure 690–65

Ex 2: The grounded dc conductor can be switched when the switch is:
Figure 690–66

  (1) Only used for array maintenance,

  (2) Only accessible to qualified persons, and

  (3) Rated for the maximum dc voltage and dc short-circuit current.

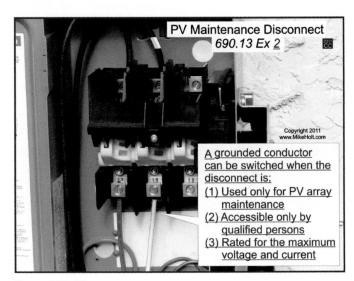

Figure 690–66

690.14 PV System Disconnecting Means.

(A) PV Disconnecting Means. The PV system disconnect (ac circuit) is not required to be marked suitable for service equipment use.

(B) Equipment. A PV source circuit isolating switch is permitted on the PV side of the PV system dc disconnect [690.14(C)(5)]. **Figure 690–67**

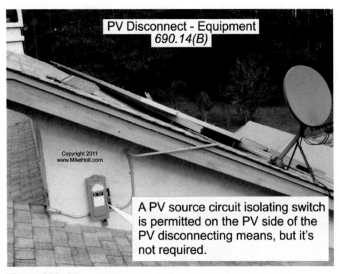

Figure 690–67

(C) Requirements for Disconnecting Means. The PV system disconnect must open all ungrounded conductors.

(1) Location. Each PV system disconnect must be located at a readily accessible location either outside the building/structure, or inside nearest the point of dc PV system conductor entry. **Figure 690–68 and 690–69**

Ex: Where the PV system disconnect(s) is not located at the point of entry, the dc PV conductors must be installed in a metal raceway, Type MC cable, or metal enclosure [690.31(E)]. Figure 690–70

(2) Marking. Each PV system disconnect must be permanently marked to identify it as the PV system disconnect. **Figure 690–71**

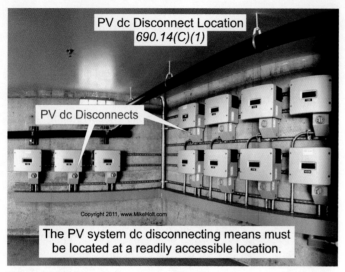

Figure 690–68

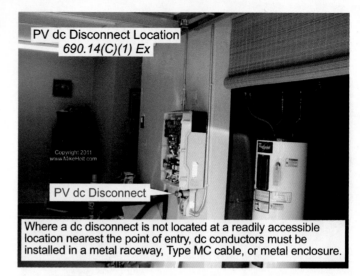

Figure 690–70

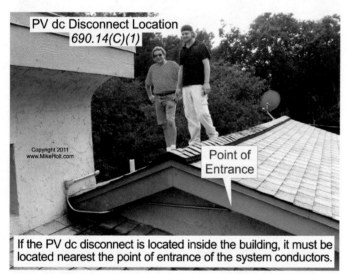

Figure 690–69

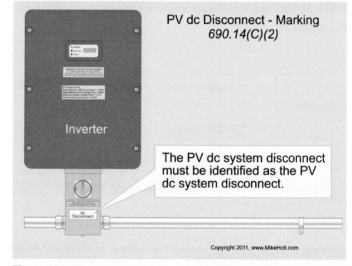

Figure 690–71

(3) Suitable for Use. The PV system disconnect(s) must be suitable for the prevailing environmental conditions.

> **Author's Comment:** Type 3R NEMA enclosures protects against falling rain, sleet, and undamaged by the formation of ice on the enclosure [110.28].

(4) Maximum Number of Disconnects. The PV system ac disconnecting means can consist of no more than six switches or six circuit breakers mounted in a single or group of separate enclosures. **Figure 690–72**

(5) Grouping. The PV system disconnect(s) must be grouped together.

(D) Inverter Disconnects. Where utility-interactive inverters are not readily accessible, dc and ac circuit disconnecting means is requires as follows:

(1) A disconnect for the inverter dc input circuit are required within sight of or in the inverter.

> **Author's Comment:** Visible and not more than 50 ft away from the equipment [Article 100].

(2) A disconnect for the inverter ac output circuit is required within sight of the inverter.

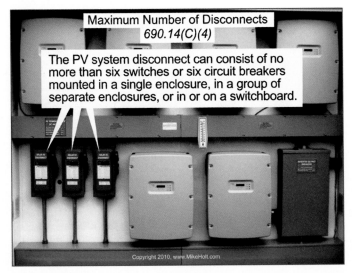

Figure 690–72

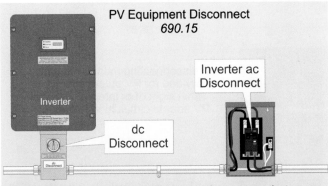

PV equipment must have a disconnecting means that opens all ungrounded circuit conductors from all sources of power, the dc and ac disconnects must be grouped together and each permanently marked to identify their purpose.

Copyright 2011, www.MikeHolt.com

Figure 690–73

(3) An additional ac disconnect located at a readily accessible location.

(4) A permanent plaque identifying the locations of the service and inverter ac disconnect(s) must be placed at service and inverter ac disconnect(s) locations.

690.15 PV Equipment Disconnect.

PV equipment must have a disconnecting means that opens all ungrounded circuit conductors from all sources of power. Where equipment is energized from more than one source, such as an inverter supplied by dc current input from the array and ac current output to the utility source, a disconnecting means is required for each and both dc and ac disconnects must be grouped together and each permanently marked to identify their purpose. **Figure 690–73**

A single disconnecting means in accordance with 690.17 can be used the ac output of one or more inverters or ac modules in an interactive system.

690.16 Disconnecting Means for Fuses

(A) PV Source Circuit. A means must be provided to disconnect each PV source circuit fuse independently of other PV source circuits fuse. **Figure 690–74**

Author's Comments:

- Combiners containing pull-out fuses and finger-safe fuse holders meet this requirement.

- Overcurrent protection devices for PV source circuits are not required to be readily accessible [690.9(C)].

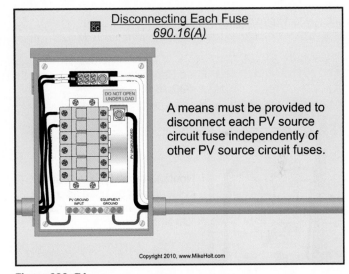

A means must be provided to disconnect each PV source circuit fuse independently of other PV source circuit fuses.

Copyright 2010, www.MikeHolt.com

Figure 690–74

(B) PV Output Circuit. A disconnecting means must be provided for PV output circuits. The PV output circuit disconnect must be within sight of or integral with the PV source circuit fuse holders, be externally operable without exposing the operator to live parts, and plainly indicating whether in the open or closed position [690.17]. Where the disconnecting means is more than 6 ft from the fuse, a directory indicating the location of the fuse disconnect must be at the fuse location. **Figure 690–75**

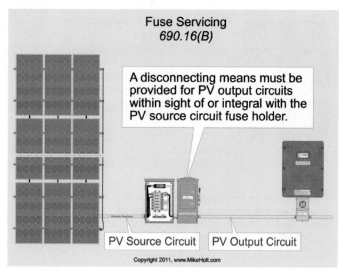

Figure 690–75

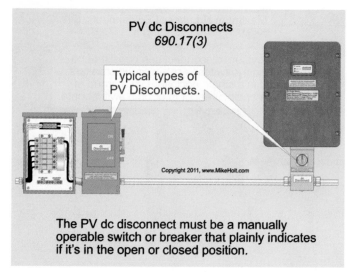

Figure 690–77

Nonload-break fuse pullouts or holders must be marked "Do not open under load. **Figure 690–76**

(4) Have an interrupting rating sufficient for the circuit voltage and the current available at the line terminals of the equipment.

For dc disconnects where line and load terminals will be energized when the switch is in the open position, a warning sign must be placed on or adjacent to the disconnect such as: **Figure 690–78**

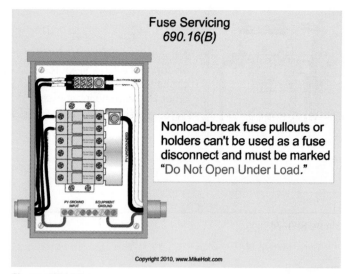

Figure 690–76

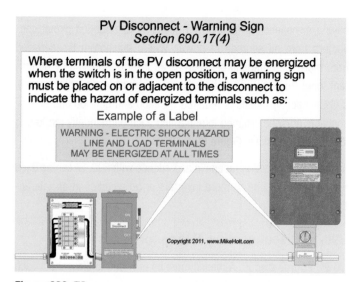

Figure 690–78

690.17 Disconnect Requirement. Disconnects must be a manually operable switch or circuit breaker meeting all of the following:

(2) Externally operable without exposing the operator to live parts.

(3) Plainly indicating whether in the open or closed position. **Figure 690–77**

⚠ **WARNING—ELECTRIC SHOCK HAZARD DO NOT TOUCH TERMINALS—TERMINALS ON BOTH THE LINE AND LOAD SIDES MAY BE ENERGIZED IN THE OPEN POSITION**

Ex: A connector complying with 690.33 can be used as a disconnecting means.

Author's Comment: The most common application of this exception is for micro-inverters that handle the output of one or two PV modules; plug connectors are used for the dc and ac disconnect. **Figure 690–79**

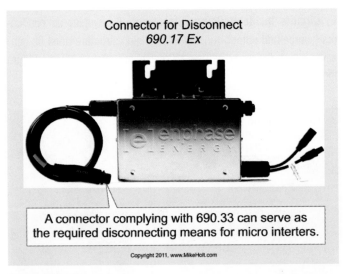

Figure 690–79

690.18 Installation and Service. Open circuiting, short circuiting, or opaque covering can disable an array or portions of an array for installation and service. **Figure 690–80**

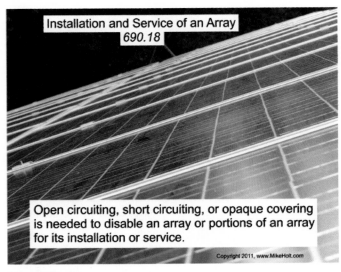

Figure 690–80

Note: The interconnecting cables for PV modules are energized whenever the module is exposed to light, including moon light! Although moonlight may not generate lethal voltages, a shock hazard may still exist. **Figure 690–81**

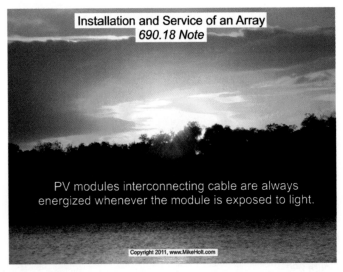

Figure 690–81

PART IV. WIRING METHODS

690.31 Wiring Methods.

(A) Wiring Systems. Chapter 3 wiring methods or single-conductors listed and identified as PV Wire. **Figure 690–82**

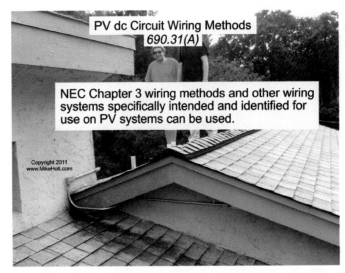

Figure 690–82

Where exposed single-conductors for PV source or output circuits operate at over 30V are located so as to be readily accessible, they must be installed in a Chapter 3 wiring method. **Figure 690–83**

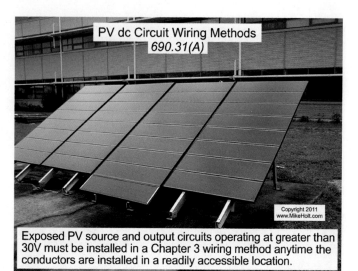

Figure 690–83

(B) Single-Conductor Cable. Single-conductor Type USE-2 or single-conductors listed and identified as PV Wire can be run exposed at outdoor locations for PV source circuits where not readily accessible [690.31(A)].

> Note: PV wire raceway fill is based on the actual area of the conductor (see manufacturer's specifications) in conjunction with Table 1 of Chapter 9. **Figure 690–84**

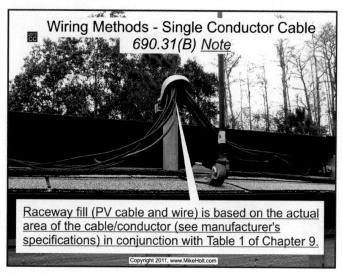

Figure 690–84

Author's Comment: See 300.17 in this textbook for information on raceway sizing based on conductor fill.

(C) Flexible Cords and Cables. Flexible cords used to connect the moving parts of tracking PV modules must be installed in accordance with Article 400 and be identified as a hard service cord or portable power cable suitable for extra-hard usage, listed for outdoor use, water resistant, and sunlight resistant.

(E) Circuits Inside Buildings/Structures. PV system dc conductors (source and output) run inside a building/structure must be contained in a metal raceway, Type MC cable, or metal enclosure. **Figure 690–85**

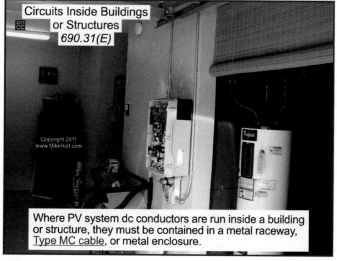

Figure 690–85

(1) Beneath Roofs. Wiring methods cannot be located within 10 in. of the roof decking or sheathing, except where located directly below the roof surface covered by PV modules and associated equipment and must be run perpendicular (90°) to the roof penetration point. **Figure 690–86**

> Note: The 10 in. from the roof decking/sheathing is to prevent accidental contact with energized conductors from saws used by firefighters for roof ventilation during a structure fire.

(2) Flexible Wiring Methods. FMC smaller than trade size ¾ or Type MC cable smaller than 1 in. in diameter installed across ceilings or floor joists must be protected by substantial guard strips that are at least as high as the wiring method. Where run exposed, other than within 6 ft of their connection to equipment, wiring methods must closely follow the building surface or be protected from physical damage by an approved means.

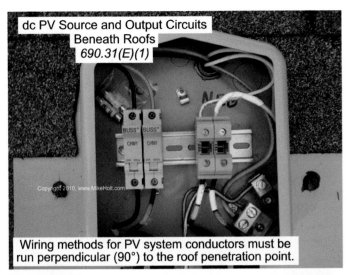

dc PV Source and Output Circuits
Beneath Roofs
690.31(E)(1)

Wiring methods for PV system conductors must be
run perpendicular (90°) to the roof penetration point.

Figure 690–86

(3) Marking/Labeling. Wiring methods and enclosures containing PV source conductors must be marked "Photovoltaic Power Source" by labels or other approved permanent marking means. **Figure 690–87**

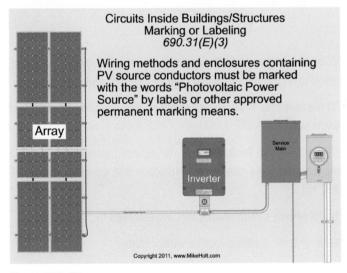

Circuits Inside Buildings/Structures
Marking or Labeling
690.31(E)(3)

Wiring methods and enclosures containing
PV source conductors must be marked
with the words "Photovoltaic Power
Source" by labels or other approved
permanent marking means.

Array

Service Main

Inverter

Figure 690–87

(4) Marking /Labeling Methods. The marking required by 690.31(E)(3) must be visible after installation and appear on every section of the wiring system separated by enclosures, walls, partitions, ceilings, or floors. Spacing between labels/marking must not be more than 10 ft and labels must be suitable for the environment. **Figure 690–88**

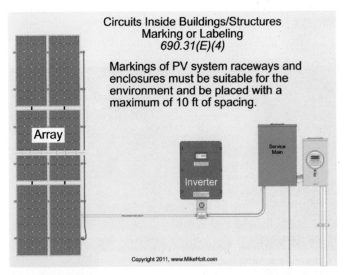

Circuits Inside Buildings/Structures
Marking or Labeling
690.31(E)(4)

Markings of PV system raceways and
enclosures must be suitable for the
environment and be placed with a
maximum of 10 ft of spacing.

Array

Inverter

Service Main

Figure 690–88

(F) Flexible, Fine-Stranded Conductors. Flexible, fine-stranded conductors must terminate in terminals, lugs, devices, or connectors identified and listed for fine-stranded conductors in accordance with 110.14(A). **Figure 690–89**

Wiring Methods Flexible Conductor Termination
690.31(F)

Flexible and fine-stranded conductors must terminate in
terminals, lugs, devices, or connectors that are identified
and listed for fine-stranded conductors [110.14].

Figure 690–89

690.32 Component Interconnections. Connectors and fittings used with building-integrated PV modules can be concealed at the time of on-site assembly.

690.33 Connectors. Figure 690–90

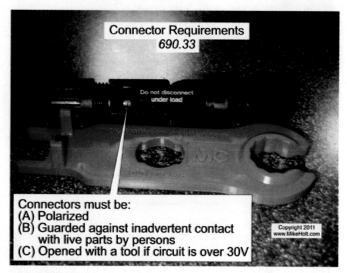

Figure 690–90

(A) Configuration. Connectors must be polarized.

(B) Guarding. Connectors must be designed so that they guard against inadvertent contact with live parts by persons.

(C) Type. Where used for circuits operating at over 30V, connectors must require a tool for opening.

(E) Interruption of Circuit. Connectors not rated for to interrupt current without hazard to the operator must require a tool to open and be marked "Do Not Disconnect Under Load." **Figure 690–91**

Figure 690–91

690.34 Access to Boxes.

Junction, pull, and outlet boxes can be located behind PV modules that are secured by removable fasteners and connected by a flexible wiring system. **Figure 690–92**

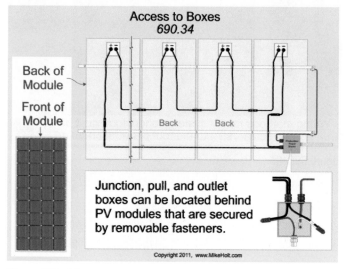

Figure 690–92

690.35 Ungrounded Systems.
PV power systems are permitted to be ungrounded if they comply with the following:

(A) Disconnects. A disconnecting means that complies with Part III of Article 690.

(B) Overcurrent Protection. All ungrounded conductors (positive and negative) have overcurrent protection that complies with 690.9 [240.15].

(D) PV source circuit conductors are installed in:

(1) Nonmetallic jacketed multiconductor cables

(2) Raceway, or

(3) Exposed single-conductors listed and identified as PV Wire.

(F) Labeled. The PV power source must be labeled with the following warning at every junction box and termination point:

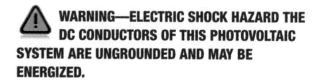

WARNING—ELECTRIC SHOCK HAZARD THE DC CONDUCTORS OF THIS PHOTOVOLTAIC SYSTEM ARE UNGROUNDED AND MAY BE ENERGIZED.

(G) Listing. Inverters or charge controllers for ungrounded PV systems must be listed for the purpose [690.4(D)].

PART V. GROUNDING

690.41 System Grounding. One conductor of a 2-wire PV system operating at over 50V and the reference (center tap) conductor of a bipolar system must be grounded. **Figure 690–93**

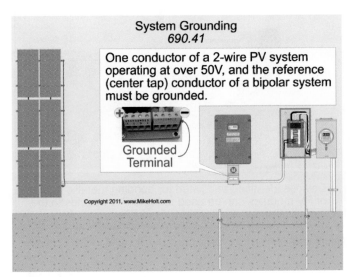

Figure 690–93

Exception: Ungrounded systems complying with 690.35.

Author's Comment: Most PV systems in the U.S. have the negative conductor of the PV system grounded in accordance with module manufacturer's instructions; this conductor is called the "grounded conductor." See 200.6 for the identification requirements of the grounded conductor.

690.42 Point of System Grounding Connection. For grounded PV systems, the grounding connection can be at any "single" point on the grounded conductor of the PV dc output circuit.

Author's Comment: This connection is typically made within the inverter by the inverter manufacturer; the installer does not make this connection.

Ex: PV systems with ground-fault protection [690.5] that incorporates the system grounding connection must not have an additional grounding connection. **Figure 690–94**

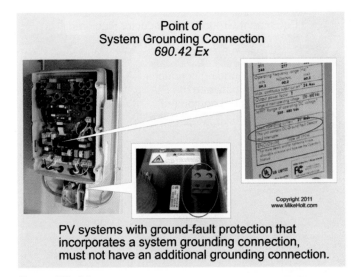

Figure 690–94

690.43 Equipment Grounding.

(A) Equipment Grounding Required. Exposed metal parts of PV module frames, electrical equipment, raceways, and enclosures must be connected to an equipment grounding conductor of a type permitted in 250.118 [250.134]. **Figures 690–95**

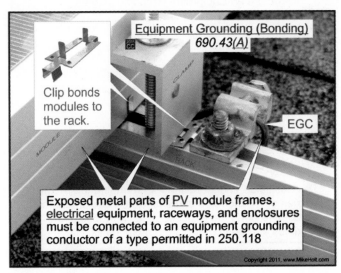

Figure 690–95

(B) Equipment Grounding Conductor Required. An equipment grounding conductor must be installed between the array and associated equipment. **Figure 690–96**

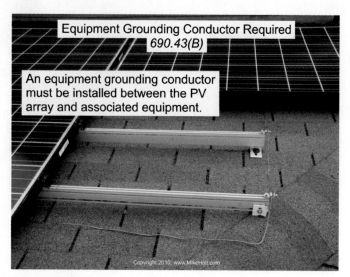

Figure 690–96

(C) Structure as Equipment Grounding Conductor. Devices listed for grounding metallic frames of PV modules and associated equipment can be used to bond exposed metal surfaces of the modules and equipment to metal racks. **Figure 690–97**

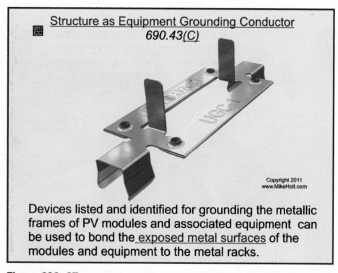

Figure 690–97

Metallic mounting racks used as an equipment grounding conductor must be identified as an equipment grounding conductor or have identified bonding jumpers/devices connected between the separate metallic racks and be connected to an equipment grounding conductor as required by 690.43(A).

(D) Securing Devices and Systems. Devices and systems securing PV modules to metal mounting racks that serve as an equipment grounding conductor must be identified for such purposes.

(E) Adjacent Modules. Devices listed for bonding metallic frames of PV modules can be used to bond PV modules to adjacent PV modules. **Figure 690–98**

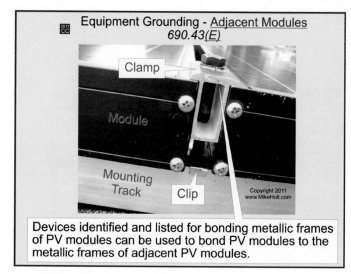

Figure 690–98

(F) Run Together. All conductors of a circuit, including the equipment grounding conductor, must be installed in the same raceway or cable, or run with single-conductor listed and identified PV wire when leaving the vicinity of the array [300.3(B)]. **Figure 690–99**

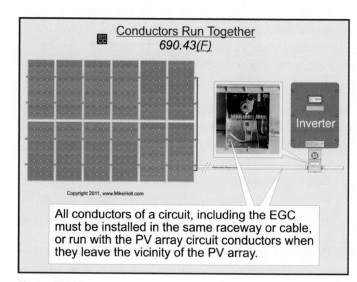

Figure 690–99

690.45 Size of Equipment Grounding Conductors.

(A) General. Equipment grounding conductors must be sized to the rating of the PV circuit overcurrent device in accordance with Table 250.122. **Figure 690–100**

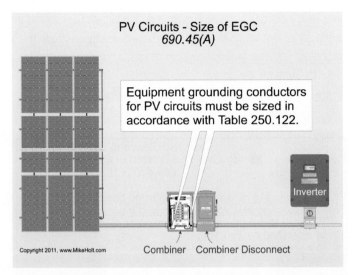

PV Circuits - Size of EGC
690.45(A)

Equipment grounding conductors for PV circuits must be sized in accordance with Table 250.122.

Combiner   Combiner Disconnect

Figure 690–100

Table 250.122 Sizing Equipment Grounding Conductor	
Overcurrent Device Rating	Copper Conductor
15A	14 AWG
20A	12 AWG
30A—60A	10 AWG
70A—100A	8 AWG
110A—200A	6 AWG
225A—300A	4 AWG
350A—400A	3 AWG
450A—500A	2 AWG
600A	1 AWG
700A—800A	1/0 AWG
1,000A	2/0 AWG
1,200A	3/0 AWG

Where overcurrent protection is not provided, as permitted in 690.9 Ex, PV equipment grounding conductors are sized to the PV circuit short-circuit current rating (Isc) in accordance with Table 250.122. **Figure 690–101**

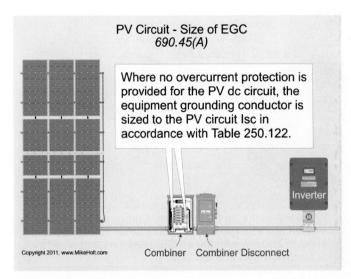

PV Circuit - Size of EGC
690.45(A)

Where no overcurrent protection is provided for the PV dc circuit, the equipment grounding conductor is sized to the PV circuit Isc in accordance with Table 250.122.

Inverter

Combiner   Combiner Disconnect

Figure 690–101

690.46 Array Equipment Grounding Conductors.

Exposed equipment grounding conductors sized 8 AWG and smaller subject to physical damage during maintenance or other events must be installed in a raceway [250.120(C)]. **Figure 690–102**

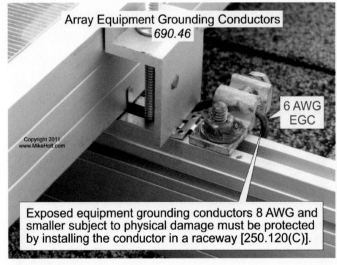

Array Equipment Grounding Conductors
690.46

6 AWG EGC

Exposed equipment grounding conductors 8 AWG and smaller subject to physical damage must be protected by installing the conductor in a raceway [250.120(C)].

Figure 690–102

690.47 Grounding Electrode System.

(A) Stand-Alone Alternating-Current PV System Grounding. For stand alone ac PV systems, a grounding electrode system must be provided in accordance with 250.50 through 250.60, with the ac grounding electrode conductor installed and sized in accordance with 250.64. **Figure 690–103**

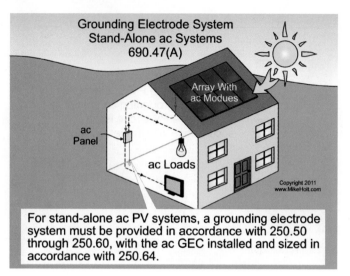

Figure 690–103

(B) Stand-Alone Direct-Current PV System Grounding. For stand-alone grounded dc PV systems, a grounding electrode system in accordance 250.50 through 250.60 must be provided, with the dc grounding electrode conductor sized in accordance with 250.166 and installed in accordance with 250.64. **Figure 690–104**

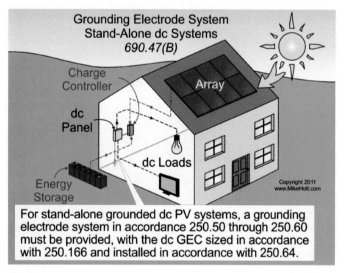

Figure 690–104

Author's Comment: The dc grounding electrode conductor is not permitted to be smaller than the largest ungrounded dc conductor or 8 AWG [250.166(B)]. When the dc GEC is connected to a ground rod, the GEC is not required to be larger than 6 AWG copper [250.166(C)], and when the dc GEC is connected to a concrete-encased electrode, the GEC is not required to be larger than 4 AWG copper [250.166(D)].

(C) PV Systems with Alternating-Current Power System Grounding. Grounded PV systems constructed of dc modules must have the dc system grounding by one of the following methods:

(1) Separate dc Electrode. A grounding electrode conductor run from the marked dc GEC point at the inverter to the dc separate dc grounding electrode sized no smaller than the largest ungrounded dc conductor or 8 AWG [250.166(B)]. The dc grounding electrode must be bonded to the ac grounding electrode with a bonding jumper sized to the larger of the the dc grounding electrode conductor [250.166] or ac grounding electrode conductor [250.66]. **Figure 690–105**

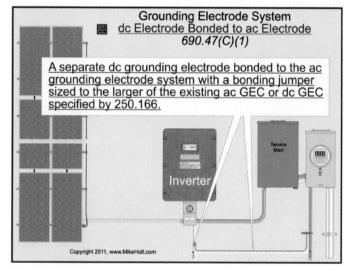

Figure 690–105

Example: What size dc GEC and minimum size dc/ac bonding conductor required for a PV system where the largest ungrounded dc inverter circuit conductors are 6 AWG?

Answer: 6 AWG, 250.166(B)

(2) Alternating-Current Grounding Electrode. A grounding electrode conductor sized in accordance with 250.166 run from the marked dc GEC point at the inverter to the ac grounding electrode. **Figure 690–106**

Where an ac grounding electrode isn't accessible, the dc grounding electrode conductor is permitted to terminate to the ac grounding electrode conductor by irreversible compression-type connectors listed as grounding and bonding equipment or by exothermic welding [250.64(C)(1)]. **Figure 690–107**

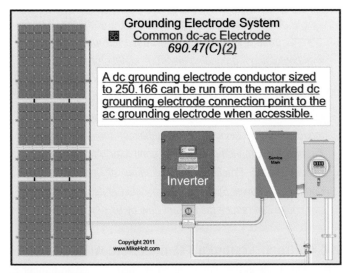

Figure 690–106

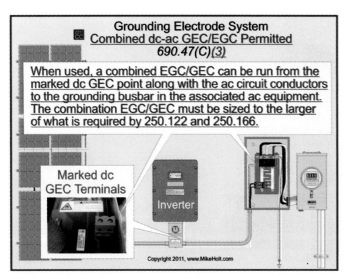

Figure 690–108

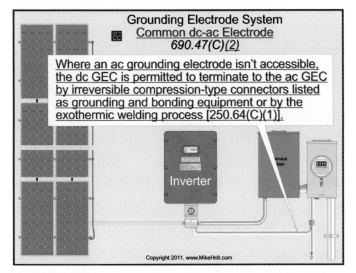

Figure 690–107

Author's Comment: The grounding electrode conductor run from the marked dc GEC point at the inverter to the ac grounding electrode must be sized no smaller than the largest ungrounded dc conductor or 8 AWG [250.166(B)].

(3) Equipment Grounding Conductor. An unspliced or irreversibly spliced, equipment grounding/grounding electrode conductor run from the marked dc GEC point at the inverter with the ac circuit conductors to the grounding busbar in associated ac equipment. The combined EGC/GEC must be sized no smaller than required by 250.122 or 250.166. **Figure 690–108**

Author's Comment: The ac equipment grounding conductor is sized in accordance with 250.122 based on the rating of the ac circuit overcurrent protection device size, and the dc grounding electrode conductor is sized no smaller than the largest ungrounded dc conductor or 8 AWG [250.166(B)].

Question: What size EGC/EGC is required for a 5 kW inverter where the dc inverter circuit conductors are 6 AWG and the inverter ac output circuit conductors are 10 AWG protected by a 30A breaker? **Figure 690–109**

Answer: Table 250.122 requires the EGC to be sized no smaller than 10 AWG, 250.166(B) requires the grounding electrode conductor to be no smaller than the largest dc circuit conductors. In this case, the EGC/GEC must be a 6 AWG or larger.

To prevent inductive choking of grounding electrode conductors, ferrous raceways and enclosures containing grounding electrode conductors must have each end of the raceway or enclosure containing the EGC/GEC bonded to the grounding electrode conductor in accordance with 250.92(B)(2) through (B)(4) [250.64(E)]. **Figure 690–110**

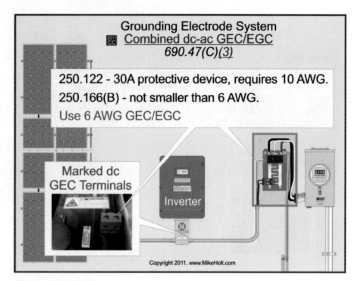

Figure 690–109

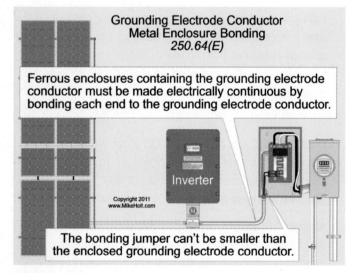

Figure 690–110

Author's Comments:

• Nonferrous metal raceways, such as aluminum rigid metal conduit, enclosing the grounding electrode conductor aren't required to meet the "bonding each end of the raceway to the grounding electrode conductor" provisions of this section.

• To save a lot of time and effort, install the grounding electrode conductor exposed if it's not subject to physical damage [250.64(B)], or enclose it in PVC conduit suitable for the application [352.10(F)].

CAUTION: *The effectiveness of a grounding electrode is significantly reduced if a ferrous metal raceway containing a grounding electrode conductor isn't bonded to the ferrous metal raceway at both ends. This is because a single conductor carrying high-frequency induced lightning current in a ferrous raceway causes the raceway to act as an inductor, which severely limits (chokes) the current flow through the grounding electrode conductor. ANSI/IEEE 142, Recommended Practice for Grounding of Industrial and Commercial Power Systems (Green Book) states: "An inductive choke can reduce the current flow by 97 percent."*

690.48 Open Grounding Connection. Where the removal of equipment opens the grounding connection, a bonding jumper is required to maintain the connection while the equipment is removed.

690.49 Open Grounding Connection for Grounded Systems. Where the removal of equipment opens the grounding electrode conductor connection required by 690.47, a bonding jumper is required to maintain the connection while the equipment is removed.

PART VI. MARKING

690.53 Direct-Current PV Power Source. A permanent label must be applied by the installer at the PV dc disconnect indicating:

(1) Rated maximum power-point current (Imp x number of combined paralleled source circuits).

(2) Rated maximum power-point voltage (Vmp x number of modules in each source circuit).

(3) Maximum system voltage (Voc).

    Note: See 690.7(A) for maximum photovoltaic system voltage calculation.

(4) Short-Circuit Current (Isc x 1.25).

    Note: See 690.8(A) for maximum circuit current calculation.

    Author's Comment: The values for maximum power-point current (Imp), maximum power-point voltage (Vmp), open circuit voltage (Voc), and short-circuit current (Isc) are indicated on the manufactures specifications sheet for the modules used for the system.

(5) Maximum rated output current of the charge controller (if installed)

Example: Determine the DC PV power source information needed for the PV power source label based on the following: array consists of twenty-three 200W modules, 11.05 Imp, 18.10 Vmp, 22.60 Voc (at 7°C), and 11.80 Isc. **Figure 690–111**

(1) Rated Maximum Power-Point Current (Imp)

Imp = Module Rated Imp × Number of Strings in Parallel

Imp = 11.05A × 1

Imp = 11.05A

(2) Rated Maximum Power-Point Voltage (Vmp)

Vmp = Module Vmp × Number of Modules per String

Vmp = 18.10V × 23 = 416V

(3) Maximum System Voltage (Voc)

PV Voc = Module Voc × Table 690.7 Correction Factor × # Modules per String

PV Voc = 22.60 Voc × 1.14 × 23 modules

PV Voc = 593V

(4) Short-Circuit Current (Isc)

Isc = Module Isc × 1.25 × Number of Strings in Parallel

Isc = (11.80A × 1.25) × 1

Isc = 14.75A

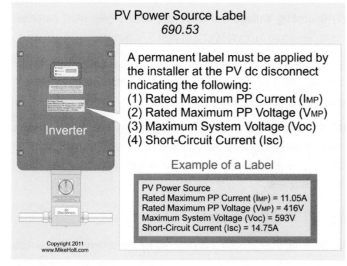

Figure 690–111

690.54 Interactive System. The point of connection of the PV system to ac power must be marked with the rated ac output current and nominal operating ac voltage. **Figure 690–112**

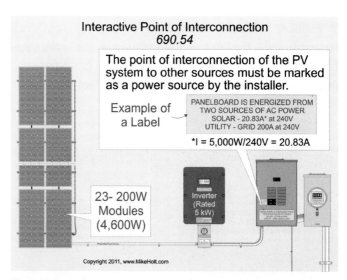

Figure 690–112

Example: What's the rated ac output current for a utility-interactive inverter rated 5 kW at 120/240V supplied by twenty-three dc modules each rated 200W?

Inverter Rated ac Output Current = Inverter kW rating/ Nominal ac Voltage

Inverter Rated ac Output Current = 5,000W/240V

Inverter Rated ac output current = 20.83A at 240V

Author's Comment: Panelboards containing ac inverter circuit breakers must be field-marked to indicate the presence of multiple ac power sources [705.12(D)(4)].

690.55 PV Systems with Energy Storage. PV systems having energy storage must be marked with the maximum operating voltage, equalization voltage, and polarity of the grounded circuit conductor.

690.56 Identification of Power Sources.

(A) Facilities with Stand-Alone Systems. Any building/structure with a stand-alone PV system (not connected to a utility power) must have a permanent plaque placed on the exterior of the building/structure at a readily visible location that is acceptable to the authority having jurisdiction. The plaque must indicate the location of the stand-alone PV system disconnecting means and that the structure contains a stand-alone electrical power system.

(B) Facilities with Utility Power and PV System. Buildings/structures containing both utility power and a PV system must have a permanent plaque placed at the service and PV system ac disconnecting means identifying the location of the other system if not located at the same location. **Figure 690–113**

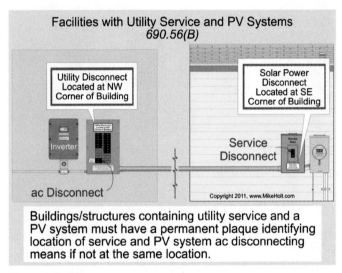

Figure 690–113

PART VII. CONNECTION TO OTHER SOURCES

690.60 Interactive Systems. Only inverters and ac PV modules listed as interactive can be used with interactive systems. **Figure 690–114**

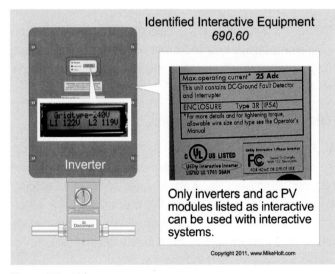

Figure 690–114

690.61 Loss of Interactive System Power. An inverter or an ac module in an interactive PV system must automatically de-energize its output to the connected electrical distribution system upon loss of voltage and remain de-energized until the electrical distribution system voltage has been restored.

> **Author's Comment:** This requirement is met if the inverter is listed as a utility-interactive inverter in accordance with UL Standard 1741—*Equipment for Use with Distributed Energy Resources.*

690.63 Unbalanced Interconnections. Unbalanced connections must be in accordance with 705.100.

690.64 Point of Connection. The output of a utility-interactive inverter must be connected to the premises wiring in accordance with 705.12.

PART VIII. STORAGE BATTERIES

690.71 Installation.

(A) General. Storage batteries for PV systems must be installed in accordance with Article 480.

(B) Dwellings.

(1) Operating Voltage. For dwellings, battery cells must be series connected so as to operate at less than 50V, nominal.

(2) Guarding of Live Parts. Live parts of storage battery systems for dwellings must be guarded to prevent accidental contact by persons or objects regardless of voltage.

(C) Current Limiting. Listed current-limiting overcurrent devices must be installed where the available short-circuit current from the battery bank exceeds the interrupting or withstand ratings of equipment it supplies.

690.72 Charge Control.

(A) General. Charge control is required for the battery system unless the PV source circuit matches the voltage rating and charge current requirements of the interconnected battery cells and the maximum charging current multiplied by 1 hour is less than 3 percent of the rated battery capacity expressed in ampere-hours or as recommended by the battery manufacturer.

> **Note:** Certain battery types such as valve-regulated lead acid or nickel cadmium can experience thermal failure when overcharged.

690.74 Battery Interconnections. Flexible cable minimum 2/0 AWG identified for hard-service use and moisture resistant in accordance with Article 400 is permitted between cells within the battery enclosure and from the battery terminals to a nearby junction box.

Flexible, fine-stranded cables must terminate in terminals, lugs, devices, or connectors that are identified and listed for fine-stranded conductors [110.14(A)].

CHAPTER 6. SPECIAL EQUIPMENT — PRACTICE QUESTIONS

Article 690 Solar Photovoltaic (PV) Systems

1. The provisions of Article 690 apply to _____ systems, including inverter(s), array circuit(s), and controller(s) for such systems.

   (a) solar photoconductive
   (b) solar photovoltaic
   (c) solar photogenic
   (d) solar photosynthesis

2. An Alternating-Current Photovoltaic Module is designed to generate ac power when exposed to_____.

   (a) electromagnetic induction
   (b) heat
   (c) sunlight
   (d) hysteresis

3. A mechanically integrated assembly of modules or panels with a support structure and foundation, tracker, and other components as required to form a dc power-producing unit, is known as a(n) _____.

   (a) pulse width modulator
   (b) array
   (c) capacitive supply bank
   (d) alternating current photovoltaic module

4. A photovoltaic array that has two outputs, each having opposite polarity to a common reference point is known as _____.

   (a) bipolar photovoltaic array
   (b) polar photovoltaic array
   (c) a or b
   (d) neither a or b

5. A blocking _____ is used to block reverse current flow into a PV source circuit.

   (a) resistor
   (b) potentiometer
   (c) diode
   (d) all of the above

6. _____ include photovoltaic cells, devices, modules, or modular materials that are integrated into the outer surface or structure of a building and serve as the outer protective surface of that building.

   (a) protective photovoltaics
   (b) building integrated photovoltaics
   (c) bipolar photovoltaic arrays
   (d) bipolar photoconductive arrays

7. A _____ controller controls dc voltage, dc current, or both, and is used to charge a battery.

   (a) charge
   (b) power
   (c) photovoltaic
   (d) b and c

8. A piece of equipment that regulates the charging process of a battery by diverting power from energy storage to direct-current or alternating current loads or to an interconnected utility service is known as a(n) _____.

   (a) alternating charge controller
   (b) diversion charge controller
   (c) direct charge controller
   (d) alternating charge regulator

9. An Electrical Production and Distribution Network, such as a utility and connected load is internal to and controlled by a photovoltaic power system.

    (a) True
    (b) False

10. Multiple power sources that may include photovoltaic, wind, micro-hydro generators, engine-driven generators, and others, but do not include electrical production and distribution network systems or batteries are best defined as _____.

    (a) hybrid systems
    (b) composite systems
    (c) mixed systems
    (d) photo transform systems

11. Other than an energy storage subsystem of a photovoltaic system, such as a battery, a(n) _____ system operates in parallel with and may deliver power to an electrical production and distribution network.

    (a) hybrid
    (b) inverted
    (c) interactive
    (d) internal

12. A(n) _____ is a device that changes direct-current input to an alternating-current output.

    (a) diode
    (b) rectifier
    (c) transistor
    (d) inverter

13. The conductors between the inverter and the battery in a stand-alone system or the conductors between the inverter and the photovoltaic output circuits for electrical production and distribution network are part of the _____.

    (a) branch circuit
    (b) feeder
    (c) inverter input circuit
    (d) inverter output circuit

14. The conductors between the inverter and an alternating-current panelboard for stand-alone systems, or the conductors between the inverter and the service equipment, or another electric power production source, such as a utility, for electrical production and distribution network are part of the _____.

    (a) bipolar photovoltaic array
    (b) monopole subarray
    (c) emergency standby power
    (d) inverter output circuit

15. A(n) _____ is a complete, environmentally protected unit consisting of solar cells, and other components, exclusive of tracker, designed to generate direct-current power when exposed to sunlight.

    (a) interface
    (b) battery
    (c) module
    (d) cell bank

16. A _____ subarray has two conductors in the output circuit, one positive (+) and one negative (-). Two of these subarrays are used to form a bipolar photovoltaic array.

    (a) bipolar
    (b) monopole
    (c) double pole
    (d) module

17. A field-installable unit including a collection of modules mechanically fastened together and wired, is called a(n) _____.

    (a) panel
    (b) array
    (c) bank
    (d) gang

18. The circuit conductors between the inverter or direct-current utilization equipment and the photovoltaic source circuit(s) is part of the _____.

    (a) photovoltaic output circuit
    (b) photovoltaic input circuit
    (c) inverter input circuit
    (d) inverter output circuit

19. A single array or aggregate of arrays that generates direct-current power at system voltage and current is the Photovoltaic _____.

    (a) output source
    (b) source circuit
    (c) power source
    (d) array source

20. The circuit(s) between modules and from modules to the common connection point(s), of the direct current system is known as the _____.

    (a) photovoltaic source circuit
    (b) photovoltaic array circuit
    (c) photovoltaic input circuit
    (d) photovoltaic output circuit

21. The photovoltaic system voltage is the direct-current voltage of any photovoltaic source or photovoltaic output circuit.

    (a) True
    (b) False

22. The _____ is the basic photovoltaic device that generates electricity when exposed to light.

    (a) solar battery
    (b) solar cell
    (c) solar atom
    (d) solar ray

23. The _____ is the total components and subsystems that, in combination, convert solar energy into electric energy suitable for connection to a utilization load.

    (a) solar photovoltaic system
    (b) solar array
    (c) a and b
    (d) neither a or b

24. A stand alone system supplies power in conjunction with and to supplement an electrical production and distribution network.

    (a) True
    (b) False

25. A _____ is an electrical subset of a photovoltaic array.

    (a) panel
    (b) module
    (c) circuit
    (d) subarray

26. Unless supplemented or modified by Article 690, Chapters 1, 2, 3, and 4 in the *NEC* shall apply. However, if any provisions of Article 690 differ with other articles of the *Code*, Article 690 requirements apply within the scope of Article 690 installations.

    (a) True
    (b) False

27. Photovoltaic systems are permitted to supply any building or other structure in addition to any other _____.

    (a) electricity supply system
    (b) telephone supply system
    (c) plumbing supply system
    (d) none of the above

28. Photovoltaic source circuits and photovoltaic output circuits are not permitted to be contained in the same raceway, cable tray, cable, outlet box, junction box, or similar fitting, with nonphotovoltaic systems unless the two systems are separated by a partition.

    (a) True
    (b) False

29. PV system conductors shall be identified by separate color coding, marking tape, tagging, or other approved means.

    (a) True
    (b) False

30. Photovoltaic source circuits shall be identified at all points of termination, connection, and splices.

(a) True
(b) False

31. The conductors of PV output circuits and inverter input and output circuits shall be identified at all points of termination, connection, and splices.

(a) True
(b) False

32. Where the conductors of more than one PV system occupy the same junction box, raceway, or equipment, the conductors of each system shall be identified at all termination, connection, and splice points.

(a) True
(b) False

33. The requirement for grouping PV source and output circuit is not required if the circuit enters from a cable or raceway unique to the circuit that makes the grouping obvious.

(a) True
(b) False

34. Where the conductors of more than one PV system occupy the same junction box or raceway with removable cover(s), the ac and dc conductors of each system shall be grouped separately by wire ties or similar means at least once, and then shall be grouped at intervals not to exceed _____.

(a) 6 in.
(b) 12 in.
(c) 36 in.
(d) 6 ft

35. The connection to a _____ shall be arranged so that removal of either from a photovoltaic source circuit does not interrupt a grounded conductor to other PV source circuits.

(a) panelboard or switchboard
(b) bus or lug
(c) module or panel
(d) array or subarray

36. All equipment intended for use in photovoltaic power systems shall be _____ for the application.

(a) identified
(b) listed
(c) approved
(d) a and b

37. The location of PV source and output conductors imbedded in built-up, laminate, or membrane roofing materials in areas not covered by PV modules and associated equipment must be clearly marked.

(a) True
(b) False

38. PV source and output conductors must be routed along building structural members _____ where the location of those structural members can be determined by observation.

(a) beams and rafters
(b) trusses and columns
(c) windows and doors
(d) a and b

39. Monopole subarrays in a Bipolar Photovoltaic system shall be physically _____ where the sum of the photovoltaic system voltages, without consideration of polarity, of the two monopole subarrays exceeds the rating of the conductors and connected equipment.

(a) separated
(b) connected
(c) joined
(d) together

40. Where inverters are remotely located from each other, a directory must be provided at each dc PV system disconnecting means, each ac disconnecting means and at the main service disconnecting means showing the location of all ac and dc PV system disconnecting means in the building.

(a) True
(b) False

41. Grounded dc photovoltaic arrays must be provided with direct current _____ meeting the requirements of 690.5(a) through (c) to reduce fire hazards.

(a) arc-fault protection
(b) rectifier protection
(c) ground fault monitors
(d) ground fault protection

42. A ground-fault protection device or system required for photovoltaic systems shall be capable of _____.

(a) interrupting the flow of fault current
(b) detecting a ground fault current
(c) provide an indication of the fault
(d) all of the above

43. Faulted circuits required to have ground-fault protection in a photovoltaic system shall be isolated by automatically disconnecting the _____, or, the inverter charge controller fed by the faulted circuits shall automatically stop supplying power to output circuits.

(a) ungrounded conductors
(b) grounded conductors
(c) equipment grounding conductors
(d) all of the above

44. A warning label applied by the _____ must be on the utility-interactive inverter stating the following: WARNING ELECTRIC SHOCK HAZARD— IF A GROUND FAULT IS INDICATED, NORMALLY GROUNDED CONDUCTORS MAY BE UNGROUNDED AND ENERGIZED

(a) home owner
(b) inspector
(c) installer
(d) power company

45. Article 690 requirements pertaining to dc PV source circuits do not apply to ac PV modules since ac PV modules have no dc output. The PV source circuit, conductors and inverters are considered as internal wiring of an ac module.

(a) True
(b) False

46. The output circuit conductor of an ac module, which has a built-in dc to ac inverter, is considered an _____ output circuit as defined in 690.2.

(a) Inverter
(b) module
(c) PV
(d) subarray

47. Photovoltaic alternating-current module systems are permitted to use one device to detect only _____ ground faults and to disable the array by removing ac power to the ac module(s).

(a) line to line
(b) direct current
(c) line to neutral
(d) alternating current

48. The _____ of a dc photovoltaic source circuit or output circuit, must be calculated as the sum of the rated open-circuit voltage of the series-connected photovoltaic modules multiplied by the correction factor provided in Table 690.7.

(a) minimum allowable ampacity of conductors
(b) maximum allowable ampacity of conductors
(c) minimum photovoltaic system voltage
(d) maximum photovoltaic system voltage

49. One source for lowest-expected ambient temperature is the Extreme Annual Mean Minimum Design Dry Bulb Temperature found in the ASHRAE Handbook — Fundamentals.

    (a) True
    (b) False

50. For one- and two-family dwellings, the maximum PV system voltage is _____V.

    (a) 240
    (b) 208
    (c) 480
    (d) 600

51. In one- and two-family dwellings, live parts over 150V to ground must not be _____ while energized.

    (a) accessible to an inspector
    (b) accessible to an electrician
    (c) accessible to an unqualified person
    (d) all of the above

52. The PV source circuit current is calculated by multiplying the sum of the parallel module nameplate short-circuit current ratings (Isc) by 125 percent.

    (a) True
    (b) False

53. The PV output circuit current is equal to the sum of parallel PV source circuit maximum currents as calculated in _____.

    (a) 690.8(A)(1)
    (b) 690.8(A)(2)
    (c) 690.8(A)(3)
    (d) none of the above

54. The maximum inverter output circuit current is equal to the _____ output current rating.

    (a) average
    (b) peak
    (c) continuous
    (d) intermittent

55. Currents of photovoltaic systems are to be considered _____.

    (a) safe
    (b) continuous
    (c) non-continuous
    (d) inverted

56. Overcurrent devices for PV systems shall be rated to carry not less than _____ percent of the maximum currents calculated in 690.8(A).

    (a) 80
    (b) 100
    (c) 125
    (d) 250

57. The overcurrent device ratings in photovoltaic systems operated at temperatures greater than _____, shall comply with the manufacturer's temperature correction factors.

    (a) 32 degrees C
    (b) 40 degrees C
    (c) 32 degrees F
    (d) 40 degrees F

58. Overcurrent devices for PV source circuits must be readily accessible.

    (a) True
    (b) False

59. Fuses or circuit breakers for PV dc circuits must be _____ for use in dc circuits and shall have the appropriate voltage, current, and interrupt ratings.

    (a) identified
    (b) approved
    (c) recognized
    (d) listed

60. In photovoltaic source circuits, one overcurrent protection device is not permitted to protect the photovoltaic modules and the interconnecting conductors.

(a) True
(b) False

61. For stand-alone systems, the ac current output from a stand-alone inverter(s) can be _____ than the calculated load connected to the disconnect, but not less than the largest single utilization equipment connected to the system.

(a) less
(b) more
(c) greater
(d) any of these

62. For stand-alone systems, energy storage or backup power supplies are required.

(a) True
(b) False

63. Plug-in type backfed circuit breakers connected to a stand-alone system are not required to be secured in place by an additional fastener that requires other than a pull to release the breaker from the panelboard.

(a) True
(b) False

64. For stand-alone systems, circuit breakers that are marked line and load can be backfed.

(a) True
(b) False

65. A disconnecting means is required to open ungrounded dc circuit conductors.

(a) True
(b) False

66. A switch, circuit breaker, or other device is permitted to open the grounded dc conductor.

(a) True
(b) False

67. A disconnecting switch is permitted to open the grounded dc conductor of a PV system when _____.

(a) the switch is used only for PV array maintenance
(b) the switch is accessible only by qualified persons
(c) the switch is rated for the maximum dc voltage and current, including ground fault conditions
(d) all of these

68. A PV source circuit isolating switch is permitted on the PV side of the PV disconnecting means, but it's not required.

(a) True
(b) False

69. The PV system dc disconnect must be placed at a readily accessible location _____ of a building or structure to disconnect the ungrounded PV system dc circuit conductors.

(a) outside
(b) inside, nearest the point of entrance
(c) anywhere inside
(d) a or b

70. The PV system disconnecting means must be _____ to identify it as a photovoltaic system disconnect.

(a) listed
(b) approved
(c) permanently marked
(d) temporarily marked

71. The PV system disconnecting means shall be suitable for _____.

(a) heat
(b) cold
(c) rain
(d) the prevailing conditions

72. Means must be provided to disconnect equipment, such as batteries, inverters, charge controllers, and the like, from all ungrounded conductors of all sources.

    (a) True
    (b) False

73. Disconnecting means must be provided to disconnect a fuse from all sources of supply if energized from both directions and shall be capable of being disconnected independently of fuses in other photovoltaic source circuits.

    (a) True
    (b) False

74. Disconnecting means must be installed for PV output circuits where fuses that must be serviced can't be isolated from energized circuits. The disconnect must be within sight and accessible to the fuse or integral with the fuse holder, be externally operable without exposing the operator to contact with live parts, and plainly indicating whether in the open or closed position [690.17]. Where the disconnecting means is located more than _____ from the fuse, a directory showing the location of the fuse disconnect must be installed at the fuse location.

    (a) 3 ft
    (b) 6 ft
    (c) 10 ft
    (d) 12 ft

75. Non-load-break rated disconnecting means for PV output circuits must be marked "Do not open under load".

    (a) True
    (b) False

76. Disconnects used for PV systems (dc and ac) must be a manually operable switch or circuit breaker _____.

    (a) located where readily accessible
    (b) externally operable without exposing the operator to contact with live parts
    (c) plainly indicating whether in the open or closed position
    (d) all of these

77. Where all terminals of a disconnecting means may be energized when the switch is in the open position, a warning sign must be placed on or adjacent to the disconnecting means. The sign shall be similar to: WARNING ELECTRIC SHOCK HAZARD. DO NOT TOUCH TERMINALS. TERMINALS ON BOTH THE LINE AND LOAD SIDES MAY BE ENERGIZED IN THE OPEN POSITION.

    (a) True
    (b) False

78. _____ must be used to disable an array or sections of an array for installation and service.

    (a) Open circuiting
    (b) Short circuiting
    (c) Opaque covering
    (d) any of the above

79. All raceway and cable wiring methods included in this *Code* and other wiring systems and fittings specifically intended and identified for use on photovoltaic arrays shall be permitted.

    (a) True
    (b) False

80. Exposed PV source and output circuits operating at greater than _____ must be installed in a Chapter 3 wiring method anytime the conductors are installed in _____ location.

    (a) 30V, accessible location
    (b) 30V, readily accessible location
    (c) 60V, accessible location
    (d) 60V, readily accessible location

81. Single-conductor Type USE-2 and single conductor cable _____ as PV wire can be run exposed at outdoor locations for PV source circuits for PV module interconnections within the PV array.

    (a) approved
    (b) listed or labeled
    (c) listed and labeled
    (d) none of the above

82. Where the source circuit operates at over 30V, single-conductor Type USE-2 or listed and labeled PV wires installed in a readily accessible location must be installed in a raceway

    (a) True
    (b) False

83. Where dc PV source or output circuits are run inside a building or structure, they must be contained in _____.

    (a) metal raceways
    (b) Type MC cables
    (c) metal enclosures
    (d) any of these

84. Wiring methods for PV systems conductors are not permitted within _____ of the roof decking or sheathing except where located directly below the roof surface that is covered by PV modules and associated equipment.

    (a) 6 in.
    (b) 10 in.
    (c) 12 in.
    (d) none of these

85. Wiring methods for PV system conductors must be run _____ to the roof penetration point until they are 10" below the roof deck.

    (a) perpendicular
    (b) 90 degrees
    (c) 120 degrees
    (d) 180 degrees

86. Which of the following that contain photovoltaic power source conductors must be marked with the wording Photovoltaic Power Source by means of permanently affixed labels or other approved permanent marking?

    (a) Exposed raceways, cable trays, and other wiring methods
    (b) The covers or enclosures of pull boxes and junction boxes
    (c) Conduit bodies in which any of the available conduit openings are unused
    (d) all of the above

87. Markings of PV system raceways and enclosures must be suitable for the environment and be placed with a maximum of _____ of spacing.

    (a) 5 ft
    (b) 10 ft
    (c) 20 ft
    (d) none of these

88. Photovoltaic wiring methods containing _____ must be terminated only with terminals, lugs, devices, or connectors that are identified and listed for such use.

    (a) flexible, fine-stranded cables
    (b) solid conductors
    (c) flexible raceways
    (d) all of the above

89. Listed fittings and connectors that are intended to be concealed at the time of on-site assembly are permitted for on-site interconnection of modules or other array components.

    (a) True
    (b) False

90. The connectors permitted by Article 690 shall _____.

    (a) be polarized.
    (b) guard against inadvertent contact with live parts by persons.
    (c) require a tool for opening if the circuit operates at over 30V nominal maximum dc or 30V ac.
    (d) All of these

91. Junction, pull, and outlet boxes can be located behind PV modules that are secured by removable fasteners.

    (a) True
    (b) False

92. To limit the voltage induced by lightning, one conductor of a 2-wire PV system operating at over _____ must be solidly grounded (connected to the earth) in accordance with 250.4(A)(1).

    (a) 15V
    (b) 30V
    (c) 50V
    (d) none of these

93. The direct-current system grounding connection must be made at any _____ point(s) on the photovoltaic output circuit.

    (a) single
    (b) two
    (c) three
    (d) four

94. A(n) _____ must be installed between a photovoltaic array and other equipment .

    (a) grounded conductor
    (b) main bonding jumper
    (c) equipment grounding conductor
    (d) system bonding jumper

95. Devices _____ for grounding the metallic frames of PV modules and other equipment can be used to bond the exposed metal surfaces of the modules and equipment to the mounting structures.

    (a) identified
    (b) approved
    (c) listed
    (d) a and c

96. Metallic mounting structures used for grounding purposes must be _____ as an equipment grounding conductors or have _____ bonding jumpers or devices connected between the separate metallic sections and be bonded to the grounding system.

    (a) listed
    (b) labeled
    (c) identified
    (d) a and b

97. Devices and systems used for securing PV modules that also provide grounding of the module frames must be _____ for the purpose of grounding PV modules.

    (a) listed
    (b) labeled
    (c) identified
    (d) a and b

98. Devices _____ for bonding the metallic frames of PV modules shall be permitted to bond the metallic frames of PV modules to the metallic frames of adjacent PV modules.

    (a) listed
    (b) labeled
    (c) identified
    (d) a and c

99. All conductors of a circuit, including the equipment grounding conductor, must be installed in the same raceway or cable, or otherwise run with the PV array circuit conductors when they leave the vicinity of the PV array.

    (a) True
    (b) False

100. Equipment grounding conductors for PV circuits having over-current protection must be sized to the rating of the PV circuit overcurrent device in accordance with _____.

    (a) 250.122
    (b) 250.66
    (c) Table 250.122
    (d) Table 250.66

101. Where no overcurrent protection is provided for the PV dc circuit, an assumed overcurrent device rated at the PV circuit short-circuit current is used to size the equipment grounding conductor in accordance with _____.

    (a) 250.122
    (b) 250.66
    (c) Table 250.122
    (d) Table 250.66

102. Where exposed and subject to physical damage, array equipment grounding conductors smaller than 4 AWG must be protected by raceway or cable armor.

(a) True
(b) False

103. A common dc grounding-electrode conductor of a PV system is permitted to serve multiple inverters with the size of the common grounding electrode and the tap conductors in accordance with 250.166. The tap conductors must be connected to the common grounding-electrode conductor in such a manner that the common grounding electrode conductor remains _____.

(a) without a splice or joint
(b) inside inverter enclosures
(c) inside a raceway
(d) supported on insulators

104. PV systems having no direct connection between the dc grounded conductor and ac grounded conductor shall have a _____ which shall be bonded to the ac grounding system.

(a) ac grounding system
(b) dc grounding system
(c) separately derived grounding system
(d) none of the above

105. PV systems with dc modules having no direct connection between the dc grounded conductor and ac grounded conductor must be bonded to the ac grounding system by _____.

(a) a separate dc grounding electrode bonded to the ac grounding electrode system with a bonding jumper
(b) a dc grounding electrode conductor sized to 250.166 run from the marked dc grounding electrode connection point to the ac grounding electrode
(c) an unspliced, or irreversibly spliced, combined grounding conductor run from the marked dc grounding electrode connection point along with the ac circuit conductors to the grounding busbar in the associated ac equipment_
(d) a, b, or c

106. Where the removal of equipment opens the bonding connection between the _____ and exposed conducting surfaces in the PV source or output circuit equipment, a bonding jumper shall be installed while the equipment is removed.

(a) equipment grounding conductor
(b) grounded conductor
(c) grounding electrode conductor
(d) ungrounded conductor

107. Where the removal of the utility-interactive inverter or other equipment disconnects the bonding connection between the grounding electrode conductor and the photovoltaic source and/or photovoltaic output circuit grounded conductor, a _____ shall be installed to maintain the system grounding while the inverter or other equipment is removed.

(a) grounding electrode conductor
(b) fuse
(c) bonding jumper
(d) overcurrent device

108. A permanent label must be applied by the installer at the PV dc power source disconnect indicating the following:

(a) the rated maximum power-point current and voltage
(b) the maximum system voltage and short-circuit current
(c) the maximum rated output current of the charge controller (if installed)
(d) all of the above

109. The point of interconnection of the PV system power source to other sources must be marked at an accessible location at the _____ as a power source and with the rated ac output current and nominal operating ac voltage.

(a) disconnecting means
(b) array
(c) inverter
(d) none of the above

110. Any building or structure with a stand-alone PV system not connected to a utility service source must have a permanent _____ installed on the exterior of the building or structure at a readily visible location acceptable to the authority having jurisdiction. The _____ must indicate the location of the stand-alone PV system disconnecting means and that the structure contains a stand-alone electrical power system.

    (a) plaque
    (b) directory
    (c) a and b
    (d) a or b

111. Buildings or structures containing both utility service and a PV system must have a permanent _____ identifying the location of the service disconnecting means and PV system ac disconnecting means if they are not located at the same location.

    (a) plaque
    (b) directory
    (c) a and b
    (d) a or b

112. Only inverters and ac PV modules listed as interactive can be used with interactive systems.

    (a) True
    (b) False

113. An inverter or an ac module in an interactive PV system must automatically de-energize its output to the connected electrical distribution system upon _____ of voltage and remain de-energized until the electrical distribution system voltage has been restored.

    (a) surge
    (b) spike
    (c) loss
    (d) unbalance

114. In dwellings, the cells must be series connected so as to operate at less than _____ nominal.

    (a) 20V
    (b) 30V
    (c) 40V
    (d) 50V

115. Live parts of storage battery systems for dwellings shall be _____ to prevent accidental contact by persons or objects regardless of voltage.

    (a) isolated
    (b) grounded
    (c) insulated
    (d) guarded

116. A listed current-limiting overcurrent device must be installed where the available short-circuit current from the battery bank exceeds the interrupting or _____ ratings of equipment it supplies.

    (a) short-circuit
    (b) withstand
    (c) ground-fault current
    (d) none of these

117. Where used for battery interconnections, flexible cables identified as hard-service use and moisture resistant in Article 400, must be a minimum size of _____ AWG.

    (a) 1/0
    (b) 2/0
    (c) 3/0
    (d) 4/0

118. Where flexible cables are installed, they are only permitted between the battery terminals to a nearby junction box where they must connect to an approved wiring method, or between batteries and cells within the battery enclosure.

    (a) True
    (b) False

119. Where used for battery interconnections, flexible, fine-stranded cables must terminate in terminals, lugs, devices, or connectors that are identified and listed for fine-stranded conductors.

    (a) identified
    (b) listed
    (c) a or b
    (d) a and b

CHAPTER 7

SPECIAL CONDITIONS

INTRODUCTION TO CHAPTER 7—SPECIAL CONDITIONS

Chapter 7, which covers special conditions, is the third of the *NEC* chapters that deal with special topics. Remember, the first four chapters of the *NEC* are sequential and form a foundation for each of the subsequent three chapters. What exactly is a "Special Condition?" It's a situation that doesn't fall under the category of special occupancies or special equipment, but creates a need for additional measures to ensure the "safeguarding of people and property" mission of the *NEC*, as stated in 90.1(A).

- **Article 705—Interconnected Electric Power Production Sources.** Article 705 relates to power sources that operate in parallel with a primary source. Typically, a primary source is the utility supply, but it can be an on-site source, instead. For instance, in addition to the requirements of Article 690, provisions of this article apply to solar photovoltaic systems.

Notes

Interconnected Electric Power Production Sources

INTRODUCTION TO ARTICLE 705—INTERCONNECTED ELECTRIC POWER PRODUCTION SOURCES

Anytime there's more than one source of power production at the same building or structure, safety issues arise. In cases where a power production source such as a generator is used strictly for standby power, the *NEC* requires transfer switches and other safety considerations as covered in Articles 700, 701, or 702 depending on whether the standby power is legally required or optional. When interactive electrical power production sources such as wind powered generators, solar photovoltaic systems, or fuel cells are present, there usually isn't a transfer switch. In fact, it can be expected that there will be more than one source of electrical supply connected simultaneously. This can raise many questions regarding how to maintain a satisfactory level of safety when more than one power source is present.

Article 705 answers these and other questions related to power sources that operate in parallel with a primary source. Typically, a primary source is the utility supply, but it can be an on-site source instead.

PART I. GENERAL

705.1 Scope. Article 705 covers the installation of electric power production sources (photovoltaic, wind, micro-hydro generators, etc) operating in parallel with a primary source(s) of electricity. **Figure 705–1**

Note: Primary sources of electricity include a utility supply and on-site electric power sources like photovoltaic or wind powered systems.

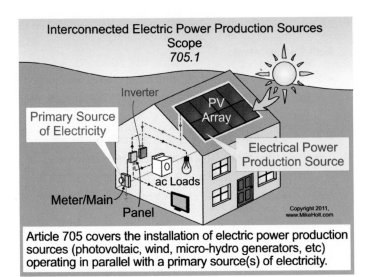

Figure 705–1

705.2 Definitions.

Hybrid System. A system comprised of multiple power sources, such as photovoltaic, wind, micro-hydro generators, engine-driven generators, and others, but not the utility power system. **Figure 705–2**

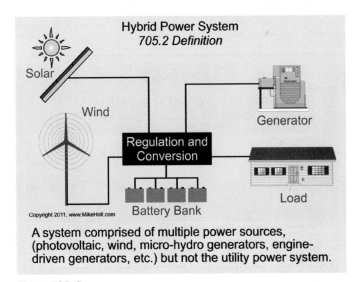

Figure 705–2

Energy storage systems such as batteries, flywheels, or superconducting magnetic storage equipment don't constitute a power source for the purpose of this definition.

Point of Common Coupling. The point where electric power production systems interface. **Figure 705–3**

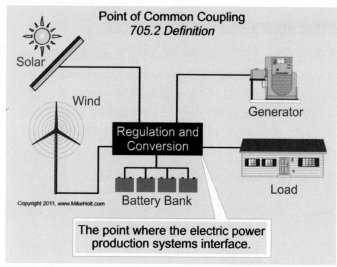

Figure 705–3

Power Production Equipment. The generating source, and all distribution equipment associated, that generates electricity from a source other than a utility supplied service. **Figure 705–4**

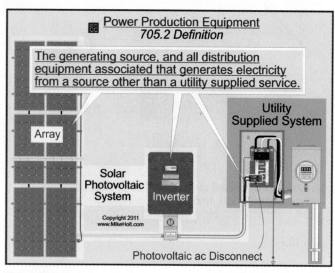

Figure 705–4

Author's Comment: Examples include generators, solar photovoltaic systems, and fuel cell systems.

705.10 Directory. A permanent plaque or directory denoting all electric power sources on or in the premises must be installed at each service equipment location and all interconnected electric power production sources.

705.12 Point of Connection.

(A) Supply Side. An electrical power production source can be connected to the supply side of the service disconnecting means in accordance with 230.82(6). **Figure 705–5**

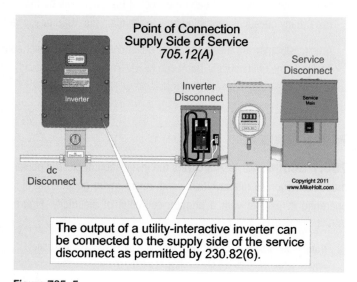

Figure 705–5

Author's Comments:

- Supply-side connection of electrical power production source is required for facilities incorporating ground-fault protection of equipment [705.12(D)].

- When determining the number of disconnects per service in accordance with 230.71(A), do not count the PV disconnect(s) connected on the supply side of service equipment, since it's not a service disconnect as defined in Article 100. **Figure 705–6**

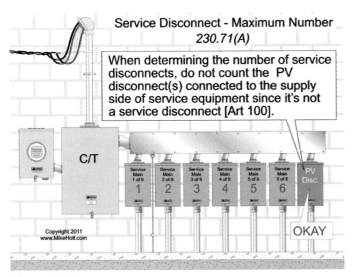

Figure 705–6

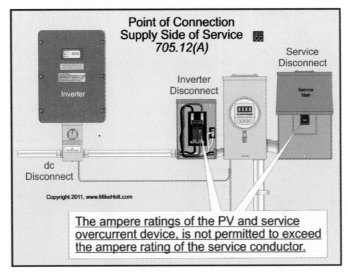

The ampere ratings of the PV and service overcurrent device, is not permitted to exceed the ampere rating of the service conductor. Figure 705–8

Figure 705–8

⚠ **CAUTION:** *The NEC does not have any specific rules governing the following, but these are suggested best practices*

- *The grounded conductor on the supply-side of service equipment for PV systems should be bonded to the PV disconnect in accordance with 250.24.* **Figure 705–7**
- *Raceways containing supply-side of service equipment conductors for PV systems should be bonded in accordance with 250.92(B).*
- *Wiring methods for supply-side of service equipment for PV systems should be limited to those identified in 230.43.*

Author's Comment: For load-side connection of PV systems to service equipment, the ampere rating of the PV and service overcurrent device is permitted to exceed.100 percent of the ampere rating of the service conductors [705.12(D)].

(D) Load Side. The output of a utility-interactive inverter can be connected to the load side of the service disconnecting means at any distribution equipment on the premises. **Figure 705–9**

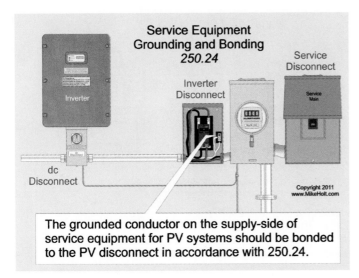

Figure 705–7

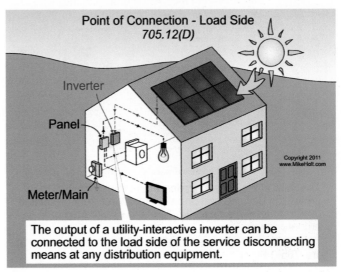

Figure 705–9

Where distribution equipment is capable of supplying multiple branch circuits or feeders or both, the interconnecting provisions for the utility-interactive inverter(s) must comply with (D)(1) through (D)(7).

(1) Dedicated Circuit. Each inverter circuit must terminate to a dedicated circuit breaker or fusible disconnect [690.64]. **Figure 705–10**

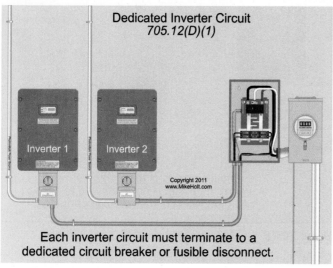

Figure 705–10

Dedicated Inverter Circuit
705.12(D)(1)

Inverter 1   Inverter 2

Copyright 2011
www.MikeHolt.com

Each inverter circuit must terminate to a
dedicated circuit breaker or fusible disconnect.

Author's Comment: The requirement that each inverter terminate to a dedicated circuit breaker or fusible disconnect does not apply to micro-inverters; all micro-inverters of a string are required to connected to single breaker in accordance with the listed instructions [110.3(B)].

(2) Panelboard Bus Rating. Where distribution equipment is capable of supplying multiple branch circuits or feeders, the sum of the ampere rating of the inverter overcurrent devices and panelboard overcurrent device must not exceed 120 percent of the panelboard bus ampere rating. **Figure 705–11**

Example: What's the maximum ampere rating of the dedicated inverter overcurrent device for a 200A bus panelboard that is capable of supplying multiple branch circuits or feeders supplied by 4/0 AWG aluminum rated 180A?

Maximum Inverter OCPD = Panelboard Bus Ampere × 1.20, less Panelboard OCPD.

Example: 150A Panelboard
Max. Inverter Device = 200A × 1.20 – 150A
Max. Inverter Device = 240A - 150A
Max. Inverter Device = 90A

Example: 175A Panelboard
Max. Inverter Device = 200A × 1.20 – 175A
Max. Inverter Device = 240A - 175A
Max. Inverter Device = 65A

Example: 200A Panelboard, **Figure 705–12**
Max. Inverter Device = 200A × 1.20 – 200A
Max. Inverter Device = 240A - 200A
Max. Inverter Device = 40A, Two 30A inverter circuits would exceed the 40A maximum current limit. **Figure 705–13**

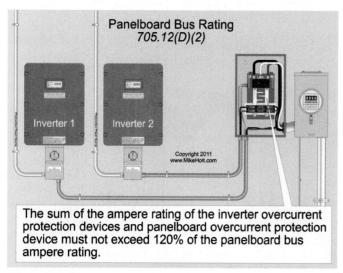

Figure 705–11

Panelboard Bus Rating
705.12(D)(2)

Inverter 1   Inverter 2

Copyright 2011
www.MikeHolt.com

The sum of the ampere rating of the inverter overcurrent protection devices and panelboard overcurrent protection device must not exceed 120% of the panelboard bus ampere rating.

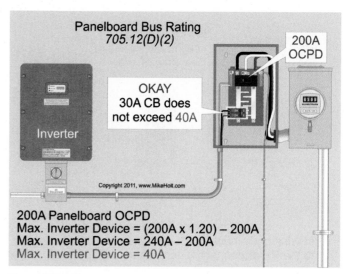

Figure 705–12

Panelboard Bus Rating
705.12(D)(2)

200A
OCPD

OKAY
30A CB does
not exceed 40A

Inverter

Copyright 2011, www.MikeHolt.com

200A Panelboard OCPD
Max. Inverter Device = (200A x 1.20) – 200A
Max. Inverter Device = 240A – 200A
Max. Inverter Device = 40A

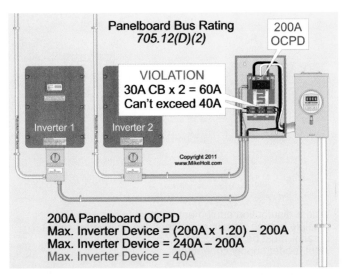

Figure 705–13

Author's Comment: The "not exceed 120 percent of the panelboard bus ampere rating" rule [705.12(D)(2)] only applies to distribution equipment that is capable of supplying multiple branch circuits or feeders or both. For example, a 225A bus panelboard protected by a 225A main circuit breaker could have four 60A inverter overcurrent protection devices, if those breakers fill all spots in the panelboard. **Figure 705–14**

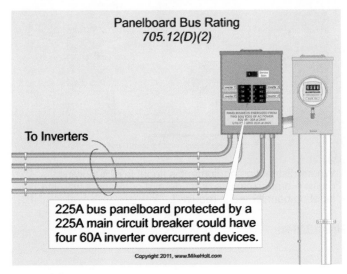

Figure 705–14

Ex: *Where the PV system has energy storage for stand-alone operation, the value used in the calculation of bus or conductor loading is 125 percent of the output inverter current.*

(3) Ground-Fault Protection. Supply-side connection of electrical power production source [705.12(A)] is required for facilities incorporating ground-fault protection of equipment as required by 215.9 and 230.95.

(4) Marking. Panelboards containing ac inverter circuit breakers must be field-marked to indicate the presence of multiple ac power sources such as: **Figure 705–15**

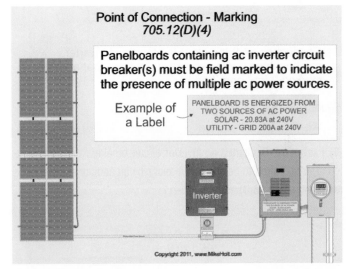

Figure 705–15

⚠ **CAUTION:** *The label must resist the environment for 25 to 40 years of system use, be suitable for the environment, and be installed so as not to void equipment listing [110.3(B)].*

(5) Suitable for Backfeed. Conductors from the ac inverter can backfed dedicated circuit breakers that aren't marked "Line" and "Load." **Figure 705–16**

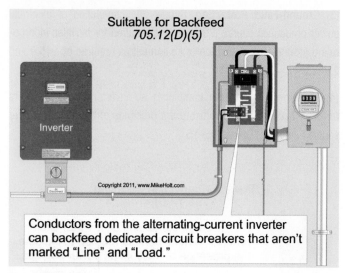

Suitable for Backfeed
705.12(D)(5)

Conductors from the alternating-current inverter can backfeed dedicated circuit breakers that aren't marked "Line" and "Load."

Figure 705–16

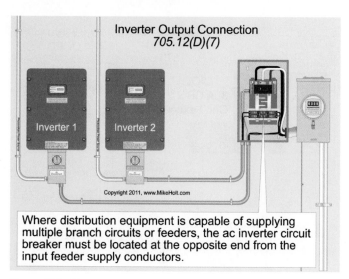

Inverter Output Connection
705.12(D)(7)

Where distribution equipment is capable of supplying multiple branch circuits or feeders, the ac inverter circuit breaker must be located at the opposite end from the input feeder supply conductors.

Figure 705–18

(6) Fastening. Dedicated ac inverter circuit breakers that are back-fed aren't required to be secured in place by an additional fastener as required by 408.36(D). **Figure 705–17**

Where distribution equipment is capable of supplying multiple branch circuits or feeders, a permanent warning label on panelboard is required to warn that the inverter output connection circuit breaker must not be relocated: **Figure 705–19**

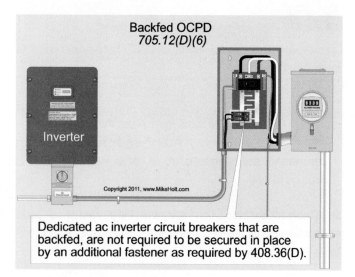

Backfed OCPD
705.12(D)(6)

Dedicated ac inverter circuit breakers that are backfed, are not required to be secured in place by an additional fastener as required by 408.36(D).

Figure 705–17

Author's Comment: Once the dedicated ac inverter circuit breaker has been removed from the panelboard, listed interactive inverter automatically power down and turns off output ac power generation from the inverter.

(7) Inverter Output Connection. Where distribution equipment is capable of supplying multiple branch circuits or feeders, the ac inverter circuit breaker must be located at the opposite end from the input feeder supply conductors. **Figure 705–18**

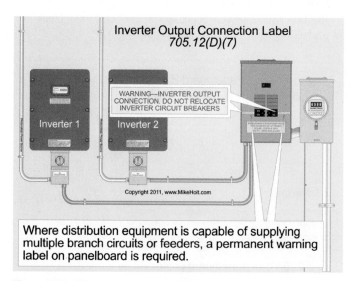

Inverter Output Connection Label
705.12(D)(7)

WARNING—INVERTER OUTPUT CONNECTION. DO NOT RELOCATE INVERTER CIRCUIT BREAKERS

Where distribution equipment is capable of supplying multiple branch circuits or feeders, a permanent warning label on panelboard is required.

Figure 705–19

 WARNING—INVERTER OUTPUT CONNECTION DO NOT RELOCATE CIRCUIT BREAKER

705.40 Loss of Primary Source. Upon loss of utility source power, an electric power production source must be automatically disconnected from all ungrounded conductors of the utility source and not reconnected until the utility source has been restored.

Ex: A listed utility-interactive inverter can automatically cease exporting power upon loss of utility source power and isn't required to automatically disconnect all ungrounded conductors from the utility source power. A listed utility-interactive inverter can automatically resume exporting power to the utility source once the utility source has been restored.

PART II. UTILITY-INTERACTIVE INVERTERS

705.100 Unbalanced Interconnections.

(A) Single Phase. Single-phase inverters connected to a 3-phase primary power source must not significant increase unbalanced system voltage.

UNDERSTANDING MAXIMUM UNBALANCED VOLTAGE AND PV SYSTEMS

Improperly connecting single-phase inverters to a three-phase system can result in an significant increase in unbalanced system voltage. Significant unbalanced voltage causes three-phase motors to motor run hotter because unbalanced voltage results in unbalanced magnetic fields created by the windings to work against each other. The NEMA formula to determine *Maximum Unbalanced Voltage = 100 x Maximum Deviation from Average Voltage/Average Voltage*. Let's review three examples.

Existing: What is the calculated maximum unbalanced system voltage at the electrical service without a PV system for the following line voltages: A – B 206V, B – C 200V, and A - C 204V?

Maximum Unbalanced Voltage = 100 x Maximum Deviation from Average Voltage/Average Voltage

Maximum Deviation = 206V

*Average Voltage = (206V + 200V + 204V)/
3 lines, 203.33V*

Maximum Deviation from Average = Maximum Deviation—Average Voltage

Maximum Deviation from Average = 206V – 203.33, 2.67V

*Maximum Unbalanced Voltage = 100 x 2.67V/
203.33V, 1.31%*

Improper Connection: If we connect two single-phase PV systems to lines A – B resulting in voltages of: A – B 208V, B – C 200V, and A – C 204V, what is the calculated maximum unbalanced system voltage at the electrical service?

Maximum Unbalanced Voltage = 100 x Maximum Deviation from Average Voltage/Average Voltage

Maximum Deviation = 208V

Average Voltage = (208V + 200V + 204V)/3 lines, 204V

Maximum Deviation from Average = Maximum Deviation—Average Voltage

Maximum Deviation from Average = 208V - 204V, 4V

Maximum Unbalanced Voltage = 100 x 4V/204V, 1.96%

Improperly placing two inverters between lines A and B increases the maximum unbalanced voltage by over 20% (1.96/1.63%).

Proper Connection: If we connect two single-phase PV systems to lines B - C resulting in voltages of: A – B 206V, B – C 202V, and A – C 204V, what is the calculated maximum unbalanced system voltage at the electrical service?

Maximum Unbalanced Voltage = 100 x Maximum Deviation from Average Voltage/Average Voltage

Maximum Deviation = 206V

Average Voltage = (206V + 202V + 204V)/3 lines, 204V

Maximum Deviation from Average = Maximum Deviation—Average Voltage

Maximum Deviation from Average = 206V – 204V, 2V

Maximum Unbalanced Voltage = 100 x 2V/204V, 0.98%

Properly placing two inverters between lines B and C significantly decreased the maximum unbalanced voltage by 50% (0.98%/1.96%)!

CHAPTER 7. SPECIAL CONDITIONS — PRACTICE QUESTIONS

Article 705 Interconnected Electric Power Production Sources

1. Article _____ covers the installation of electric power production sources operating in parallel with a primary source(s) of electricity.

   (a) 700
   (b) 701
   (c) 702
   (d) 705

2. For interconnected electric power production sources, a hybrid system is comprised of multiple power sources, such as _____, but not the utility power system.

   (a) photovoltaic
   (b) wind
   (c) micro-hydro generators
   (d) all of these

3. For interconnected electric power production sources, a hybrid system includes the utility power system.

   (a) True
   (b) False

4. For interconnected electric power production sources, a hybrid system includes _____.

   (a) storage batteries
   (b) flywheel storage equipment
   (c) superconducting magnetic storage equipment
   (d) none of these

5. For interconnected electric power production sources, the point of common coupling is the point where electric power production systems interface.

   (a) True
   (b) False

6. For interconnected electric power production sources, the circuit conductors from the inverter output terminals that supplies ac power to the utility powered electric system is known as the utility-interactive inverter output circuit.

   (a) True
   (b) False

7. The generating source, and all distribution equipment associated with it that generates electricity from a source other than a utility supplied service is called a _____.

   (a) service drop
   (b) power production equipment
   (c) service point
   (d) utilization equipment

8. For interconnected electric power production sources, utility-interactive inverters must be _____ for interconnection service.

   (a) listed
   (b) labeled
   (c) identified
   (d) a and c

9. Installation of one or more electrical power production sources operating in parallel with a primary source(s) of electricity must be installed only by _____.

   (a) qualified persons
   (b) utility company
   (c) the authority having jurisdiction
   (d) b or c

10. For interconnected electric power production sources, a permanent _____, denoting all electric power sources on or in the premises, must be installed at service equipment location and all interconnected electric power production sources.

    (a) label
    (b) plaque
    (c) directory
    (d) b or c

11. For interconnected electric power production sources, an electric power production source is permitted to be connected to the supply side of the service disconnecting means.

    (a) True
    (b) False

12. For interconnected electric power production sources, the sum of the ratings of all overcurrent devices connected to power production sources is permitted to exceed the rating of the service.

    (a) True
    (b) False

13. For interconnected electric power production sources, the output of a utility-interactive inverter can connected to the load side of the service disconnecting means at any distribution equipment on the premises.

    (a) True
    (b) False

14. For interconnected electric power production sources, each utility-interactive inverter connection must terminate to a dedicated circuit breaker or fusible disconnect.

    (a) True
    (b) False

15. For interconnected electric power production sources, panelboards containing ac inverter circuit breakers must be field marked to indicate the presence of multiple ac power sources.

    (a) True
    (b) False

16. For interconnected electric power production sources, conductors from the ac inverter can backfeed dedicated circuit breakers that are not marked _____.

    (a) line
    (b) load
    (c) a or b
    (d) a and b

17. For interconnected electric power production sources, dedicated ac inverter circuit breakers that are backfed, must be secured in place by an additional fastener as required by 408.36(D).

    (a) True
    (b) False

18. For interconnected electric power production sources, dedicated ac inverter circuit breakers must be located at the opposite end from the input feeder supply conductors.

    (a) True
    (b) False

19. For interconnected electric power production sources, a permanent warning label must be applied to the panelboard to warn others that the inverter output connection circuit breaker must not be relocated.

    (a) True
    (b) False

20. For interconnected electric power production sources, upon loss of utility source power, an electric power production source must be manually disconnected from all ungrounded conductors of the utility source and not reconnected until the utility source has been restored.

    (a) True
    (b) False

Notes

FINAL EXAMS

Notes

Final Exam A

Final Exam A

Use the 2011 *NEC Code* book to answer the following questions.

1. A box or conduit body shall not be required where cables enter or exit from conduit or tubing that is used to provide cable support or protection against physical damage.

   (a) True
   (b) False

2. A common dc grounding-electrode conductor of a PV system is permitted to serve multiple inverters with the size of the common grounding electrode and the tap conductors in accordance with 250.166. The tap conductors must be connected to the common grounding-electrode conductor in such a manner that the common grounding electrode conductor remains _____.

   (a) without a splice or joint
   (b) inside inverter enclosures
   (c) inside a raceway
   (d) supported on insulators

3. A connection between equipment grounding conductors and a metal box shall be by _____.

   (a) a grounding screw used for no other purpose
   (b) equipment listed for grounding
   (c) a listed grounding device
   (d) any of these

4. A disconnecting means is required to open ungrounded dc circuit conductors.

   (a) True
   (b) False

5. A disconnecting switch is permitted to open the grounded dc conductor of a PV system when _____.

   (a) the switch is used only for PV array maintenance
   (b) the switch is accessible only by qualified persons
   (c) the switch is rated for the maximum dc voltage and current, including ground fault conditions
   (d) all of these

6. A listed expansion/deflection fitting or other approved means must be used where a raceway crosses a _____ intended for expansion, contraction or deflection used in buildings, bridges, parking garages, or other structures.

   (a) junction box
   (b) structural joint
   (c) cable tray
   (d) unistrut hanger

7. A permanent label must be applied by the installer at the PV dc power source disconnect indicating the following:

   (a) the rated maximum power-point current and voltage
   (b) the maximum system voltage and short-circuit current
   (c) the maximum rated output current of the charge controller (if installed)
   (d) all of the above

8. A piece of equipment that regulates the charging process of a battery by diverting power from energy storage to direct-current or alternating current loads or to an interconnected utility service is known as a(n) _____.

   (a) alternating charge controller
   (b) diversion charge controller
   (c) direct charge controller
   (d) alternating charge regulator

9. A PV source circuit isolating switch is permitted on the PV side of the PV disconnecting means, but it's not required.

   (a) True
   (b) False

10. A switch, circuit breaker, or other device is permitted to open the grounded dc conductor.

    (a) True
    (b) False

11. A switching device with a marked OFF position shall completely disconnect all _____ conductors of the load it controls.

    (a) grounded
    (b) ungrounded
    (c) grounding
    (d) all of these

12. A(n) _____ must be installed between a photovoltaic array and other equipment .

    (a) grounded conductor
    (b) main bonding jumper
    (c) equipment grounding conductor
    (d) system bonding jumper

13. Admitting close approach, not guarded by locked doors, elevation, or other effective means, is referred to as _____.

    (a) accessible (as applied to equipment)
    (b) accessible (as applied to wiring methods)
    (c) accessible, readily
    (d) all of these

14. All conductors of a circuit, including the equipment grounding conductor, must be installed in the same raceway or cable, or otherwise run with the PV array circuit conductors when they leave the vicinity of the PV array.

    (a) True
    (b) False

15. All conductors of a circuit, including the grounded and equipment grounding conductors, shall be contained within the same _____, unless otherwise permitted elsewhere in the *Code*.

    (a) raceway
    (b) cable
    (c) trench
    (d) all of these

16. All conductors of the same circuit shall be _____, unless otherwise specifically permitted in the *Code*.

    (a) in the same raceway or cable
    (b) in close proximity in the same trench
    (c) the same size
    (d) a or b

17. All equipment intended for use in photovoltaic power systems shall be _____ for the application.

    (a) identified
    (b) listed
    (c) approved
    (d) a and b

18. All raceway and cable wiring methods included in this *Code* and other wiring systems and fittings specifically intended and identified for use on photovoltaic arrays shall be permitted.

    (a) True
    (b) False

19. An effective ground-fault current path is an intentionally constructed, permanent, low-impedance path designed and intended to carry fault current from the point of a ground fault on a wiring system to _____.

    (a) ground
    (b) earth
    (c) the electrical supply source
    (d) none of these

20. An Electrical Production and Distribution Network, such as a utility and connected load is internal to and controlled by a photovoltaic power system.

    (a) True
    (b) False

21. An equipment grounding conductor shall be identified by _____.

    (a) a continuous outer finish that is green
    (b) being bare
    (c) a continuous outer finish that is green with one or more yellow stripes
    (d) any of these

22. An insulated grounded conductor of _____ or smaller shall be identified by a continuous white or gray outer finish, or by three continuous white stripes on other than green insulation along its entire length.

    (a) 8 AWG
    (b) 6 AWG
    (c) 4 AWG
    (d) 3 AWG

23. An inverter or an ac module in an interactive PV system must automatically de-energize its output to the connected electrical distribution system upon _____ of voltage and remain de-energized until the electrical distribution system voltage has been restored.

    (a) surge
    (b) spike
    (c) loss
    (d) unbalance

24. Any building or structure with a stand-alone PV system not connected to a utility service source must have a permanent _____ installed on the exterior of the building or structure at a readily visible location acceptable to the authority having jurisdiction. The _____ must indicate the location of the stand-alone PV system disconnecting means and that the structure contains a stand-alone electrical power system.

    (a) plaque
    (b) directory
    (c) a and b
    (d) a or b

25. Buildings or structures containing both utility service and a PV system must have a permanent _____ identifying the location of the service disconnecting means and PV system ac disconnecting means if they are not located at the same location.

    (a) plaque
    (b) directory
    (c) a and b
    (d) a or b

26. By special permission, the authority having jurisdiction may waive specific requirements in this *Code* where it is assured that equivalent objectives can be achieved by establishing and maintaining effective safety.

    (a) True
    (b) False

27. Capable of being reached quickly for operation, renewal, or inspections without resorting to portable ladders and such is known as _____.

    (a) accessible (as applied to equipment)
    (b) accessible (as applied to wiring methods)
    (c) accessible, readily
    (d) all of these

28. Chapters 1 through 4 of the *NEC* apply _____.

    (a) generally to all electrical installations
    (b) only to special occupancies and conditions
    (c) only to special equipment and material
    (d) all of these

29. Compliance with the provisions of the *NEC* will result in _____.

    (a) good electrical service
    (b) an efficient electrical system
    (c) an electrical system essentially free from hazard
    (d) all of these

30. Concrete, brick, or tile walls are considered _____, as it applies to working space requirements.

    (a) inconsequential
    (b) in the way
    (c) grounded
    (d) none of these

31. Conductors in ferrous metal raceways and enclosures shall be arranged so as to avoid heating the surrounding ferrous metal by alternating-current induction. To accomplish this, the _____ conductor(s) shall be grouped together.

    (a) phase
    (b) grounded
    (c) equipment grounding
    (d) all of these

32. Conductors in raceways shall be _____ between outlets, boxes, devices, and so forth.

    (a) continuous
    (b) installed
    (c) copper
    (d) in conduit

33. Conductors shall be installed within a raceway, cable, or enclosure.

    (a) True
    (b) False

34. Conductors with the color _____ insulation shall not be used for ungrounded or grounded conductors.

    (a) green
    (b) green with one or more yellow stripes
    (c) a or b
    (d) white

35. Conduits or raceways through which moisture may contact live parts shall be _____ at either or both ends.

    (a) sealed
    (b) plugged
    (c) bushed
    (d) a or b

36. Connectors and terminals for conductors more finely stranded than Class B and Class C, as shown In Table 10 of Chapter 9, must be _____ for the specific conductor class or classes.

    (a) listed
    (b) approved
    (c) identified
    (d) all of these

37. Currents of photovoltaic systems are to be considered _____.

    (a) safe
    (b) continuous
    (c) noncontinuous
    (d) inverted

38. Devices _____ for bonding the metallic frames of PV modules shall be permitted to bond the metallic frames of PV modules to the metallic frames of adjacent PV modules.

    (a) listed
    (b) labeled
    (c) identified
    (d) a and c

39. Devices _____ for grounding the metallic frames of PV modules and other equipment can be used to bond the exposed metal surfaces of the modules and equipment to the mounting structures.

    (a) identified
    (b) approved
    (c) listed
    (d) a and c

40. Devices and systems used for securing PV modules that also provide grounding of the module frames must be _____ for the purpose of grounding PV modules.

    (a) listed
    (b) labeled
    (c) identified
    (d) a and b

41. Disconnects used for PV systems (dc and ac) must be a manually operable switch or circuit breaker _____.

    (a) located where readily accessible
    (b) externally operable without exposing the operator to contact with live parts
    (c) plainly indicating whether in the open or closed position
    (d) all of these

42. Each disconnecting means shall be legibly marked to indicate its purpose unless located and arranged so _____.

    (a) that it can be locked out and tagged
    (b) it is not readily accessible
    (c) the purpose is evident
    (d) that it operates at less than 300 volts-to-ground

43. Electrical equipment shall not be connected to the supply side of the service disconnecting means, except for a few specific exceptions such as _____.

    (a) Type 1 surge protective devices
    (b) taps used to supply legally required optional standby power systems, fire pump equipment, fire and sprinkler alarms, and load (energy) management devices
    (c) Solar photovoltaic systems
    (d) all of these

44. Electrical equipment with _____ and having adequate fire-resistant and low-smoke-producing characteristics can be installed within an air-handling space (plenum).

    (a) a metal enclosure
    (b) a nonmetallic enclosures listed for use within an air-handling (plenum) space
    (c) any type of enclosure
    (d) a or b

45. Electrical installations in hollow spaces, vertical shafts, and ventilation or air-handling ducts shall be made so that the possible spread of fire or products of combustion is not _____.

    (a) substantially increased
    (b) allowed
    (c) inherent
    (d) possible

46. Enclosures for overcurrent devices shall be mounted in a _____ position unless impracticable.

    (a) vertical
    (b) horizontal
    (c) vertical or horizontal
    (d) there are no requirements

47. Equipment grounding conductors for PV circuits having over-current protection must be sized to the rating of the PV circuit overcurrent device in accordance with _____.

    (a) 250.122
    (b) 250.66
    (c) Table 250.122
    (d) Table 250.66

48. Equipment grounding conductors, grounding electrode conductors, and bonding jumpers shall be connected by _____.

    (a) listed pressure connectors
    (b) terminal bars
    (c) exothermic welding
    (d) any of these

49. Equipment or materials included in a list published by a testing laboratory acceptable to the authority having jurisdiction is said to be _____.

    (a) book
    (b) digest
    (c) manifest
    (d) listed

50. Explanatory material, such as references to other standards, references to related sections of the *NEC*, or information related to a *Code* rule, are included in the form of Informational Notes.

    (a) True
    (b) False

51. Exposed PV source and output circuits operating at greater than _____ must be installed in a Chapter 3 wiring method anytime the conductors are installed in _____ location.
    (a) 30V, accessible location
    (b) 30V, readily accessible location
    (c) 60V, accessible location
    (d) 60V, readily accessible location

52. Factory-installed _____ wiring of listed equipment need not be inspected at the time of installation of the equipment, except to detect alterations or damage.

    (a) external
    (b) associated
    (c) internal
    (d) all of these

53. Fittings and connectors shall be used only with the specific wiring methods for which they are designed and listed.

    (a) True
    (b) False

54. For circuits over 250 volts-to-ground, electrical continuity can be maintained between a box or enclosure where no over-sized, concentric or eccentric knockouts are encountered, and a metal conduit by _____.

    (a) threadless fittings for cables with metal sheath
    (b) double locknuts on threaded conduit (one inside and one outside the box or enclosure)
    (c) fittings that have shoulders that seat firmly against the box with a locknut on the inside or listed fittings
    (d) all of these

55. For interconnected electric power production sources, a permanent warning label must be applied to the panelboard to warn others that the inverter output connection circuit breaker must not be relocated.

    (a) True
    (b) False

56. For interconnected electric power production sources, an electric power production source is permitted to be connected to the supply side of the service disconnecting means.

    (a) True
    (b) False

57. For interconnected electric power production sources, conductors from the ac inverter can backfeed dedicated circuit breakers that are not marked _____.

    (a) line
    (b) load
    (c) a or b
    (d) a and b

58. For interconnected electric power production sources, dedicated ac inverter circuit breakers that are backfed, must be secured in place by an additional fastener as required by 408.36(D).

    (a) True
    (b) False

59. For interconnected electric power production sources, each utility-interactive inverter connection must terminate to a dedicated circuit breaker or fusible disconnect.

    (a) True
    (b) False

60. For interconnected electric power production sources, panelboards containing ac inverter circuit breakers must be field marked to indicate the presence of multiple ac power sources.

    (a) True
    (b) False

61. For interconnected electric power production sources, the output of a utility-interactive inverter can connected to the load side of the service disconnecting means at any distribution equipment on the premises.

    (a) True
    (b) False

62. For interconnected electric power production sources, the sum of the ratings of all overcurrent devices connected to power production sources is permitted to exceed the rating of the service.

    (a) True
    (b) False

63. For interconnected electric power production sources, upon loss of utility source power, an electric power production source must be manually disconnected from all ungrounded conductors of the utility source and not reconnected until the utility source has been restored.

    (a) True
    (b) False

64. For interconnected electric power production sources, dedicated ac inverter circuit breakers must be located at the opposite end from the input feeder supply conductors.

    (a) True
    (b) False

65. For one- and two-family dwellings, the maximum PV system voltage is _____ V.

    (a) 240
    (b) 208
    (c) 480
    (d) 600

66. For stand-alone systems, circuit breakers that are marked line and load can be backfed.

    (a) True
    (b) False

67. For stand-alone systems, the ac current output from a stand-alone inverter(s) can be _____ than the calculated load connected to the disconnect, but not less than the largest single utilization equipment connected to the system.

    (a) less
    (b) more
    (c) greater
    (d) any of these

68. Fuses or circuit breakers for PV dc circuits must be _____ for use in dc circuits and shall have the appropriate voltage, current, and interrupt ratings.

    (a) identified
    (b) approved
    (c) recognized
    (d) listed

69. Grounding electrode conductors _____ and larger that are not subject to physical damage can be run exposed along the surface of the building construction if it is securely fastened to the construction.

    (a) 10 AWG
    (b) 8 AWG
    (c) 6 AWG
    (d) 4 AWG

70. Grounding electrode conductors shall be made of _____ wire.

    (a) solid
    (b) stranded
    (c) insulated or bare
    (d) any of these

71. Grounding electrodes of the rod type less than _____ in. in diameter shall be listed.

    (a) ½ in.
    (b) 5/8 in.
    (c) ¾ in.
    (d) none of these

72. Hazards often occur because of _____.

    (a) overloading of wiring systems by methods or usage not in conformity with the *NEC*
    (b) initial wiring not providing for increases in the use of electricity
    (c) a and b
    (d) none of these

73. If the *NEC* requires new products that are not yet available at the time a new edition is adopted, the _____ may permit the use of the products that comply with the previous edition of the *Code* adopted by that jurisdiction.

    (a) electrical engineer
    (b) master electrician
    (c) authority having jurisdiction
    (d) permit holder

74. In judging equipment for approval, considerations such as the following shall be evaluated:

    (a) mechanical strength
    (b) wire-bending space
    (c) arcing effects
    (d) all of these

75. In locations where electrical equipment is likely to be exposed to _____, enclosures or guards shall be so arranged and of such strength as to prevent such damage.

    (a) corrosion
    (b) physical damage
    (c) magnetic fields
    (d) weather

76. In photovoltaic source circuits, one overcurrent protection device is not permitted to protect the photovoltaic modules and the interconnecting conductors.

    (a) True
    (b) False

77. In the *NEC*, the words _____ indicate a mandatory requirement.

    (a) shall
    (b) shall not
    (c) shall be permitted
    (d) a or b

78. Internal parts of electrical equipment, including _____, shall not be damaged or contaminated by foreign materials such as paint, plaster, cleaners, abrasives, or corrosive residues.

    (a) busbars
    (b) wiring terminals
    (c) insulators
    (d) all of these

79. Junction, pull, and outlet boxes can be located behind PV modules that are secured by removable fasteners.

    (a) True
    (b) False

80. Listed fittings and connectors that are intended to be concealed at the time of on-site assembly are permitted for on-site interconnection of modules or other array components.

    (a) True
    (b) False

81. Listed or labeled equipment shall be installed and used in accordance with any instructions included in the listing or labeling.

    (a) True
    (b) False

82. Live parts of storage battery systems for dwellings shall be _____ to prevent accidental contact by persons or objects regardless of voltage.

    (a) isolated
    (b) grounded
    (c) insulated
    (d) guarded

83. Markings of PV system raceways and enclosures must be suitable for the environment and be placed with a maximum of _____ of spacing.

    (a) 5 ft
    (b) 10 ft
    (c) 20 ft
    (d) none of these

84. Means must be provided to disconnect equipment, such as batteries, inverters, charge controllers, and the like, from all ungrounded conductors of all sources.

    (a) True
    (b) False

85. Metal enclosures for switches or circuit breakers shall be connected to the circuit _____.

    (a) grounded conductor
    (b) grounding conductor
    (c) equipment grounding conductor
    (d) any of these

86. Metal raceways, cable armors, and other metal enclosures shall be _____ joined together into a continuous electric conductor so as to provide effective electrical continuity.

    (a) electrically
    (b) permanently
    (c) metallically
    (d) none of these

87. Monopole subarrays in a Bipolar Photovoltaic system shall be physically _____ where the sum of the photovoltaic system voltages, without consideration of polarity, of the two monopole subarrays exceeds the rating of the conductors and connected equipment.

    (a) separated
    (b) connected
    (c) joined
    (d) together

88. Non-load-break rated disconnecting means for PV output circuits must be marked "Do not open under load".

    (a) True
    (b) False

89. Nonmandatory information annexes contained in the back of the *Code* book _____.

    (a) are for information only
    (b) aren't enforceable as a requirement of the *Code*.
    (c) are enforceable as a requirement of the *Code*
    (d) a and b

90. One source for lowest-expected ambient temperature is the Extreme Annual Mean Minimum Design Dry Bulb Temperature found in the ASHRAE Handbook — Fundamentals.

    (a) True
    (b) False

91. Only inverters and ac PV modules listed as interactive can be used with interactive systems.

    (a) True
    (b) False

92. Only wiring methods recognized as _____ are included in this *Code*.

    (a) expensive
    (b) efficient
    (c) suitable
    (d) cost-effective

93. Openings around electrical penetrations into or through fire-resistant-rated walls, partitions, floors, or ceilings shall _____ to maintain the fire-resistance rating.

    (a) be documented
    (b) not be permitted
    (c) be firestopped using approved methods
    (d) be enlarged

94. Overcurrent devices for PV source circuits must be readily accessible.

    (a) True
    (b) False

95. Overcurrent devices for PV systems shall be rated to carry not less than _____ percent of the maximum currents calculated in 690.8(A).

    (a) 80
    (b) 100
    (c) 125
    (d) 250

96. Overcurrent devices shall be readily accessible and installed so the center of the grip of the operating handle of the switch or circuit breaker, when in its highest position, is not more than _____ above the floor or working platform.

    (a) 2 ft
    (b) 4 ft 6 in.
    (c) 5 ft
    (d) 6 ft 7 in.

97. Overcurrent devices shall not be located _____.

    (a) where exposed to physical damage
    (b) near easily ignitible materials, such as in clothes closets
    (c) in bathrooms of dwelling units
    (d) all of these

98. Overcurrent protection for conductors and equipment is designed to _____ the circuit if the current reaches a value that will cause an excessive or dangerous temperature in conductors or conductor insulation.

    (a) open
    (b) close
    (c) monitor
    (d) record

99. Photovoltaic alternating-current module systems are permitted to use one device to detect only _____ ground faults and to disable the array by removing ac power to the ac module(s).

    (a) line to line
    (b) direct current
    (c) line to neutral
    (d) alternating current

100. Photovoltaic source circuits and photovoltaic output circuits are not permitted to be contained in the same raceway, cable tray, cable, outlet box, junction box, or similar fitting, with nonphotovoltaic systems unless the two systems are separated by a partition.

    (a) True
    (b) False

Final Exam B

Use the 2011 *NEC Code* book to answer
the following questions.

1. Photovoltaic source circuits shall be identified at all points of termination, connection, and splices.

   (a) True
   (b) False

2. Photovoltaic systems are permitted to supply any building or other structure in addition to any other _____.

   (a) electricity supply system
   (b) telephone supply system
   (c) plumbing supply system
   (d) none of the above

3. Photovoltaic wiring methods containing _____ must be terminated only with terminals, lugs, devices, or connectors that are identified and listed for such use.

   (a) flexible, fine-stranded cables
   (b) solid conductors
   (c) flexible raceways
   (d) all of the above

4. PV source and output conductors must be routed along building structural members _____ where the location of those structural members can be determined by observation.

   (a) beams and rafters
   (b) trusses and columns
   (c) windows and doors
   (d) a and b

5. PV system conductors shall be identified by separate color coding, marking tape, tagging, or other approved means.

   (a) True
   (b) False

6. PV systems having no direct connection between the dc grounded conductor and ac grounded conductor shall have a _____ which shall be bonded to the ac grounding system.

   (a) ac grounding system
   (b) dc grounding system
   (c) separately derived grounding system
   (d) none of the above

7. PV systems with dc modules having no direct connection between the dc grounded conductor and ac grounded conductor must be bonded to the ac grounding system by _____.

   (a) a separate dc grounding electrode bonded to the ac grounding electrode system with a bonding jumper
   (b) a dc grounding electrode conductor sized to 250.166 run from the marked dc grounding electrode connection point to the ac grounding electrode
   (c) an unspliced, or irreversibly spliced, combined grounding conductor run from the marked dc grounding electrode connection point along with the ac circuit conductors to the grounding busbar in the associated ac equipment_
   (d) a, b, or c

8. Raceways shall be _____ between outlet, junction, or splicing points prior to the installation of conductors.

   (a) installed complete
   (b) tested for ground faults
   (c) a minimum of 80 percent complete
   (d) none of these

9. Raceways shall be provided with expansion fittings where necessary to compensate for thermal expansion and contraction.

(a) True
(b) False

10. Raceways, cable assemblies, boxes, cabinets, and fittings shall be securely fastened in place.

(a) True
(b) False

11. Raceways, cable trays, cablebus, auxiliary gutters, cable armor, boxes, cable sheathing, cabinets, elbows, couplings, fittings, supports, and support hardware shall be of materials suitable for _____.

(a) corrosive locations
(b) wet locations
(c) the environment in which they are to be installed
(d) none of these

12. Rigid metal conduit that is directly buried outdoors shall have at least _____ of cover.

(a) 6 in.
(b) 12 in.
(c) 18 in.
(d) 24 in.

13. Short sections of metal enclosures or raceways used to provide support or protection of _____ from physical damage shall not be required to be connected to the equipment grounding conductor.

(a) conduit
(b) feeders under 600V
(c) cable assemblies
(d) none of these

14. Short sections of raceways used for _____ shall not be required to be installed complete between outlet, junction, or splicing points.

(a) meter to service enclosure connection
(b) protection of cables from physical damage
(c) nipples
(d) separately derived systems

15. Single-conductor Type USE-2 and single conductor cable _____ as PV wire can be run exposed at outdoor locations for PV source circuits for PV module interconnections within the PV array.

(a) approved
(b) listed or labeled
(c) listed and labeled
(d) none of the above

16. Single-throw knife switches shall be installed so that gravity will tend to close the switch.

(a) True
(b) False

17. Special permission would be the written consent from the _____.

(a) testing laboratory
(b) manufacturer
(c) owner
(d) authority having jurisdiction

18. Switches and circuit breakers used as switches can be mounted _____ if they are installed adjacent to motors, appliances, or other equipment that they supply and are accessible by portable means.

(a) not higher than 6 ft 7 in.
(b) higher than 6 ft 7 in.
(c) in the mechanical equipment room
(d) up to 8 ft high

19. Switches and circuit breakers used as switches shall be installed so that they may be operated from a readily accessible place.

    (a) True
    (b) False

20. Switches or circuit breakers shall not disconnect the grounded conductor of a circuit unless the switch or circuit breaker _____.

    (a) can be opened and closed by hand levers only
    (b) simultaneously disconnects all conductors of the circuit
    (c) opens the grounded conductor before it disconnects the ungrounded conductors
    (d) none of these

21. Switches shall be marked with _____.

    (a) current
    (b) voltage
    (c) maximum horsepower, if horsepower rated
    (d) all of these

22. The _____ has the responsibility for deciding on the approval of equipment and materials.

    (a) manufacturer
    (b) authority having jurisdiction
    (c) testing agency
    (d) none of these

23. The _____ of a dc photovoltaic source circuit or output circuit, must be calculated as the sum of the rated open-circuit voltage of the series-connected photovoltaic modules multiplied by the correction factor provided in Table 690.7.

    (a) minimum allowable ampacity of conductors
    (b) maximum allowable ampacity of conductors
    (c) minimum photovoltaic system voltage
    (d) maximum photovoltaic system voltage

24. The _____ rating of a conductor is the maximum temperature, at any location along its length, which the conductor can withstand over a prolonged period of time without serious degradation.

    (a) ambient
    (b) temperature
    (c) maximum withstand
    (d) short-circuit

25. The ampacity of a conductor can be different along the length of the conductor. The higher ampacity can be used beyond the point of transition for a distance of no more than _____ ft, or no more than _____ percent of the circuit length figured at the higher ampacity, whichever is less.

    (a) 10, 10
    (b) 10, 20
    (c) 15, 15
    (d) 20, 10

26. The authority having jurisdiction has the responsibility _____.

    (a) for making interpretations of rules
    (b) for deciding upon the approval of equipment and materials
    (c) for waiving specific requirements in the *Code* and permitting alternate methods and material if safety is maintained
    (d) all of these

27. The *Code* contains provisions considered necessary for safety, which will not necessarily result in _____.

    (a) efficient use
    (b) convenience
    (c) good service or future expansion of electrical use
    (d) all of these

28. The *Code* isn't a design specification standard or instruction manual for the untrained and unqualified.

    (a) True
    (b) False

29. The conductors and equipment from the electric utility that deliver electric energy to the wiring system of the premises is called a _____.

    (a) branch circuit
    (b) feeder
    (c) service
    (d) none of these

30. The conductors of PV output circuits and inverter input and output circuits shall be identified at all points of termination, connection, and splices.

    (a) True
    (b) False

31. The connection of the grounding electrode conductor to a buried grounding electrode (driven ground rod) shall be made with a listed terminal device that is accessible.

    (a) True
    (b) False

32. The connection to a _____ shall be arranged so that removal of either from a photovoltaic source circuit does not interrupt a grounded conductor to other PV source circuits.

    (a) panelboard or switchboard
    (b) bus or lug
    (c) module or panel
    (d) array or subarray

33. The connectors permitted by Article 690 shall _____.

    (a) be polarized.
    (b) guard against inadvertent contact with live parts by persons.
    (c) require a tool for opening if the circuit operates at over 30V nominal maximum dc or 30V ac.
    (d) All of these

34. The derating factors in 310.15(B)(3)(a) shall be applied to a metal wireway only where the number of current-carrying conductors in the wireway exceeds _____.

    (a) 30
    (b) 40
    (c) 50
    (d) 60

35. The direct-current system grounding connection must be made at any _____ point(s) on the photovoltaic output circuit.

    (a) single
    (b) two
    (c) three
    (d) four

36. The equipment grounding conductor shall not be required to be larger than the circuit conductors.

    (a) True
    (b) False

37. The grounding conductor connection to the grounding electrode shall be made by _____.

    (a) listed lugs
    (b) exothermic welding
    (c) listed pressure connectors
    (d) any of these

38. The independent support wires for supporting electrical wiring methods in a fire-rated ceiling assembly shall be distinguishable from fire-rated suspended-ceiling framing support wires by _____.

    (a) color
    (b) tagging
    (c) other effective means
    (d) any of these

39. The largest size grounding electrode conductor required is _____ copper.

    (a) 6 AWG
    (b) 1/0 AWG
    (c) 3/0 AWG
    (d) 250 kcmil

40. The location of PV source and output conductors imbedded in built-up, laminate, or membrane roofing materials in areas not covered by PV modules and associated equipment must be clearly marked.

    (a) True
    (b) False

41. The material located in the *NEC* Annexes are part of the requirements of the *Code* and shall be complied with.

    (a) True
    (b) False

42. The maximum current in amperes a conductor can carry continuously, where the temperature will not be raised in excess of the conductor's insulation temperature rating is called its _____.

    (a) short-circuit rating
    (b) ground-fault rating
    (c) ampacity
    (d) all of these

43. The maximum inverter output circuit current is equal to the _____ output current rating.

    (a) average
    (b) peak
    (c) continuous
    (d) intermittent

44. The minimum height of working spaces about electrical equipment, switchboards, panelboards, or motor control centers operating at 600V, nominal, or less and likely to require examination, adjustment, servicing, or maintenance while energized shall be 6½ ft or the height of the equipment, whichever is greater, except for service equipment or panelboards in existing dwelling units that do not exceed 200A.

    (a) True
    (b) False

45. The *NEC* applies to the installation of _____.

    (a) electrical conductors and equipment within or on public and private buildings
    (b) outside conductors and equipment on the premises
    (c) optical fiber cables
    (d) all of these

46. The *NEC* is _____.

    (a) intended to be a design manual
    (b) meant to be used as an instruction guide for untrained persons
    (c) for the practical safeguarding of persons and property
    (d) published by the Bureau of Standards

47. The *NEC* requires that electrical work be _____.

    (a) installed in a neat and workmanlike manner
    (b) installed under the supervision of a licensed person
    (c) completed before being inspected
    (d) all of these

48. The next higher standard rating overcurrent device above the ampacity of the ungrounded conductors being protected shall be permitted to be used, provided all of the following conditions are met:

    (a) The conductors are not part of a branch circuit supplying more than one receptacle for cord-and-plug-connected portable loads.
    (b) The ampacity of the conductors doesn't correspond with the standard ampere rating of a fuse or circuit breaker.
    (c) The next higher standard rating selected doesn't exceed 800A.
    (d) all of these

49. The number and size of conductors permitted in a raceway is limited to _____.

    (a) permit heat to dissipate
    (b) prevent damage to insulation during installation
    (c) prevent damage to insulation during removal of conductors
    (d) all of these

50. The output circuit conductor of an ac module, which has a built-in dc to ac inverter, is considered an _____ output circuit as defined in 690.2.

    (a) Inverter
    (b) module
    (c) PV
    (d) subarray

51. The overcurrent device ratings in photovoltaic systems operated at temperatures greater than _____, shall comply with the manufacturer's temperature correction factors.

    (a) 32 degrees C
    (b) 40 degrees C
    (c) 32 degrees F
    (d) 40 degrees F

52. The point of interconnection of the PV system power source to other sources must be marked at an accessible location at the _____ as a power source and with the rated ac output current and nominal operating ac voltage.

    (a) disconnecting means
    (b) array
    (c) inverter
    (d) none of the above

53. The PV output circuit current is equal to the sum of parallel PV source circuit maximum currents as calculated in _____.

    (a) 690.8(A)(1)
    (b) 690.8(A)(2)
    (c) 690.8(A)(3)
    (d) none of the above

54. The PV source circuit current is calculated by multiplying the sum of the parallel module nameplate short-circuit current ratings (Isc) by 125 percent.

    (a) True
    (b) False

55. The PV system dc disconnect must be placed at a readily accessible location _____ of a building or structure to disconnect the ungrounded PV system dc circuit conductors.

    (a) outside
    (b) inside, nearest the point of entrance
    (c) anywhere inside
    (d) a or b

56. The PV system disconnecting means must be _____ to identify it as a photovoltaic system disconnect.

    (a) listed
    (b) approved
    (c) permanently marked
    (d) temporarily marked

57. The PV system disconnecting means shall be suitable for _____.

    (a) heat
    (b) cold
    (c) rain
    (d) the prevailing conditions

58. The requirement for grouping PV source and output circuit is not required if the circuit enters from a cable or raceway unique to the circuit that makes the grouping obvious.

    (a) True
    (b) False

59. The space above a hung ceiling used for environmental air-handling purposes is an example of _____, and the wiring limitations of _____ apply.

    (a) a specifically fabricated duct used for environmental air, 300.22(B)
    (b) other space used for environmental air (plenum), 300.22(C)
    (c) a supply duct used for environmental air, 300.22(B)
    (d) none of these

60. The temperature rating associated with the ampacity of a _____ shall be so selected and coordinated so as not to exceed the lowest temperature rating of any connected termination, conductor, or device.

    (a) terminal
    (b) conductor
    (c) device
    (d) all of these

61. The upper end of a ground rod electrode shall be _____ ground level unless the aboveground end and the grounding electrode conductor attachment are protected against physical damage.

    (a) above
    (b) flush with
    (c) below
    (d) b or c

62. The working space in front of the electric equipment shall not be less than _____ wide, or the width of the equipment, whichever is greater.

    (a) 15 in.
    (b) 30 in.
    (c) 40 in.
    (d) 60 in.

63. There are four principal determinants of conductor operating temperature, one of which is _____ generated internally in the conductor as the result of load current flow, including fundamental and harmonic currents.

    (a) friction
    (b) magnetism
    (c) heat
    (d) none of these

64. This *Code* covers the installation of _____ for public and private premises, including buildings, structures, mobile homes, recreational vehicles, and floating buildings.

    (a) optical fiber cables
    (b) electrical equipment
    (c) raceways
    (d) all of these

65. To limit the voltage induced by lightning, one conductor of a 2-wire PV system operating at over _____ must be solidly grounded (connected to the earth) in accordance with 250.4(A)(1).

    (a) 15V
    (b) 30V
    (c) 50V
    (d) none of these

66. Ungrounded describes not connected to ground or a conductive body that extends the ground connection.

    (a) True
    (b) False

67. Unless identified for use in the operating environment, no conductors or equipment shall be _____ having a deteriorating effect on the conductors or equipment.

    (a) located in damp or wet locations
    (b) exposed to fumes, vapors, liquids or gases
    (c) exposed to excessive temperatures
    (d) all of these

68. Unused openings for circuit breakers and switches in switchboards and panelboards shall be closed using _____ or other approved means that provide protection substantially equivalent to the wall of the enclosure.

    (a) duct seal and tape
    (b) identified closures
    (c) exothermic welding
    (d) sheet metal

69. Unused openings other than those intended for the operation of equipment, intended for mounting purposes, or permitted as part of the design for listed equipment shall be _____.

    (a) filled with cable clamps or connectors only
    (b) taped over with electrical tape
    (c) repaired only by welding or brazing in a metal slug
    (d) effectively closed to afford protection substantially equivalent to the wall of the equipment

70. What is the minimum size copper equipment bonding jumper for a 40A rated circuit?

    (a) 14 AWG
    (b) 12 AWG
    (c) 10 AWG
    (d) 8 AWG

71. When a single equipment grounding conductor is used for multiple circuits in the same raceway, cable or cable tray, the single equipment grounding conductor shall be sized according to _____.

    (a) combined rating of all the overcurrent devices
    (b) largest overcurrent device of the multiple circuits
    (c) combined rating of all the loads
    (d) any of these

72. When determining the number of current-carrying conductors, a grounding or bonding conductor shall not be counted when applying the provisions of 310.15(B)(3)(a) _____.

    (a) True
    (b) False

73. When equipment grounding conductors are installed in panelboards, a _____ shall be secured inside the cabinet.

    (a) grounded conductor
    (b) terminal lug
    (c) terminal bar
    (d) none of these

74. When installing PVC conduit underground without concrete cover, there shall be a minimum of _____ of cover.

    (a) 6 in.
    (b) 12 in.
    (c) 18 in.
    (d) 22 in.

75. When normally enclosed live parts are exposed for inspection or servicing, the working space, if in a passageway or general open space, shall be suitably _____.

    (a) accessible
    (b) guarded
    (c) open
    (d) enclosed

76. When the *Code* uses _____, it means the identified actions are allowed but not required, and they may be options or alternative methods.

    (a) shall
    (b) shall not
    (c) shall be permitted
    (d) a or b

77. When the opening to an outlet, junction, or switch point is less than 8 in. in any dimension, each conductor shall be long enough to extend at least _____ outside the opening of the enclosure.

(a) 0 in.
(b) 3 in.
(c) 6 in.
(d) 12 in.

78. Where circuit conductors are spliced or terminated on equipment within a box, any equipment grounding conductors associated with those circuit conductors shall be connected to the box with devices suitable for the use.

(a) True
(b) False

79. Where conductors are run in parallel in multiple raceways or cables and include an EGC of the wire type, the equipment grounding conductor must be installed in parallel in each raceway or cable, sized in compliance with 250.122.

(a) True
(b) False

80. Where corrosion protection is necessary for ferrous metal equipment and the conduit is threaded in the field, the threads shall be coated with a(n) _____, electrically conductive, corrosion-resistant compound.

(a) marked
(b) listed
(c) labeled
(d) approved

81. Where dc PV source or output circuits are run inside a building or structure, they must be contained in _____.

(a) metal raceways
(b) Type MC cables
(c) metal enclosures
(d) any of these

82. Where exposed and subject to physical damage, array equipment grounding conductors smaller than 4 AWG must be protected by raceway or cable armor.

(a) True
(b) False

83. Where inverters are remotely located from each other, a directory must be provided at each dc PV system disconnecting means, each ac disconnecting means and at the main service disconnecting means showing the location of all ac and dc PV system disconnecting means in the building.

(a) True
(b) False

84. Where no overcurrent protection is provided for the PV dc circuit, an assumed overcurrent device rated at the PV circuit short-circuit current is used to size the equipment grounding conductor in accordance with _____.

(a) 250.122
(b) 250.66
(c) Table 250.122
(d) Table 250.66

85. Where portions of a cable raceway or sleeve are subjected to different temperatures and condensation is known to be a problem, the _____ shall be filled with an approved material to prevent the circulation of warm air to a colder section of the raceway or sleeve.

(a) raceway
(b) sleeve
(c) a or b
(d) none of these

86. Where raceways contain insulated circuit conductors _____ AWG and larger, the conductors shall be protected from abrasion during and after installation by a fitting that provides a smooth, rounded insulating surface.

(a) 8
(b) 6
(c) 4
(d) 2

87. Where six current-carrying conductors are run in the same conduit or cable, the ampacity of each conductor shall be adjusted by a factor of _____ percent.

    (a) 40
    (b) 60
    (c) 80
    (d) 90

88. Where the conductors of more than one PV system occupy the same junction box or raceway with removable cover(s), the ac and dc conductors of each system shall be grouped separately by wire ties or similar means at least once, and then shall be grouped at intervals not to exceed _____.

    (a) 6 in.
    (b) 12 in.
    (c) 36 in.
    (d) 6 ft

89. Where the conductors of more than one PV system occupy the same junction box, raceway, or equipment, the conductors of each system shall be identified at all termination, connection, and splice points.

    (a) True
    (b) False

90. Where the source circuit operates at over 30V, single-conductor Type USE-2 or listed and labeled PV wires installed in a readily accessible location must be installed in a raceway

    (a) True
    (b) False

91. Where used for battery interconnections, flexible cables identified as hard-service use and moisture resistant in Article 400, must be a minimum size of _____ AWG.

    (a) 1/0
    (b) 2/0
    (c) 3/0
    (d) 4/0

92. Where used for battery interconnections, flexible, fine-stranded cables must terminate in terminals, lugs, devices, or connectors that are identified and listed for fine-stranded conductors.

    (a) identified
    (b) listed
    (c) a or b
    (d) a and b

93. Which of the following is not standard size fuses or inverse time circuit breakers?

    (a) 45A
    (b) 70A
    (c) 75A
    (d) 80A

94. Which of the following switches must indicate whether they are in the open (off) or closed (on) position?

    (a) General-use switches
    (b) Motor-circuit switches
    (c) Circuit breakers
    (d) all of these

95. Which of the following that contain photovoltaic power source conductors must be marked with the wording Photovoltaic Power Source by means of permanently affixed labels or other approved permanent marking?

    (a) Exposed raceways, cable trays, and other wiring methods
    (b) The covers or enclosures of pull boxes and junction boxes
    (c) Conduit bodies in which any of the available conduit openings are unused
    (d) all of the above

96. Wiring methods for PV system conductors must be run _____ to the roof penetration point until they are 10" below the roof deck.

    (a) perpendicular
    (b) 90 degrees
    (c) 120 degrees
    (d) 180 degrees

97. Wiring methods for PV systems conductors are not permitted within _____ of the roof decking or sheathing except where located directly below the roof surface that is covered by PV modules and associated equipment.

    (a) 6 in.
    (b) 10 in.
    (c) 12 in.
    (d) none of these

98. Within sight means visible and not more than _____ ft distant from the equipment.

    (a) 10
    (b) 20
    (c) 25
    (d) 50

99. Working space distances for enclosed live parts shall be measured from the _____ of equipment or apparatus, if the live parts are enclosed.

    (a) enclosure
    (b) opening
    (c) a or b
    (d) none of these

100. Working space shall not be used for _____.

    (a) storage
    (b) raceways
    (c) lighting
    (d) accessibility

Notes

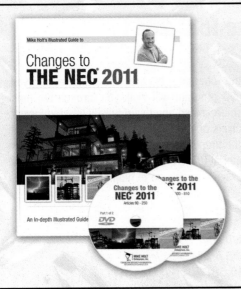

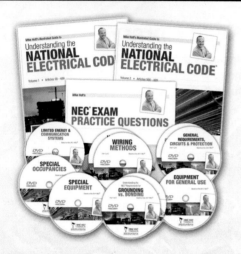
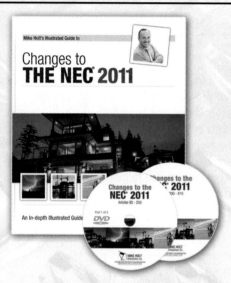

Index

A FREE Magazine By and For the Solar Workforce

Independently published by solar industry veterans, *SolarPro* is a technical training resource available by free subscription to qualifying trade professionals. Written and edited by and for North American system engineers, designers, integrators and installers, each bimonthly issue delivers a comprehensive perspective on equipment, tools, safety and best practices for optimizing the design, installation and performance of photovoltaic systems.

SolarPro and solarprofessional.com are the hub of a growing, professional community made up of over 20,000 solar industry peers sharing their knowledge and experience.

To take part, subscribe today at solarprofessional.com/subscribe.